AMERICAN MASSACRE

AMERICAN MASSACRE

THE TRAGEDY AT MOUNTAIN MEADOWS,
SEPTEMBER 1857

SALLY DENTON

ALFRED A. KNOPF

NEW YORK   2003

THIS IS A BORZOI BOOK
PUBLISHED BY ALFRED A. KNOPF

Copyright © 2003 by Sally Denton
All rights reserved under International and Pan-American Copyright
Conventions. Published in the United States by Alfred A. Knopf,
a division of Random House, Inc., New York, and simultaneously in Canada
by Random House of Canada Limited, Toronto.
Distributed by Random House, Inc., New York.
www.aaknopf.com

All photographs and illustrations are from the author's personal collection,
with the exception of the portraits of Thomas Leiper Kane and John Cradlebaugh,
which are courtesy, respectively, of the American Philosophical Society
and the Nevada Historical Society.

Knopf, Borzoi Books, and the colophon are registered
trademarks of Random House, Inc.

Library of Congress Cataloging-in-Publication Data

Denton, Sally.
American massacre : the tragedy at Mountain Meadows,
September 1857 / Sally Denton.—1st ed.
p.   cm.
Includes bibliographical references and index.
ISBN 0-375-41208-5 (alk. paper)
1. Mountain Meadows Massacre, 1857. I. Title.

F826 .D44 2003
979.2'47—dc21   2002043085

Manufactured in the United States of America
First Edition

For my sons,

Ralph, Grant, and Carson

In pursuing the bloody threat which runs through this picture of sad realities, the question of how this crime, that for hellish atrocity has no parallel in our history, can be adequately punished often comes up and seeks in vain for an answer.

—Brevet Major James H. Carleton, *Special Report to Congress,*
May 25, 1859

Live in tune with the Holy Spirit.
Seek the truth always. Be not
afraid to learn the truth of anything,
for no truth will be revealed to you as such
that will be in conflict with God's kingdom.

—Mormon patriarchal blessing

Contents

PART THREE: THE LEGACY

EPILOGUE

Author's Note

In the following pages, all recorded acts, all thoughts or feelings, all states of mind public or private, all conditions of weather and terrain, and any other circumstance, however detailed, are based on documentary evidence—especially the often literarily elegant and graphically descriptive journals and diaries kept so faithfully in that age. In telling a story so violent and bloody, so controversial, and in many ways so alien to modern sensibility, I have taken no liberties with the factual record. Sources for the narrative and all quoted remarks appear in the notes.

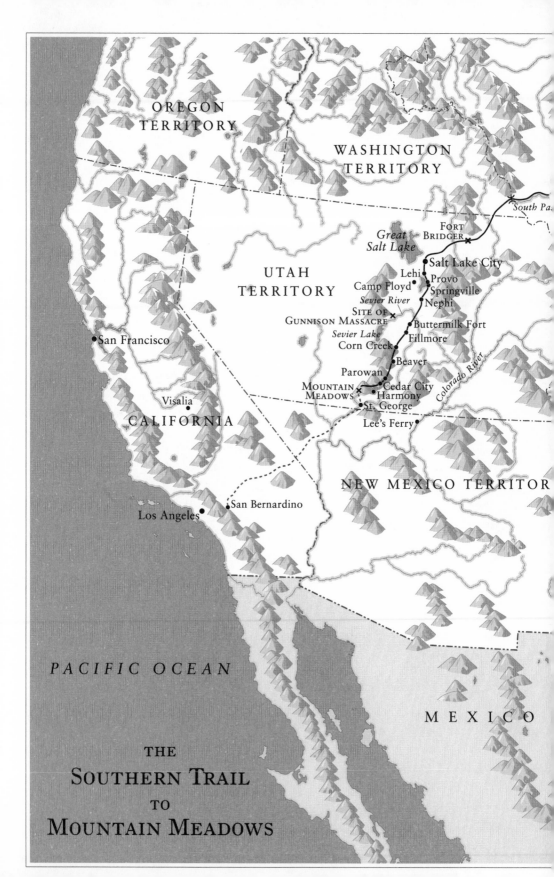

OREGON TERRITORY

WASHINGTON TERRITORY

South Pa

UTAH TERRITORY

Great Salt Lake

FORT BRIDGER

Salt Lake City

Lehi

Camp Floyd

Sevier River

SITE OF
GUNNISON MASSACRE

Sevier Lake

Corn Creek

Parowan

MOUNTAIN
MEADOWS

Provo

Springville

Nephi

Buttermilk Fort

Fillmore

Beaver

Cedar City

Harmony

St. George

Lee's Ferry

San Francisco

Visalia

CALIFORNIA

Colorado River

NEW MEXICO TERRITOR

San Bernardino

Los Angeles

PACIFIC OCEAN

MEXICO

THE

SOUTHERN TRAIL

TO

MOUNTAIN MEADOWS

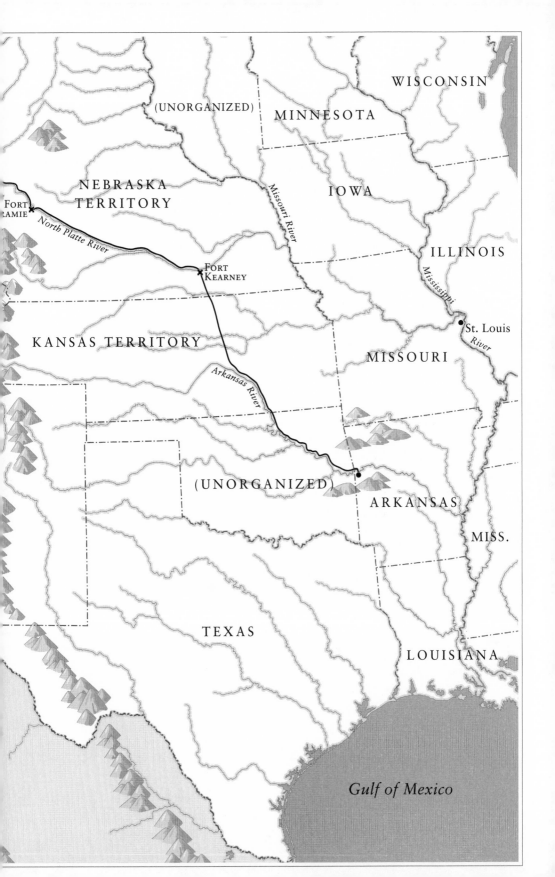

PROLOGUE

Jacob Hamblin's Ranch,
September 11, 1857

It is a late summer afternoon and the valley is at its most beautiful. Just weeks away from the first snows, bitter storms that close suddenly over the rim of the Pine Valley range, the days now are soft and mild, alabaster clouds stark against a sapphire sky. On the nearby ridges, native Paiute families are moving unseen on the shadowed slopes facing the valley to harvest the piñon trees already bulging with cones. The quaking aspen on distant peaks are beginning to turn golden.

Emigrants along this wagon train trail to California describe their surprise and joy coming upon the pasture. At a six-thousand-foot divide between rivers emptying into the Great Basin and the watershed of the Colorado, the floor of the valley is not large, a few hundred yards wide and less than five miles long north to south. But the lush high-country grasses fed by three strong and clear springs create a precious oasis between the craggy plateaus behind and the great desert ahead to the west. Even seasoned travelers are impressed. "The best grazing tract in Utah Territory," a respected U.S. Army explorer, Brevet Major James H. Carleton, will say of it when he and his company of dragoons ride onto the site twenty months later. For almost everyone who comes here, Mountain Meadows is a haven, a refuge, a place of life and renewal.

Hard against the foothills of the northern slope, Jacob Hamblin's summer home is still unfinished from building begun months earlier. The Church of Jesus Christ of Latter-day Saints, which Hamblin serves as a devout member and obedient agent, has granted him ten square miles of land here, encompassing the whole of Mountain Meadows, and his new stone and adobe ranch house has a commanding view of the valley. Today, standing expectantly in front of the house, his wife, Rachel, and their hired hands have been listening to some commotion from the fields beyond. Now they can see rocking open wagons straining up toward them on the rutted track from the pasture.

Hundreds of cattle bray in alarm as they are herded north toward Cedar City. Two hundred horses, most of them valuable Kentucky thoroughbreds, rear and shriek at strange hands and the smoke of blazing pyres nearby. Forty prairie schooners and four ornate carriages rumble and creak under new drivers, coming back up out of the valley on the same trail by which they entered it days before. Buzzards caw impatiently as they circle above, and wolves have already begun to gather and howl at the edge of the valley, waiting for the living to clear out. The enclosing ravines and ridges magnify the din. But as two regimental baggage wagons draw nearer the Hamblin ranch, the screaming and moaning of the more than twenty children they carry drown out every other sound. The children, who range in age from nine months to seven years, are all under the age of eight, young enough to be considered "innocent blood" in the Mormon faith. They have had no fresh water and little to eat for five days. The blood of their parents, sisters, and brothers still wet on their skin and clothes, they are hysterical from what they have just seen. Two of them are severely wounded and one will soon die.

One of the men walking behind their procession up to the Hamblin house, a sun-leathered figure named John Doyle Lee who has commanded and joined in the mass murder that has just taken place, will soon decide how this cargo of terrified children will be distributed along with the other loot, brothers and sisters to be separated as chattel among households in the region. Lee seems untroubled by what has happened. That evening, exhausted by his work in the day's carnage, he stretches out on a grassy mound beside the ranch house and, using his saddle as a pillow, sleeps easily until the next morning.

The men left in the meadow that night to guard what has not been hauled to Cedar City are not so fortunate. They huddle silently near their campfires while in the darkness beyond, packs of wolves and coyotes yip with delight at their feast of some 140 unburied corpses. Strangely, unnaturally apart from the wild feeding on the floor of the meadow, one wolf stands at the tree line above them, howling incessantly through the night. Some of the men will stay awake until dawn.

At the Hamblin ranch, the helpless children exert a kind of hold of their own on their guardians. Rachel Hamblin and the others who have taken them in, the murderers of their families who have escorted them there, sympathizers who ride to the ranch to inspect the scene later that evening—all of them will be haunted afterward by the unbroken sobs and wailing, the inconsolable, unforgettable grief of the young survivors. "The children," one man will remember, "cried nearly all night."

The Cairn, August 3, 1999

The work has only begun and the morning is already heavy with the heat of the day. A neighbor has come down to watch as the backhoe operator powers his shovel into a hard-packed mound of earth. To the shock and dread of them both, the bucket pulls and lurches and then emerges with more than thirty pounds of human skeletal remains. The driver anxiously jumps down, and the two men, wearing baseball caps and blue jeans, circle warily around the bones, discussing what they know has happened, what they feared. Their first inclination, as one of them would later admit, is to dump the load right back in the hole they made in Mountain Meadows and swear each other to secrecy.

The once magnificent valley not far off Utah Highway 18 between St. George and Cedar City has turned a dozen shades of brown. Scrub pine and sagebrush dot the low hills. The cottonwoods—or *alamosas,* as the locals call the huge shade trees that once graced the meadow— are gone. The belly-high emerald grass for which the valley is legendary no longer grows. State officials attribute the blight of the land to over-grazing and torrential floods in 1861 and 1873. But natives of the area say that the meadow was never the same after that day in September 1857 when the emigrants were slaughtered there. Word was passed down from generation to generation around the valley. "We were told never to plant a garden in certain locations," remembers a great-grandson of a pioneer landholder.

In the late 1980s, a group of John D. Lee's descendants—including former interior secretary Stewart Udall—began working to clear their ancestor's name of the murders at Mountain Meadows. The Church of Jesus Christ of Latter-day Saints had long denied any official responsibility for the killings, but others, including most descendants of the victims, had remained unconvinced. Simultaneously, descendants of the victims pressed the federal government to erect a suitable memorial at the site. The church, which controlled the land, decided to restore the site, and built a granite wall on Dan Sill Hill overlooking the meadow containing the etched names of the murdered pioneers, which was dedicated in a private ceremony. The inscription on that monument read: "In Memoriam: In the valley below, between September 7 and 11, 1857, a company of more than 120 Arkansas emigrants led by Capt. John T. Baker and Capt. Alexander Fancher was attacked while en route to California. This event is known in history as the Mountain Meadows Massacre."

That wall fell into disrepair, and by the late 1990s descendants were once again pushing for a new monument. Their Mountain Meadows Association—what the *Salt Lake Tribune* described as "an unusual mix of historians and descendants of massacre victims and perpetrators"— had been meeting annually at the meadow on the anniversary of the atrocity. Increasingly concerned by what they called "the deplorable condition of the site," the group had begun imploring the church to restore and rebuild the primitive rock-cairn memorial at the location. In 1998, LDS officials agreed to a renovation.

Brigham Young University archaeologists examined the area before sending in earthmoving equipment. "There are a million different stories about how many victims there were and where their bodies are buried," a Salt Lake City journalist would explain at the time, "and the last thing the church wanted was to dig up any bones and set off a public controversy."

During July 1999, in the weeks before necessary excavation for the refurbished monument began, scientists working for the church used every modern device available for a noninvasive study of the locale— aerial photographs, metal detectors, core soil sampling, and ground-penetrating radar. Forensic geologists and geophysicists searched for anomalies in the soil pattern, such as chemical concentrations of calcium that would indicate where burials had taken place. All the while, church leaders had gone to great lengths to keep the planned renovation secret from the public and the press. Then, on August 3, assured that the digging would reveal no surprises—"the archaeological evidence was one hundred percent negative," one of the scientists had reported to Mormon headquarters in Salt Lake City—the excavation began.

But this August morning, the two men at the backhoe, members of the association, were looking at the very discovery the church had gone to such lengths to avoid. Knowing that Utah laws now existed for the handling of human remains unearthed anywhere in the state, they called the local sheriff, who drove out to the valley to meet them. "It was a very humbling experience," Sheriff Kirk Smith said later. "I saw buttons, some pottery and bones of adults and children. But the children—that was what really hit me hard."

Smith reported the findings to church leaders in Salt Lake City. After a flurry of meetings and telephone discussions, Utah state archaeologist Kevin Jones reaffirmed to church and law enforcement officials the legal requirement that any unidentified remains uncovered must be forensically examined, and failure to comply would be a felony. Jones issued the necessary permit for the state and church scientists to examine the remains to determine age, sex, race, stature, health condition, and cause of death. Intrigued by the discovery and aware of the political controversy—what one newspaper editor called Utah's "unique church-state tango"—a team of anthropologists, archaeologists, and other church and state scientists from around Utah began working long hours poring over the remains. "It was a marathon forensic study," one of them said.

As the scientists from around the region gathered, news of the discovery leaked to the national press, unleashing a storm of public controversy over the unexpected skeletons and adding new urgency and tension to the scientific inquiry. Delicately removing hundreds of pieces of bone from the opening dug by the backhoe, the scientists worked eighteen hours a day to determine how and when the victims were killed.

Before the examination could be completed, however, it was stopped. For descendants of both victims and perpetrators, for institutions of church and state implicated in what the bones signify, the issue was as volatile and ominous as it had been nearly a century and a half before. Utah governor Mike Leavitt, himself a direct descendant of someone who participated in the murders, ordered the bones be reburied as quickly as possible; he then directed state officials to find administrative or other means to do just that.

U.S. Forest Service archaeologist Marian Jacklin, like many others, fought the state's decision to halt the inquiry. "Those bones could tell the story, and this was their one opportunity," she said. "I would allow my own mother's bones to be studied in a respectful manner if it would benefit medicine or history." Before the probe came to a standstill, the scientists reconstructed eighteen different skulls and reported publicly that the killings were more complicated than previously believed.

But the dead would not be allowed to speak. Once more, when it seemed there might be new answers to old questions, the voices were silenced. But what happened at Mountain Meadows is hardly a secret.

PART ONE

***

THE GATHERING

CHAPTER ONE

Palmyra, 1823

JOSEPH SMITH knelt in a small upstairs bedroom in rural New York, a farm boy beseeching God to forgive him his sins. Suddenly, he would say later, a light as bright as the midday sun grew around him, and a personage draped in exquisite white robes—"a countenance truly like lightning"—addressed the seventeen-year-old by name. This spirit, Moroni, then delivered the celestial decree: "That God had a work for me to do; and that my name should be had for good and evil among all nations, kindreds, and tongues."

This "work," Smith said he was told, involved locating a book inscribed on golden plates that Moroni had buried on a mound in nearby Cumorah fourteen hundred years earlier. Contained in the leaves was an account of the aborigines of America, a lost tribe of Israel, which included "the everlasting Gospel . . . as delivered by the Savior to the ancient inhabitants." To assist Smith in translating the Egyptian-like symbols on the tablets would be two sacred seer stones, the Urim and Thummim, fastened to a breastplate and deposited with the book.

Quoting numerous biblical prophecies regarding the Second Coming of Christ to earth—"For behold the day cometh that shall burn as an oven"—Moroni, Smith said, conveyed the gravity of Smith's mission. Then, the mysterious light enveloped the angel, who "ascended until he entirely disappeared." Moroni visited Smith two more times that night—for, as Smith biographer Fawn Brodie wrote, "to be authentic, celestial truth must be thrice repeated."

The visitations on that evening of September 21, 1823, were neither the first nor the last of what Smith would describe as God's direct communication with him. The tall athletic boy claimed he had received his first prophetic directive three years earlier, when, as a mere fourteen-year-old, he accidentally came upon the New Testament passage that would lead him on his religious journey. Written "to the twelve tribes which are scattered abroad," it read: "if any of you lack wisdom, let him ask of God, that giveth to all men liberally and upbraideth not; and it shall be given him."

On a crisp spring day in 1820, he had decided to test the passage literally—to seek advice from God himself as to which of the local Methodist, Presbyterian, or Baptist sects he should join. In answer, "a pillar of light" surrounded him, and in that moment the charismatic teenager claimed to have become God's chosen instrument to reveal to the world that all religions were false and corrupt. Stung by the derision that greeted his excited proclamations to the public, Smith drew the inevitable martyr's comparison to one of Jesus' apostles. "I felt much like Paul," he would later write, "when he made his defense before King Agrippa, and related the account of the vision he had had when he saw a light and heard a voice; still, there were but few who believed him." It would be the first of hundreds of mythical persecutions that would mark Smith's life and death, and portend a future of oppression and vengeance unlike anything America had seen.

In the intervening years between supernatural visions, Smith continued to till his father's soil while spending his "leisure leading a band of idlers in digging for buried treasure," as one account put it. Dabbling in the occult, Smith apprenticed with a man described as "a peripatetic magician, conjurer and fortuneteller," from whom he learned the era's folk concepts of crystal gazing, divining rods, seer stones, and rituals associated with treasure hunting. He advised others in their pursuits, once instructing a neighbor he could locate buried money on his property by slitting the throat of a black sheep and leading it in a circle on the land. Increasingly ridiculed as a necromancer and money digger, Smith kept details of his continuing revelations to himself, confiding only in his parents, siblings, and, by early 1827, in young Emma Hale, with whom he had eloped. All the while he patiently awaited an order from the angel Moroni that it was time to retrieve the golden book.

It was an auspicious night for communing with spirits, according to the astrological handbooks of the day. "Jews throughout the world celebrated the Feast of Trumpets, which initiates the Days of Awe," or Rosh Hashanah, academic journals later noted in an attempt to seek association between Smith and Judaism. Almanacs published near Smith's home reported the date was "both the autumnal equinox and a new moon, an excellent time to commence new projects." A publication in nearby Canandaigua reported "the moon was also in Libra, when one should 'Delve and Dig.' "

The twenty-one-year-old Smith dressed himself in black, then borrowed a black horse and sleigh for the ride to the hill of Cumorah. He had been "commanded to go on the 22d day of September 1827 at 2 o'clock," Smith's sister later wrote. Emma rode with him in the carriage, but she knelt and prayed with her back to her husband, so she never saw Moroni as Smith climbed the slope to receive the hand-delivered sacred plates from the angel. If by carelessness Smith lost control of the hallowed book, Moroni warned, he would be "cut off" as the chosen revelator. There would be swirling controversies and exaggerated fables surrounding the golden plates, Smith himself claiming he hid them in a hollow black oak tree before racing back to his family home with the magic spectacles. His mother, Lucy, could barely contain her excitement over "the two smooth three-cornered diamonds set in glass and the glasses set in silver bows," and though vowing secrecy could not resist the impulse to gossip roundly. "Joseph's former troubles were as nothing to what followed after he obtained possession of the plates," the nineteenth-century journalist T. B. H. Stenhouse would observe.

"No comet appeared in the sky at his coming," wrote a historian of Joseph Smith's birth into a poverty-stricken Vermont family on December 23, 1805. The third boy in a family of four children, he was named for his father, a failed ginseng merchant who vainly cultivated a rocky parcel set above the rugged White River. Joseph's mother, the former Lucy Mack, maintained a lively intellectual quest for spiritual guidance despite an unschooled mind. Bonded by their nonconforming contempt for organized religion, the parents were avid seekers of God and a church they felt to be true.

Married in 1796, at the height of the international "Treason of the Clergy" movement—the era's revulsion against clerical dominance and corruption—the couple was keenly aware of the religious skepticism sweeping the world and nation, embodied by the French philosopher Voltaire and the English writer Thomas Paine. Paine's *Age of Reason* challenged Christianity as "too absurd for belief, too impossible to convince, and too inconsistent to practice." The Smiths were apparently drawn into the dialogue. "As a result of Paine's work, the Bible desperately needed support," wrote Smith biographer Robert D. Anderson. "A second witness for Christ was necessary for those who needed, in a psychological sense, a future life better than this one." Finding that second witness would define the Smith family's future.

Each parent brought a clan history of a complex blending of magic and religion that would take root in the revivalism of the moment. Lucy, a descendant of Scotch clergymen, abandoned traditional Protestantism for a devotion to mysticism and miracles. Joseph Sr. had been raised by a father who "frankly gloried in his freedom from ecclesiastical tyranny," as one writer described him, and, because he was prone to fits, was called "Crook-Necked Smith." Joseph Sr. was further swayed by his great-grandfather's accusations of witchcraft against two women, which had resulted in their hanging in Salem, Massachusetts.

But by the time young Joseph Smith began navigating his own spiritual path, his parents were wallowing in more temporal matters. Living through an economic depression, the family had moved three times in Smith's first five years of life. Then, the typhoid fever epidemic of 1813 struck each of the Smith children. While all eventually recovered, the eight-year-old Joseph fought a heroic battle in his pain and suffering that would become legendary in the valleys of Vermont. As infections and angry sores spread throughout his body, he was bled, purged, and poulticed by a local physician—all to no avail. When Lucy refused to allow her son's leg to be amputated, the "barber-surgeon . . . had to content himself with chiseling out a piece of bone beneath the child's knee," according to one account of the gruesome and bloody procedure. "Great things were expected of the child whose mettle had been tested in so fearsome an ordeal," wrote one biographer, while another psychological interpreter claimed the painful episode led to a fixation on compensatory fantasies of omnipotence that would obsess Smith all his life.

Future ramifications aside, the epidemic took a toll on the family stability as Lucy sank into emotional depression while the Smiths' financial security collapsed with three years of barren harvests. In desperation, Joseph Sr. moved in 1816 to the western New York town of

Palmyra, hoping to facilitate his family's escape from its bleak existence and unrelenting hunger. Called the Burned-Over District for the ubiquitous faith healers and evangelists swarming into the area—"leaving behind a people scattered and peeled, for religious enthusiasm was literally being burnt out of them"—the town of thirty-five hundred was vibrant with "convulsive revivals." Peopled by Puritan descendants of those who had burned witches two hundred years earlier, the locale served as an underground station for what one resident called "runaway Negroes" from Missouri to Canada.

Greeted by a booming economy, Joseph Sr. immediately sent word for Lucy and the children to join him. Seizing a speculative moment, he was able to borrow enough to build a log cabin on one hundred acres of unimproved land. As he cleared and planted and Lucy sold root beer and painted oilcloths, Joseph Jr. scorned the land—"he detested the plow as only a farmer's son can," wrote a historian—turning his future, instead, to buried treasure. Before long, the entire family was "digging for money for subsistence," according to some reports.

Affable and gregarious, with a devil-may-care attitude and boundless exuberance, Joseph Smith grew into a large and dynamic young man, whose exaggerative and enigmatic storytelling captivated many. A "lake-country prototype of Huckleberry Finn," biographer Carl Carmer described him, "proverbially good-natured—yet he was never known to laugh." Though his formal education was stunted, his intellect undisciplined, his perspicacity and towering ego inspired confidence. He "would have made a fine stump speaker if he had had the training," a friend later recalled.

His embellished tales were most often spun around the mystery of the Mound Builders—a thousand-year-old lost race fabled to have been slaughtered and buried on the outskirts of Palmyra. The conelike ruins there spawned theories of a highly advanced civilization exterminated by evil ancestors of the Indians indigenous to the area, and Joseph Smith Jr. was determined to write a book about the mass graves. Accepting in entirety the prevailing legend of the lost race—folklore that would later be discredited by archaeological evidence—Smith entertained his family with tales of the ancient inhabitants, every conceivable detail of their lives so elaborated his mother thought it seemed "as if he had spent his whole life with them." The theories and anecdotes he tested so effusively and successfully on his own clan would prove the germ of his forthcoming Book of Mormon.

During the winter of 1827–28, he began translating the golden plates he said he had found in September, making use of the seer stones and dictating the book to his wife. Emma dared not disturb the plates that were wrapped in linen, for Joseph had warned her of instant death if her eyes fell upon them. Though mystified by her husband's ability to interpret the characters from the plates without unwrapping them but by merely gazing into a hat that contained the Urim and Thummim, she was faithful from the start. "I, Nephi, having been born of goodly parents"—she wrote down his words, and the book was thus begun. Bearing a striking resemblance to the King James Bible, the book told the story of the young Hebrew prophet Nephi who had left Jerusalem in 600 B.C., sailing to America with his father, Lehi. Nephi's two older brothers, Laman and Lemuel, were evil sinners, causing God to curse them and all of their descendants with a red skin. But Nephi and his three younger brothers, Sam, Jacob, and Joseph, were devout and godly, so God blessed them and all of their descendants with white skin. Hence, the saga of the Nephites and Lamanites would be an expansion and explanation of the most common theories of the day—that the Indians of North America were a remnant of one of the mythical ten lost tribes of Israel. The Nephites were what Smith called a "white and delightsome people," while the baneful Lamanites were bloodthirsty combatants.

Emma the scribe dutifully recorded what one writer called the "stream of prose that flowed from her husband's lips"—the colorful history of these two warring factions, and the origin of the founding fathers of all Americans. "He began the book," wrote Fawn Brodie, "by focusing upon a single hero, Nephi, who like himself was peculiarly gifted of the Lord." This narrative device allowed Smith to follow the formula of the Bible's Old Testament, the prophetic writings divided into books.

Pregnant with a baby that would soon be delivered stillborn, and penniless from the devotion to the couple's joint endeavor, Emma soon sought a replacement for her position as secretary. In April 1829, a young Palmyra schoolmaster named Oliver Cowdery began taking dictation from Smith, and in just over two months the two men had miraculously completed a 275,000-word manuscript. This new adventure story was much improved in pacing and excitement, but still "lacked subtlety, wit, and style," as one critic put it. "He began the book with a first-class murder, added assassinations, and piled up battles by the score." Complex and intricate, the plot centered largely around the story of Mormon—a military figure who led his people, who populated North America, and Nephi, an early migrant from Palestine to America. Moroni, the angel who directed Smith to the tablets, was Mormon's son and the last diarist of the events.

Covering a thousand years and brimming with heroes and villains, bloodshed and miracles, army generals and covert operations, rich biblical symbols and autobiographical themes, what was to be called the Book of Mormon was reflective of the unsophisticated mystical leanings of the day. At root was the conviction that all believers were on the road to Godhood, that a heaven existed where all men could be saved and then go on to create their own worlds.

Less than a year later, the illiterate Joseph Smith published the highly commercial manuscript, creating at the same time an entirely new theology. The Book of Mormon first went on sale in Palmyra on March 26, 1830. "BLASPHEMY—BOOK OF MORMON, ALIAS THE GOLDEN BIBLE," the *Rochester Daily Advertiser* wrote in drawing the first imprecation. Two weeks later the Church of Christ was formally established, and Smith announced to his six followers that his official title was now "Seer, a Translator, a Prophet, an Apostle of Jesus Christ, and elder of the Church through the will of God the Father, and the grace of your Lord Jesus Christ."

A month later the ranks would number forty, and within a few years would swell into the thousands. Though ignored by literary critics, the Book of Mormon would soon bring hundreds of thousands of immigrants to America. But the "catapult that flung Joseph Smith to a place in the sun," as one historian described the Book of Mormon, "could not be responsible for his survival there."

In 1828, the United States, only a half century old, was home to fewer than thirteen million souls. Andrew Jackson was elected that year in one of the bitterest presidential elections in American history. Internal dissent gripped the country, pitting Jackson's popularity as a military hero among America's Midwest farmers, workers, and small tradesmen against the privileged Eastern postrevolutionary establishment. The staid Protestantism of the early colonies was now fraught with radical reinterpretation and revisionism, and Smith's proposed theocracy of evangelical socialism, a precursor of Marxian communism, was seductive to many. In this epoch of theological and political schisms, America was "ripe for a religious leader wearing the mantle of authority," as one historian described the moment. Smith envisioned a revolutionary utopia, and his Book of Mormon would be one of the most significant and powerful contributions to American religious thought. He had written "a supernatural history filled with superheroes and miracles," wrote biographer Anderson, "capable of touching the heart of every person who has felt small, helpless, and alone."

Neither Judaic nor Christian, the true church should now be "restored" in North America by its prophet Smith, who would gather the remnants of Israel to a latter-day Zion and await the impending millennium. Smith and his successors would "progress" to the same divinity as the God of the Old Testament—a corporeal being residing on a planet orbiting a star called Kolob and sexually active with a Heavenly Mother and other wives. Smith "had received the keys of the holy priesthood from the apostles, Peter, James, and John," one historian wrote, and he was ablaze with his mission. Because he had the "poor man's awe of gold," his promises of afterlife included a paradise "laden with jewels and gold."

With a keen eye toward martyrdom, the inventive and resourceful new prophet would quickly learn to manipulate the myth and reality of persecution as a means to his own ends—a manipulation that would culminate in the massacre decades later at Mountain Meadows. Like other new religions of the day, the sect would have its share of fanaticism and zealotry, gaining ardor with every slight, and, like other millennialist movements, a holy war passion sowed for the first time on American soil.

Theology notwithstanding, it would ultimately be Smith's own charisma that would define the movement and its extraordinary, unprecedented growth in the country. Stunningly handsome—"except for his nose, which was aquiline and prominent," according to one description—Smith had oversized and appealing features. Deep-set translucent blue eyes rimmed with luxuriant black lashes, a six-foot stature and a portly countenance, a contagious smile and gregarious spontaneity, and, perhaps especially, a "mysterious illumination" drew immediate disciples to Smith. This bewitching, forceful character wasted no time gathering his flock, which he ruled through divine revelation. Flanked by able orators—"worthy male" converts upon whom he flatteringly bestowed such New Testament titles as apostle, elder, priest, deacon, and patriarch, all puffed up with the exaltation of restoring the house of Israel—Smith proselytized with historic fruition. Whole congregations and their learned ministers fell sway to this homegrown American prophet, eager to join the ranks of the chosen people for God's new covenant and convinced that Smith brought "the Dispensation of the Fullness of Times" that would immediately precede the much-anticipated Second Coming.

The "fortune-teller turned baptizer," as one of his biographers called him, met his first official persecution when an angry mob destroyed a dam built by his followers for the immersion baptisms Smith was performing in record numbers. The jeers of "false prophet" mounted, as conflicts with neighbors increased. Arrested on charges of disorderly conduct and fearing for his life, Smith turned his sights away from Palmyra. His church was not yet five months old when he began seeking a new location for his Zion. He dispatched his apostles to the west to find a site upon which to build the New Jerusalem and to persuade the Indians, whom Smith's followers now called Lamanites, that the Book of Mormon was the history of their ancestors. The natives proved reluctant converts, and the proselytizing effort was a colossal failure. "Joseph was offering the red man, not restoration, but assimilation," wrote one historian, "not the return of his continent, but the loss of his identity."

Enthusiastically welcomed by a communistic colony already established in Kirtland, Ohio, the Mormon disciples converted and baptized the entire community, returning excitedly to Palmyra to lobby for the wholesale migration to Kirtland. The twenty-five-year-old Smith announced that Kirtland was the easternmost boundary of the Promised Land. Reticence and strife infected his sixty followers, most preferring an inhospitable New York to an uncertain Ohio. But one of Smith's most remarkable, and politic, revelations quelled all dissent: there existed a place of such allure and temptation, he said—"a land flowing with milk and honey, upon which there shall be no curse when the Lord cometh. And I will give it unto you for the land of your inheritance, if you seek it with all your hearts"—that no true believer dared stay behind. By May 1831, the entire congregation had relocated three hundred miles west to the small Ohio community on the south shore of Lake Erie, where, before long, they would dominate the region economically and once again spark the ire of their neighbors.

CHAPTER TWO

Kirtland/Far West, 1831

INDUSTRIOUSNESS, abundance, and collectivism would fuel the rebuke the Mormons faced wherever they settled. The inevitable phases of curiosity followed by envy, fear, then ultimately rage, though predictable, seemed strangely underestimated by the young prophet. Setting themselves apart as the chosen ones—calling all non-Mormons "Gentiles"—created a suspicion and animosity not easily assuaged. The "us" versus "them" mentality, begun as a survival tool and forged into a pathology, would serve as both cohesion and division, and, in any case, plague the new religion for years to come.

From the beginning, a peculiar force of Mormonism lay in a devotion to material wealth that was destined to alienate others. Unlike the asceticism espoused by many movements of the day, Smith's Church of Christ pursued affluence with unabashed vigor. Prosperity was a path to godliness in a utopian religion where financial acumen corresponded with spiritual perfection.

In Kirtland the Mormons began what journalist James Coates called a "pattern of colony building, prosperity, persecution, and collapse" that would distinguish them for decades to come. Kirtland was awash with easy money and credit, a city in the throes of a speculative craze. Its 62 percent increase in population in the 1830s amplified the real estate boom, and Smith himself was "infected with the virus of speculation." Profiting in the land bubble and boldly founding a church bank in which he advised his followers to invest their entire savings, Smith awaited the revelation that would direct him to Zion. All the while, scuffles between Mormons and Gentiles erupted in the vicinity, as hostilities swelled.

With the beginning seeds of the grandiosity that would eventually overtake his personality, Smith announced in the spring of 1833 that the first of a dozen temples should be built. Revelation determined the dimensions of the three-story, fifty-five-by-sixty-five-foot structures. A week after the first cornerstone was laid in Kirtland, Smith ordered the building of a temple in the new Zion, now identified as Independence, Missouri. That locale, Smith told his followers, was the site of the original Garden of Eden. Twelve miles away in Far West—now Kansas City—was where Cain killed Abel, he said, and therefore where Adam and Eve began the human race. Disturbing to many of his followers was Smith's revelation that the "redemption of Zion must needs come by power." He proclaimed he would lead them "like as Moses led the children of Israel," and preparations began for another mass departure. Revelations came rapidly as Smith established an economic order, an authoritarian church structure, a military apparatus, an expanding doctrine of secret sacraments, and a political ideology in preparation for the march to Zion.

Through what he called the United Order of Enoch, converts were commanded to consecrate all property to the church. They would then be provided according to their individual need. "Those, who like me, had full faith in the teachings of God as revealed by Joseph Smith, His Prophet, were willing to comply with *every* order," wrote early convert John Doyle Lee. But most were skeptical. "I feared the people would not give up all their worldly possessions, to be disposed of by and at the will and pleasure of three men." A unanimous vote for the consecration was what Lee called "a show of hands, but not a show of hearts." When more-well-to-do members of the church rebelled, the communalism gave way to a strict system of tithing 10 percent of one's gross personal wealth.

What had begun with a pyramidal lay clergy—a device that provided a bonding camaraderie and loyalty for all male church members—Smith formalized into a priesthood. Those who had balked at the Order of Enoch were excluded from the inner circle, which now consisted of twelve apostles—each young man as overconfident and robust as the next—and a quorum of seventy men. Those who had responded with generosity he repaid with elevated positions in the hierarchy. He gave special appellations to two of his most formidable supporters—"The Lion of the Lord" for his new convert Brigham Young, and "The Archer of Paradise" for his early disciple Parley P. Pratt—and even ordained some of his men as high priests.

Nine of the apostles and the entire Quorum of Seventy, as it was formally known, became members as well of Smith's newly formed private militia. Dividing his army into companies of twelve—Smith designated himself "head" of the "war department" of the "Lord's Host"—the prophet surprised his followers with his superb marksmanship. Now a swaggering general in his Army of Israel, Smith carried a rifle and several pistols, while also heeling a vicious bulldog at his side. Disciplining his minions with the harsh tenor of the gospel, he called to them every night, like Moses, with a blast upon a sacred ram's horn. Drilling and pageantry were quite suddenly pervasive aspects of a once-pacific Kirtland existence. His newly formed bodyguard would be but the first in numerous incarnations of a church internal security contingent.

The dogma thickened too, and Smith became reckless with his prolific prophecies. In 1833 he dictated the "Word of Wisdom" forbidding tobacco, alcohol, coffee, and red meat. In the church and in family households, a rigid white male patriarchy ruled the tightly knit sect. Smith changed the name of his denomination to the Church of Latter-day Saints in 1834, hoping to replace the despised nickname "Mormons" with the more elevated "Saints." He then initiated the secret rituals that would further repel their conventional Christian neighbors—anointings, endowments, proxy baptisms, visions, healings, writhing ecstasies, and, especially, the concepts of "eternal progression" and "celestial marriage." Some high officials were secretly practicing polygamy by the mid-1830s, though the principle was not formally condoned and was even publicly denied by the church. Rumors abounded that Smith had seduced a comely seventeen-year-old orphan living in his home. "The breath of scandal was hot upon his neck," wrote one historian of the relationship that would become Smith's first of forty-eight polygamous wives. "Emma was furious and drove the girl, who was unable to conceal the consequences of her celestial relation with the Prophet, out of her home." It was widely believed that Emma's defiant behavior prompted Smith's 1835 public statement to his female followers: "Wives, submit yourselves unto your own husbands . . . for the husband is the head of the wife." By the end of the decade, Kirtland, Ohio, would be identified with plural marriage.

Smith's attraction to national politics had begun in 1832 with a trip to New York City to secure loans in the name of the Kirtland United Order. The city was alive with debate over how President Jackson should deal with a rebellious South Carolina, and Smith's exposure to such heated dialogue would mark the beginning of the church's theocratic expansion. On Christmas Day, a month after his return from New York, Smith prophesied about "the wars that will shortly come to pass." Smith's prescience of a looming civil war would be evidence of his divinity for thousands of future converts, though it would be eighteen more years before the prediction was fulfilled. "The Southern States shall be divided against the Northern States," he railed, "slaves shall rise up against their masters." There followed a series of revelations on government and war—the birth and evolution of Smith's vision for a political Kingdom of God. In this theocratic nation of his dreams, he would be the ruler of all things spiritual and temporal, overseeing his empire from the promised land of Far West, Missouri.

Smith's bank collapsed in the national panic of 1837, prompting several creditors to file lawsuits against the prophet. He was arrested seven times in a four-month period. Church members who had lost money in the bank joined armed non-Mormons against the church leader. Finally, upon hearing of criminal bank fraud charges filed against him, Smith fled Kirtland in the middle of the night—"his horse turned toward Zion." After he traveled an exhausting eight hundred miles to his colony in Far West, Smith's high spirits returned when he was greeted by fifteen hundred passionate converts. But the peace and gaiety of that first homecoming would soon fade.

Missourians had watched with bitter rancor as the Mormons pooled their resources, building towns and opening banks and other businesses while shunning Gentile establishments. Under what seemed the radical political leadership of Smith, who not only espoused a controversial socialism but was a vocal opponent of slavery as well, the Mormons once again faced contempt. Missouri was a hotbed of proslavery factions that greeted the Mormons with disdain from the start. The Mormons' millennialist fervor, coupled with assertions that their scriptures were equal to the Bible and their faith the only true one, added to the conflict, as did what two historians described as "the antidemocratic tendencies of their dogmatic, crusading spirit." Believing in the relative insignificance of the moment, the Celestial Kingdom holding out a larger reward than any earthly pleasure or accomplishment, the Mormons held little fear of death. They were peculiarly oblivious to "the provocative nature of their more radical doctrines"—including their apocalyptic goal of ushering in the new messiah—which led to what two historians called "the myth of persecuted innocence."

As hostilities escalated outside the church, Smith would face internal dissension as well. Members accused Smith of apostasy for dropping "Christ" from the church title, and in 1838 a new revelation would guide the prophet to yet another name: the Church of Jesus Christ of Latter-day Saints. Throughout the year, Smith and his church were fighting for survival against coalitions of Gentiles and apostates. He excommunicated dozens of dissenters, and set the stage for the siege mentality that would shape and dominate future events.

Paranoia and fear now added to his imposing vision, Smith took steps to organize a secret group of loyalists. The Danites—or Sons of Dan, as they were known, taking their name from the biblical prophecy of Daniel—would become one of the most legendarily feared bands in frontier America. Later nicknamed the "Avenging Angels," the group "developed an infamous reputation for its intimidation of Mormon dissenters and its warfare against anti-Mormon militia units," according to the scholar D. Michael Quinn.

The creation of this consecrated, clandestine unit of divinely inspired assassins, organized into units of tens and fifties, would have implications far beyond the seemingly minor conflicts of Ohio and Missouri. For they would introduce the most divisive and fanatical doctrine of all—the ritualized form of murder called blood atonement. In such a killing of higher purpose, the victim's blood must be spilled into the earth in order for his spirit to ascend into heaven, the murderer in effect providing the victim with eternal salvation by slitting his throat. There would follow untold numbers of such murders, euphemistically called savings, at the hands of the Danites. Among the first charter members to be personally selected by Joseph Smith for his elite avenging army was John Doyle Lee.

Lee was born on September 6, 1812, "on the point of land lying between and above the mouth of the Okaw," as he described his birthplace in Kaskaskia in Illinois Territory, a river-bottom locale with more wild horses than people. Though the grandson of a Revolutionary War hero, and a relative of Robert E. Lee, John—and his immediate family—would be marred by tragedy and alcoholism. Elizabeth Doyle—"a pale and listless mother," as he described her—was the daughter of a successful linguist who held the position of Indian agent. But any prosperity was dissipated before John was born. In 1799, Elizabeth married William Oliver, a young landowner with whom she then had two children. But following a dispute of unknown origin with another local man, Oliver was bludgeoned to death in his bed while sleeping; Elizabeth and her infant son were seriously injured by the assailant. Two years later, the baby died. "It affected her all the rest of her life," Lee said of his mother's trauma.

In 1811 she married Ralph Lee, a Catholic cattleman and carpenter, and gave birth to John the following year. By all accounts the marriage was rocky from the start, Elizabeth unable to pull herself out of a depression and Ralph an insolvent gambler. When John was three years old, his mother suddenly deeded all her property to be held in trust for the boy and his stepsister, Eliza. Elizabeth died shortly thereafter. His father, "a slave to drink, seldom sober," as John recalled, would eventually disappear altogether, leaving his young son "thrown upon the wide world, helpless." Raised an unwanted child in the French-speaking home of an aunt and uncle who appropriated his mother's estate for their own use, John forgot his native language and was ridiculed by townspeople, who called him "Gumbo." "I was robbed of all," he later wrote, "treated worse than an African slave," regularly whipped and beaten. "If it had not been for my strong religious convictions I would have committed suicide."

From this hardship he would develop a rugged independence, a vow to marry for love, a disdain for gambling, and the outsider's search for belonging. He wanted to live a life far beyond the borders of his childhood. With only three months of formal schooling, Lee was determined to better himself, devouring books and seeking out new ideas. He bounced around the territory, taking jobs as a mail carrier earning seven dollars a month—where he "developed the love and pride he always took in a fine horse," according to one account—a bartender in mining camps, a firefighter on a Mississippi River steamboat. In 1831, at nineteen, Lee volunteered in the Black Hawk War, fighting with the whites against the Indians of northern Illinois. During that skirmish he became a skilled horseman and a strong fighter and encountered more of life's lessons that would shape him. "Men who will lead you into trouble will seldom stand by you to get you out of it," his wartime experiences taught him. "I determined to live within my income . . . to be prompt and punctual . . . making my word my honor and my bond."

Grown into a handsome, well-muscled man, the blue-eyed Lee had what one scholar called "a strong sense of his own destiny and a healthy respect for himself, his abilities, his self-discipline and goodness." In 1833 he courted a young woman named Aggatha Ann Woolsey while visiting relatives in Vandalia, Illinois. They married almost immediately and settled on Luck Creek near Aggatha's extended family into a secure, even prosperous existence.

Five years later he had fathered three children—one dead, one dying, one a suckling infant. The evening his second child, Elizabeth Adaline, slipped from life, Lee picked up a copy of a book given to him months earlier by a missionary passing through. "The night she lay a corpse I finished reading the Book of Mormon," Lee later remembered. "I never closed my eyes in sleep from the time I commenced until I finished the book."

Drawn to what he called "the glory of the Latter Day Work," Lee determined that night to throw himself into the creation of Joseph Smith's Kingdom of God on earth. "Everything but my soul's salvation was a matter of secondary consideration," he wrote in his memoir forty years later. "I had a small fortune, a nice home, kind neighbors, and numerous friends, but nothing could shake the determination I then formed, to break up, sell out, and leave Illinois and go to the Saints at Far West, Missouri."

On June 4, 1838, Lee, Aggatha, and their last living child arrived on the outskirts of Zion. Six days later he saw his new prophet for the first time. He thought him majestic. By June 17, Lee found himself submerged in Shady Grove Creek. "As he came up, his hair washed back from his face, his clothes dripping," according to one account, "he felt cleansed in spirit, as though all that was dross and cheap in his nature literally had been washed away."

The Fourth of July brought the largest exhibition of Mormon pomp and pageantry yet. Lee and thousands of others marched to the site where the first cornerstone for the new temple would be laid, alarming their fellow Missourians with an ominous display of infantry, floats, bands, and cavalry. "Hosanna," the crowd yelled wildly as they awaited the presentation. Vowing a "war of extermination" against Mormon persecutors, a church official delivered one of the more inflammatory speeches in church history and ignited yet more strife in their new locale. More threatening to neighbors than the vitriolic rhetoric, however, was the posturing of the Danites, who seemed to have grown bored with practice and were now "thirsting for action."

Resolute and devout, quick and accomplished, Lee aroused the attention of Smith's confidants, who immediately inducted him into the Danites. Though he personally had no axes to grind, no persecutions to avenge, he embraced his inclusion into what he thought an honorable secret society, and he vowed to defend his fellow Saints to the end. His first engagement was only weeks away.

Lee stretched out on the lawn in the public square of tiny Gallatin, Missouri, awaiting the trouble he knew was brewing. Lee "knew that the two political parties were about equally divided," he would write later, "and that the Mormons held the balance of power." Numbering more than ten thousand, the Mormons were now the largest organized group in the state. That day, August 6, 1838, would mark the first time the Mormons had chosen to vote in a bloc, and the local settlers were determined to keep them from the polls.

"Mormons don't vote, no more than niggers," a Missourian taunted the first who approached the polls. A fight broke out, with men on all sides grabbing four-foot-long oak beams from a nearby building site. "The sign of distress was given by the Danites," Lee remembered, "and all rushed forward." It would be Lee's first chance to battle the persecution of which he had heard so much. "I had seen the *sign*," he wrote, "and, like Sampson when leaning against the pillar, I felt the power of God nerve my arm for the fray." This sign, Lee would later reveal, "is made by placing the right hand on the right side of the face, with the points of the fingers upwards."

The election riot "set the match to the powder keg," as historian Juanita Brooks described it, the Danites rendering nine Gentiles unconscious and badly beating two dozen more. There followed a state of siege in which mobs of Mormons and non-Mormons terrorized each other. The Danites plundered rural farms, stealing livestock and homestead implements. "Alarm seized the stoutest hearts," Lee wrote, "and dismay was visible in every countenance." But in the upcoming conflict and violence, Lee and his fellow Danites would muster a passionate bravado and fervid belief that God would fight their battles for them. "I thought that one Danite would chase a thousand Gentiles and two could put ten thousand to flight." Sworn to secrecy—"to divulge the name of a Danite to an outsider, or to make public any of the secrets of the order . . . was to be punished with death," remembered one who later broke the covenant—the Danites were "placed under the most sacred obligations that language could invent."

A warrant was issued for Smith's arrest, and Governor Lilburn Boggs ordered out six companies of militia to put down the unrest. At the Battle of Crooked River in October 1838, a handful of men on both sides were killed in a brawl, resulting in exaggerated rumors of a church-led massacre and prelude to an all-out civil war. Igniting the already aroused tempers, Smith delivered a vitriolic address on October 14 in the town square that would go down in history as the "Mohammed speech." "If the people will let us alone we will preach the gospel in peace," he ranted. "But if they come on us to molest us, we will establish our religion by the sword. We will trample down our enemies and make it one gore of blood from the Rocky Mountains to the Atlantic Ocean. I will be to this generation a second Mohammed, whose motto in treating for peace was 'the Alcoran [Koran] or the Sword.' "

The Mormons were now formally, if not officially, at war. Responding to embellished allegations of looting, as well as reports of the Mohammed speech, Governor Boggs took an even bolder stance, issuing what would become known as the "Extermination Orders." "The Mormons must be treated as enemies and must be exterminated," he wrote to one of his commanders on October 27, "or driven from the state, if necessary for the public good. Their outrages are beyond all description."

Within days almost all the Mormons had abandoned their outlying settlements—all except Jacob Haun and his fellow settlers at Hauns Mill, who refused to leave their small community and newly built flour mill on a creek a few miles from Far West. On October 30, more than two hundred militiamen stormed the village, brutally slaughtering seventeen men and boys. When a nine-year-old was dragged from his hiding place in a blacksmith shop, one of the Gentiles was heard to say: "Don't shoot, it's just a boy." But in a coldblooded murder that would become legend in the decades that followed, a man shot the child in the head from point-blank range. The Hauns Mill Massacre, as it came to be known, would thus become a rationale and justification for future vengeance and bloodshed—the undeniable evidence of the persecution so central to the growing faith.

John D. Lee's home in Ambrosia, twenty miles southeast of Far West, had been reduced to charred logs when Lee arrived back from the conflict. His wife and small daughter clung to each other in a corner of the demolished house. Now that he knew firsthand the depredations suffered by the Saints, his armchair ardor forged into zealotry. He considered the patriarchal blessing he received a few weeks later as "next to a boon of eternal life." He memorized every word, taking to heart the full implication of the benison, eventually carrying it, with irony and prophecy, to his own grave. "Thou shalt have power over thine enemies," Lee was promised. "Thou shalt come forth in the morning of the first resurrection, and no power shall hinder, except the shedding of innocent blood, or consenting thereto." From that moment forward, Lee would "pray for strength to face a frowning world."

"You are brave and good men," the prophet told his troops. "But we are faced by 10,000 soldiers with instructions for our extermination." He then surrendered to Missouri lawmen on November 30 to face charges of treason, murder, arson, burglary, robbery, larceny, and perjury. Expecting immediate execution, he would instead languish heavily chained for four months in a stone jail cell in Liberty, Missouri. All the while his appointed surrogates planned for another mass exodus—this time to adjacent Illinois.

As the months passed, the state lost its appetite for a public trial of Smith, which was sure to cause mayhem and more violence. On April 6, 1839, as Smith's jailers transported him from Liberty to Gallatin, he was able to escape his captors with little fanfare. Mounting a "fine chestnut stallion," according to one account, he "pounded up the road toward his old settlement, where he joined the last remnant of the Mormons who were headed for the Mississippi."

CHAPTER THREE

Nauvoo, 1840

T HE NAME IS of Hebrew origin," Smith would say of Nauvoo the Beautiful—the new Zion. "It is situated on the eastern bank of the Mississippi River, at the head of the Des Moines Rapids, in Hancock County; bounded on the east by an extensive prairie of surpassing beauty; and on the north, west, and south by the Mississippi." The word "Nauvoo" had what one writer called "the melancholy music of a mourning dove's call and somehow matched the magic of the site."

Smith, thirty-three upon his arrival in Nauvoo in 1839, envisioned a commonwealth on the limestone flat so powerful, wealthy, and industrious as to dwarf every other city in the United States. Here, in the land of Abraham Lincoln and Stephen Douglas, would be the last City of Joseph, the final theocratic state ordained by God and conveyed to Smith, to usher in the Second Coming.

By the time John D. Lee arrived in April 1840, Nauvoo was a thriving boomtown of twelve stores, two gunsmiths, three blacksmiths, three hotels, a bakery, a newspaper and printing office, several doctors and lawyers, two sawmills and a massive flour mill, a tool factory and foundry, and a handful of bootmakers, carpenters, tailors, teachers, and the other requisite contributors to a civilized society. The city would boast three thousand souls by the summer of 1840 where none had been only months before. The city's population would double every year for the next three years, culminating in the melded society the Mormons had envisioned.

Skilled converts were pouring into Nauvoo from England in record numbers—"gathering like bees to a swarming limb," wrote one historian—crossing the dangerous Atlantic Ocean before trekking halfway across the continent as new adherents to Joseph Smith's vision. Having suffered beatings and tarrings at the hands of Mormon baiters years earlier, and having faced impending death at various junctures, Smith sensed rightly that events in Nauvoo would be the grand finale of his life. Now he worked with a newfound passion to bring national attention to the plight of his people, "resolving to make Missouri a byword for oppression and Boggs a synonym for tyranny." Carrying hundreds of petitions to President Martin Van Buren in Washington demanding punishment of the perpetrators of the Hauns Mill Massacre, Smith was disgusted with the complacency he found in the capital. "Your cause is just, but I can do nothing for you," Van Buren wrote Smith, apparently reluctant to alienate Missourians on the cusp of a presidential election. The response turned Smith away from Van Buren's Democratic Party in favor of the Whigs, and fueled Smith's own political ambitions and grandiose ideas of a separatist city-state that would rival Washington, with Smith as God's chosen leader.

Smith controlled all real estate deals in Nauvoo and dictated numerous business transactions through divine revelation; the wealthy metropolis of wide streets and lush adjacent farms was on its way to becoming one of the largest cities in the state. "It was the policy of Joseph Smith to hold the city lots in Nauvoo at a high price, so as to draw money from the rich, but not so high as to prevent the poor from obtaining homes," Lee would recall. Smith "classed the poor in three divisions: The Lord's poor, the devil's poor, and the poor devils."

Building a spired marble temple took precedence over everything else—"each man required to do one day's work every ten days in quarrying rock." Smith himself was not only spiritual leader of his burgeoning religion, but he was now mayor, hotelier, judge, temple architect, realtor, merchant, and banker in his model city as well. He relished his role as purveyor of the Mormon voting bloc so soon to be influential in Illinois politics. In January 1842 the *New York Herald* reported a population of ten thousand in Nauvoo proper and thirty thousand in the nearby countryside, editor Gordon Bennett calling it "a new religious civilization . . . that may revolutionize the whole earth one of these days."

That year, John C. Bennett (no relation to the journalist), perhaps Smith's closest friend and the second most powerful man in Nauvoo, had a bitter falling-out with Smith over a woman each desired as a plural wife. Bennett would angrily leave Nauvoo and write a series of malicious news articles exposing the Danites and Smith's militaristic plans to implement by force a nationwide theocracy, and denouncing "Smith for being an insatiable libertine." He also claimed to have heard the prophet offer $500 to any Danite who would assassinate Governor Boggs, declaring that "the exterminator shall be exterminated!" In early May, while reading by candlelight in his Missouri home, Boggs was shot three times in the head by an unknown sniper. Miraculously surviving, Boggs accused Smith of being an "accessory" to his attempted murder.

By this time Smith's Nauvoo Legion, or Army of God, was the largest militia in the state, with its twenty-six companies totaling two thousand troops, nearly a quarter the size of the U.S. Army. Smith's dream come true, Nauvoo was indeed the first genuine theocracy in American history. Commissioned lieutenant general by the Illinois governor, Smith—the first American to hold the position since George Washington—"jested about his outranking every military officer in the United States." Abandoning his church title of "president" for the more lofty designation of "general," he began calling out the legion for trumped-up celebrations. He designed a navy blue military uniform for himself, resplendent with gold braiding and brass buttons, and wore shiny black knee-high boots over taupe trousers. As he rode a black stallion at the front of his legion, his fancy spurs and high-crowned Napoleon-style hat—"gilt stars tossed there among black ostrich plumes"—unmistakably set him apart as commander-in-chief.

Noting the military despotism arising in Smith's realm, newspapers from New York to Illinois expressed alarm. Smith's personal and political aspirations were also growing beyond his once limited boundaries. Taken with the Texas fever sweeping the nation, he claimed for the Mormon empire a huge swath of land to be carved out of Mexico. To implement the vision of this new, imposing Kingdom of God in the West perched in a high mountain range, he organized a top-secret Council of Fifty, a group of princes who would rule this new sovereignty. "So secret was its very existence," wrote historian David L. Bigler, "that any breech was held to be a serious sin that could only be atoned by the blood of the offender." In March 1844, Smith brazenly asked Congress to appoint him an officer in the U.S. Army and vest him with the authority to raise 100,000 men to guard the United States all the way from Texas to Oregon. Considered overreaching, if not delusional, Smith's petition was denied.

With equal audacity, he then announced he was running for president of the United States, advocating a "Theodemocracy," he told a Nauvoo newspaper, "where God and the people hold the power to conduct the affairs of men," the abolition of slavery, the annexation of Texas, the reform of prisons, and the reduction of Congress by two thirds. One of history's more unusual presidential candidates, Smith claimed church membership of 200,000 when fewer than 30,000 were on the official rosters. He saw rival politicians James Buchanan and Millard Fillmore as threats to his quixotic dominion.

"Using the same techniques they used to win souls," wrote one observer of the Mormons, "they worked to win votes instead." Smith dispatched one hundred of his loyalists to go forth as missionaries, campaigning for Smith while also seeking converts. "It was hard enough to preach the gospel without purse or scrip," John D. Lee, now a major in the Nauvoo Legion, would recall of the strange assignment. "But it was as nothing compared to offering the Prophet Joseph to the people as a candidate for the highest gift of the nation."

In these last few months of his life Smith acted with uncharacteristic heedlessness. As he organized for war—securing thirty cannons and hundreds of small arms—he prophesied the impending overthrow of the nation and in a bizarre coronation appointed himself a "king" while also seeking the presidency. He set apart twelve of his most fierce Danites, including Lee, as destroying angels "whose business it was to spy out the Prophet's enemies," wrote a historian, "and assassinate them at midnight, garbed in white robes, and wearing a wide red sash about their waists."

Despite his popularity within the sect and the favorable publicity his campaign received, the hatred he inspired was perilous. "Those who took Joseph's campaign seriously," Fawn Brodie would write a century later, "saw him as an evil symbol of the union of church and state."

But in the end, it would be his own emerging and much disputed doctrines, his inability to accurately assess and neutralize his enemies—especially from within—and his narcisisstic "theme of deceiving self and others," as one scholar put it, that would lead to his downfall. He "moved from one self-made crisis to another."

"You don't know me; you never knew my heart. . . . No man knows my history." Smith spoke these words at a funeral in the spring of 1844 when, as a candidate for the highest office in the land, he was secretly the husband of nearly fifty wives and the church he had founded had been transformed into what was widely seen as a "mystery cult."

Nauvoo, unlike Kirtland, had become the sanctuary for strange ceremonials and shrouded rites many members found increasingly alien and offensive. Purification rituals with sexual overtones, endowment ceremonies with fertility worship, phallic symbolism, and allegorical dramas with shocking similarities to freemasonry all moved the church further away from the traditional movements of the day and led to a rise in critical apostates. The principle most difficult for many men and women to abide was that of polygamy.

"Monogamy seemed to him—as it has seemed to many men," one of Smith's biographers wrote of his belief, "an intolerably circumscribed way of life." Though practiced covertly by Smith and some of his intimates for nearly a decade, the revelation of the Law of Jacob— named for the Old Testament polygamist—was not officially presented as a commandment from God until 1842. Careful to keep the system concealed so as not to "bring down the wrath of the Gentiles," Smith revealed the "blessing" one by one to his inner circle. On May 5 of that year he divulged the details of plural marriage to his apostle Brigham Young, who, "after much hesitation" according to one account, took a plural wife within weeks.

In August 1843, the revelation was finally committed to writing and read to the High Council. After what one author described as an "initial period of shock and spiritual torment," some men were won over. Depicted as part of "celestial" or everlasting marriage, "spiritual wifery," as it was called, was appealing to many. "To men who loved their wives, it was pleasant to hear that death was no separation," as one account put it, "and to men who did not, it was gratifying to hear that there could be no sin in taking another." The concept of eternal progression and celestial marriage, wrote a Mormon historian, "allowed the most ordinary backwoodsman to become a god and rule over worlds of his own creation with as many wives as his righteousness could sustain."

But many church members, male and female, found the practice appalling. Smith "plunged into new sealings to married women, sisters, and very young girls," as one historian described the prophet's promiscuity; he even propositioned the wives of friends, prompting a schism in the congregation. Church officials split into two camps—those in favor of polygamy and those opposed.

Defections were rampant and accusations incendiary. "My life is more in danger from some little dough-head of a fool in this city than from all my numerous and inveterate enemies abroad," Smith said of his critics. Meanwhile, he ordered reinforcements of his personal guard, the Nauvoo Legion swelled to four thousand members, and John D. Lee was assigned the coveted and trusted role of protecting Smith during the prophet's conjugal visits with his various wives. Two of the most vehement renegades from Smith's clandestine brotherhood, the Council of Fifty—"men who knew too much," as they were described—founded the *Nauvoo Expositor* in order to reveal publicly the widespread practice of polygamy. The exposés quickly grew to include seedy details of Smith's financial shenanigans with the temple building funds, as well as other lascivious propensities unseemly for a prophet. "The paper had put him on trial before his whole people," wrote Brodie. Smith "tried to be a law-abiding citizen," as Lee saw it, "but he had a motley crew to manage."

Smith grew increasingly outspoken in his hostility. "Here is wishing that all the mobocrats of the nineteenth century were in the middle of the sea in a stone canoe, with an iron paddle; that a shark might swallow the canoe, and the shark be thrust into the nethermost part of hell, and the door locked, the key lost, and a blind man hunting for it," the prophet offered in a celebratory toast.

In a rash and ultimately fatal move—the fateful blunder of his life—Smith ordered the Nauvoo Legion to storm the newspaper, destroy the press, and burn all extant issues. The vandalism set loose the latent hostilities seething in Illinois, prompting constitutional defenders of the First Amendment to call for Smith's arrest. Refusing to submit to the authorities of Illinois, Smith declared martial law in his independent city-state.

On June 18, 1844, he called out the legion to keep order, as angry anti-Mormon mobs from Missouri, Iowa, and Illinois gathered in nearby towns, "attracted like flies to the smell of blood," as one writer depicted the mood. The thirty-eight-year-old prophet led his legion in a parade up Main Street, his stallion Charlie prancing at the head of the line. Addressing his subjects for the last time, he mounted a reviewing stand—"his blue and buff uniform blazoned with gilt buttons and epaulets"—as his men marched into formation to the cadence of a brass band. "Will you stand by me to the death?" he shouted out, and was answered with a thunderous "Aye!" Dramatically pointing his sword to the sky, he yelled, "I call God and angels to witness that I have unsheathed my sword." A "Christlike sacrificial figure willing to die for the Saints," as Smith in his final public moments was described, he faced thousands of his followers, tears streaming down their faces. "I am ready to be offered, for what can they do, only kill the body."

As the legion patrolled the riverbanks, scouts rode into town every hour to report the growing turmoil in the countryside. When word arrived of a posse from nearby Carthage en route to arrest him, Smith took to hiding in a secret chamber built into his Mansion House and began acting like a doomed man while addressing the problem of naming a successor. Betrayed by members of his Council of Fifty who had violated their secrecy oaths, he and three other men sneaked onto the Mississippi at midnight on June 22 in a small dinghy. They hid in Iowa, having left "word for the brethren to hang onto their arms and take care of themselves the best way they could," a witness remembered. Smith's faithful followers were horrified at his hasty departure, prompting panic in Nauvoo.

Begged by his first wife, Emma, and others to return, a dispirited Smith responded to those charging him with cowardice. "If my life is of no value to friends it is of none to myself," he said before surrendering at the Carthage jail. "I am going like a lamb to slaughter . . . my blood shall cry from the ground for vengeance."

The morning of July 27, 1844, he sent orders to his legion to immediately attack the jail and free him, and when he heard at five p.m. that a large militia was approaching the stone jail, he assumed they were his rescuers. But soon it was clear that this was a vigilante mob that had no intention of saving him. Standing in the window of his second-story cell, he faced a hundred bayonets, and "behind every bayonet there was a hideously painted face," his attackers disguised with war paint. Lore has it that he gave the Masonic distress signal before calling out: "Oh Lord my God. Is there no help for the widow's son?" As he looked out on the crowd, some of his enemies had made their way up to his cell. A musket ball struck him in the back, and he plunged out the window and to the ground.

It was a brutal and ironic end for a man of such grand ambition and accomplishment. The presidential candidate, church leader, mayor, and military commander seemed predestined for a far more dramatic and historic death—at the hands of the U.S. Army, perhaps, or in some other clash of epic theological and political proportions. Instead, he had been arrested as a common criminal, charged with ordinary acts of hooliganism, and killed by a rabble in an unassuming midwestern hamlet. Undaunted by the banality of Smith's end, his followers cleaved to the mythology of the man. For them, their Prophet, Seer, and Revelator was now ascending to his rightful place in the Celestial Kingdom of martyrs, his death second in importance only to that of Jesus Christ. He was the first American religious leader ever to be assassinated. "For never, since the Son of God was slain, has blood so noble flow'd from human vein," wrote one of his secret polygamist wives, the talented poetess and high priestess Eliza Snow.

"Joseph is killed!" shouted the head of the Danites, galloping his horse into the streets of Nauvoo on June 28, 1844. Paralyzed by shock and grief, the Mormons were at first unbelieving. When their martyr's body arrived in a wooden coffin draped by a colorful Indian blanket and sprays of prairie grass, twenty thousand of his weeping followers formed a final procession. "The death of the modern Mahomet," the *New York Herald* somewhat gloatingly remarked of the passing, "will seal the fate of Mormondom. . . . [T]he 'latter-day saints' have indeed come to the latter day."

The horror of the loss soon turned to outrage. Allen J. Stout gave words to feelings widely held, roiling emotions and steadfast vows that would manifest themselves in the next decades of a church and its disciples. "I hope I live to avenge [his] blood," the Danite wrote in his journal. "But if I do not, I will teach my children to never cease to try to avenge [his] blood and then teach their children and children's children to the fourth generation as long as there is one descendant of the murderers upon the earth."

The death of the prophet threw the sect into chaos, and the following weeks were mired in confusion and power struggles over the right of succession. "If Smith anticipated the possibility of his death," wrote a historian, "he failed to clarify for the highest leadership of the church the precise method of succession God intended."

"Who should rule the church was now an open question," wrote T. B. H. Stenhouse. More than a dozen cabals sought to seize control, while many of the Quorum of Twelve were scattered throughout the eastern states campaigning for Smith's presidency. Sidney Rigdon, who had been a church leader for fourteen years and once the prophet's close confidant, had recently apostatized over Smith's attempted seduction of his daughter into a polygamous marriage. He now returned to claim the throne. "Pretenders began to assemble at Nauvoo, each claiming the right to succeed the fallen martyr," as one writer described the crisis. Ferocious internal struggles threatened the stability of the church itself.

The far-flung apostles reported a prescience in the hours surrounding Smith's death. On a boat in Utica, New York, at the time of the murder, Parley Pratt felt a "strange and solemn awe [come] over me, as if the powers of hell were let loose. I was so overwhelmed with sorrow I could hardly speak."

Brigham Young was in Boston about to board a train to Salem. "In the evening, while sitting in the depot waiting, I felt a heavy depression of spirit, and so melancholy I could not converse with any degree of pleasure," he wrote in his diary.* "Not knowing anything concerning the tragedy enacting at this time in Carthage jail, I could not assign my reasons for my peculiar feelings."

Upon learning of the death, the apostles dashed back to Nauvoo, where they converged with fellow aspirants all competing for control of the church. On August 8 at ten o'clock in the morning, the Saints met for a climactic meeting in an open grove above the riverbank. Rigdon was the first to speak, but the wind made it difficult to hear his interminably long address, and his nervousness and diffidence annoyed the audience.

What happened when the stocky, redheaded Brigham Young clambered onto the wagon being used as a makeshift stage would become legendary. For when he opened his mouth to speak, it was not his voice that emanated, according to many of those in the audience, but a voice uncannily like that of Joseph Smith. Many in the crowd rushed the platform to see if their prophet had risen from the dead, only to be fur-

---

*The extent of Brigham Young's literacy is a subject of historical debate and speculation. While we know that he was virtually uneducated and that his apostles often read documents to him, surprisingly articulate letters in Young's handwriting attest to his abilities.

ther mystified by the same "supernatural radiance" that had enveloped Smith now illuminating Young.

"Brigham Young arose and roared like a young lion," John D. Lee later recalled, "imitating the style and voice of Joseph." While many of Lee's brethren "saw the mantle of Joseph fall upon him," Lee believed the rightful successor should be Smith's young son Joseph, and that Young should merely hold the presidency until Joseph Smith III grew to manhood. But Young waged a tenacious and mesmerizing battle, and had no intention of safeguarding the seat of power for a twelve-year-old boy. Lee listened as the prophet's mother begged Young "with tears, not to rob young Joseph of his birthright," which she claimed his father had bestowed upon him. Young, while acknowledging the validity of the claim, warned her to stop promoting the issue. "You are only laying the knife to the throat of the child," Young told her, implying that the Missourians would kill the boy, while he promised that "no one shall rob him" of the position as leader of the church. Thousands, including Lee, would eventually grow to see Young as a usurper. But for now, his dynamic ascendancy went relatively unchallenged. "Brigham Young was at the head of the Quorum of the Twelve," wrote Stenhouse. "No one questioned his fidelity to the Prophet up to this time; but, personally, he was remarkable for nothing—except being 'hard-working Brigham Young.'"

Young would lead the Saints from that day forward. Though the quorum in its entirety was the designated official first presidency of the church—Young would not formalize his ascendancy for three more years—by the end of that month he was in command of the Nauvoo Legion. Knowing he could not compete with Smith as a seer, Young sought to dispense the power of divine manifestation to his flock. "Instead of vaulting to the prominence of the 'Revelator,' Brigham brought down the revelations to the grasp of the people," wrote a contemporaneous insider. "The soul and inspiration of Mormonism were gone. Brigham might occupy Joseph's seat on the platform, but he could never fill his place in the Church, and no one knew this better than Brigham himself." Young, however, assured the Saints that Joseph had left behind enough revelations to guide them over the next twenty years—Young himself preferring industry, fortitude, and planning over visionary dispensations.

While murmurs of usurpation abounded, most Saints committed

themselves unquestioningly to their new leader. "There is a tinge of Cromwell and Napoleon about Brigham that is really charming to the very humble Mormons," was how one writer described the growing devotion and admiration for Young. From the beginning, Young ruled with an iron fist, attempting to control everyone and everything, molding the seductive thirst for vengeance into an adhesive to bind his disparate forces. All who had passed through their temple endowments were now "placed under the most sacred obligations to avenge the blood of the Prophet, whenever an opportunity offered, and to teach their children to do the same," wrote John D. Lee, who had received the order. Thus the "entire Mormon people [became] sworn and avowed enemies of the American nation."

Lee sat in Young's office one day and watched as the new leader raised his right hand: "I swear by the eternal Heavens that I have unsheathed my sword, and I will never return it until the blood of the Prophet Joseph . . . is avenged." Then, in perhaps the first hint of what would mark the next decades, Young turned to the men in the room. "Now," he said, "betray me, any of you who dare to do so."

At only sixteen years of age, the orphaned John Young, Brigham's father, had enlisted in the Revolutionary War, then served in four engagements under George Washington. Five years later, in 1785, he returned to his birthplace, Hopkinton, Massachusetts, and married Abigail "Nabby" Howe, a young girl from a respectable family. The Puritan New Englanders had two daughters in short order before wandering through the wilderness of rural New York in search of fertile farmland. Young, a harsh and laconic man whose primitive instincts had been honed by wartime experiences, was more comfortable in nature than Nabby, who was sensitive, delicate, and frail in spirit and health. Once, when attacked by an enormous raging bear, John, short and wiry, rammed a rudimentary spear down the bear's mouth and throat and killed the animal after a fierce and legendary struggle. When John's father-in-law demanded that he return with Nabby and their now three children to the more civilized Hopkinton, John did so begrudgingly, in the winter of 1790. Five more children were born to the couple in the next decade, and except for the unfortunate maiming of two-year-old Phinehas by his older brother—"Joseph cut off my right hand . . . with an ax while we were at play"—life was by all accounts uneventful.

Responding to an offer from a Young relative who had subdivided farmland in Whitingham, Vermont, the family moved eighty miles northwest in January 1801 and bought fifty acres of virginal woodlands for fifty dollars. The family made the journey in two bobsleds pulled by oxen through blinding snowstorms. Six months later, on June 1, Brigham was born. "The heavens were heard to resound slightly," later disciples would claim, "and towards evening a star is said to have twinkled more irregularly than usual, indicating thereby that God was manifesting particular interest in this one of his many children."

By the time of Brigham's birth, the Youngs were among the poorest families to settle in Whitingham, having somehow lost their land, living in a sixteen-foot-square one-room cabin, and owning neither a cow nor a horse. John, now a hot-tempered, destitute basket maker, moved his family yet again before Brigham was three. This time it was to the Finger Lakes area of western New York, where John tried to cobble together a living out of unforgiving soil. Brigham grew to manhood under the harsh eye of parents plagued with the religious fervor then sweeping upstate New York. Superstitious and ignorant, the Youngs were obsessed with the revivals taking place in their region.

John disciplined Brigham with what the latter called "a word and a blow . . . but the blow came first." In later life, Brigham would boast of his eleven and a half days in school, but as a youth—like Joseph Smith—he longed for something beyond the clearing, chopping, plowing, planting, and reaping that defined his childhood. Just after his fourteenth birthday, his mother died of consumption, adding domestic chores to Brigham's farming responsibilities. "I learned to make bread, wash the dishes, milk the cows, and make butter," he would later reminisce. Such resourcefulness would serve him well when, at sixteen, his stern father told him to "go and provide for yourself."

"I have been a poor boy and a poor man," Brigham Young later said, but when he set out to become a craftsman, it was with an eye toward improving his lot in life, committed to what he called "honest, reliable work." As a builder and an artisan, a painter and a glazier, Young developed the patience and meticulous attention to detail that would have historic consequences. Independent and stubborn—"I am naturally opposed to being crowded"—Young rejected the Reformed Methodism of his parents that disallowed dancing, music, and card-playing, refusing at one point to sign a temperance pledge his father was demanding. Because he recognized "weakness, sin, darkness, and ignorance" within himself, he decided to live an upstanding life while formulating his own faith. Unable to reconcile the Bible's teachings with the religious agitation surrounding him, he refused to join any of the copious sects in the Burned-Over District.

"I saw them get religion all around me," Young recalled. "Men were rolling and holloring [sic] and bawling and thumping but it had no effect on me." Young kept his head and his counsel in what has been described as an "unremitting warfare of theologies." But when it came time to marry and start a family, he began in earnest to consider "these eternal things."

Eighteen-year-old Miriam Works, a stunning, affable blue-eyed blonde, married the rugged, responsible twenty-three-year-old carpenter on October 8, 1824. He had developed into what a neighbor would call "as fine a specimen of young manhood as I have ever known." To coincide with his marriage, he was finally baptized a Reformed Methodist, "to prevent my being pestered any more." Not long after, he relocated to the Canandaigua-Mendon area to be near his cousin Heber Kimball, who would become his lifelong best friend. There he abandoned his new religion and joined a group of "primitivists," who viewed traditional churches as corrupt and stressed a need in the sectarian conflict for the restoration of the primitive faith.

On the moonless night of September 22, 1827, Brigham and Miriam observed a strange apparition in the sky above nearby Palmyra. They gazed, astonished, at the lights that formed a battalion in the night's darkness. "The light was perfectly clear and remained several hours," Brigham would describe the vision. "It formed into men like as if there were great armies." Kimball too remembered the night: "I distinctly heard the guns crack and the swords clash."

But it would be a few more years before they came to believe the lights they saw were those that had illuminated the angel Moroni delivering the golden plates to their neighbor Joseph Smith.

Brigham, said to be a tender and devoted family man, assumed the care of his young daughters when Miriam was stricken with tuberculosis.

After cooking breakfast and dressing the girls, he "carried his wife to the rocking chair by the fireplace and left her there until he could return in the evening." Though there would be later allegations by a Canandaigua newspaper that he neglected Miriam and the girls, an acquaintance of the family called these charges "most unjust."

Miriam's decline contributed to a growing despondency in Brigham so profound that he once said he was so "sick, tired, and disgusted with the world" that he felt like withdrawing from society. At twenty-nine, he was still poor, disappointed in his unfulfilled ambitions, pessimistic about his future, and contemptuous of mankind.

When his brother Phinehas brought him a copy of the Book of Mormon just weeks after it had been published a few miles away, Brigham expressed little interest. For eighteen months, "the more he wrestled with [the book] the truer it seemed," wrote one historian. Still, he wavered. Though at least two of his brothers, his father, and a sister had converted to Mormonism, Brigham held out with a tentativeness that would prompt later critics to question his dedication. It was the simple affirmation by an inarticulate missionary that ultimately convinced him. "The Holy Ghost proceeding from that individual illuminated my understanding," Young would later explain, "and light, glory, and immortality were before me. I was encircled by them, filled by them, and I knew for myself that the testimony of the man was true." This plainspoken elder, Young claimed, set off "fire in my bones."

On a frigid, snowy Sunday in April 1832, Young was baptized in his "own little mill stream." Before his clothes were dry, he knew he wanted to spread this revolutionary restored gospel. "I had to go out and preach, lest my bones should consume within me." A week later, the elders asked him to give his first speech. Though uneducated and inexperienced—"I was but a child so far as public speaking"—he found himself possessed by supernatural powers. "I opened my mouth and the Lord filled it."

In a style that many say came to resemble those of the famous revivalist Charles Finney and the seminarian Lyman Beecher, Young perfected the conversational delivery of powerful preaching. "Simple language, short sentences, and a colloquial manner, with frequent repetition and parables," as a Mormon scholar described the method that would come naturally to Young. "Pump yourselves brim full of your subject until you can't hold another drop," Beecher would lecture, "and then knock out the bung and let nature caper."

Miriam died the following September, setting Brigham free to pursue his new calling. Selling or giving away his possessions, ridding himself of all encumbrances that tied him to the material world, and depositing his daughters with Heber Kimball and his wife, he "set out Quixote-like to change the world," as one scholar described it. "I wanted to thunder and roar out the Gospel to the nations," was how Young later referred to his mission.

Two months later, in November 1832, Joseph Smith was chopping wood in the forest near his home when some friends brought the new convert to meet him. Smith invited the men into his cottage, then turned to Brigham Young and asked him to pray. "In my prayer I spoke in tongues," Young remembered, which alarmed those present, as Smith had been trying to repress such behavior. But rather than condemn him, Smith announced that the incomprehensible gibberish was in fact the "true Adamic language." The gift of tongues "thus acquired status in the church," as one account put it, providing "the most inarticulate convert with a spontaneous, mysterious, and immensely satisfying form of self-expression."

Stocky and corpulent, energetic and alert, intelligent and forceful, Young endeared himself to the new prophet at their very first meeting. "That man," Smith is said to have remarked at the time, pointing toward Brigham, "will yet preside over this church." Others would claim in later years that they heard Smith say instead: "If Brigham Young ever becomes president of the church, he will lead it to hell." The truth, no doubt, lay somewhere in between.

By August 1844, Young ruled the church. The most pressing matter for Young now was to reinforce his personal and political security while disposing of his rivals. "Engulfed by dissension from within and without," as one of Young's biographers, Stanley P. Hirshson, described the moment, "Young established in Nauvoo a police state." From the very beginning, John D. Lee was an integral component in the new power structure. While Lee had "maintained a half-worshipful distance from Joseph Smith," Juanita Brooks wrote, "he had worked hand in glove with Brigham Young." Young appointed Lee as his personal bodyguard, purchasing a nearby house for him. He then ordered Lee to "organize all the young men into Quorums of Seventy" and to be the clerk and recorder for the group. Threatened by internal enemies, separatist movements, and Missouri lawmen seeking justice for the attempted murder of their governor, Young kept hidden during most of the fall of 1844. "In the meantime," Lee later wrote, "his 'destroying angels' were diligently on the watch." If necessary, they would "treat with great kindness" suspected invaders, "and in that way decoy them to some out-of-the way place and 'save them.' "

The twelve apostles excommunicated Sidney Rigdon, who was orchestrating a widespread propaganda campaign against Young, and they shunned Emma Smith. Refusing to acknowledge Young's ascendancy, Emma and other Smith relatives would eventually return to Far West and found the Reorganized Church of Jesus Christ of Latter Day Saints, which would thrive and become an outspoken voice against polygamy.

In Nauvoo the Saints worked feverishly to finish the temple that they believed God had commanded be built. The huge stone structure would be the site for the "endowments" so crucial to true believers— the spiritual blessings and ritual ceremonies of eternal progression central to the faith. One of Joseph Smith's last exhortations to his followers was to complete the temple in order to receive the requisite endowments for the "Mormon road to Heaven." Prodded by church leaders, "men were as thick as blackbirds busily engaged upon the various portions," a participant wrote in his diary. At a cost of $600,000, the temple was to exhibit "more wealth, more art, more science, more revelation, more splendor, and more God, than all the rest of the world."

The following months were uncharacteristically calm. As a master proselytizer, Young had served ten missions to the British Isles before Smith's death, and was thought to be personally responsible for the astonishing number of those who had converted and emigrated. In England, missionaries capitalized on the intolerable social and economic conditions—ramshackle tenements, overflowing sewers, rampant unemployment, and what Fawn Brodie has described as "a fearful burden of taxes weighing on the thin shoulders of the poor"—to win adherents. That fall of 1844 would see four thousand converts pouring into Nauvoo, the diligent and practical Young overseeing every aspect of their relocation. "Though they missed their Prophet," as Brooks described the peculiar peace and prosperity that now reigned in the city, "they knew that his passing had eased tensions generally, so that building went on and social life was gay."

Inevitably, though, by the spring of 1845 hostilities began escalating once again, as controversial doctrines and proclamations were pronounced in Young's fulminating sermons. Polygamy had expanded, and thanks to John D. Lee's high standing in the church he became one of the elite who could practice celestial marriage. In March, Young preached that women "have no right to meddle in the affairs of the Kingdom of God." Brutality also flourished. In April, Young commended his police for nearly beating to death an apostate within the walls of the temple—a commendation that shocked neighboring Gentiles.

But one of the primary catalysts for events to follow was the "Proclamation of the Twelve Apostles," which notified the world that the "Kingdom of God has come, as has been predicted by ancient prophets." In the document written by Parley Pratt and addressed to all the kings on earth, the president of the United States, and the governors of each American state, the governing body of every nation was ordered to "take sides either for or against" this kingdom, to choose between good and evil. In preparation for Christ's return, the Indians, or Lamanites—"a remnant of the tribes of Israel, as is now made manifest by the discovery and revelation of their ancient oracles and records"—must now be gathered and civilized.

The proclamation was published, translated, and circulated in England, Scotland, Ireland, Wales, the Isle of Man, Spain, France, Norway, and Germany. Newspapers throughout the world were asked to report on this "news." In America the church printed 100,000 copies, translating some into Cherokee and other Native American tongues, and providing them "gratis" to all "presidents, governors, legislators, judges, postmasters, rulers, and people, not forgetting the clergy."

"Know ye not that the millennium has commenced?" Young blared to a general conference on April 6, the day the proclamation was signed. In June, the temple was completed—the "top stone laid with Praises and Hosannas," an observer recalled—and on June 27, the one-year anniversary of Smith's murder, the Quorum of Twelve presented a formal prayer, or oath, of vengeance against the murderers of their prophet.

The arrogance of the proclamation, the alienating practice of polygamy, the whisperings of vengeance, the beatings and murders of Gentiles, the influx of converts, and the increasingly caustic sermons all led to renewed conflict. The pending indictment of two leaders of the church on counterfeiting charges spurred more agitation. Trouble grew in the nearby settlements, and soon thousands of armed Mormons and Gentiles faced off. By September more than a hundred Mormon homes had been burned, and, as one observer wrote, "the Saints were no less ruthless." Young ordered his secret Council of Fifty to send a fact-gathering company of fifteen hundred men to scout for land further west as yet another exodus seemed imminent.

While the idea of finding a Zion in the remote, uncivilized Rocky Mountain region took hold in Young's mind, a meeting was arranged between church leaders and Illinois senator Stephen Douglas to negotiate a cease-fire. At a convention held in Carthage near the site of Smith's murder, the parties agreed they would live in peace until "the grass grows and water runs in the spring, when they shall all dispose of their property and leave the state." Now, with a welcome respite but a looming deadline, plans for a mass migration took shape. Mormons saw it as "an episode in the cosmic struggle between God and the devil"—with the believing Mormons innocent and the nonbelievers wicked—and it fanned their zeal.

CHAPTER FOUR

Winter Quarters—
Council Bluffs, 1846

N o ONE unacquainted with the history of the Saints at this time could possibly imagine the recrimination and bitterness of feeling that existed," T. B. H. Stenhouse wrote. "It was worse than civil war, worse than a war of races; it was religious hate! It was fed by fanaticism on both sides."

To strengthen his position, Young now acted on his belief that when a "worthy male" ascended to Godhood he would want to be joined by his "able assistants." Brigham had been "sealed" to Joseph as part of this covenant, and now selected thirty-eight men he wanted sealed to him. The second chosen, John D. Lee, would always resent the placement. "I should have been his first adopted son," Lee wrote long afterward. All the same, he would be among the first to receive his "washings and anointings . . . which made me an equal in the order of the Priesthood." It was a quid pro quo—"I was to seek his *temporal* interests here and in return he was to seek my *spiritual* salvation." Embracing the gravity of the rite, Lee signed his correspondence "J. D. L. Young" for many years to come.

The devotion between Brigham and John was tested briefly in upcoming weeks. Lee planned to marry a virginal beauty named Emmeline Free, but Young demanded that Lee relinquish her to him. Young held out amorphous promises from the everlasting kingdom. Lee reluctantly acquiesced, though with an odd strutting boast that he went immediately home and "frigged all the women he had in his house."

Despite the treaty with Missouri officials, skirmishes continued, and by December Young had intensified efforts to locate a new Zion in the West. Violence broke out as anti-Mormons reported widespread larceny, and by February 1846 it was clear the Saints would have to move before the spring. "Flee Babylon by land or by sea," Young ordered his people that month, and the fifteen thousand converts now residing in Nauvoo began preparations, though no one yet knew where they would be going. The men established shops where green timber, the only wood available, was boiled in brine to make it malleable and sturdy enough for wagon construction. Young dispatched two of his apostles to Washington, D.C., to request government approval to resettle in Oregon Territory, and to be provided a massive armed escort of American soldiers. In Washington, Senator Douglas gave the men a copy of Colonel John Charles Frémont's report of his recent explorations, which Parley Pratt is said to have read to Young. At the time, very little was known about the geography, topography, and indigenous tribes west of the Missouri River.

Retreating "from Christians," as Young called his enemies, he, his twelve apostles, and the first of two thousand Mormons crossed the "Great Father of Waters" to the Iowa shore at eleven o'clock the morning of February 15. Though the landscape was knee-deep in snow, a fleeting mild snap had thawed much of the solid ice in the Mississippi. "The crossing of the river was superintended by the police," Young's diary reads. "They gathered several flatboats, some old lighters, and a number of skiffs, forming altogether quite a fleet, and were at work night and day crossing the saints." Men, women, children, and their animals and furnishings crammed onto the ferries—"American refugees fleeing a city under threat," Bernard DeVoto sympathetically called them. Nine babies were born to freezing refugee parents at the makeshift compound—"their squalling a muted note against the winter wind"—and the infants were warmed by the hot coals of enormous bonfires. Trudging ten miles inland, they encamped at Sugar Creek, where temperatures dropped to twenty degrees below zero. Young, the chosen leader of the migrating party, called all his men together for a council. He mounted a wagon and gave instructions for maintaining order in the hegira to come. Calling on the "captains of his 100s, 50s, and 10s" to conduct a census recording the name, age, and birthplace of every Mormon at the camp, he then ordered the men to build a central crib for livestock feed.

It was here that Brigham Young received a letter from an eastern emissary informing him that the U.S. government intended to disarm the Mormons and prevent them from continuing westward. Young was told that a "syndicate" of men—allegedly including President James K. Polk, "though his name was not to be used in the matter"—had offered to exert the necessary national influence to avoid such action if the "Mormons would agree in writing to assign every alternate lot of land in the new home they chose to this syndicate of gentlemen." Insulted, and refusing to be intimidated by what he called a "covenant with death," Young ignored the blackmail.

Muddy ravines scarred the wagon trails, the streams and rivers swelled with the incessant rains of March and April, and the nights were "so cold that grass could not grow." By mid-May the best-organized and best-outfitted groups left Nauvoo with thousands of starving Mormons traversing Iowa toward the rendezvous point of Council Bluffs. "A great deal of grumbling, and in some cases almost open rebellion, was indulged in," wrote Danite George Washington Bean. Overtaken by events and only marginally prepared, Young—the "leader of this band of misery"—was wracked with worry. The once beefy man, now gaunt and rangy—the buttons on his coat "lapped over twelve inches"—sought to anticipate and thereby mitigate the hardship to come. Still, he convinced his followers that God would provide their safety, and even insisted they maintain the gaieties of life that had imprinted Nauvoo. Captain Pitt's Brass Band, a feisty combine of English converts, played polkas, minuets, and Scotch reels for the dancing expatriates, though Young branded the waltz inappropriate.

With thousands of hungry, destitute, and ailing Mormons left behind in Nauvoo, and even more arriving regularly from Europe, it became clear to Young that it would not be feasible to push ahead that summer. Instead, in what they called their Camp of Israel, they forged across the plains, setting up a chain of campsites from Council Bluffs to Winter Quarters, near present-day Omaha. Migrating as a people, they methodically established a network of way stations, "building the roads and the bridges," as a western historian put it, "halting companies of the Saints at strategic locations to put in crops for harvesting by brethren yet to take the trail."

All the while, Young sought a rapprochement with the government. In one of his final official acts before abandoning Nauvoo, he dispatched Jesse C. Little, a New England convert, to preside over the

Mormons remaining in the East. "If our Government shall offer any facilities for emigrating to the Western coast," Young wrote to Little, "embrace those facilities." It was the postscript in this appointment that the missionary would take most to heart: "Whenever you find a good man and want to . . . make him an agent to transact any business, spiritual or temporal, pertaining to the Church, you are authorized to call and appoint the same in the name of the Lord."

Clutching this letter, Little made his way toward the nation's capital. At a stopover in Philadelphia on May 13, 1846—the day Congress was declaring war on Mexico—he convened a conference of Mormons. There, "in the forenoon," a delicately built and conceited young man approached him. "His object in seeing me was to obtain information relative to our people going to California," Little would report to Brigham Young, "having a desire to travel with them."

Though neither man could have fully grasped the consequence at the time, their encounter would change the fate of a religion and alter the course of American history. Thomas Kane, the son of one of the most powerful Democrats in the country, would then and there resolve to be the Mormons' Good Samaritan and serve as a decisive liaison between the church and the federal government. Kane, who would later come to be genuinely taken with the Mormons' plight, was now simply pursuing his own quest for glory. Privy to secret intelligence operations involving American expansion and the not-yet-announced war, and fueled by unquenchable sibling rivalry, Kane adopted the Mormons, at least initially, as a vehicle for his own rather grand ambitions.

Kane's heritage was a moneyed if slightly checkered one. His great-grandfather John O'Kane was a well-to-do landlord from Ireland who came to the colonies in 1750 and married into a prominent Puritan family. But O'Kane had remained defiantly loyal to the British Crown during the Revolution, and when the Americans confiscated his New York estates, he fled to Canada, where he promptly made a new fortune trading in contraband with both rebels and redcoats. The family name was changed to the Scottish "Kane," and after the war succeeding generations returned to the United States. Prestigious marriages obscured the Tory taint and the profiteering scandal while maintaining the wealth. The smuggler's merchant son married a Van Rensselaer, the heiress to an old Dutch colonial fortune as well as that of a respected general of George Washington's army. In turn, their son, John Kintzing Kane, was matched to Jane Duval Leiper, "one of the most beautiful women of her time," as a biographer described her, and the daughter of another Revolutionary War hero.

Christened for his maternal grandfather, Thomas Leiper Kane was born in Philadelphia in 1822, the second of five children in a family in which he would struggle to live up to its expectations. From an early age, as throughout his life, he suffered bouts of sudden, undetermined illnesses that seemed near fatal and then vanished as quickly and mysteriously as they appeared. By his own account it was a remarkably coddled, sheltered childhood, surrounded by a nervously doting mother and a house full of servants who performed every task for the unpredictably vulnerable little boy. "Leaving all responsibility upon servants, tailors and trades-people," he once described his life growing up, "I could not tie a shoestring."

At the same time he took up a vigorous but vain competition with his older brother, pushing himself to learn to ride, shoot, and play musical instruments, though never so well as Elisha, who was two years his senior and had the robust health, unrefracted intellect, and easy charm Thomas would always lack. As children excitedly hovering over the family globe and atlas, they mapped together great expeditions to uncharted lands. But it was Elisha Kent Kane who went on to become a naval hero, a world traveler, and nineteenth-century America's preeminent Arctic explorer, his exploits and even his romantic marriage to a spiritualist memorialized from geographical history to children's literature. "My handsome brother, Surgeon Kane of the Navy," the younger man wrote of his competitor when they were in their late twenties, "a sort of 'Admirable Crichton,' who, bearing the scars of five honorable wounds on his goodly person, still spends his life doing the fine brave things that ladies love and men envy."

Like the rest of the family and much of their social circle, both older sons were in the shadow of their formidable father. By 1829, John Kane was one of Philadelphia's most eminent lawyers, a future federal judge, and an intimate of President Andrew Jackson, whom Thomas and Elisha visited in the White House on several occasions as boys. At that, Jackson was only the first of a succession of presidents over three decades, Whigs as well as Democrats—Martin Van Buren, James Polk, Zachary Taylor, Millard Fillmore, Franklin Pierce, and the Kanes' Pennsylvania neighbor James Buchanan—whom the elder Kane and then his sons would know on a first-name basis.

Beyond their Philadelphia town house or rolling country estate in nearby Kanesville, the inherited friendships with national leaders made for a world of advantage in Washington and the country at large as well as at home. The Kanes were part of an intricate system of personal political influence—what historian Mark Summers called the "web of family connection, preferment, privilege and patronage"—that ruled antebellum America often beyond party or region. Invoked simply by signing a name to a letter or announcing it to a servant at the door, the cachet was considerable. Like his frailty and rivalry with his brother, that presumed power was an integral part of Thomas Kane's rarefied world.

Contacts were crucial from the beginning. While Elisha went to medical school at the University of Pennsylvania, Thomas had remained at home to be educated under the watchful care of his mother and the household staff, though nothing seemed to stem his recurrent afflictions. In the summer of 1840, an effeminate young man of eighteen barely five feet five inches tall and weighing little more than a hundred pounds, he was suddenly sent to live with a relative in London, "to recover his health," as his biographer Albert Zobell described the purpose of the trip, "which had been somewhat broken by study." There would be no record, even in Kane's prolix correspondence with his parents, of how Britain affected his condition, only the perhaps apocryphal family story that he rejected a large inheritance from an elderly English kinsman when it required renunciation of U.S. citizenship.

What was clearer was that Kane recuperated enough after a few months to spend "much time," as one version put it, away from London and in the salons and cafés of Paris. By 1841 he had taken up residence in the French capital, his father's writ in Washington securing him appointment as attaché of the U.S. legation with admission to the court of Louis-Philippe. As it was, Thomas enjoyed a personal relationship with the French king through yet another Kane family tie, this one with Robert Morris, the Philadelphia financier and a signer of the Declaration of Independence, who had been a patron of Philippe before his accession in 1830. By similar clan connections Kane also engaged as an instructor in French an aged abbé who had once been a secretary to the revolutionary leader Robespierre. The tutor in turn introduced his student to a circle of radical politicians, as well as to the philosopher Auguste Comte, the social reformer whose doctrine of positivism, preaching tolerance, cultural harmony, and a humanistic religion shorn of metaphysical dogma, Kane would adopt as his own.

For the young expatriate it was a heady, even risky fraternization with opposing camps of left and right, orthodox and heretical, in the swirl of republican, imperial, and clerical intrigues around France's beleaguered constitutional monarchy. "Erratic appearance in such varying company," one account portrayed the Paris social circle of the "fiery but dapper little lad." Still, Kane seems to have lunged into French politics and ideology with the presumption that in Paris, as in Washington, his passions of the moment were a family prerogative. When Paris police detained the nineteen-year-old attaché on suspicion of liaison with the pretender to the throne, Louis Napoleon, Kane "threatened the officers," as Zobell wrote, "with what his father in Pennsylvania would do to them." As Thomas told the story afterward, a suitably chastened prefect apologized, and to make amends took the young American on a gendarme-guided tour of the fleshpots of Paris.

Kane came back to Philadelphia in the spring of 1843, at twenty-one visibly matured and self-assured by the years abroad. "Practiced in the arts of diplomacy to the point that I should undertake it if needs be in any righteous cause," he described himself to his sister just before leaving Paris, "and certain that I must be guided not by pride or particular belief but by the general rule of the greatest welfare for all."

For the next three years he dutifully apprenticed in the law in his father's office, and in March 1846 was admitted to the bar in Philadelphia, where he was already known less for any legal practice than for his dedication to various reforms. The periodic bouts of acute illness now reappeared. But in a fitful rhythm repeated through much of his life—"I do not know how I shall do it but only that I will!" he wrote a friend at the time—Kane alternated between sickbed, legal briefs, and a flurry of writing, speaking, touring, and general philanthropy on behalf of what he called "our urgent work."

His causes were a roll call of some of the most heated issues that had emerged in American politics and society while he was still in Europe—the abolition of slavery, cessation of capital punishment, prison reform, higher education for women. Yet his enthusiasms were also impulsive, and left very different impressions. "This man never knowingly passed by anyone needing his help," wrote one admirer. "A sentimental humanitarian," a historian of the period judged him, "the kind who loved all good works . . . and obstructed the path of serious reformers."

Always too frail for military service, he would watch with undisguised envy in the spring of 1846 as Elisha was given a hero's sendoff from Philadelphia for active duty in the looming war with Mexico. "I wished him Godspeed, as I always must," Thomas told a friend afterward, "and have to console myself with fighting the foes of humanity here."

It was a few weeks later, as the military planned an "Army of the West" to march from Fort Leavenworth to Santa Fe to seize New Mexico, California, and much of Utah, that Kane would formulate his idea for infiltrating the Mormons. After several hours of conversation at Kane's lavish Locust Street residence about "the subject of emigration to which he listened with great attention," as Little recalled the discussion, the twenty-four-year-old aristocrat generously offered to introduce the Mormon elder to President Polk. With "tact and patience and a little maneouvring [sic]," as Kane later bragged of his courtship of the Mormon who "rules all of the Church east of the Mississippi with despotic sway," Kane won Little's trust.

Giving his new acquaintance some "valuable hints" about what Little called "affairs at Washington" on the brink of a war, Kane also armed the Mormon with a letter to his father's good friend Vice President George M. Dallas. This was the first of untold times that Kane would advise church leaders in political expediency, saving them from ruin. In time, Kane would almost single-handedly keep the Mountain Meadows Massacre from being investigated.

For now, in return for his efforts, Kane had but one request: a letter of introduction to Brigham Young. As always with this complex and calculating man, his motives were wider than his sympathy for the Mormons and their persecutions. His correspondence and conversations made clear he envisioned that he would join them in this trek to the wild uncharted country of the American frontier, writing a bestselling adventure story of such splendor and magnitude as to ensure his superiority over his dashing brother Elisha. If such a literary enterprise brought less fame or fortune than imagined, Kane nurtured the attendant and zealous dream that through his father's singular political influence he could be appointed the first governor of California.

On May 25, 1846, President Polk learned that a Mormon agent had arrived in Washington with a request for aid in his people's emigration. That day, Polk was devising plans for Colonel Stephen Watts Kearny to invade the Southwest on a mission that would coincide with a naval shipment of weapons and ammunition to the Pacific Coast. Polk speculated as to how the Mormons and their peculiar dilemma could be turned to the nation's advantage. In previous months, he had taken what historian Dale L. Morgan described as an "aloof attitude . . . no more disposed to interfere with the Mormons than with the Baptists or any other sect." But now the world looked very different to the president. Congress had authorized an army of fifty thousand men and appropriated $10 million for the war effort, and American sentiments were emotionally divided about entering into war with neighboring Mexico.

"Devoid of all personal magnetism," as Allan Nevins portrayed Polk and his bland personality, his seven terms in Congress and stint as governor of Tennessee had "taught him to deal expeditiously with public business." Having decided to go to war, "he carried out his program with Machiavellian adroitness." Evolving from mundane appeaser to imperial expansionist, Polk recognized the value of a Mormon covert operative team in his aggressive conquest of the Southwest. The accommodation between Washington and the Mormons was the work of neither heroes nor villains, but of self-serving and scheming men calculating their advantages at every turn. Keenly aware of the controversy over his foreign policy, Polk was interested in conciliating the Mormons in order to avoid extraneous contention and even possible disaster. "If, in a hostile mood, they [Mormon antagonists] turned up in California at some delicate moment in the progress of the conquest," Morgan described the prickly dynamics, "they might throw all plans out of joint."

Little's entreaty to the president was no doubt molded by Kane's inside information about the Polk administration's plans and was meant, especially, to exploit Polk's anxiety over a British plot to seize California. "We are true-hearted Americans, true to our native country, true to its laws, true to its glorious institutions," Little wrote the president. "And we have a desire to go under the outstretched wings of the American eagle." Then, to assuage the president—or perhaps to veil a threat that the Mormons would become allies of Great Britain, as was the rumor of the day—he continued: "We would disdain to receive assistance from a foreign power. If you will assist us in this crisis, I hereby pledge my honour, as the representative of this people, that the whole body will stand ready at your call." Great Britain was disputing

America's claim to Oregon, so war seemed a possibility, and it was no secret that the Mormons had been "actively courting British support" for resettlement on Vancouver Island. "Little's respectfully worded, but not so subtle, threat," as one account described the letter, "is among the most important documents in the history of the Mormon movement in the nineteenth century."

"It was with the view to prevent this singular sect from becoming hostile to the U.S. that I held the conference with Mr. Little," Polk wrote in his diary on June 3. Kane joined Little in Washington on the morning of June 7, and together they lobbied the president and other high government officials to form an infantry unit of Mormons to serve in Kearny's army. Polk opposed the plan at first, reluctant to have Mormons among the first troops to reach California. He refused to accept the twenty-five hundred Mormon volunteers Kane and Little proposed, but through Kane's personal persuasion the president finally relented and assented to five hundred.

Polk entrusted Kane to carry the top-secret orders for the "Mormon Battalion" to Kearny at Fort Leavenworth, which instructed Kearny that the number of Mormon volunteers should not under any circumstance exceed one third of Kearny's command of fifteen hundred men. The president then offered Kane compensation for his efforts with the Mormons, Kane later claimed, promising him "*carte blanche* as to what I could ask for on my return," as Kane put it. Starting off from Washington on June 12, Kane and Little traveled together as far as St. Louis, where they separated, Little returning to a camp near Council Bluffs and Kane seeking out Kearny in Kansas. Captain James Allen, designated by Kearny to lead the Mormon soldiers, arrived at the Mount Pisgah camp on June 26 with the U.S. Army's First Regiment of Dragoons. "The call could hardly have been more inconveniently timed," as the journalist Stenhouse put it. The able-bodied Mormon men were already stretched to their capacity, having abandoned their Nauvoo homes, now struggling to provide for their poverty-stricken families, and facing sweeping illness and hardship.

"This thing is from above, for our good," Young declared, exhorting every Mormon man in all the camps and settlements between the ages of eighteen and forty-five to join. "None wanted to enlist," wrote Juanita Brooks. "Brigham Young had to use all his persuasive powers, visiting all the camps and back stations, encouraging, urging, almost commanding men to join."

"Go and serve your country," Young implored. "And if you will do this, and live your religion, I promise you in the name of Israel's God that not a man of you shall fall in battle." He told these "ragged and hungry refugees" that he had been guaranteed by the U.S. government that they would see no fighting, serving as a regiment for exploration rather than battle. Alarmed at the resistance—"President Young had pulled all the strings he could through Jesse C. Little to get this call, but now he was to have some difficulty to raise the quota"—the church leader pressured and cajoled. He saw it as divine providence, an opportune if ironic way to transport his ablest men west at government expense, while also collecting forty-two dollars per man—not to mention the provisions of shoes and clothing for his ragtag militia. "A considerable portion of the camp would be transported to California and there released with arms and accouterments after a year's service," one historian wrote of the outcome.

On July 11, 1846, Thomas Kane rode into one of the Mormon camps strung out along the bluffs above the Missouri. Covered with angry mosquito bites from the journey through the hot muddy country to the south, Kane could still barely suppress his excitement. "Reminded of the Seine," as one account put it, he was captivated by the Mormon women washing their brightly colored clothes along the riverbank. Expecting the subjects of his planned book to "exhibit much of queer life: yankee & fanatic," as he had written in a letter to his family, Kane would find himself irresistibly and surprisingly drawn to these people.

He had plunged immediately into what one Mormon elder remembered as "animated conversation" about the fugitives, their history, and their faith. Some suspected Kane of being another Gentile spy. Then he flourished a letter of reference written fulsomely by their eminent missionary Jesse Little, and asked to be taken to Brigham Young. Within days the stranger had his audience with Young. Afterward he almost seemed one of them, helping to recruit the volunteers to fight in the war against Mexico, invited to meetings of the leaders, taking instruction in the gospel, weeping as he moved among the stricken and destitute refugees, and stopping to hear them offer up their devout prayers.

More soldiers were needed, and Kane was able to recruit them. "In three days the force was reported, mustered, organized, and ready to march," Kane later recorded; a worn American flag was brought out of storage and "hoisted to the top of a tree mast." The ingenious Kane-inspired battalion represented a fresh deliverance for the Church of Jesus Christ of Latter-day Saints at its most desperate hour, while conveniently neutralizing it as a sworn enemy of the United States—thus endearing Kane to all sides.

By July 18, Brigham had his five companies, 526 men, ready to march, with orders that "we should go into the Great Basin, which is the place to build Temples." A massive farewell ball was held at Mount Pisgah—"a more merry dancing rout I have never seen," Kane wrote, "though the company went without refreshments and their ball-room was of the most primitive." Remarking on the women's unadorned dress—all earrings, pendants, and watches had been sold before leaving Nauvoo—Kane thought them "decorous maidens" nonetheless. He was unabashedly charmed by the "neatly darned white stockings, and clean bright petticoat, the artistically clear-starched collar and chemisette . . . the well-washed gingham gown that fitted modishly to the waist of its pretty wearer."

Kane now advised Young to write a letter to President Polk to court goodwill. Not only should the Saints express gratitude "for his benevolent design," but they should also beseech especially that he not appoint Missouri's Lilburn Boggs as governor of California, as was rumored. Kane, with his own ambition, thus shared a mutual enemy with the Mormons. Kane continued his political machinations by requesting that his father, back in Philadelphia, be hospitable to the "prolatary Little," who would be calling on him. He cautioned the wealthy judge not to be too "familiar." "It is necessary to impress him with the heaviest sense of your *omnipotence* (nothing short of it)," as Kane underlined in a letter to his father, "and our family dignity and wealth. . . . On no consideration, let him have more than five minutes talk with you . . . let him not take a meal with the family." Kane was obviously trying to foster the general impression on the Mormons' part of his family's stature and class distinction.

The battalion left behind a camp at Mount Pisgah overcome with disease. So many of the Mormon refugees were dying of cholera, pneumonia, and malnutrition, especially the young, that burial parties working day and night could not keep up with the calamity. In dozens of cabins and shelters, parents sat a gruesome vigil over their dead children until graves were dug, constantly waving off the plump bluebottle Iowa flies that swarmed over the bodies. A plague of "black canker" that darkened the limbs had wiped out a third of the settlers—"the graveyards on the bluffs filling so fast that some of the dead could not even be given burial robes," wrote DeVoto.

In the first week in August, Kane collapsed with a raging fever. Desperate for superior care, Kane asked Young to deliver a letter to Kearny at Fort Leavenworth invoking Kane's rank of colonel, an honorary title he had received from the Pennsylvania state militia. Young dutifully pleaded for the kind of expert attention for Kane that none of his own Saints received. When Dr. H. J. W. Edes arrived soon thereafter to attend to Kane, it was clear to all at the camp that Kane was indeed someone with great influence.

It was this near-death experience that seemed to transform Kane's commitment to the Mormons from one of political and personal expedience to a devotion of spiritual affinity. During his agonizing convalescence he observed the Saints in their worship, in their perseverance against horrible circumstances, and in their optimistic gaiety, and he emerged a different man. His caretakers shaved his head and sponged his body, and Brigham Young laid hands upon him, promising future vitality and even parenthood. Mormon legend has it that Kane was baptized during this period, his membership in the church kept secret so as not to mitigate the appearance of neutral intervention in Washington. Though evidence of such a ritual would never surface, a deep and abiding friendship of historic proportions was forged between Kane and Young, "with all the beauty of that of David and Jonathan, of Ruth and Naomi, or of Damon and Pythias," as one writer described it.

Before leaving the camp in September, Kane would request of Young a patriarchal blessing, a copy of which he would carry with him throughout the rest of his life: "not an hair of thine head shall ever fall by the hand of an enemy, for thou art appointed to do a great work on earth and thou shalt be blessed in all thine undertakings."

His health restored, Kane returned to Philadelphia, where the "small, nervous hypochondriac," as one writer called him, predictably suffered from more bouts of illness. Often toiling from his sickbed, he continued to champion the Mormons' cause in the national arena, romanticizing their persecution and victimization, intervening with government officials for assistance in their relocation to the Great Basin, and orchestrating a public relations campaign that would ultimately be their salvation. In gratitude the Mormons sent him a buffalo robe, which hung in his office until he gave it to his brother in celebration of Elisha's completing his first polar expedition.

The winter of 1846–47 was as harsh at the Camp of Israel as the previous season had been, with hunger and despair still rampant. Young built a gristmill but charged "a heavy toll for all that the mill ground," according to John D. Lee. Without fresh fruits and vegetables the Saints were forced to rely exclusively on a diet of corn and bacon, resulting in an epidemic of scurvy.

The Mormon Battalion had marched from Fort Leavenworth to Santa Fe and then on to San Diego, many of them ill with the fever they had contracted at the Camp of Israel. "Bonaparte crossed the Alps," it was said, "but these men have crossed a continent." In September 1846, disturbed that battalion members had privately sent their salaries back to their wives, Brigham Young dispatched John D. Lee Young, as Lee now called himself, to follow the battalion to Santa Fe and intercept the battalion payroll to be consecrated to the church. Calling it a most "dangerous but responsible mission," Young entrusted Lee with confidential correspondence to Kearny demanding that the U.S. Army release all funds to Lee instead of to the individual soldiers. The purpose of Lee's journey was so secret he was not allowed to tell his wives where he was going or when he would return.

When Lee returned months later, carrying the money as well as clothing, groceries, and other supplies Young had ordered him to procure along the way, he was aghast at the condition of his family. "President Young, how does this compare with your promises to me, when I trusted all to you?" he said to express passionate disappointment to his adopted father. "I took my life in my hands and went into that Indian country on that perilous trip, a distance of two thousand two hundred miles, through savage foes to carry out your orders." Though Young had promised Lee he would care for Lee's family, they had been left to the forces of nature and the indignity of want. "Now I see all my family exposed to the storm; they, of all the camp, are without houses. My best cattle have been butchered and eaten, but not by my family. The choice beef has been given to your favorites, and the refuse given to my wives and children." Young admitted he was ashamed but quickly laid the blame on others. "Come, cheer up," Young told Lee, placing a hand on his shoulder and offering to pay him $100 from the army's pay. The money never materialized. It would not be the last time that Lee put the word and direction of Brigham Young above all else only to face betrayal in the end.

In the entrepreneurial spirit that became his trademark, Young used the battalion earnings to purchase food to stock a store he owned, which he then sold back to his starving Saints at inflated prices. Claiming $20,000 had been appropriated in this way, some dissenters left the faith. "Some of the women, being entirely destitute, desired their husbands' share, and some cried for the want of it," a battalion member recorded.

Lee, who "considered Brigham Young infallible," as one writer described his devotion, put his enmity aside and reported to Young on the land around Great Salt Lake. "Buffalo, elk, deer, antelope, mountain sheep and goats, white and grizzly bear, beaver and geese [are] in great abundance" in the area, he said, and a plentiful supply of salt, precious minerals, and freshwater streams made it a perfect location for the new Zion.

Over the past three years Young had evolved from a simple obscure carpenter to a more dictatorial pragmatist, gaining confidence with each oration and bolstered by his new kinship with Thomas Kane. But he had been leading only as de facto president since Smith's death. Now he was ready to appropriate the role of "Prophet, Seer, and Revelator" and formalize his presidency. On January 14, 1847, he disclosed his first, and only recorded, divine revelation, which concerned how the Camp of Israel was to be organized for the pilgrimage to the Great Basin. There should be singing, dancing, and praying along the way, he said, and plans for the thousand-mile journey were to begin that very moment. Within a week, members of the Quorum of Twelve were visiting the far-flung camps to spread the word, moving in a procession of small parties at regular intervals strung out for three hundred miles. "The angels of God will go with you," Young told his followers, "even as they went with the children of Israel when Moses led them from the land of Egypt."

On February 16 he proclaimed he was "entitled to the Keys of the Priesthood according to lineage and blood," and the next day he stunningly claimed his own death and resurrection. "Distressed in the stomach and bowels," as Lee documented Young's illness in his journal, Young "fainted away, apparently dead, for several moments." Revived back to consciousness, Young told Lee he had died in those minutes. "It is hard coming to life again," he told his followers the next Sunday, "but I know that I went to the world of spirits." Ten days later he reported to the High Council that he had conversed with Joseph Smith, whom he had taken by the hand and kissed on both cheeks. "I turned away and saw that Joseph was in the edge of the light, but where I had to go was as midnight darkness."

Consulting with his devotee Lee every day, Young solidified his takeover plans. His proposal for the creation of an autonomous First Presidency that diminished the power of the Quorum of Twelve met significant opposition. "Stirred up to do this by the spirit of the Lord," Young successfully overcame the resistance and finalized his own ascendancy. Now officially ensconced and elevated to a deity, he would govern with increasing totalitarianism for the next thirty years, an authoritarian dictatorship that led to the Mountain Meadows Massacre.

Young organized the mass movement with a brilliance and compulsion never seen in the annals of the American experience. His headquarters teemed with "an immense bookkeeping, a constant dispatch and arrival of couriers, an almost nightly convocation of the counselors, the Prophet's fingers on the controls of an organization that stretched from the Missouri River all the way eastward across America and halfway across Europe," DeVoto wrote.

The first group left the Camp of Israel on March 1 in a calm and harmonious fashion. Young had ordered that each wagon train be divided into "hundreds" or "fifties" under the command of one captain, and further subdivided into "tens" under the commandment of a lieutenant who organized the travelers, mediated disagreements, and determined camp locations. Navigating through snowbanks and torrential rains, the group lurched along, covering only half a mile a day. "The only comfort we had," recalled one emigrant, "was that Joseph our Prophet saw in vision our homes in the Mountains . . . and we faced the West unafraid."

Kane had presented Young with valuable and rare maps of Texas, Oregon, and northern California. Those, along with Lansford W. Hastings's *Emigrant Guide to Oregon and California,* provided the leader with the requisite knowledge of their destination. Father Pierre-Jean de Smet, the Jesuit adventurer, had ridden into Council Bluffs the previous year; afterward he reported lengthy interrogations by Young about his explorations in the Great Basin. Drawn to the area around Great Salt Lake as one of the most isolated locales on the continent, surrounded by a formidable mountain range and inhospitable desert, Young designated it the haven for escaping the Gentile, American world. "In the cove of mountains along its eastern shore, the lake is bordered by a plain where the soil is generally good, and a greater part fertile, watered by a delta of prettily timbered streams," Frémont had written in the report Young had in his possession. Even more attractive to Young than the excellent opportunity for farming was the fact that the several thousand square miles of land he envisioned for his empire belonged to Mexico and therefore lay outside the long reach of American sovereignty.

Brigham Young and a band of some 148 people struck out in early April, heading west on the Oregon Trail, which had been blazed by earlier trappers and fur traders and followed the north side of the Platte River. Young had obtained two sextants, two barometers, telescopes, thermometers, and other necessary equipment to guide them. The party comprised mostly brawny men, but at least three women—favorite wives of Young, Heber Kimball, and Young's brother, Lorenzo—and two young children also went along. Carefully selected for their strength and ability, the men were between thirty and fifty years old and included the requisite "farmers, artisans, and craftsmen" for building a new settlement, and at least eighteen members of the secret Council of Fifty. Including natives of twenty states and seven foreign countries, and three black slaves, this group was fully representative of the astonishing breadth of the Mormon movement.

Seventy-two prairie schooners and an untold number of carts and trundles carried the personal belongings of the party. Ninety-three horses, fifty-two mules, nineteen cows, sixty-six oxen, seventeen dogs, a handful of domestic cats, and several chickens accompanied the entourage. John D. Lee procured thirty-three of the wagons, "including the mules and harness to draw them," for Young. Lee also forgave Brigham a debt in the amount of $285 and made an additional gift of seventeen ox teams. "He accepted them and said 'God Bless you, John,'" Lee wrote in his journal. "In giving property to Brigham Young I thought I was loaning it to the Lord." Still, Lee resented being ordered by Young to stay behind at a 2,600-acre farm known as Summer Quarters, sixteen miles from Winter Quarters. There he was directed to plant crops for the Saints who would follow later, and under Lee's cultivation the land would produce abundant fields of corn, squash, beans, and grain. Lee would form his own wagon train and begin the journey later in the season.

Young's convoy made good time, not stopping until eight-thirty every night. Like an army, the Saints were awakened at five a.m. with the blast of a trumpet. Another blast in the evening ordered everyone to pray and retire for the night. One of the women discovered that the lurching of the wagons provided sufficient turbulence to churn milk into butter; bread was baked in hollows dug into hillsides at campsites. At night the Mormons sought the identified planets of the Bible through primitive telescopes, and by day they marked their mileage with a rudimentary odometer devised by one of the Saints. Efficiently organized under Young's stern eye, the gunsmiths kept the rifles in good repair and shoemakers replaced the soles on the men's boots. All the while they "preserved their illusion that innumerable mobbers, politicians, and especially Pukes [a derogatory term for Missourians] were after them," according to one account, though there was never any evidence that anyone in the country "intended them any harm whatever."

Crossing the plains was horribly monotonous—there was "an inescapable, depressing quality to the prairies, which was felt by even the most sanguine dispositions," as one writer described the desolation. The boredom was broken when the prairies turned black with buffalo in herds numbering as many as 200,000. The primary dangers were prairie fires whipped up by dry lightning or accidents that usually involved women's long skirts catching in wagon parts. Young broke the tedium by courting Indian women along the way. Having been "sealed" to two Sioux squaws before leaving Winter Quarters, he attempted to persuade others he met to unite with him on the spiritual journey.

They followed the river north to Fort Laramie, which had been built in 1841 by the American Fur Company, and then to what is now Casper, Wyoming, where they stopped to build a boat to cross the Platte. Nine men from the expedition stayed behind to operate a toll ferry as the rest proceeded south along the Sweetwater River to Independence Rock— a sixty-mile stretch of rocks and alkali soil called Hell's Reach. On the third anniversary of Joseph Smith's murder, they transversed the Continental Divide at the 7,700-foot-high South Pass, where they heard a disquieting report. Jim Bridger, the famous mountain man, warned them that the only crops that could be grown in the arid desert around the Great Salt Lake were sagebrush and cactus. Bridger even taunted Brigham Young with an offer of $1,000 for the first bushel of corn harvested in the valley. Undeterred, the Mormons traveled along the mean-dering Big Sandy to its conjunction with the cottonwood-lined Green River, reaching Fort Bridger on July 7. There they stopped to repair their wagons and to trade with other emigrants, obtaining buffalo robes, western attire, tobacco, ponies, raisins, sugar, beef, and other luxuries.

Along the way other Mormon groups, including a contingent from the Mormon Battalion who had been detained in Colorado due to ill-ness, joined them. One of these Saints urged Young to redirect to Cali-fornia's lush San Joaquin valley, but Young held firm, believing, as one writer put it, that "a choice and rich land would attract the Gentiles, and the Saints would soon be overwhelmed and rooted out." "God has made the choice—not Brigham Young," he calmly replied.

Leaving the Oregon Trail, they proceeded west over the recently explored and mapped Hastings Cutoff. This steep, rocky, barely visible trail was already infamous for its severity, yet they were grateful for the clearing of dense scrub oak done the previous year by the doomed Donner-Reed party. "This last group had spent precious time here chopping through the trees, moving rocks, and cutting away banks," one writer said, "time which lost them their lives."

Passing through a ninety-mile-long "chain of defiles," as one observer described a natural swath through the Wasatch Range of the Rockies, "as if an ancient Titan had dragged a stock through the region," they reached the summit of the Bear Divide on July 10. Just after crossing the Bear, Young became violently ill with Rocky Moun-tain spotted fever. Delirious, he ordered everyone but a few to push for-ward as he stayed behind to recuperate.

On July 21, those who had gone ahead caught their first glimpse of the valley. "A broad and barren plain hemmed in by mountains, blister-ing in the burning rays of the midsummer sun," was how one reflected the initial disappointment. "No waving fields, no swaying forests, no verdant meadows . . . but on all sides a seemingly interminable waste of sagebrush . . . the paradise of the lizard, the cricket, and the rat-tlesnake." When John D. Lee saw the valley, he envisioned the New Jerusalem, paraphrasing Nehemiah from the Old Testament: "Zion shall be established in the tops of the mountains and exalted above the hills, and all nations shall flow unto it."

On the morning of July 24, Young was well enough to travel. The apostle Wilford Woodruff helped the prophet into a wagon and took him to an escarpment to view the valley below. Mormon legend would later contend that Young rose from his pallet and announced, "This is the place!" But there is no contemporaneous evidence that he uttered such a remark, which in any case would not be attributed to him until thirty-three years later.

"A hard, resistant folk had found a hard, resistant land," wrote DeVoto, "and they would grow to fit one another." Descending onto the ancient bed of Lake Bonneville, which in prehistoric times had been a tremendous body of freshwater, the Saints unhitched their horses and plowed the soil the very afternoon of their arrival. Digging canals to divert the mountain runoff to their fields, they were unwittingly creating the most sophisticated irrigation system in the history of the West—"laying the foundation," as a historian put it, "of the most ambitious desert civilization the world has seen." Already by Sunday morning, July 25, all the potatoes and most of the seeds for the corn, beans, and peas they brought with them had been planted. By late afternoon Brigham finally felt strong enough to address his flock. After consecrating this land of Canaan, with its own river Jordan flowing from a freshwater lake into the Dead Sea they would call the Great Salt Lake, he gave an ominous warning to all who had come. From this point forward, anyone who refused to live the laws about to be set forth was free to leave. Those who remained would have to submit to the new covenants of this promised land.

Over the next weeks, as Young fully recovered from his illness, he carved out his empire and established his utopia. As he directed the building of the kingdom, he launched the most successful socialist experiment in American history, even more autocratic and communistic than any previous Mormon colonies. Using the divining rod that had belonged to Joseph Smith's Book of Mormon collaborator Oliver Cowdery, Brigham selected a forty-acre lot as the site for the temple. Following the cardinal points of a compass, the Mormon men laid out 132-foot-wide streets—so a wagon pulled by an ox team could make a full U-turn—originating at the temple and radiating due east and west, north and south. The two-square-mile city was divided into lots of one and a quarter acres, eight lots in a block for homes with small yards. A nearby six-square-mile enclosure was divided into parcels ranging from five to eighty acres for farming.

Revealing the plan he had devised with the twelve apostles, Young told the Mormons there would be no private ownership of property, since the land belonged to the Lord. Rather, each man would be assigned two plots, one for a home and one for a farm. The beehive became the symbol of the industrious and hardworking Saints. "The communal food gatherers, or farmer bees," a historian said in explaining the agrarian system, "were to live in the city, or hive, and harvest food from assigned plots in nearby fields for central storage from which all would share, according to their needs."

Just turned forty-six, and now the preeminent colonizer in the nation's history, Brigham Young—the man George Bernard Shaw would later call the "American Moses"—prepared to usher in the "Dispensation of the Fullness of Times" that signaled Christ's return. Here he would gather his nation under the umbrella of the "only true church" as prophesied by Joseph Smith. From this no-man's-land, he would wage a long and bitter struggle with the U.S. government to establish a theocracy apart from the rest of the country. The Mormons' clannishness and radical theology would be both their strength and their curse. The atmosphere of persecution and insularity, piety and spiritual supremacy, zealotry and vengeance heated by Smith's death and martydom would inevitably culminate in a clash of historic proportions. But for now, the vision seemed within reach.

"It would be a history of a mad prophet's visions turned by an American genius into the seed of life," wrote DeVoto, "in the memory of suffering and the expectation of eternal glory, while the angels hovered overhead and portents flamed in the sky."

CHAPTER FIVE

Salt Lake City,
August 24, 1849

I N JULY 1849, a St. Louis newspaper account from May 9 had finally made its way to Salt Lake City with the disquieting report that the U.S. government was sending an army expedition for a "trigonometrical and nautical survey of the Great Salt and Utah lakes." Characteristically, Brigham Young fomented mistrust in his followers—five thousand Saints had poured into the city in only two years—about the government's stated purpose, suggesting instead that Captain Howard Stansbury's prestigious unit of topographical engineers was cover for a secret military operation to expel the Mormons from their new homeland. By the time Young learned of the expedition heading toward his empire, the group was already camped at Fort Laramie on the North Platte River. The company of eighteen men, five wagons, and forty-six horses and mules arrived at Fort Bridger within a few weeks.

At the once quiet fort they found dozens of prospectors, cattle drovers, and merchants seeking supplies, swapping stories of Indian activities, and trading advice about trails and cutoffs for the final push over the mountains to the coast. The previous year's discovery of gold at Sutter's Mill on the South Fork of the American River in California, combined with the Treaty of Guadalupe Hidalgo, signed a few weeks later (the second largest land acquisition in American history, which transferred the Pacific Southwest from Mexico to the United States), had created a new sense of urgency and excitement at Fort Bridger. With a grandiosity that shocked members of Congress and other American officials, Young had claimed for his Mormon domain a landmass encompassing not only the later states of Utah and Nevada, but also two thirds of Arizona, more than a quarter of California, a third of Colorado, and thousands of square miles of southern Idaho, south-western Wyoming, and western New Mexico. Called Deseret—a word in the Book of Mormon meaning honeybee—the planned Mormon dominion would have consumed well more than half the territory ceded in the Mexican War. To justify this imperial claim, Young pointed to his tiny, barely self-sustaining missions as far south as San Bernardino and as far west as Genoa in the Sierra Nevada foothills as evidence of his colonizing.

But the proposed free and independent state of Deseret had been "deliberately snubbed" by Congress, as Mark Twain reported it, which created Utah Territory "out of the same accumulation of mountains, sagebrush, alkali and general desolation." It was bounded on the "west by the State of California, on the north by the Territory of Oregon, on the east by the summits of the Rocky Mountains, and on the south by the 37th parallel of north latitude," and the official document also included a proviso that "Congress should be at liberty . . . to cut it up into two or more Territories."

Stansbury, aware of isolationist if not secessionist proclivities in Brigham Young's government and warned by political colleagues of trouble with the Mormons—he was advised "they would never permit any survey of their country to be made" and if he proceeded his "life would scarce be safe"—divided his party into two groups. He took a few men with him on the longer northern approach into the Salt Lake Valley through Ogden's Hole, dispatching the main body of the expedition under his second-in-command, thirty-seven-year-old John Williams Gunnison, through the shorter, more direct route. Gunnison led the first party into the valley on August 24, 1849. Though he had been ill for weeks, traveling much of the way bedded down in the back of a government spring wagon used for transporting instruments, racked with fever and chills, he had insisted on the long horseback ride into the imposing and formidable region.

By the time Gunnison arrived in Young's infant and guarded realm, he had already served in the Seminole War and had helped in the re-location of Cherokees as part of President Andrew Jackson's Indian policy. Born in 1812 to a New Hampshire farmer of colonial blood-lines, Gunnison was educated at a private academy in the Sunapee Mountains and then taught in a one-room log schoolhouse while awaiting entrance to West Point. "The idol of his school and the whole neighborhood," as someone described the affable and handsome seventeen-year-old, Gunnison, bold and adventurous, received his appointment following a recommendation from family friend and then congressman Franklin K. Pierce. He was thoroughly familiar with "Cicero's Select Orations and the Aeneid of Virgil," as a former teacher wrote, and "well-versed in the elements of Philosophy and Chemistry."

Reading "nearly one thousand pages a week," the cadet wrote his father, he was consumed with ambition, graduating in 1836 with high honors as a second lieutenant of the Second Artillery. "One of the U.S. Army's brightest ornaments," as a historian described him, Gunnison had then mapped most of Georgia as well as much of Wisconsin, Michigan, and the Great Lakes area. Spared combat duty in the Mexican War, he would now have one of the most coveted assignments for an army engineer—mapping the vast new American territory.

The first thing Gunnison did upon his arrival in Salt Lake City, intelligent and politic as was his nature and breeding, was to seek out his unofficial but unmistakable host. Reaching the center of town before nightfall, he inquired as to the whereabouts of Brigham Young; when he was unsuccessful, he guided his men as conspicuously and unthreateningly as possible to a camp on the northern edge of the community. Early the next morning, an emigrant who had traveled from Fort Leavenworth with the expedition, and who had borrowed a mare from Gunnison, appeared at the camp. Gratefully returning the horse, this "Mr. Blodgett," as he was later identified, invited Gunnison to tea that afternoon at the home of a Mormon bishop. Gunnison would write in his journals of the strange "tea," where he was introduced to a Mormon explorer named Albert Carrington, and Brigham Young was—coincidentally—at the house next door. As Gunnison proceeded toward the neighbor's house, the Mormon prophet appeared just as expectantly. They spoke for only a few minutes, but Gunnison discerned a tacitly hostile tone. "Under much apparent indifference he showed anxiety," was how Gunnison described their initial conversation in the street, "and I hear from various sources that our survey is regarded with great jealousy—and have had warning that secret means would be used to prevent any maps being made of the valley—even that our lives are in danger." Gunnison noted in his diary that the admonitions had come from the leader of Young's Danites, and was therefore to be taken somewhat seriously.

Two days later, Captain Stansbury arrived at Gunnison's camp, recounting how he and his group had been denied lodging by Mormons the night before in nearby Brown's Settlement, and, further, had been refused eggs, milk, and other provisions for purchase. The captain had heard his share of veiled threats, and when his lieutenant expressed comparable alarm, the two decided they should cultivate Young's co-operation and goodwill—without which, it was clear, the mission could not be accomplished. "No means would be left untried, short of open opposition, to prevent the success of a measure by them deemed fatal to their interests and safety," Stansbury wrote, in his official report, of the need to obtain Young's official blessing.

Stansbury and Gunnison sought to convince Young of "the true object of the expedition," as one account put it, the two engineers striving to allay Young's apprehensions that the government intended to divide his territory into sections without regard for Mormon sovereignty. Stansbury counseled Young that the opening of a central route to the Pacific would benefit the sect's "gathering to Zion," and further curried favor with the prophet by offering to supply arms, ammunition, and soldiers to fight the unruly Utah Indians in the outlying settlements. Young took the matter under advisement, though not before subjecting the two soldiers to the usual harangue of persecutions the Saints had suffered in Missouri and Illinois, and, most significantly, insinuating Council of Fifty member Carrington onto Stansbury's staff of engineers. Eventually Young offered his full support of the survey, and "kindness was shown to the members individually," Gunnison would later recall. "This was done, however, after it was ascertained that the advantages of the exploration would accrue to themselves." But to the end of the assignment, distrust and skepticism prevailed on all sides.

Gunnison and Carrington were thrust into partnership through much of the early-autumn survey, the two men riding horseback together to the south shore of the twenty-thousand-year-old Salt Lake, swimming in the buoyant salt water of America's inland Dead Sea. Gunnison was captivated by the sheer mystery of the place, its "having inhospitable tracts to the north and south, and the untimbered slope of the Rocky Mountains, nearly a thousand miles wide, on the east, and nearly a thousand miles of arid salt-deserts on the west, broken up by frequent ridges of sterile mountains." Soon monsoon rains impeded the mapmakers working near the expansive lake and surrounding desert. Then Ute Indians caused delays by begging for food. Then "unsaintly Saints," as they have been described, plagued Gunnison's camp, stealing their cattle. By early October the operation was stymied.

When early and severe snows paralyzed the valley, Gunnison took up winter quarters in Salt Lake City, where he and Stansbury kept to themselves. "We are very quiet, everybody is too busy to visit us & we too comfortable alone to make acquaintance of such *distant* neighbors," Gunnison wrote his wife, Martha. Though the Mormons would later go to great lengths to portray Gunnison's Salt Lake sojourn that winter of 1849–50 as one of extreme pleasantness and even Young-hosted feting, Gunnison's correspondence with his wife contradicted that. Bemoaning his accommodations, in which "the snows of a cold February" drifted through the ceiling and rough walls of his adobe "home," and for which he and Stansbury were charged an exorbitant fifty dollars a month, Gunnison depicted Mormon hospitality as leaving much to be desired. "Wood can scarcely be had at any price," he wrote, describing the primitive working and sleeping arrangements so at odds with his refined New England beginnings. "The room in the roof which I have used for a plotting room (plotting maps, not mischief) is my bed room." Gunnison, turning the unwelcome hiatus to opportunity, observed the Mormons in their natural habitat, and in time would incorporate those observations in a book that would provide a first objective account to a nation baffled, if not appalled, by their peculiarities. "It was conceived," Gunnison would write of his study, "that what is influencing the conscientious character of . . . [these] souls, is worth a serious investigation, though not pertinent to official report under government auspices." He proceeded to interview as many Mormons as would speak with him, on subjects ranging from the origins of the religion to its more controversial doctrines. "I shall have some curious notes to make up hereafter, if I live," he wrote Martha. "Some things happen . . . which would astonish people in the States."

When the spring thaw came, Gunnison rejoined his family, and while on paid leave for a year drafted the official report to Congress of the Stansbury expedition while simultaneously writing a book on his time with the Saints. *The Mormons, or Latter-Day Saints, In the Valley of The Great Salt Lake: A History of Their Rise and Progress, Peculiar*

Doctrines, Present Condition, and Prospects, Derived from Personal Observation, During a Residence Among Them was published in 1852 and brought immediate attention to Gunnison. Advocating a national policy toward the Mormons that would allow their self-rule—what he described in their own terms as "let them severely alone"—Gunnison became a much sought after authority on the Mormon question, earning for him a historic role in the political fervor of the moment.

The debate surrounding the Mormons had changed drastically since Gunnison's excursion to Salt Lake just three years earlier, and some congressmen were pushing for military action against Brigham Young. Mexican War hero Zachary Taylor, elected as president in 1848, was avowedly hostile to the Mormons as both religious fanatics and a rival power center in the West. But Taylor had died suddenly of apparent food poisoning only a few months after taking office. In the summer of 1850, Thomas Kane had beseeched Taylor's successor, Millard Fillmore, to appoint Young as territorial governor of newly drawn Utah Territory, a landmass comprising Utah, Nevada, and a portion of western Colorado. The territory was far smaller than what Young had presumptuously suggested. Fillmore, looking toward the 1852 election, was reluctant to antagonize the Mormons, and his attitude toward them was further tempered by his own Unitarian religious convictions. Still, he had heard the allegations of Young's practice of plural marriage, and he offered the job of governor to Kane instead. Kane declined, personally guaranteeing the president that "charges against Brigham Young's Christian morality were unfounded." Fillmore then appointed Young to the position on September 28. The new territorial governor only learned the news four months later, on January 27, 1851, when mail bound for California arrived in the Salt Lake valley. Despite elaborate celebrations—with fireworks, a triumphal civilian and military procession, and a gratuitous naming of the territory's capital city "Fillmore" and the county in which it was situated "Millard"—Young's followers deeply resented the U.S. government's interference in their affairs.

Gentile officials appointed by Fillmore turned up in Utah during the summer of 1851, where they were uniformly greeted with "scowls and insults," as one contemporaneous account put it. One official wrote to Fillmore of Young's disgraceful behavior at a public celebration in which he cheered President Taylor's death. "Taylor is dead and in hell, and I am glad of it," Young shouted, raising his arms toward the sky and threatening that "any President of the United States who lifts his finger against this people shall die an untimely death, and go to hell." When Young called one of Fillmore's judicial appointees to the territory "profoundly ignorant" and then "went on to refer darkly to the 'cutting of throats,' " as one history of the era described it, several of the new officials fled the territory. Alleging that polygamy was widely practiced, that a well-trained and well-armed Mormon militia routinely murdered dissidents—apostates and Gentiles alike—and that the entire territory was infected with sedition if not outright revolt, these "runaway officials," as the Mormons sneeringly called them, presented a grim portrait. They would be the first of sixteen officers who would flee Utah over the next twelve years, abandoning their federal positions. "[The Mormons'] conduct shows that they either disregard, or cannot appreciate, the blessing of the present form of government established for them by the United States," wrote one of those departing.

Gunnison was in Washington at the height of the "runaway" scandal, and when several congressmen denounced both Young and Fillmore—David K. Cartter, of Ohio, called Young a "Prophet of hell"—Gunnison played a pivotal role in mitigating the controversy. "A matter of moonshine, fright and homesickness," Gunnison said in dismissing the officials' complaints about Utah, advising legislators to patiently allow "reason to regain its sway" rather than send an army to quash what was seen in the nation's capital as a rebellion. Inspired by the current debate, Gunnison had written a new final chapter to his book called "Self Government," in which he assured legislators the Mormons were loyal citizens whose quest for autonomy was rooted in the earlier persecutions aimed at them. His sensitivity toward the sect gained notoriety in itself, as he swayed not only the congressmen but also, at the season's many balls, their wives and daughters, likening the conflict to colonial America's struggle against Great Britain.

Gunnison's argument was seen differently, however, once his book was published and read widely by an avid national and international audience. Though considered basically favorable toward the church by a highly skeptical nation—the best, most objective book about the Mormons and their western expansion yet written—Gunnison's underlying message was indeed more complex. With an eloquence and clarity never before brought to the topic, Gunnison was urging a federal hands-off policy toward the Mormons due to his conviction that the cornerstone of the movement, its essential element for survival, lay in what he termed a "tempest" of persecution. "Smarting under a bitter recollection of violence, that people could easily be goaded into rebellion, or rather into a warfare," he wrote. "The whole United States army would probably be insufficient to garrison and control a hostile population on a line of five hundred miles." Leave the Mormons alone and they will dissolve from within, was his clear message. "Separated now from those who can persecute them," he claimed, "it is hard to keep up the enthusiasm of the mass, by reference to the persecutions heretofore endured." For the U.S. government to fill that role would be folly. "If they were allowed to govern themselves in their isolated location," a Utah historian later summarized Gunnison's conclusions, if they could not claim persecution, "the internal weaknesses and inconsistencies of the religion would lead to division and remove any threat the Mormons might hold for the American Union."

Gunnison proclaimed that Young's hold was anything but secure. Eloquent and thoughtful, Gunnison passionately conveyed his belief in the power of freedom to overcome all tyranny. More specifically, Gunnison set forth divisive aspects of the religion that would weaken the whole. Not least offensive was the author's portrait of what he called Joseph Smith's "inspired" translation of the Bible, and the sect's strange origins. "Mormonism is an eclectic religious philosophy, drawn from Brahmin mysticism in the dependence of God, the Platonic and Gnostic notion of Eons . . . Mahomedan sensualism, and the fanaticism of the sects of the early church . . . with the convenient idea of the transmigration of souls, from the Persian." As Mormons became more educated, Gunnison argued, new converts would reject the authoritarian theocracy in favor of a modernized, more traditional version of Christianity and a return to the ideals of the separation of church and state.

Time was on America's side as well, Gunnison argued. Numerous apocalyptic predictions and elaborate prophecies from Young continually failed to materialize—"in a few short years, they see the great city of New York, its people, its temples, and its wealth, going down into the opening earth." The administration of justice by means of pagan rituals would also face challenge and dissent within the church as it matured—"a criminal code called 'The Laws of the Lord' which has been given by revelation," as Gunnison described the doctrine of blood atonement. In what must have been met with disbelief, if not disgust, by his eastern audience, he described in shocking detail the church's "common mountain law," in which "all grave crimes will be punished and atoned for by cutting off the head of the offender . . . as an act of mercy to the criminal." Included in the transgressions punishable by such beheading were apostasy and adultery. "They make it both a religious and a social custom, a point of personal honour," Gunnison wrote, "for a man whose wife, daughter, or sister has been led astray, to kill the seducer."

But for all the shocking revelations in Gunnison's treatise, none had a greater impact than the exposé of polygamy. Gunnison's confirmation of the widespread practice of plural marriage in Utah—vehemently, repeatedly, and vociferously denied by Young and his apostles throughout the world—made his book a best-seller in the nation and abroad. Verification from such an authoritative source as Gunnison fueled the anti-polygamist zealots in the country.

President Fillmore felt personally deceived by Thomas Kane, whose own writings, discourses, and intensive personal lobbying of the president in support of the Mormons denied the sect's stranger proclivities as described by Gunnison. Kane "was long enough among the Mormons, and familiar enough with them on their journey between Nauvoo and Council Bluffs, to have learned that polygamy was a fact in Mormonism," Fillmore later wrote.

Gunnison's portrait of "spiritual marriage" was not one of moral judgment—though it went against his own deeply held religious convictions—but rather of reinforcement for his claim of schisms within the fold. Mormon women would not long tolerate their unequal status, he said, in which the exaltation of the gender was to be found in childbearing and caregiving. Polygamy introduced a "great cause of disruption and jealousies" in families from which women would naturally and predictably rebel. "The contemplation of plurality is highly distasteful to the young ladies of any independence of feeling."

This core doctrine of the faith, upon which the family values, patriarchal traditions, and early rituals of the religion were based, had been condoned since 1831, though never publicly acknowledged. At its root was the journey to the Celestial Kingdom—"the pinnacle of postmortal existence," as one scholar described it, where the "faithful will evolve into gods in their own right and come to rule universes of their own." In the patriarchy of Mormondom, a woman could enter this eternal heaven only as an appendage to a man, yet a man could take as many women "through the veil" as he pleased. Otherwise they would be stalled for eternity in the limbo of the Telestial Kingdom. "Some women," Gunnison wrote, "distrusting the title of their spouses to enter at all, have been desirous to take hold of the skirt of an apostle or high-priest with superior credentials." Such matrimonial complications were dictated by Brigham Young himself, for he alone had the power to grant a man the privilege of taking another wife, just as he alone had the power to dissolve a marital relationship. "Out of this matter grows an immense power, based upon his knowledge of all the domestic relations in the colony; such delicate confidence begets a reverence and fear."

Gunnison's "personal observation" meant that celestial marriage could no longer be denied, and its exposure would have far-reaching, negative consequences for the church. At an emergency conference of Young's apostles organized in August 1852, Young said Joseph Smith had in fact received a divine revelation from God a decade earlier, on July 12, 1843, that "all worthy men" should cleave to as many women as possible. Evoking a biblical justification for the principle, Young avowed that Adam was God and a polygamist, and Eve but one of his many wives. Pandemic apostasy and sharply stunted proselytizing in the once fertile fields of Great Britain and Scandinavia were the immediate and devastating result. In fact, polygamy would eventually "lead to the downfall of the political Kingdom of God . . . planted in the American West," according to David Bigler.

For all his evenhandedness and objectivity, for all his praising of the Mormon virtues of perseverance and resourcefulness, generosity and benevolence, communal spirit and organizational skills, Gunnison had deconstructed what the Mormons held most sacred—polygamy and blood atonement. The topographical engineer apparently presumed his impassioned support of their quest for self-rule would ingratiate him with Brigham Young to such an extent that Young would overlook the more critical aspects of the portrayal. Gunnison had written several letters to his onetime Mormon friend Carrington, and when they went unanswered he pleaded that Carrington respond, "no matter how severe." But his own father seemed to grasp the impact of the book more than the author did: "I . . . am astonished that people in this enlightened age can be made such fools." With an innocence characteristic of his time and place, the man the Mormons now considered neither objective nor friendly would return to Utah, as one author put it, "to test that hospitality a second time." Gunnison proceeded as though unaware he was now marked as an enemy of the Church of Jesus Christ of Latter-day Saints, and as if he didn't know what that meant.

As much as Gunnison knew and wrote about the Mormons, there was nothing in his behavior or reflections to suggest he believed he was taking a mission into a powerful and hostile foreign nation. For all his study of the Mormons—which was more religious and cultural examination than political—he did not fully comprehend how alien and separatist they had truly become in their isolated theocracy. No evidence exists to suggest that Gunnison believed the Mormons would seriously contemplate a civil war with the United States or that they would be blatantly hostile to a representative of the U.S. government such as himself. In the end, the supremely self-confident Gunnison apparently felt he could placate Brigham Young. He planned to write Young to let the prophet know of his impending arrival. "As their interest lies in promoting this work," he wrote his anxious wife, "the Mormons will doubtless keep the peace."

It was an intoxicating time for the country. As rail historian David Haward Bain wrote, there was "a quality of madness abroad in the land . . . the nation's 'manifest destiny' had prevailed over barriers both natural and political." The dream of a transcontinental railroad was gathering momentum, and Gunnison, a passionate adherent, was an outspoken promoter in Washington for a train route following the trail he had taken with Stansbury—an itinerary also espoused by railroad visionary Asa Whitney. Gunnison recommended a line "crossing the North Platte into the South Pass, over the Coal Basin, skirting the Bear River Mountains at the northern base, near Bridger's fort; and through the Bear and Weber Kanyons . . . to the Timpanogos, and course down its banks to the Valley of Lake Utah." His contemporary engineering knowledge of the terrain, coupled with his unique insight into Brigham Young's mentality—such a railroad would have to traverse land Young governed—brought him to the attention of congressmen, senators, and government department heads.

The primary opponent of Gunnison's recommendation was Missouri senator Thomas Hart Benton. "Old Bullion" Benton, as he was known, had his own scheme for linking St. Louis and San Francisco, following a trail not mapped by West Point topographers or compasses, but paths worn by buffalo, antelope, and elk. If his concept was short on science and engineering, it still reflected his desire to control the political and financial spoils of the enterprise. Whitney eventually accused Benton of turning the venture from an altruistic, government-sponsored project into a "gambling, stock-jobbing Wall Street and Threadneedle street concern, backed by some hundred millions of Government bonds, with an annual subsidy from the Treasury to meet the expenses for its management, to be provided for by an enormous and burdensome tax upon the labor of the country to pay the European stockholder his rich dividends."

In the winter of 1852–53, the subject had consumed the second session of the Thirty-second Congress, with all factions agreeing only on the need for immediate government surveys. Benton flagrantly angled to secure the leadership of the expedition for his braggart son-in-law, Colonel John C. Frémont, who, in anticipation of the railroad, had already purchased California land that would enrich him and his wife, Jessie Benton Frémont, commonly thought the brains of the marriage. With Frémont living in Paris—"having his first leisure and rest," as his wife described it—and therefore unable to organize an operation of such seriousness and magnitude, Benton went so far as to suggest that a surrogate explorer serve as an advance party until Frémont could catch up. But many interested parties opposed Frémont, recalling his ill-fated exploits to the Colorado Rockies in the winter of 1848–49, in which he lost many of his men to starvation and hypothermia, and others were rumored to have survived on cannibalism, reminiscent of the infamous Donner party.

While legislators and journalists debated the issue, a $150,000 rider attached to an appropriations bill passed on March 2, 1853—a literal fortune at the time—authorized War Secretary Jefferson Davis to establish a Bureau of Explorations and Surveys and dispatch his Army Topographical Corps to survey five possible routes. John Gunnison was promoted to captain the next day, and following the inauguration of his close friend Franklin Pierce as president two weeks later, Gunnison was selected to survey between the thirty-eighth and thirty-ninth parallels from the Arkansas headwaters to the Great Basin, by way of the Santa Clara River in southwestern Utah.

Now forty years old and the father of three small children, Gunnison greeted this choice assignment with excitement, if also with slight ambivalence about venturing so far from his home and family. "The crowning work of the century," he pronounced the undertaking, "it would be so wonderful in its results on trade and the destinies of the race, that all other human efforts sink in insignificance." He especially believed his route would prove the most feasible, and with his completed survey his name would be "prominently before the public," he told his family. By late spring he was "hurrying everyone from the President on down," as he wrote his mother from Washington, to get his expedition started. Secretary Davis scrambled to amass a historic body of explorers, engineers, geographers, geologists, artists, illustrators, botanists, zoologists, cartographers, meteorologists, and paleontologists. "Not since Napoleon had taken his company of savants into Egypt had the world seen such an assemblage of scientists and technicians marshaled under one banner," wrote western historian William H. Goetzmann. Gunnison selected his own staff, including two topographers, an artist, an astronomer, a botanist, a surgeon, a geologist, and a wagon master.

Though anxious to begin the long and challenging journey, Gunnison stayed an extra day in the nation's capital for a meeting with the president. Ironically, his final agenda was to plead the Mormons' cause with the nation's highest leader, a task grown more difficult with some of Young's recent statements. In the year since the publication of Gunnison's book, any favorable analysis of the Mormons seemed less accurate. Young's public proclamation of polygamy as "divinely inspired" had been greeted by nationwide scorn, and some northern congressmen began comparing it to slavery—the embryonic Republican Party eventually vowing to eradicate what were called twin relics of barbarism. Young had drawn more negative attention to his movement by threatening to "unsheathe" his bowie knife against a group of internal dissenters calling themselves the "Gladdenites." A widely read article in the *New York Herald* called the Mormons the "Mohametans of the Nineteenth Century," whose religion would one day be the religion of America, and this further drew what the author called "the anxious eye of the statesman on the Utah settlement."

Young "never had taken the trouble to conceal his inflexible opposition to any attempt to build a railroad through his empire," as one writer described the church leader's frame of mind at the time. Among those in Congress and the Pierce administration most knowledgeable about the political as well as physical complications of the transcontinental route, there were apparently few illusions about what awaited the survey in Utah. "The Government knew all too well," said one observer, "that Gunnison's reappearance in the Territory would be viewed with intense hostility by Brigham Young." Yet Gunnison and his Washington superiors were also confident he could once again deal with the prophet. Gunnison thought Young a rhetorical bully but nothing more threatening than that.

Upon Gunnison's arrival in St. Louis, he received the confirmation that his book had not been well received in Utah. His letters to Carrington had been met with a silence he initially took as disapproval, though he soon characteristically gave the Saints the benefit of the doubt. "You know full well," he had written his closest friend from the Stansbury expedition, "my desire to do justice to the character, doctrine, and polity of the Mormons." Now, only weeks away from striking off into the fastness and singular political culture of the Great Basin, he would learn beyond any doubt that he had fallen into the dangerous, if not doomed, category of the sect's "enemy." The June 5 *St. Louis Intelligencer,* which Gunnison read on his arrival in the city, carried a brief but graphic dispatch on a recent address made by Mormon bishop Edward Hunter at the laying of the cornerstone of the new tabernacle in Salt Lake City—an occasion, Gunnison well understood, for only the most serious statements of policy and orders to the faithful as directed and approved by the prophet. Bishop Hunter, the paper reported, "was inflammatory against the persecutors of the Mormons, among whom he seemed to include the people generally of the United States, not altogether sparing Lt. [sic] Gunnison, (the surveyor of their territory) who is referred to as an *unsolicited* chronicler."

Clearly alarmed, the paper's editor took the extraordinary step of accompanying the article with a warning that the army expedition should proceed with caution in Utah. Gunnison's book had given detailed descriptions of the meaning and often lethal result of this kind of imprecation pronounced on Gentiles and apostates. Hoping for a fuller, more contextual report on remarks he could only view as ominous, Gunnison anxiously scoured St. Louis for a copy of the Saints' *Deseret News* reporting the cornerstone ceremony. But he found no further account of the temple dedication, and once again, typically, his confidence that the Mormons would not provoke an expedition of the U.S. government apparently outweighed any misgivings.

Whatever the balance of concern and self-assurance in Gunnison personally—his letters and journal are inconclusive on the point—no officer or civilian member of the survey, including the second-in-

command at St. Louis, Lieutenant Edward G. Beckwith, himself a journalist, left any evidence that Gunnison shared his apprehension at what
amounted theologically, if not legally, to a Mormon declaration of war
on the party. Gunnison did, however, confide something of his anxiety
in a letter to his mother written in his cabin on the paddle wheeler
Honduras as it steamed up the Missouri toward Fort Leavenworth.
"These people, I understand, do not spare me in their remarks," he told
her, though conveying nothing of the historic implications of such condemnation. He then assured his mother and Martha that he had no
"fears," and that they should not worry unduly about insults thrown at
him by the Mormons. "No one can take a step beyond the humdrum of
society without getting a few raps on the knuckles or giving a few to
others," he wrote on June 12. He instructed them to open any letters
that might still arrive from Carrington, and "thereby judge what my
reception will probably be."

Arriving on June 13 at Fort Leavenworth, Gunnison mobilized
teamsters and purchased the necessary livestock to outfit the expedition. There he met his designated military escort of thirty troopers
commanded by Brevet Captain R. M. Morris, a Mexican War hero promoted for his "gallant and meritorious conduct" in the battle of Cha-
pultepec and specially selected by Washington to guard the survey.
Soon they pushed twenty miles west to their base camp, crossing both
Shawnee and Delaware territories, where the once warlike Indians were
now establishing farms. In a letter home from the prairie—echoing his
career-long views that Native Americans should be peaceful yet not
forced into an alien way of life imitating the whites—Gunnison seemed
melancholy about the relocated, newly agrarian Indians. Deeply missing his family, dispirited in general, he also lamented the lateness in the
season, obviously dreading another possible winter in Great Salt Lake
City [Salt Lake City]. His mission was now "pure pandemonium," he
wrote Martha; the more experienced laborers and famous Missouri
mules had joined earlier expeditions, leaving the survey only unruly,
untrained men and bedraggled Mexican livestock whose scars of cru-
elty from former owners told tales, he thought, worth "volumes on
parchment." The only bright spot, Gunnison concluded, was the
prospect of a constructive relationship with the ruling theocracy he
knew so well in Utah.

CHAPTER SIX

Sevier River, October 26, 1853

"T HE HAWK of the Mountains," Wa-kara, the most famous chief of the Ute Indians, was fluent in Spanish, spoke the dialects of numerous indigenous tribes, and could communicate in English as well. The irreverent and flamboyant Chief Walker, as the white men called him, led his warriors on the finest horses stolen from Mexican rancheros, their saddles embellished with silver, their manes and tails braided with colorful trappings. He wore fine linen shirts and a stylish broadcloth suit, adding his own eclectic flourish of colored blankets draped like a Roman toga over his outfits. His braves wore smooth buckskin leggings, vermilion-painted faces, and moccasins decorated with beads and porcupine quills.

The Mormon sect's essential doctrine, deeply rooted in the story of how the wicked Lamanites defeated their white relatives and went on to become the American Indians, stipulated as a condition and precursor of Christ's return to earth that the Lamanites would rejoin the faith. Since the founding of the church, missionaries had poured out to convert their Indian brethren. They met with some success in Illinois and Missouri, but far less when they moved among the Utes. "From their earliest memory, these tribes had waged sporadic warfare at their disputed boundary in Salt Lake Valley," wrote one historian. "Now there settled between them an American millennial movement that had never lived anywhere with its neighbors in peace."

"These Utah Indians went by different names, such as Timpa-Utes, Pi-Utes, Yampa-Utes, and Gosh-Utes, each having its chief, fishing and hunting grounds . . . but in reality they were all the same tribe," wrote Bill A. Hickman in his 1872 "confessions" as a Danite soldier for Young. Revered by them all was Wa-kara, whose four brothers were the chiefs Kanosh, Ammon, Arapene, and Sowiete—all of whom had some Spanish blood. "The Mormons got permission of them to settle there, and made them presents," Hickman wrote, "and they [the Indians] were glad to have them come and raise grain." Adopting the policy that it was better to feed than to fight, Young made accommodations with Wa-kara, even baptizing him in 1850, though most doubted Wa-kara's conversion.

The Utes were fine archers and horsemen who thought agricultural life "beneath the dignity of a warrior," as one U.S. government agent described them. Instead, they "depended upon the chase, the hunt, and raids upon other tribes or settled communities for their subsistence," a historian wrote of their livelihood. Another government agent said there was "not a braver tribe to be found." Wa-kara had worked out an arrangement in 1849 with Dimick Baker Huntington, the prophet's special Indian interpreter and intermediary. Wa-kara would steal herds of horses in California and return with them to Salt Lake, where Huntington would sell them to emigrants, taking a 1 percent fee off the top. Wa-kara also had a thriving slave trade, kidnapping children from other Great Basin tribes and trading them for horses in New Mexico. "This [Wa-kara] is the man who, regarded in the mountains as a petty adventurer," Gunnison wrote in his book, "has often been so romantically eulogised in the States, and furnishes a theme of praise among the Mormons, being esteemed a trophy to the power of their religion, a kind of first-fruits of their policy."

In the early years of Mormon settlement, the Utes welcomed the pioneers, Wa-kara's band frequently serving as an enforcement arm of the church, bound by a mutual hatred of the Gentiles passing through in growing numbers. But then thousands of Mormons began pouring into the territory by wagon trains. The church's Perpetual Emigrating Fund advanced money to northern Europeans converted by missionaries gathering Israel's children from the outside world of Babylon. Between 1849 and 1851 new settlements were built along the southern trail to California, Mormons encroaching deeper and deeper into the Indian homelands with a rapidity and rapacity startling to the tribes. All Mormon men between the ages of eighteen and forty-five were ordered to enroll in the theocracy's army, the Nauvoo Legion, creating an intimidating militia in the heartland of the Utes. The tribe, driven from valley to valley, their deer and elk herds dwindling, their best fishing streams overtaken, their burial grounds despoiled, became increasingly contentious. Random skirmishes broke out, Indians ambushing small parties and stealing cattle, sometimes seeking vengeance—one life for one life—for earlier depredations.

On July 2, 1853, Salt Lake City came to a standstill as a procession moved slowly through its wide streets. Chief Wa-kara rode the band's most coveted horse, wearing his trademark beaver hat and native decorations; 150 of his warriors trailed in formation, and hundreds of women and children walked behind. "As he rode at the head of his braves with their gayly accoutered steeds and embroidered saddles glittering with metal ornaments," Hubert Howe Bancroft wrote, "he might have been taken for a Soldan among the dusky Panims of the west."

The thirty-eight-year-old chief was coming to lodge a bitter complaint with the Mormons' "Great Father," who had betrayed them. With the help of a Spanish interpreter, Wa-kara expressed his anger to Brigham Young for attributing to the Indians the recent murder of a white American trader. Such scapegoating was becoming commonplace—"blue-eyed, white-faced Indians," as they were commonly called, were masquerading as Utes—and his people were suffering the consequences. Wa-kara also complained that Young was interfering in his tribe's long established trade with the Mexicans, that the prophet's colonizing was displacing them, and that Mormons were severely abusing, if not murdering, his people. In sum, Young had broken his promise to live in harmony with them.

Wa-kara had come in peace, by all historical accounts, and expressed no intent to wage war on the Mormons. Yet Young seized the opportunity to mobilize and incite his followers, who he believed had become lax in their faith, their outlying villages and scattered homesites nourishing an independence Young believed threatened the budding theocracy, if not his ultimate power. Now there was an "enemy" he could use to spark the religious zeal that he found to be slacking. Within days, well-placed stories in the *Deseret News* appeared with vague statements that seemed to imply the chief had declared war on the Mormons. The predictable fuel of "persecution," as Gunnison had so eloquently described in his book, was being lit once more, and its misnomer now was the "Walker War." Young "used the fear of Indian aggressions as his most effective device," wrote R. Kent Fielding, "to prepare his people for the more dangerous and more important future predicted by Mormon theology." Under the guise of "Indian trouble," Young could fulfill his dream of the ancient biblical fortress.

Now calling their Lamanite brethren the "Scourge of God," Young reversed the Book of Mormon prophecies and ordered the immediate fortification of all villages. "Owing to the present position of our Indian relations," he proclaimed on July 21, "it has become apparent that the policy of constructing forts and occupying them . . . should now be adopted and rigidly enforced." Such structures were to be permanent forts built to exclude Indians, apostates, Gentiles, and all "others" of the outside world, and to serve as what one historian called "protection against the mobs and armies of the world that would come against Zion."

To Young's anger and dismay, his flock was hesitant in responding. Most had lived peacefully and happily among the Utes and were reluctant to credit the peril, much less to leave their homes. "No person must be allowed to give, sell, or in any way dispose of to any Indian man, woman, or child, any gun, powder, lead, caps, flints or any other weapon," Young proclaimed. The order seemed overwrought to many, if not a complete reversal of Joseph Smith's earlier prophecies that the Indians must be made "white and delightsome people" before Christ's return to earth. Four days later, Young ordered all surplus livestock be driven to Salt Lake and placed in the control of church officials— a directive many Mormons heeded only after further threats of severe penalties.

Behind the scenes Young took action that belied his public stance and affirmed his conviction that the Utes posed no danger. Dimick Huntington brought a peaceful message from Young to Wa-kara. "I send you some tobacco for you to smoke in the mountains when you get lonesome. You are a fool for fighting your best friends, for we are the best friends and the only friends that you have in the world. Everybody else would kill you if they could get a chance." Patronizing and condescending, as was his usual demeanor toward the Indians, he continued: "When you get good natured again, I would like to see you. Don't you think you should be ashamed? You know I have always been your best friend."

Wa-kara was hardly pacified—a war with the Utes was imminent, and tensions were building between both sides. Young placed the territory under martial law, ordering all settlements abandoned except Parowan and Cedar City in the south. An American expedition passing through central Utah under the command of California Indian superintendent Edward Beale saw the activity around Parowan, mystified by the unwavering allegiance to Young by the settlers. "It was a strange sight to witness the alacrity with which these people obeyed an order which compelled them to destroy in an instant, the fruits of two years' labor," wrote Gwynn Heap, the journalist for the party. Though urged by Mormon militia colonel George A. Smith to alter their course, the expedition pushed south to Cedar City, having heard more reports of Mormon hostility against Americans than of any Indian depredations. John D. Lee had moved his entire settlement from Fort Harmony, in what is now southwestern Utah, to nearby Cedar City, where he and other Mormon men were busy constructing a fort. The town center was "blocked up with wagons, furniture, tents, farming implements and baggage," Heap wrote, a chaotic scene "difficult to describe."

Many farmers refused to turn over their cattle to church officials in Salt Lake City, prompting first excommunications and then court-martial trials for the "enemies of the Territory," as they were designated, that consumed the remaining summer weeks. Still others fled the territory, joining passing caravans. Lee was ordered by Young to identify and chastise the disaffected among them, which Lee did with a zeal portentous of later events. "I was determined to carry out the instructions and requirements contained in the general orders if it need be by the shedding of the blood of those cursed wicked apostate fault-finding wretches," Lee wrote of his fellow Mormons. "I would rather walk into them than to slay Walker and his Bands."

For his part, Wa-kara was baffled by the forts being constructed— "how can we shake hands across a wall?" asked the chief, who by that time had been baptized and ordained as an elder. Other Utes seemed oblivious to the new state of affairs and still attempted to trade with their previous friends. In the turmoil of the era, some abandoned villages were burned and livestock stolen, but there were few reports of actual engagement between Indians and settlers. On July 29, one hundred warriors stole two hundred head of cattle and horses bound for Salt Lake City from Allred's Settlement. Then, on August 17, 1853, four Mormon men hauling lumber near Parley's Park, present-day Park City, were shot in an apparent ambush, though the killers were never identified. Pointing to the same kind of evidence that would be tellingly ignored in a far more significant crime four months later, Mormon authorities now made much of the fact that the Parley's Park victims had not been scalped, and thus clearly could not have been killed by the Utes. Instead, they blamed the murders on a figure they increasingly suspected of allying with both the United States and local tribes to subvert the theocracy—the fiercely independent and buccaneering mountain man Jim Bridger.

Young had long resented Bridger's control of the trading post on the Black Fork of the Green River. The envy festered with John Gunnison's recent recommendation, which the Mormons saw as all the more threatening, that the post be the headquarters "to control and aid the emigrant travel to Oregon and California" and that Bridger himself be the man to run it. "With a buffalo-skin and piece of charcoal," Gunnison described Bridger in unusually romantic terms, "he will map out any portion of this immense region, and delineate mountains, streams, and the circular valleys . . . with wonderful accuracy."

On August 19, with reports Bridger was "furnishing the Indians with powder and lead to kill Mormons," as Danite chief Bill Hickman recalled, Young ordered his Nauvoo Legion to seize the fort. "A posse of one hundred and fifty men" rode the 110 miles to arrest Bridger, according to Hickman, and to "capture his ammunition and destroy all his liquors." Bridger, hearing of the impending attack, fled the fort. "Bridger had eluded too many Blackfeet war parties to be caught by a herd of militiamen thundering over the trail from Salt Lake Valley," David Bigler wrote. No ammunition was found, Hickman reported back to Young, "but the whisky and rum, of which he had a good stock, was destroyed by doses"—among the Mormon troopers, whose drunken spree provoked scandalized whispers in the Saints' capital.

There followed more scuffles. On September 13, nine Indians came to the Mormon community of Manti seeking food. All were killed. That same day, the usually friendly Pahvant Indians under Chief Kanosh killed a man at Fort Fillmore. That was followed two weeks later with a fatal attack on three Mormons bound from Manti to a church conference in Salt Lake City. Avenging those deaths, Mormons in Fillmore killed nine starving Indians in cold blood. "They came into our camp looking for protection and bread with us because we promised it to them," wrote a woman resident in her diary, and they "were shot down without one minute's notice." Two days later, a Mormon settler and his son were shot and killed by Indian warriors near Manti. If "Indian trouble" had begun as an expedient for Young to whip his followers into what he termed "walling up," it had not only served that purpose, but also had created deadly conflict.

This was the treacherous climate that Gunnison and his unsuspecting company would enter.

In September, the party, still on the Colorado Plateau, had first come across Utes while camping in one of the Indians' primary hunting grounds, which teemed with antelope, deer, and elk. When a grass fire "began suddenly to burn and thick smoke rose," as survey geologist Dr. James Schiel noted, "instantly another pillar of smoke began to rise in the distance." This tradition of "telegraphing the presence of strangers," as Schiel put it, alerted Gunnison and his men that they were being watched, though it would be many days before they would have any contact. "We found ourselves surrounded within minutes by a crowd of Tabawatshi Utahs, who seemed to grow literally out of the floor," Schiel said, describing what took place as the expedition descended from a mesa to set up camp on the bank of Cebolla Creek. Several hundred well-dressed men, women, and children, riding "beautiful Navajo horses," surrounded the expedition. The women, in a manner scandalous to these cultured eastern men, straddled their own mounts. After much "haughty" posturing, "a few warriors wheeled their horses back and forth in a wild race," as Schiel recounted, before calming down and joining in the smoking of a peace pipe. "The chief gave a long speech, assuring us that the Utahs have always been the best friends of the Americans," and then returned the next day to receive gifts.

Beckwith, a journalist who had been Gunnison's second-in-command on the earlier expedition to Utah, described another encounter with the Utes. He called the Indians they met in the Uncompahgre Valley on the western slope of the Rockies "these poor objects of humanity," having observed their weather-beaten skin, arthritic hands, and filthy clothing made from deer hides. A small horse approached the Gunnison camp, every square inch of its back covered by a mother and her children, "leaving no place on the horse unoccupied, from neck to tail." The family scene left many of the troopers touched and nostalgic about their own homes. Chief Sireechiwap, leader of this band, accompanied by his son, ventured into Gunnison's camp to share tobacco and conversation. The captain informed the chief that the president of the United States "had sent him to look for a good road by which his people, who live toward the rising sun, can visit those who live upon the great water where it sets," Beckwith reported. Assuring the chief that the president was their friend, Gunnison proceeded to distribute gifts of woolen blankets and trinkets in the name of Gunnison's own good friend, President Franklin Pierce.

"This is your land and you can go over it at any time," the chief told the party. "The Utahs are good, and glad to see the Americans," whom they called Mericats. Parting with this reassurance, the expedition continued until it reached the Green River, where it met another band of Indians eager to trade with them as well. This jovial and boisterous tribe welcomed the group, indicating no sign of danger or exhibiting any animosity. "A bleary-eyed, hard faced old savage, partially clothed in tattered buckskin, with whom I shared my luncheon of bread and bacon," Beckwith wrote, "quite laughed aloud with joy at his good fortune." Gunnison tried, to no avail, to enlist the aid of a guide. But they had a great fear of the Mormons, who they claimed had entered into a war with Chief Wa-kara.

Such news came as a surprise to Gunnison, who was thoroughly familiar with the prophecy of the Lamanites. He had long had doubts about the success of Wa-kara's baptism, which the Mormons held up as a prime example of their Indian policy, but believed nonetheless that the relationship between the chief and the prophet was one of mutual and enduring benefit. With that in mind, he dismissed the "war" as a minor clash.

As the group followed the Old Spanish Trail toward the Wasatch Mountains, they met more Utes who greeted them with excitement, hoping, according to Beckwith's later reports, they were an advance party of the U.S. Army coming to assist the Utes in their war with the Mormons. One of the Utes, Tewip Narrienta, "Powerful Earth," guided them through the confusing and overwhelming terrain to the eleven-thousand-foot summit of Wasatch Pass. From there they turned south, crossing numerous ravines and valleys, toward the Sevier River. Here, noticeably apprehensive as they drew closer to Mormon communities, Narrienta warned them again of Mormon atrocities and refused to continue. His services were invaluable, and his knowledge of the trails had saved them weeks of travel, he was told. But no amount of inducement could persuade him to continue. As the expedition proceeded on its own, nothing in any of the party's contacts with the tribe had made Gunnison change his view that the so-called Walker War was of no consequence and that the Indians themselves posed no threat to the survey.

As Gunnison rode to a rise overlooking the magnificent and enticing Sevier River valley, he seemed overcome with pride in his men and their historic mission. In their four-month crossing from Kansas, they had traveled nearly seven hundred miles over uncharted wilderness and "across five mountain ranges . . . and a dry desert of seventy miles . . . without deserting one of our nineteen wagons, and leaving but one animal from sickness," Gunnison wrote proudly. "On reaching this plain a stage is attained which I have so long desired to accomplish," he began his report. "The great mountains have been passed and a new wagon road opened across the continent—a work which was almost unanimously pronounced impossible by the men who knew the mountains and this route over them."

Only the final phases of the survey remained. The gritty floor of the prehistoric Lake Bonneville spread before him, the parched desert land rising in the unseen distance to alpine lushness. Pleased to see wagon tracks in the distance, they followed them toward the first white settlement they would reach in the territory, Manti. There, Gunnison knew, he would learn, finally and after much anticipation, how Brigham Young intended to receive the expedition. There was no hint in the elation of his journal entries or letters home that danger lay ahead.

What he found in Manti, to his dismay, was apparently just the opposite of what he had believed about the absence of serious hostility between the Mormons and Indians. The entire village was barricaded under martial law, with hundreds of people crammed into a small fort. Most disconcerting to Gunnison and his weary men was the lack of advance preparations for the services he had requested personally from Young and Carrington, nor was there a message for him from either man. "We have arrived in the vicinity of the Mormons and today I rode some twenty miles with three men to this settlement," he wrote on the evening of October 19 in his last letter to Martha. "I have to go back to find my camp in the morning. There is a war between the Mormons & the Indians. We did not know what a risk we have lately been running until coming here. May the favor of Heaven attend us until the work is accomplished in like manner as heretofore. It will be impossible to cross back this winter with the Survey. I have hurried hard to escape the awful tedium of this wintering in the mountains, as you know, but the route has been longer, harder & more laborious than anticipated."

"By the blessing of God you see I am again near the old grounds where we were friends together," he wrote Carrington that night, in the final letter of his life. In Manti he hired two guides, Gardiner Godfrey Potter, or "Duff," the local Mormon militia captain, and his younger brother William. Adding two "endowed" Saints, each wearing the sect's undergarment unique to the "holy priesthood," to the seemingly unwelcome excursion was more pragmatic and political than essential. The group was hardly in need of assistance for the well-traveled trail down the Sevier River, nor were they fearful of Indians, having received universal assurances that the hostilities were aimed solely at Mormons and not at the Americans. Beckwith himself reported seeing "only a single Indian who scampered away at the sight of us, leaving only the print of his bare feet in the dust of the road."

On October 22, Gunnison went to the nearby territorial capital of Fillmore to fix a wagon, obtain supplies, and cash a government draft for $500. Anson Call, a Danite who had moved every step of the way with the sect since their expulsion from Kirtland, Ohio, and who was now residing in Fillmore, would later claim he warned Gunnison of the Indian hostilities, though no reference to such an admonition was ever recorded. To the contrary, Dimick Huntington, whom the mapmaker had known since his earlier 1849 trip and trusted completely, guaranteed the "war," such as it was, had ended. Huntington insisted the local Pahvant tribe was now at peace. Their chief, Kanosh, was a celebrated friend of Brigham Young's and would not go against the Mormons. So it was with a sense of relief and peace of mind that Gunnison proceeded.

The weather had turned harsh and cold, dropping to fourteen degrees. "Heavy snowstorms raced from time to time over the country," Schiel recorded, and it became urgent for the group to expedite their survey to Fort Bridger in time to return to Salt Lake City to set up winter quarters. At sunrise the next morning, the weather had not improved and fresh snowfall had powdered the nearby peaks. As the sun gained strength, the party pushed ahead to the Pahvant Valley in south-central Utah, relying upon the local Potter brothers to find the streams that would not yet be frozen. The men spent another bone-chilling night wrapped in their blankets circled around a sagebrush fire that required constant refueling, their horses and mules foraging in the snow-covered plains.

By dawn it was clear a decision had to be made. A lively discussion ensued; those who trusted the Mormons clashed with those who did not. But Gunnison, who was "too confiding and unsuspecting," as one of his astronomers described him, expressed "an unusual sense of security." He gave now what many later remembered as an unpopular command. "In order to accelerate our work we formed two divisions," Schiel recalled. The two contingents planned to rendezvous on the west side of the river in five days.

Gunnison directed one force to head northeast up the Sevier River to explore a canyon in the Unkookuap Mountains through which the river breaks to reach the plain. The smaller detachment of eleven men under Gunnison's command included topographer and artist Richard Kern and the survey botanist F. Kreutzfeldt. Kern had been ill for several days, and Kreutzfeldt had nearly died in Frémont's Colorado expedition five years earlier, and they were particularly reluctant to split from the main group. Gunnison also chose the younger Mormon guide, William Potter, to join him, since Potter had recently surveyed the route with Carrington. Lance Corporal Barton would lead the "corporal's guard," which included several privates; Gunnison's black manservant, John Bellows, would remain with his captain. Despite a drinking problem that had concerned Gunnison, Bellows always accompanied the captain at Martha's insistence, so certain was she of the man's devotion to her husband.

Tracing the river southwesterly for sixteen miles, "through wetlands lined with willows and alive with waterfowl," as one observer described the area, Gunnison's group set up camp in early afternoon near a tranquil and sheltered bend in the river among a grove of cattails near present-day Delta. Their tents pitched and wood gathered for the night's fire, several of the men went geese hunting while the captain stayed behind to make his routine journal entries.

With dusk the weather calmed, the clouds cleared, and a majestic sunset emblazoned the sky. Gunnison and his corporal assigned the customary sentinel watch: all men would stand guard, including the captain—two sentries every two hours. A meal of duck and goose was served. The night passed without incident.

The men rose just before first light, and stoked the fires to begin breakfast for what was planned to be their longest and most decisive day, charting the headwaters of the Sevier before beginning a triumphant return into Fort Bridger. Bellows had started the coffee and Gunnison was still dressing when the first salvo of gunfire broke through the camp. The group was taken by complete surprise, and its accomplished commander was unbelieving to the end. Gunnison burst from his tent as if to quell the furies with a gesture. His arms were outstretched in a pleading profession of friendship when the next volley cut him down.

It was three and a half years later, on an April morning in 1857, that Judge William W. Drummond sat down in his stately home on Chicago's near north shore to reply as soon as possible to the poignant letter he had received from Martha Gunnison. Two weeks earlier, after seeing a newspaper account of Drummond's resignation as a federal judge in Utah Territory, where he had served the previous eighteen months, John Gunnison's widow had written him. She hoped that he might shed some light on the murder of her husband, which she and others continued to believe unsolved and unpunished. Ironically, Martha had received letters from Carrington and Young, the men her husband had once hoped might write to welcome his mission to Utah; a lock of Gunnison's hair had accompanied Young's. "I have always held myself, that the Mormons were the directors of my husband's murder," Martha wrote Drummond on April 14, 1857, "notwithstanding I have, both from Brigham Young and Albert Carrington, received the kindest letters of condolence." She went on to beg the judge for "particulars of such information as you have gleaned."

"My dear strange friend," Drummond began his letter to Mrs. Gunnison at Bethlehem, Pennsylvania, "this information I will cheerfully give you, not only as a sense of duty to you as the wife of a good man, who fell prematurely at his post doing duty, but as a matter of fact, which should go to the world as a portion of the history of that barbarous transaction." He went on to recite the details of the murder of her husband and eight of his party—"one of whom was a Mormon"—and the aftermath in Utah, where the "report was quite current that they were murdered by the Indians." At a grand jury in Juab County, Utah, he explained to her, with Judge John F. Kinney presiding, twenty-six "Parvante [sic]" Indians were indicted for the murder. Through an arrangement between U.S. Army Colonel E. J. Steptoe and Chief Kanosh, "eight Indians (some of whom were squaws, and one old blind Indian man) were put on trial for murder," in the Mormon town of Nephi. "Strange to say," Drummond continued, "a Mormon jury found the Indian warriors were not guilty, and as against the old, crippled, and measurably blind Indians, three in number, found a verdict of manslaughter" and sentenced them to three years' imprisonment in the Utah penitentiary.

Judge Kinney was so "wounded and mortified" over the verdict, Drummond wrote, "that he at once adjourned the court, unavoidably coming to the conclusion that there was false dealing somewhere." Kinney was joined in his indignation, according to Drummond, by Steptoe, federal prosecutor Joseph Hollman, Indian Agent Garland Hurt, Army Captain James B. Leach, and one Columbus L. Craig—"all of whom were cognizant of the influences brought to bear on the trial." The verdict was "by order of the church," and the man who "bore the decree" to the jury was Dimick Huntington, "Indian interpreter, and spiritual brother-in-law of Brigham Young."

Drummond then related to Martha an event that provided him with his own unique information about her husband's death. In November 1855, two years after the Gunnison murders, Drummond presided over the trial of Levi Abrams, "a Jewish Mormon" who had been charged with the murder of a Pahvant warrior. "During that trial, much was said by both Indian and white witnesses relative to the murder of Captain Gunnison and his party, which raised strong presumptions in my mind that certain white men were *particeps criminis* to that cruel murder, but not wholly conclusive." A Mormon jury found Abrams not guilty, but Drummond noted the testimony suggesting Mormon involvement in the murder of Gunnison.

Then, "at the same court a favorite Indian warrior of Gov. Young, by the name of Eneis," was also tried for the murders of the Gunnison party. "Upon his trial I became convinced beyond the possibility of a doubt," Drummond wrote, "that the whole affair was a deep and maturely laid plan to murder the whole party of engineers, or surveyors, and charge the murders upon the Indians." Trial evidence revealed that Eneis was "the property of Governor Young, and that he could speak English quite fluently, and that when he left the city of Salt Lake, he went under the order of Governor Young and the church." Further, much testimony indicated that Eneis was in the company of "several white men on the day before the murder, and that they were all on their way toward the engineers' camp."

Indian witnesses in Eneis's trial had maintained that "only four shots were fired by the Indians, and that all the rest were fired by the Mormons, and that, by order and direction of the Mormons the Indians sprang out of the ambush, where they lay disguised during the night before the firing, which occurred about sunrise . . . and went across the river to scalp and otherwise maltreat the men in their agonies of death, but more particularly to save the Mormon" who had accompanied the party. The Indians knew very well how to distinguish the Mormon from the Gentile officers—"which was by certain peculiar marks" on the priestly garment which he wore next to his body. But the "unfortunate" Mormon had died in the melee as well.

"The white men [the murderers] were so accurately described," Drummond continued, that he felt certain in identifying them. "This I do for the benefit of those men who may go to Utah as appointees under the present administration, viz: William A. Hickman, Anson Call, Alexander McRay, Ephraim Hanks, James W. Cummings, Edward D. Wolley, George Peacock, Levi Abrams, and————Bronson, all of whom are in good standing to this day in the church."

His tale of mountain justice almost complete, Drummond turned his attention to the most difficult part of the correspondence. "Painful and revolting as it is," he proceeded to inform Martha of the gruesome details of the killings. After the surveyors had been shot, their arms and legs had been cut off. Most brutal of all was Eneis's final act. He "cut Capt. Gunnison's body open and took out his heart while he was yet alive, and the heart so full of blood that it bounded on the ground after being taken out; and not content with this, but cut out his tongue."

Drummond recounted "this dark and bloody picture [that] will prostrate every nerve of your tender form" out of his conviction not to participate in or perpetuate the suppression of the facts, ghastly as they were. "Duty to you, duty to the country, duty to a broken and violated law, duty to bleeding and down-trodden humanity, duty to correct history in connection with the dark and bloody code of the order of the High Priesthood of the Utah Mormons."

Bidding her blessings for her future, he wrote in closing that he hoped she would "see the day when the foul stain of Mormon oppression and tyranny shall be effectually checked in this our happy country, your husband's untimely death vindicated by the courts and laws of this land."

The sensational correspondence between the widow and the federal judge was printed in the *New York Times* on May 1, 1857, setting off a national public outcry. Drummond was among a new group of "runaway" officials reminiscent of the summer six years earlier when Gunnison had downplayed the complaints of the first exodus of government agents from the Mormons. By May 1857, there was only one U.S. official remaining in Utah Territory. A slander campaign waged in the *Deseret News* denounced Drummond for cohabiting with a woman who was not his wife—his morals offending, somewhat ironically, the polygamist Mormons, whose elders were in the habit of confiscating at will younger wives of less ranking members of the church—and accused Gunnison, driven by personal ambition, of recklessly and rashly failing to heed the Mormons' warnings. This would not be the last time the Mormons would defame the victims while blaming the Indians.

In Washington, in response to the charges by Drummond and others, the newly inaugurated president James Buchanan submitted evidence to Congress citing treason, disloyalty, and other offenses. Congress declared Utah Territory to be in a state of insurrection. Not least in moving Congress to approve the military force was Drummond's allegation that Captain John Williams Gunnison had been murdered "under the orders, advice, and direction of the Mormons."

On May 28, 1857, General Winfield Scott ordered one sixth of the U.S. Army to march to Utah as a *posse comitatus* to install a new governor to replace Brigham Young and a slate of federal judges and marshals. Young, for his part, called all able-bodied men to enroll in a newly reorganized militia under Lieutenant General Daniel H. Wells of the Nauvoo Legion. Troops on both sides were assembling for what would be called the Utah War.

But the previous month, April 1857, as Judge Drummond wrote to Martha Gunnison, an equally dramatic event was in the making: the richest wagon train ever to enter Utah Territory was gathering in northwest Arkansas. "Into this cauldron of suspicion," a historian wrote, "came the unfortunate Fancher party en route from Arkansas to California."

PART TWO

THE PASSAGE

CHAPTER SEVEN

Harrison, March 29, 1857

ALEXANDER FANCHER first heard about California from his brother John, who had heard about the "rush" from a neighbor. Gold nuggets were lying unconcealed in creek beds; there was no digging necessary, you just reached down and grabbed one, the neighbor told John as he paid for a bushel of turnips. "Are you as tired of looking at the damn double-shovel plow as I am?" Alexander responded in the summer of 1849, when John asked him if he wanted to go west. Nomads by breeding and spirit, the Fanchers were easily seduced by the lure of California, not for gold, like most emigrants of the day, but for the wide-open range and ready cattle market.

The two brothers, who were also best friends, now embraced a romantic notion of a bountiful future in the West. Life in northwest Arkansas had been fruitful and rewarding, but the idea of year-round grazing, ideal weather conditions for growing hay, and high prices for beef paid by miners appealed to the hardworking and adventurous Fancher clan. "Good grass coupled with a mild climate was a rancher's dream," wrote one of their relatives. As a war veteran, Alexander was entitled to a free land grant in the new frontier, and the promise seemed boundless. John, thirty-nine, and Alexander, a year younger, planned to leave for California by the following spring. This first trip would be a preliminary exploration in search of the most aesthetic yet practical locale, so their wives and children were invited to participate in the selection of their new homes. Leasing out their Carroll County farms for one year, the Fanchers began preparations for the journey. John and

Alexander would drive a herd of cattle overland on the Oregon Trail. Their families would travel in comparative luxury on a steamer from New Orleans to Panama, ride mules across the isthmus, and then catch a ship bound for San Diego. There they planned to rendezvous and head north through central California, seeking the largest, most enticing ranch property they could find.

Descended from a long line of French sheepherders, their Huguenot ancestors persecuted by religious fanatics, the Faucher family had turned to cattle once they emigrated to Long Island, New York, in 1724 and Americanized their surname to Fancher. A hardy and upright strain marked the bloodline, which endured religious wars in France and fought in the American Revolution, the War of 1812, and the Black Hawk War. They were known for their horsemanship as well as their laid-back but attentive demeanor, and they generally subscribed to the adage that one should "keep one's nose out of religion and politics." Though slow to anger, they would not turn their back on a wrong. "If they owed you money, they would pay you," was the Fanchers' reputation. "And if you wanted to fight, they would fight you." But no ancestry, valor, wisdom, or aptitude could prepare them for their ultimate confrontation with the Mormons of southern Utah.

Born in 1812 in Tennessee, Alexander spent his childhood in Coles County, Illinois, the son of Isaac and Sarah Fancher. Father and son served together in the Black Hawk War of 1832, and Isaac was wounded in the arm by a musket ball in the Battle of New Orleans. In one of the stranger ironies of their lives, the two men fought as militia members alongside John D. Lee, and their fates would be entangled dramatically again years later at Mountain Meadows.

Alexander then returned to Illinois and married Eliza Ingram in 1836. Their first two children, Hampton and William, were born soon after. They moved temporarily into the Big Richwoods Township of Miller County, Missouri, where "an abundance of good mast," according to a later descendant, "of acorns, beechnut, hickory nuts" provided choice range for raising pigs. Two more children, Mary and Thomas, were born there before Alexander decided to join his uncles Alexander and James, who had recently relocated in the new state of Arkansas. Spies in the War of 1812, the uncles had taken advantage of the land grants available to them. On a verdant Arkansas farm bordering the Osage Creek, they would broaden their livestock operation and become affluent.

Three more little girls were born to Alexander and Eliza—Martha in 1846, and the twins, Sara and Margaret, in 1849—and when they struck out the following year for the first trek to California, the family included seven young children. John, who had joined the Arkansas branch of the family a few years earlier, and Alexander, along with their uncles, had assembled one of the finest breeding stock operations in the southern United States. Running their longhorns in the highlands of the Ozark Mountains, they spent most of their time astride a horse, gathering and moving their herds on the free range between Carroll and Boone Counties. They had accumulated a sturdy group that could sustain the arduous trail drive to California. Once there, the brothers intended to fatten up the longhorns on the golden grasses of their new domain before trailing them north to the mining camps, where they could make a 500 percent profit on the venture. "A restless wind was blowing over both brothers," was how one writer described the Fancher trailblazing streak.

In late April 1850, the two mothers and their numerous infants, toddlers, and adolescents booked passage from Cape Girardeau, Missouri, for the first leg of their voyage. By the time they arrived in San Diego, John and Alexander and their outfit of several Arkansas men were leading cows through what is now northwestern Nevada, according to one account. Other accounts would dispute that assertion, claiming the Fanchers would be among the first wagon trains to depart from the better traveled California Trail to take the primitive wagon road from Salt Lake City to Los Angeles through central Utah, camping at the luxuriant Mountain Meadows. The distinction would become significant, when, seven years later, Alexander Fancher decided to take this same southern route.

However they traversed the Great Basin, the brothers and their families were recorded in the 1850 census as living in San Diego County. Depositing their gold in a San Diego bank, they each purchased a carriage and began exploring California, deciding to settle a couple of hundred miles north, near the tiny town of Visalia. They staked out a ranch site along a creek and registered the first livestock brand in Tulare County in 1852—a connected "JF" for John Fancher, since Alexander intended to go back to Arkansas with his family to accumulate another cattle herd and return in a couple of years. The western slope of the Sierra Nevada bound a pocket of high desert—the Four Creek Country where the Fanchers' cattle could graze year-round. At the edge of the Great Mojave, a 25,000-square-mile wasteland, Visalia had snow-free winters. "There was plenty of wood and water and grass," wrote an early settler. The brothers built the basic facilities for their enterprise in the sparsely populated county, including a house for John and his family as well as essential corrals, outbuildings, and fences. Keeping their prime brood cattle, they sold the rest of their herd in nearby locales even as they acquired more Mexican livestock.

By the spring of 1852, Alexander and Eliza, now pregnant with her eighth child, Christopher "Kit Carson" Fancher, left Visalia to return to Arkansas. Retracing the journey via steamer to Panama, once again riding mules across to the Caribbean to catch a northbound steamer to New Orleans, the family then caught a riverboat up the Arkansas River to Fort Smith. There, Alexander "purchased a team of horses and a carriage for their trip overland to Carroll County," according to an account by a Fancher descendant.

Throughout 1853 and 1854, Alexander amassed some four hundred cattle, which he branded with an *F* for a second trip to Visalia. Leading a wagon train of thirteen families in April 1854, he followed the trail from Fort Bridger across Nevada and south along the western foothills of the Sierra range to the new homeplace. As they passed through the gold fields, he sold many of his steers, making an astronomical profit, while keeping the best females to replenish the ranch.

Alexander stayed with John a few months before returning a final time to Arkansas to recruit an outfit, gather a tremendous herd, and retrieve his family for their permanent move to California. After this last trip, "the brothers would have their California ranch fully stocked to meet the market demands of the miners and the growing cities of the area," a descendant wrote. When he reached home he learned that Eliza had given birth to Triphenia, their ninth and last child.

Alexander immediately set about securing one of the largest wagon trains in America's western expansion. At forty-three his skills were impeccable, his experience confidence-inspiring, his instincts reliable. By the time he was ready to handpick the friends and family members he wanted as his California neighbors, word had spread through the

Arkansas "hollers," and many were clamoring to join him. It seemed like a golden opportunity.

Alexander would share command of the "Fancher Train," as it came to be known, with an equally accomplished Arkansan by the name of John Twitty Baker. "Captain Jack," fifty-two, was a "farmer, cattleman, and slave owner" who lived on Crooked Creek near Harrison. Part Cherokee and the son of an Alabama plantation owner, Jack had acquired plentiful land holdings in his own right. He was the patriarch of a close-knit clan of about twenty-five. For the next two years, Fancher and Baker would oversee the intensely detailed organization of the entourage, with Fancher in charge of the people and wagons and Baker the "herd boss." Each would be designated a "captain."

Lifelong neighbors, woven together by familial bonds and long-standing friendships, the two hundred men, women, and children on the wagon train constituted what T. B. H. Stenhouse called "a bevy of families related to each other by ties of consanguinity and marriage." Fancher was highly selective in his recruits; he knew from experience that "whining people would soon erode the morale of a wagon train and then they would turn on each other," said one observer. Those he had in mind were solid and responsible, their abilities honed by military service in various wars or local skirmishes, their horsemanship superior, their tenacity and loyalty without equal. "Sober, hard-working, plain folks," was how a nineteenth-century chronicler described them, "but well-to-do and, taken all in all, as respectable a band of emigrants as ever passed through."

In addition to the Fanchers, the original families were the Bakers, Mitchells, Millers, Dunlaps, and Camerons. Eventually between twenty and thirty families came aboard. For more than a year, the wives organized the domestic items. Clothing, camp stoves, sewing machines strong enough to sew buckskin, water buckets, dishes, and bulk provisions of flour, rice, sugar, beans, butter, syrup, and coffee were among the dozens of items listed on meticulous memoranda. The husbands outfitted the wagons, collecting their livestock, ammunition, tools, and blacksmith forges for shoeing the animals. Alexander convinced his cousins, James and Robert Fancher, to join, promising the sons of his deceased uncle Alexander a "wage in cattle" to begin their own ranches in California. Captain Jack's sons George W. and Abel agreed to go along, though Jack's wife of twenty-two years refused. "Arkansas is plenty good enough for me and Arkansas is where I'm going to stay," Mary Ashby Baker said, claiming she had "seen signs" that convinced her "it's death to go." Jack left with 138 "head of fine stock cattle . . . all three years old," described as "well selected and likely," the estimated value ranging from $4,000 to $10,000. "An industrious man and a shrewd, good trader," was how an Arkansas neighbor described Baker. He was sharply informed about comparative livestock prices between Arkansas and California, and he knew he stood to make a fortune with his unusual longhorns. He also took along five yoke of work oxen, mules, a mare, "one large wagon, provisions, clothing, and camp equipage for himself and five heads," according to one accounting. He owned eight slaves, though it's not certain they accompanied him. Since slaves would be free men in California, and lacking any contemporaneous reports of black men or women in the group, most historians have speculated that Baker traded them for gold before leaving Arkansas.

George Baker, twenty-seven, the owner of "a considerable amount of cash and personal property," brought his young wife, Manerva Beller Baker; their four children ranging in age from seven years to nine months; and two teenage siblings of Manerva's, Melissa and David Beller, who were under his care. George's belongings included two ox-drawn wagons, three mares worth $100 each, a rifle, a double-barreled shotgun, and 136 cattle valued at over $4,000. "A good outfit and his family was well provided for in the way of evening apparel, provisions, etc.," said a witness. He was also said to have two hired hands in his party. A Baker relative, twenty-year-old Allen P. Deshazo, added seventeen heifers to Captain Jack's herd, and brought a ten-dollar violin for music along the way.

The Camerons of Carroll County, perhaps the wealthiest family in the group, numbered nearly twenty, ranging from infants to grandparents. William and Martha Cameron traveled with six of their unmarried children and William's twelve-year-old niece. Two married daughters, Malinda Cameron Scott and Mathilda Cameron Miller, accompanied their husbands and seven of William Cameron's grandchildren. William carried a "very large amount of gold coin" for purchasing land in California, which he secreted in a specially built compartment under his wagon. He also had thirty choice dairy cows for fresh cream and butter, and a Hambletonian racing mare named

One Eyed Blaze. Descended from famous trotting-horse bloodstock, the horse was indisputably the fastest mount in the party, drawing the attention of everyone who came into contact with the train. One Eyed Blaze was worth an untold fortune, and the Camerons expected her to be the seed of their breeding operation in the West.

The interrelated Dunlap and Mitchell families constituted another large contingent. Jesse Dunlap Jr., thirty-nine, a merchant from what is now Marion County, took his wife, Nancy, and their ten children, ranging in age from one to eighteen. Jesse's brother brought his wife and their eight children. Nancy's father was William C. Mitchell, a senator in the recently formed Arkansas State Legislature, and though Mitchell decided against the move, he actively helped his two sons prepare their outfits. Charles Mitchell was married to Captain Baker's twenty-one-year-old daughter, Sarah, and they had a newborn baby named John. His brother Joel was unmarried.

Between them, the Dunlaps had at least three wagons, twenty-one yoke of oxen, ninety-two cattle, and "guns, pistols, Bowie knives, camping gear, and other property," according to an inventory. In addition to the sundry "camp fixins, cooking articles, &c," Senator Mitchell later estimated they carried some $600 in cash, and valued their entire outfit at $2,513.

Three more households from Johnson County hooked up with the train as it was departing. John Milum Jones and his younger unmarried brother Newton owned four yoke of work oxen and a large wagon. John took responsibility not only for his wife, Eloah Angeline Tackitt, and their two small children, but also for Eloah's five siblings and their widowed mother, Cynthia Tackitt, who, at forty-nine, was the oldest person, next to Captain Jack, on the train. A related young couple, the minister Pleasant Tackitt and his wife, Armilda, traveled with their four-year-old and nineteen-month-old sons. This group brought approximately sixty beef cattle with them as well as a "heavily loaded wagon" brimming with household belongings.

Alexander Fancher owned the lion's share of cattle, his contribution of five hundred swelling the herd to nearly one thousand. His Egyptian Arabian stallion, legendarily called Ebony King, rivaled One Eyed Blaze in value and speed, and stood out in the rich collection of more than two hundred horses of varying pedigrees. Alexander, Eliza, and their nine children represented the smallest group of kinfolk. He would rely heavily on the help of his cousins, James and Robert, as well as his nineteen-year-old son, Hampton. Hampton was particularly adept at riding, so he and Tilghman Cameron were the designated scouts.

Dozens more participated in the trek, though few historical details about them have survived the subsequent generations. An unknown number of single men and teenagers signed on, many as riflemen, wranglers, bull-whackers, and drovers. They all eagerly anticipated prosperous futures in California. Their names and those of entire families associated with the caravan, as well as their fates, would vanish from later accounts.

By late April 1857 the voyagers began gathering at Baker's Prairie, "where the huge spring gushed from the hillside," as one of them described the base camp. It would take fifteen days to assemble the company, organize the leadership, designate the scouts, allocate the chores and responsibilities, practice defensive maneuvers, and assign wagon placement in the convoy. The local newspaper noted the excitement, as townspeople from the neighboring villages turned out to see the fantastic convocation. "Joyous people," one writer described them, "longing for the better, richer life that they envisioned California would hold for them."

Forty wagons rolled out on May 7. The men rode horses in the lead; the women and children, who made up the majority of the train, rode in wagons or walked alongside. They had converted their life savings into gold and were transporting it along with only their most precious household belongings. Among the valuables hidden in the floorboards of the wagons or in the ticking of the featherbeds was as much as $100,000 in gold coins and other currency—at a time when the annual salary of the president of the United States was $25,000—leading to speculation that it was indeed the wealthiest wagon train to cross the continent. The group carried quality weapons and a stockpile of expensive ammunition. Three elegant carriages, their panels emblazoned with stag's heads, transported certain women in relative comfort—"Several riding carriages, which betokened the social class of life in which some of the emigrants had moved before setting out on the adventure of western colonization," as one writer put it. It was an "exceedingly fine company of emigrants, such as was seldom seen on the plains."

The rich assortment of livestock—the rare longhorn cattle, healthy heifers and beef steers, pampered dairy cows, and agile horses—stood out among the multitude of wagon trains slowly heading west that spring and summer. "A prize to tempt unscrupulous men," was how an Arkansas writer described the collection.

Their route was the established wagon road of the Cherokee Trail, which had been opened in 1849 by a gold-seeking group of Arkansans, possibly including Jack Baker, and members of the tribe for which it was named. It was especially suitable for the train's cattle herd—"it was less traveled and offered abundant grass early in the season," wrote David Bigler—and provided an unhurried approach to its convergence with the Santa Fe Trail.

They traversed northwest Arkansas, "crossing the White River," according to one account. "[T]he horses and cattle swam . . . while the wagons and carriages were ferried to the other side." Heading into Indian territory, they passed through the northeast corner of modern-day Oklahoma from Tahlequah up to Goessel, Kansas, heading west along the Arkansas River and on to Bent's Fort, which had been a supply base for the Mexican War. The route then ran north to Pueblo, Colorado, paralleling the front range of the Rocky Mountains. The course linked the Arkansas and Platte River systems, and connected the Santa Fe Trail to the south with the California Trail to the north, and had been used by pre-Columbian Indians.

The Fancher Train crossed the Continental Divide near Twin Groves, then veered west across the Laramie Plain, taking the Sweetwater Cutoff to Fort Bridger, where the Cherokee Trail merged with the Oregon-California Trail. Planning to arrive there by late July, the captains counted on dropping down into Salt Lake City with plenty of time to fortify their supplies and rest their livestock for the strenuous last haul over the Sierra Nevada.

Basil G. Parker, a Tennessee native on his way to California, started out with an outfit of twenty wagons at the same time, traveling with the Fancher party through the Cherokee Nation. Parker was alarmed that the men in the Fancher Train wasted their ammunition on killing game—a squandering that would have catastrophic ramifications. Parker's company of "fifty or sixty souls" gradually fell behind by two days; he would never see his old and dear friend Captain Jack again.

One of the largest wagon trains to travel that summer, the Fancher Train ambled along at ten to twelve miles a day instead of the average fifteen or more, slowed by their immense herd and "cutting down trees to cross" the many creeks and rivers, according to a descendant of one of the travelers. Fearing Indian attacks, they rotated each wagon's position in line one wagon each day, the last wagon moving to the front of the line and so forth. The fear was perhaps unwarranted. "Because of its size and [the] vigilance of its leaders," wrote William S. Wise, "there never had been much likelihood that the Fancher Train would experience great difficulty with the Indians whom they met along the trail." The summer days grew hotter, the evenings cooled by violent and terrifying afternoon thunderstorms. They "traveled leisurely, with the view of nursing the strength of their cattle, horses, and mules," wrote T. B. H. Stenhouse. Each night they had fiddle music, and every Sunday they "observed as a day of sacred rest for man and beast." A Methodist preacher was among them, as most of the adults belonged to that faith, and he assembled his flock under a large tent erected in the middle of their wagon-circled enclave. "There, on the low, boundless prairies, or in higher altitudes at the base of snow-capped mountains, he addressed them as fervently, and with as much soul-inspiring faith, as if his auditory had been seated comfortably within the old churchwalls at home."

The men often made hunting forays for antelope and buffalo; Basil Parker reported bands of buffalo so gigantic they sometimes brought the convoy to a standstill for hours. The captains constantly reassigned jobs to keep everyone "from becoming bored with their routines." The women gathered wild greens "to keep a supply of vitamins available." The trip to Fort Bridger—halfway to their new homeland—was relatively uneventful until Peter Huff died of a spider bite in Wyoming, but the train passed innumerable hastily dug graves along the way. The captains had made good time, considering their easy pace; even pregnant women and newly delivered babies were in fine health.

Still, all the travelers eagerly anticipated a rest in Salt Lake City, where "according to long-standing Mormon solicitations and advertisements," as one account put it, they could fatten their livestock and supplement their own diets with fresh fruits, vegetables, corn, and flour from the Saints' famously plentiful harvests. Beginning with the California gold rush in 1849, Salt Lake City had become a busy stopping-off point for wagon trains heading westward. In a mutually beneficial commercial relationship, the Mormons had welcomed the migrants in transit. The travelers would buy more than foodstuffs, and Mormons were traditionally eager to trade provisions for coveted household furnishings; the emigrants would often be willing to exchange fine paintings, modern cooking stoves, porcelain china, quilts, pianos, and other heirlooms they had carted this far but now had decided were too unwieldy to convey over the Sierra.

The Mormons had so prospered from the burgeoning commerce over the past eight years that they had come to depend upon it. Likewise, emigrants stocked their trains knowing they could resupply in Salt Lake City. So lively and amicable had the interchange evolved that the *Deseret News* systematically reported the arrival of emigrant trains, a public service to assist people in locating friends and family members.

But as the Fancher Train passed from Fort Bridger down through the rugged and romantic scenery of Echo and Emigrant Canyons, which broadened finally into the valley of the Great Salt Lake, it was entering a Mormon capital that had recently undergone radical change. The *Deseret News* uncharacteristically failed to note their arrival, a harbinger that would only later seem conspicuous.

On August 3, 1857, Alexander Fancher led the wagons into a grove of cottonwoods on the Jordan River to a favorite campsite he knew from his previous cross-country treks, while Baker and the cattlemen directed the impressive herd to the Wasatch foothills, where they could graze on public domain.

"From that day," wrote one historian, "the Arkansas party appeared to be a marked train."

CHAPTER EIGHT

Deseret, August 3, 1857

T HE PREVIOUS YEAR, disaster had struck Deseret on various
fronts, threatening to destroy the entire kingdom and setting in
motion what has been called "the culmination of a rising tide of fanaticism that long had been creeping on the land."

Insects—the Mormon cricket, as it came to be known—decimated
the crops in the valley, leaving the Saints with a severe shortage of food.
Meanwhile, Brigham Young had committed a series of historic miscal-
culations and errors with regard to transporting converts. "We cannot
afford to purchase wagons and teams as in times past," he told a missionary in Great Britain. "I am consequently thrown back upon my old
plan—to make handcarts, and let the emigration foot it." This divinely
inspired experiment led English immigrants to walk across the continent resolutely pushing small handcarts Young had modeled after what
he had once seen porters using in a New York rail station. Colorfully
painted placards announcing "Going Home to Zion" and "Truth Will
Prevail" decorated the carts. But the hopeful journey led to the deaths
of sixty-seven in one blizzard alone, and most Salt Lake Mormons laid
the blame squarely at Young's feet.

He was even more tormented by defections in his own ranks.
Unhappiness with the daily realities of Mormon life led to widespread "escapes" into what was then western Utah (eventually northern Nevada). Apostasy was spreading throughout the Mormon
settlements, Young's advisors warned him. Though thousands of
mostly impoverished Scandinavian "fisherfolk" were risking their lives

traversing the plains, the rank and file Mormons were becoming increasingly apathetic to the Zionist call.

Downcast and defiant, Young responded swiftly with his "Mormon Reformation"—"an LDS version of the Chinese Cultural Revolution," wrote one historian, "during which survival often hinged upon one's ability to convince roving mobs of enforcers of one's ideological solidarity with the cause." At the helm of this massive spiritual inquest was Jedediah "Jeddy" Morgan Grant, "the Sledgehammer of Brigham." Speaker of the Utah House of Representatives, Grant was second counselor to Young and the prophet's favorite advisor. "A tall, thin, repulsive-looking man, of acute, vigorous intellect, a thorough-paced scoundrel, and the most essential blackguard in the pulpit," wrote the *New York Times*.

Cleansing the flocks of sin and disobedience was necessary, Grant contended, to prepare for divine intervention in the growing conflict between Utah Territory and the United States. Young's church elders swept through the outlying communities in the winter of 1856–57 "in an orgy of recrimination and rebaptism," as one account put it, followed by the constant scrutiny of those who had been found lacking. Young declared that all backsliders should be "hewn down."

The horrifying spree included a printed catechism of thirteen questions conceived by Young and expanded by Grant.

1. Have you shed innocent blood or assented thereto?
2. Have you committed adultery?
3. Have you betrayed your brother?
4. Have you borne false witness against your neighbor?
5. Do you get drunk?
6. Have you stolen?
7. Have you lied?
8. Have you contracted debts without prospect of paying?
9. Have you labored faithfully for your wage?
10. Have you coveted that which belongs to another?
11. Have you taken the name of the Lord in vain?
12. Do you preside in your family as a servant of God?
13. Have you paid your tithing in all things?

Further obsessed with purity, Grant added the question "Do you wash your bodies once a week?"

At the heart of the reformation was the revival of blood atonement, the principle originally introduced by Joseph Smith but now restored by Grant and Young. Hundreds of Saints were aghast, as the doctrine had never been published or openly acknowledged before, and many schemed to leave the territory. Young's Avenging Angels gained new notoriety in what one scholar called "the era's prodigious reign of terror." Based on the words from Hebrews in the New Testament—"Almost all things are purified with blood, and without shedding of blood there is no remission"—the canon ushered in a wave of violence: "A season of community madness, like that which afflicted Salem in the witch excitement of 1692," as one account described it.

Young himself was unguarded in his promotion of the doctrine, at one point publicly proclaiming, "I want their cursed heads cut off that they may atone for their sins." John D. Lee, who several years earlier had been ordered by Young to move three hundred miles south to establish an iron industry, believed passionately in blood atonement. As a Danite, after all, he had been familiarized with the doctrine years earlier in Missouri by Smith, and saw it as the obligation of obedience: "The killing of Gentiles was considered a means of grace and a virtuous deed," he wrote.

Those who dared to flee Zion were hunted down and killed. William R. Parrish, an elderly Mormon of high standing, had "grown cold in the faith" and decided to emigrate with his family to California. But he was caught near his Springville, Utah, home, his throat slit during an ambush. Killed with him was Gardner "Duff" Potter, one of the guides who had been with Gunnison at the Sevier River massacre. "Ever since that event," his widow would be quoted in the *New York Times,* "the Mormons have been very suspicious and have been watching him continually, supposing that he knew more about the [Gunnison] affair than was consistent with the safety of certain men, particularly if he should escape the Territory."

In Manti, a party led by Bishop Warren Snow seized a young man who was engaged to a woman Snow wanted to take for a plural wife. Accusing his rival of sexual misconduct, Snow and the others castrated him "in a brutal manner, tearing the chords right out," one witness later recalled, "and then took the portion severed from his victim and hung it up in the schoolhouse on a nail, so it could be seen by all who visited the house afterwards." Rumors of slayings pervaded the realm, yet none of the crimes were ever reported in the *Deseret News,* nor was anyone brought to justice, "although what they had done was common knowledge in their settlements," according to David Bigler. Then, as quickly as the bloody regime began, it ended with Grant's sudden death, on December 1, 1856.

In the meantime, the outside world had focused its attention on the recalcitrant Mormons of Utah Territory, continuing to liken polygamy to slavery in the raging national debate. The *New York Times* carried lurid reports of lascivious prominent Mormons purchasing girls for polygamous marriages. "Vague rumors," according to Young biographer M. R. Werner, "reached the East that Brigham Young and his Mormons were guilty of personal deeds of murder and crime." A further charge that the Mormons were disloyal to the United States took hold as well, gaining credence with reports that missionaries were hauling lead ore from Las Vegas to Salt Lake to manufacture weapons. "If Brigham Young did not intentionally provoke war with the United States," wrote Will Bagley, "he was busily preparing for it."

The church, hovering on the brink of bankruptcy, and with apostates and internal dissenters at an all-time high, now suffered yet another devastating blow. A bill had been introduced in Congress that would make polygamy illegal, and the Mormons now had a vociferous and articulate enemy in their former champion Senator Stephen A. Douglas. In a widely reported speech given in Springfield, Illinois, Douglas characterized Mormonism as a "loathsome ulcer." As a presidential candidate, Douglas became increasingly venomous on the issue, ultimately advising a "cure": "The knife must be applied to the pestiferous disgusting cancer which is gnawing into the very vitals of the body politic. It must be cut out by the roots and served over by a red hot iron of stern and unflinching law." If Young celebrated the victory of James Buchanan over Douglas—and was relieved and optimistic about Buchanan's close personal relationship with the Mormons' friend Thomas Kane—the jubilation was short lived.

Buchanan, a sixty-four-year-old elder statesman known for his brilliant oratory, had been a Pennsylvania congressman for a decade before becoming secretary of state under President Polk. Buchanan had made three unsuccessful bids for the presidential nomination, in 1844, 1848, and 1852, and his long political career had molded him into a pragmatic consensus seeker. "Cautious and unimaginative," William E.

Gienapp wrote of him, "he took a narrow legalistic view of problems." The nation's only unmarried president—he became a confirmed bachelor following the sudden death of his estranged fiancée—Buchanan surrounded himself with hardened political cronies. Severely averse to conflict, he inherited a country that could not have been more discordant.

Typically, he attempted to keep the "sacred balance" between proslavery and antislavery factions even as he was inaugurated on March 4, 1857. But following the Supreme Court's Dred Scott decision two days later forbidding Congress from prohibiting slavery in any territory, Buchanan was forced to take a strong stance reaffirming national control in the provinces. Exploiting the need for a unifying diversion from the onrushing crisis of civil war, Buchanan set his sights on Utah Territory as a "test case." Intervening in the roundly objectionable issue of polygamy would be far safer and more palatable than dealing with the political morass of slavery.

That month, in an act as seditious as anything in the South, Brigham Young's government announced it would decide which American laws were to be obeyed in Utah—a brazen proclamation the new president considered treasonous. By the time Buchanan took office, "public sentiment favoring both a firm assertion of federal authority in Utah and the curbing of Brigham Young's political power had made some kind of response on his part almost mandatory," wrote Kenneth M. Stampp in *America in 1857*. Federal appointees to Utah Territory had found it all but impossible to function in the theocracy; prosecutors and federal marshals were unable to challenge the vigilante tactics of the Danites. Surveyor General David Burr had fled for his life in February. "These people repudiate the authority of the United States in this country, and are in open rebellion against the general government," he wrote the General Land Office commissioner.

With increasing brazenness, Young flaunted his long-standing secessionist convictions, whipping his audiences into an antigovernment frenzy. The stage was set for federal intervention. Buchanan initiated a forlorn search for a new governor of Utah Territory. The post, considered political oblivion, held no appeal for the candidates Buchanan felt were most qualified. His first choice, Ben McCulloch, a onetime leader of the Texas Rangers, declined twice. Others refused until finally a Georgian named Alfred Cumming was persuaded by Thomas Kane to accept the position.

That spring and summer Buchanan also settled on other federal appointees for the territory, including three new federal judges, a U.S. marshal, and a superintendent of Indian affairs, and he designated more than twenty-five hundred troops to man and protect the huge supply trains accompanying the new officials. The Mexican War hero General Winfield Scott placed three regiments—the Second Dragoons, the Fifth Infantry, and the Tenth Infantry—under the command of Brigadier General William Harney to enforce the law and keep peace as the new federal officers were installed.

President Buchanan explained his decision in his first annual message to Congress, pointing out that as governor of Utah, superintendent of Indian affairs, and president of the Church of Jesus Christ of Latter-day Saints, Brigham Young had a despotic and absolute power over the dominion. "The people of Utah, almost exclusively, belong to this church, and believing with a fanatical spirit that he is governor of the Territory by divine appointment, they obey his commands as if these were direct revelations from Heaven." Quick to acknowledge that the government had no right to interfere with their religious beliefs—though they might be "revolting to the moral and religious sentiments of all Christendom"—Buchanan thought it his duty to "restore the supremacy of the Constitution and laws."

Particularly incendiary were the supporting documents Buchanan provided Congress, including Judge Drummond's allegations that Gunnison had been murdered "under the orders, advice, and direction of the Mormons" as well as charges by the president that Brigham Young had been "tampering with the Indian tribes and exciting their hostile feelings against the United States."

General orders were issued on May 28 for the troops to be dispatched from Fort Leavenworth, with Harney specially instructed not to attack any citizens but to act only in self-defense. Although Young would not be notified officially of the movement until several weeks later, he learned of it almost immediately from his emissaries in Washington.

Two weeks earlier, the beloved apostle Parley Pratt, the "Archer of Paradise," was brutally murdered near the Arkansas-Oklahoma border. Like Joseph Smith's assassination, this martyrdom was testimony to the passions inspired by polygamy. Though in fact little more than a tawdry scene of domestic violence, Pratt's death would be used by Young to further foment unrest.

Mormons revered and adored Pratt far more than the stern Brigham Young. Born in 1807 in Burlington, New York, Pratt was one of the earliest Mormon converts and one of the original twelve apostles. A merchant, author, publisher, minister, lyricist, legislator, explorer, and missionary, Pratt had been an officially designated "Prophet and Seer" for twenty years. He had single-handedly converted hundreds of Saints, who idolized him.

He had dark brows that framed deep-set luminous eyes, and his receding hairline was counterbalanced by tufts of curls at the base of his neck. An air of spirituality and confidence attracted his women proselytes, with sexual overtones marking his steady rise in the church. In the mystical and sensual temple endowment ceremonies, Pratt most often played the choice role of Adam, where, in the elaborate drama, women were thrust into his "temptation" in the staged Garden of Eden. Only if they failed to succumb were they considered godly enough to receive their anointings.

As early as 1846 a fellow apostle claimed that, while a missionary, Pratt would "seduce girls and females and sleep & have connexion with them contrary to the law of God." In his defense, Pratt attributed the allegations to his misunderstanding of celestial marriage. The following year, Young accused Pratt of committing adultery but stopped short of excommunicating him. "He was not woman-crazy, but Gospel-crazy," a great-granddaughter would say. In the spring of 1857, Pratt's pursuit of his twelfth wife led to his sensational murder. It began and ended like many tales of infidelity, with the response of a jealous, cuckolded, and vengeful spouse.

Elenore McLean, the attractive wife of a Customs House worker in San Francisco, joined the Mormon Church in 1851 over the strong objections of her husband. Her conversion effectively destroyed the marriage, though she and Hector McLean stayed together for the sake of their three young children. One Sunday night, while she was singing from an LDS hymnal, Hector grabbed the book from her hands, severely beat her, and threw her into the street. The brutality only galvanized her convictions, and though she remained married to Hector she refused to have intimate relations with him from that point forward.

Shortly after her baptism, in 1854, she met the charismatic Pratt, who convinced her to secretly baptize her two sons—though she had vowed to Hector she would never co-opt the children into the faith.

Furious, Hector attempted to have Elenore declared insane, while shipping all three children aboard the *Sierra Nevada* to Elenore's parents in New Orleans. They arrived in Louisiana on February 13, 1855, and just over two weeks later the distraught mother joined them. "Closely guarded" during her visit, and unable to persuade her parents to let her take her children to Zion, she left for Utah alone, arriving "heartbroken and in poor health." Just two months after her arrival in Great Salt Lake City she married Pratt, though she had not divorced Hector. "I do not deny that I washed his feet, combed his hair, and often walked, that he might ride," she described her devotion. Supporting herself as a tutor for Pratt's and Young's children, she longed for her own children, and by late summer 1856 had devised a scheme to kidnap them.

Parley and Elenore left Utah together, she bound for her parents' New Orleans mansion, he for St. Louis, where he would wait until spring, when they planned to rendezvous in the Cherokee Nation near Fort Gibson and join a wagon train back to Utah. Spending months cultivating her parents' trust, claiming she had abandoned the church never to return, she gradually regained her freedoms. On March 4 she emboldened herself, fleeing with the children by steamer to Galveston, Texas. Her family immediately notified Hector, who, with a band of vigilantes, began tracking Pratt. Upon learning that Elenore and the children were heading to Indian Territory to meet up with Pratt on the Arkansas River, McLean and his party picked up their trail.

While searching for Elenore, Pratt was apprehended by a marshal and several rangers who had a warrant for his arrest. Since there were no courts in Indian Territory, they shackled him in leg irons and took him across the border to the nearest town, Van Buren, Arkansas. At his hastily held trial Pratt faced a jeering crowd agitated by the famous polygamist in its midst. The trumped-up charges of stealing the Pratt children's clothing were so flimsy the magistrate released Pratt quietly in the early-morning hours. But his horseback escape was futile; McLean and two companions overtook him near the border. Following a galloping chase, McLean came close enough to fire his gun at Pratt. When he missed, he drew alongside him, spooking Pratt's horse to rear in fright. This allowed McLean to plunge a bowie knife into his victim's left armpit. When Pratt fell to the ground, McLean shot him in the neck with a derringer and left him for dead. A nearby couple watched as Pratt tried to "staunch his wounds with wads of paper from his pock-

ets," afraid of retribution if they assisted him. Elenore found her way to
his side in time to watch him die a slow and excruciating death.
McLean was said to have returned to Van Buren, where he boasted of
the killing for a few hours before fleeing to avoid apprehension on murder charges.

Whether reports of the episode reached members of the Fancher-
Baker party, who had not yet left their base camp one hundred miles to
the northeast in Arkansas, is not known. What *is* known is that news of
the apostle's murder reached Young in Deseret on June 23—along with
correspondence from Thomas Kane—where it was greeted, predictably,
with calls for vengeance. "[T]o overheated emotions in Utah," wrote
David Bigler, "the apostle was killed for his religious beliefs."

A three-day jubilee was soon to be held to celebrate the anniversary of
the Mormons' deliverance by God into Zion. The event would take
place at spectacular Big Cottonwood Lake, at the top of a rugged
canyon ten thousand feet above sea level in the mountains east of Salt
Lake. The event was timed to end on July 24, 1857, ten years to the day
after the pioneers first entered the Great Salt Lake Valley. Everyone in
the territory was invited to attend the extravaganza, and all who could
make the twenty-four-mile trek through the steep canyons did so. The
Pioneer Day picnic was jammed with 2,587 Saints. Their one thousand
horses and three hundred oxen were corralled at one end of the narrow
valley, and hundreds of tents were pitched in a temporary campground.

They spent hours eating, fishing, hiking, playing cricket, making
music. The Saints who gathered there in the grandeur of the breath-
taking wilderness knew nothing of the enormity of what their leader
was about to impart. However difficult the circumstances, the prophet
was not about to succumb.

At the end of the celebratory event, a bugle sounded and Daniel
Wells of the Nauvoo Legion assembled the gathering for what they
thought would be instructions on an orderly breakup of camp. Mormon lore would have it that four exhausted men then rode breathlessly
into the camp to bring disheartening news, though contemporary evidence suggests Young shrewdly orchestrated the dramatic mountaintop
scene that now unfolded. An announcement was made that a huge federal invasion force was on its way to squelch the Mormons. This was no
surprise to Young, who had been corresponding with Thomas Kane

about the eventuality of troops. New York newspapers had reported the military operation in early May, and Young had heard from his missionaries in the East that the army was mustering its authority to depose him. But there couldn't have been a more climactic moment to announce such news.

Young now rose to address his assembled disciples. Portly and ruddy, Young fixed his steely eyes on his audience. He made a declaration of independence that startled the throng. They were no longer to acknowledge the designated territory of Utah, but henceforth would be the free and independent state of Deseret. "Whisperings ran through the crowd like a sudden breeze across a field of grain," Juanita Brooks wrote. The people were baffled by the American flag "floating" that very moment "above the pavilion."

But the initial confusion gave way to characteristic resolve, convinced as they were by their prophet that it was all part of the millennialist prophecies, and that God would fight their war for them. "With such glory before their wondering eyes," a journalist reported, "the simple-hearted people sang again their songs of joy . . . and when the day was fully spent they returned happily to their tents, more than ever satisfied that the angels had charge concerning them."

A zeal emerged as Mormon leaders wasted no time in delivering their burning pronouncements issuing a call to arms. "God Almighty helping me, I will fight until there is not a drop of blood in my veins," Heber Kimball raged at the following Sunday service. "God knew that Zachary Taylor would strike against us, and He sent him to hell." Young took every opportunity to assure his congregation his prediction was now coming true. "This American Continent will be Zion," he reminded them, "for it is so spoken of by the Prophets." The godless American government's moving against them signaled the beginning of their Armageddon scenario, which they believed would end, happily and unfailingly, with the ascendancy of Young and the Mormon priesthood to rule the Kingdom of God on earth.

The bland notification from the War Department to Brigham Young dated July 28, more benign than confrontational, did little to allay the frenzied machinations in Utah Territory. General Harney likened the expedition to those in other parts of the country, such as Kansas, another current site of civil unrest, where it had become necessary to install a military department. Notorious throughout the frontier as the "Squaw Killer" for his ruthless treatment of the Sioux Indians, Harney wrote to Young of the army's intent to establish headquarters at "some suitable position." Appealing to Young's more mercenary proclivities, the general indicated the army was willing to pay liberal prices for much-needed supplies.

Meanwhile, troops strung across the country were ordered to report to Fort Leavenworth. The hastily called expedition stalled as necessary cattle, horses, teamsters, laborers, food supplies, weapons, and soldiers trickled in. By July, Harney, who was reluctant from the inception, knew it was impossible to proceed to Utah so late in the season. When he and the Second Dragoons were reassigned to Kansas, the remaining force was left without a commander until a Kentuckian, Colonel Albert Sidney Johnston of the Second U.S. Cavalry, could take over in late August. He inherited a mess, but was ready for action.

Brigham Young's military strategy centered on the Saints' intimate knowledge of the harsh and mountainous terrain that had been their home for a decade, and his Nauvoo Legion set out to block and fortify the mountain passes and canyon narrows that provided the only access from the east into Zion. The Utah legislature had voted seven months earlier to reorganize the militia under the command of General Daniel H. Wells. Now designated a "Prophet, Seer, and Revelator" in addition to commander-in-chief, Wells had placed all military forces in southern Utah under William H. Dame.

Meanwhile, Young dispatched agents to the far-flung missions of Genoa, in what is now Nevada and San Bernardino, California, ordering the Saints to sell their property and return home to fight the United States. "Buy all the powder, Lead, and Caps you possibly can," Young wrote to the "Brethren" on August 15.

The soul of the prophecy of Christ's return lay in the gathering of the Lamanites, and Young set forth with new ardor to enlist them. He wrote to "Elder Jacob Hamblin," who lived at Mountain Meadows, 250 miles to the south, notifying him of his new appointment as president of the Santa Clara Indian mission: "Seek by words of righteousness to obtain their love and confidence, for they must learn that they have either got to help us or the United States will kill us both."

He sent his trusted Indian advisor, Dimick Huntington, to incite the Indians and bring them into the fold as mutual enemies of the detested Mericats. Young's inflammatory and overblown sermons suggested the

Indians were in an excited frame of mind, and that the bloodthirsty natives would murder all Gentiles if not for the prophet's efforts to restrain them. In reality, Indians throughout the nation had killed fewer than thirty-seven emigrants during the one-year period that saw an estimated 14,500 people traverse the continent to the West Coast. And nearly all of those reports of "Indian" massacres in Utah Territory carried with them tales of white-faced Indians who used Mormon slang. For their part, the Utes were unwilling allies, having been mistreated by the Mormons since the sect's arrival among them. Indian agent Garland Hurt was loved by many and held more sway with them than Huntington or Young, and the Utes believed Hurt's assurances that the U.S. government would deal with them more favorably than the Mormons had.

Much of Young's posturing was just that, for he fully expected a political solution before the spring of 1858, the earliest the troops could make it across the Wasatch. He felt certain Kane could stave off any invasion, and sent Elder Samuel D. Richards to Washington bearing a conciliatory letter for Kane to hand-deliver to President Buchanan. Young knew full well that the Kane family was extremely close to James Buchanan.

Still, in Zion he preached war and rebellion, vengeance and ultimate redemption. On August 5, as the Fancher Train lodged nearby, the prophet issued a proclamation to the citizens of Utah declaring "we are invaded by a hostile force who are evidently assailing us to accomplish our overthrow and destruction." An order went out to all outlying settlements to hoard their grain, and to "report without delay any person in your District that disposes of a Kernel of grain to any Gentile merchant or temporary sojourner." The result of this "violent and treasonable proclamation," a Utah resident wrote several years later, "was to incite the people to revenge and bloodshed." Everyone in Utah was now "looking forward to the time when the prophecies of Joseph, the Seer, should be fulfilled, and the Son of Man should come," wrote Fanny Stenhouse.

George A. Smith was sent south to personally deliver the orders to church leaders along the southern route to California in the communities of Provo, Springville, Nephi, Fillmore, and Parowan. Gratified by the militia units mustered and drilling in the outlying colonies, the blustering, overweight, and overwrought apostle fueled the Saints' fanaticism and fear of annihilation. Accompanied by William H. Dame and

Dame's assistant, James H. Martineau, Smith toured every settlement in the area. Dame reported to Wells that he had made an inventory of the weapons available: "Muskets, 99; Rifles, 190; Colt's Revolvers, 17; Pounds of Powder, 192¾; Pounds of Lead, 335½; Swords, 24." Further, Dame wrote Wells, "the command feel calm, quiet, and willing to act upon any command that may be given and any orders from head Quarters will be cheerfully obeyed."

In late August, Smith carried Brigham Young's orders to John D. Lee in Harmony. The two men had much in common. "Both were tried and trusted," a historian wrote. "Both were zealots, dedicated to establish the Kingdom of God as a condition of Christ's millennial reign; and both were members of the ultra-secret Council of Fifty." So fiery were Smith's rantings in Harmony that one of Lee's wives, Rachel, recorded them in her diary as "full of hostility and virulence." Smith made it clear that the southern provinces would be expected to fulfill the orders of the church hierarchy in the weeks to come. "I have been sent down here by the old Boss, Brigham Young," Smith claimed. "Suppose an emigrant train should come along through this southern country, making threats against our people and bragging of the part they took in helping to kill our Prophets," Smith posed to Lee. "What do you think the brethren would do with them? Would they be permitted to go their way, or would the brethren pitch into them and give them a good drubbing?"

Lee impressed upon Smith that the southern Saints remained under the influence of the recent reformation, and were still "red-hot for the gospel." Lee told Smith in no uncertain terms that *any* emigrant train that passed through in the near future would be "used up"—a euphemism all Mormons understood to mean slaughtered. "I really believe that any train of emigrants that may come through here will be attacked, and probably all destroyed," Lee told Smith, making it clear that any desired outcome *other* than complete destruction should be specifically ordered by the hierarchy. "You must inform Governor Young that if he wants emigrants to pass, without being molested, he must send orders to that effect to Colonel Wm. H. Dame or Major Isaac C. Haight."

Much pleased with the response—"he laughed heartily," Lee recalled—Smith expressed his satisfaction that the brethren "will do just as you say they will with the wicked emigrants that come through."

For his part, Lee never doubted his instructions—"to prepare the people for the bloody work"—or wavered in his obedience. "General George A. Smith held a high rank as a military leader," Lee wrote. "He was one of the twelve apostles of the Church of Jesus Christ of Latter Day Saints, and as such he was considered by me to be an inspired man. His orders were to me sacred commands, which I considered it my duty to obey, without questions or hesitation."

Smith's mission, Lee fervently held, was to order the extermination of the approaching Fancher Train. Even more, he believed wholeheartedly that he was now under "the direct command of Brigham Young."

CHAPTER NINE

The Southern Trail,
August 8–September 4, 1857

T HE CALIFORNIA TRAIL from Salt Lake City through Nevada had been a highly successful route for Alexander Fancher during his previous crossings to Visalia. He and Baker had determined they would take that trail this time too. But something changed their minds. The mystery of the Fancher Train hinges on the decision to take the Southern Trail—why it was made, who influenced it, and, ultimately, what the motives were of those who suggested it.

Arriving in the Salt Lake Valley late in the afternoon of August 3, the Fancher-Baker party and livestock were in remarkable health, though appreciative of a rest. The travelers had more than enough time to traverse the daunting seven-thousand-foot Donner Pass before the legendary Sierra snowfall would begin in late October or early November, and they intended, by all accounts, to rest near the Great Salt Lake for several days if not weeks.

Encamped six miles from the Mormon capital on the Jordan River (the exact location of their camp is disputed), the train "expected to refit and replenish their stock of provisions," according to one who traveled with the party up to this point. "But it was there that they first discovered that feeling of enmity which finally resulted in their destruction." They divided their camp "on the advice of the Mormons" so that the stock would have sufficient feed. "The two were to rejoin on the other side of Salt Lake City and continue on to California via the Northern or Humboldt Route," according to a member of the party.

Fancher and Baker "rode about Salt Lake City trying to buy grain for bread and horse feed," according to Burr Fancher, a descendant of the captain. "At each livery barn and feed store, the men met hostility. Although they had 'for sale' signs in place, the business owners rejected their offers. When asked what was wrong, they were given evasive answers." The two returned to the camp to assess the situation, and a short time later apostle Charles C. Rich, a longtime Danite, rode in with an order for them to break up their camp and depart the following day. Animated discussions ensued, during which the captains were persuaded to follow the southern route to the stream-fed Mountain Meadows. There they could refresh their cattle before embarking on the final dangerous crossing of the Mojave after the desert's 120-degree summer temperatures had subsided.

"On the morning of the 5th of August," remembered Malinda Cameron Scott, "my father [William Cameron] came to our wagon and said 'I think I am going to take the southern route.' " Charles Rich had convinced her father that the Southern Trail had more grass for their herds. But her cantankerous husband, Henry Dalton Scott, resisted the change in direction. Malinda later testified that Scott asked his father-in-law why he wanted the change. "And my father said that he had heard there was good feed and plenty of water." Unconvinced, Scott insisted on sticking with the "main road," and Malinda, nine months pregnant, had little choice but to remain with her husband. That very day she clambered into her wagon with her husband and three small children, and along with eight more emigrants they moved out toward the California Trail. Days later, a fellow emigrant murdered her husband. She would never see her parents or brothers and sisters again.

Some have written that Rich, a Council of Fifty member who himself had just returned from San Bernardino via the southern route, knowingly provided false information about early snows in the Sierra as well as reports of hostile Indians on the northern route in order to lure the train south. Some twenty years later, Brigham Young would contend that Rich had tried to warn them off the southern route, recommending they go north to Bear River and catch the California Trail. Young's later claim would be presented as fact by "a historian sympathetic to the Mormons," Hubert H. Bancroft, and it served to misrepresent and obfuscate details of the event for generations to come. "Few men have played a more decisive part in concealing the truth about the Mountain Meadows Massacre than the eminent nineteenth-century American historian Hubert H. Bancroft," wrote William Wise, disturbed by the historical inaccuracy. "His account of the massacre and its aftermath . . . has been accepted for almost a century without further question or study by later historians—an acceptance that inevitably has led to a complete distortion of the facts." It seems most likely that Rich advised the Fancher Train to take the Southern Trail.

Whatever the impetus, the train set out toward southern Utah on August 5; they had rested only a day and a half and were desperately low on supplies. Rich ordered that they move on, knowing full well that the southern settlements had been specifically directed not to sell them food. "This, considering their need of provisions, was much the same as condemning them to certain death," wrote T. B. H. Stenhouse. That day, William Eaton, an Illinois farmer who had joined the group at their Arkansas departure, wrote to his wife saying all was fine. It would be the last word from the party.

Basil Parker and his outfit arrived two days after his friends had departed. Having trailed the Fancher Train every step of the way, they had planned to rendezvous in the Salt Lake Valley and proceed to California together and all settle near Visalia. In his memoir, published forty-four years later, Parker recalled that when he arrived in Salt Lake City he found a vicious slander campaign against the Arkansans under way, including allegations of misconduct thoroughly uncharacteristic of the people he knew so well. A Mormon approached Parker's tent, making threats against the train. "The Mormons claimed that the emigrants of Baker's train had insulted their women, and had accused the Mormons of poisoning the water that had killed some of the emigrant's [sic] cattle."

Parker noted Brigham Young's current sermons vowing to "turn [the Indians] loose" on the emigrants, and he thought the "large bands of indians [sic] in the City" who seemed "bent on mischief" gave credence to the warning. Trying to "keep my temper and appear cool," Parker regretted for the rest of his life that he was unable to warn his friends; to do so would have endangered himself and his family. He immediately left the territory on the northern route.

I can now see that I was in a very close place just at that time and it can easily be seen that the way they acted with the Baker train, all they wanted was to create a disturbance as an excuse to slaughter the entire train, and I can see that the Mormons were cleverly planning a shield for themselves in allowing the Indians to be the public aggressors, and on whom they could throw the blame of the awful crime they intended to commit at Mountain Meadows a few days later, for there is every reason to believe that the Baker party was doomed to destruction before it left Salt Lake City.

Apart from the firsthand accounts of Parker and Malinda Scott, "all information about the emigrants' conduct came from men involved in their murder or cover-up," concluded Will Bagley.

Rebuffed in Salt Lake City, and apparently calculating that their only hope of obtaining supplies would be the outlying colonies, the forty wagons and huge cattle herd lumbered off, heading due south. Theirs would be the first emigrant company to take the route that summer, though two more trains would follow behind them. "Once the Fancher party left Salt Lake, it disappeared into a historical maze built of lies, folklore, popular myth, justifications, and few facts," Bagley wrote of the month-long journey. Many of the conflicting versions of events serve to protect Brigham Young and the Church of Jesus Christ of Latter-day Saints, while establishing a scenario for Indian culpability and vilification of the Fancher-Baker party. The few contemporaneous eyewitness sources remain the best, most accurate depictions, not colored by bias or motivated by self-preservation.

Inching along the rough trail, passing small irrigated farms strewn every few miles between Big Cottonwood Fort and American Fork, the party noticed abundant ripening crops in the fields. "It was no secret among travelers on the road that the Saints' stocks of flour, bacon, vegetables, poultry, butter, cheese and eggs were not only large that year but far in excess of their requirements," wrote Wise.

At American Fork, they "essayed to trade off some of their worn-out stock for the fresh and reliable cattle of the Mormons, offering fine bargains," according to a "high priest" in the church who later publicly accused Brigham Young of conspiring in the events. But at every attempt they were met with sullen refusal and hostile slurs, and their hopelessness grew into despair.

Perhaps calculating that the farther they traveled from Salt Lake City, the better their chance of obtaining provisions, Fancher and Baker pushed their party on to Lehi. The thriving community of six hundred known for its potatoes and vegetables met the group with what had become a pattern of antagonistic rejection. Grazing their nine hundred head of cattle on what they believed to be "Uncle Sam's grass" contributed to the mounting strife with the Mormon settlers.

They passed on to Battle Creek at the northeastern edge of forty-five-mile-long Utah Lake, where they tried unsuccessfully to trade work oxen for fresher animals. As they were setting up camp in a large grass field west of Provo, they were ordered by a local official to pull up stakes and keep moving. At some point south of Provo, the train was approached by William A. Aden, a twenty-year-old Tennessee artist and illustrator. He had been in Utah Territory for several weeks, apparently, according to his last correspondence home, intending to stay until the following spring, but by August was eager to join a Gentile train to California. The blue-eyed, fair-skinned young man had sketched the Overland Trail to Utah and had produced "scenic paintings for the Provo Dramatic association."

The next town was Springville, a hotbed of apostates and zealots all agitated by the previous year's murders of Parrish and Potter as well as other violent crimes during the reformation. An unknown number of "backouts" joined the train in the area around Springville, seeking asylum with the large, well-armed caravan. An apostate leader from the community addressed the Fancher company with a speech "well calculated to inflame the minds of the Strangers and Confirm all their preconceived opinions and sentiments, against the Mormons." A Mormon mail carrier who followed the train also noted a large number of defectors "who had joined the California emigrant train for security in traveling." Mysteriously, no Mormon apostates traveling to Mountain Meadows with the Fancher Train have ever been identified.

The train continued through Spanish Fork and Payson, where, according to Fanny Stenhouse, "the reception was still the same—the word of the Mormon Pontiff had gone forth, and no man dared to hold communion or to trade with them." Samuel Pitchforth recorded the group's arrival in verdant Nephi in an August 17 diary entry: "The company of Gentiles passed through this morning—they wanted to purchase Flour." Pitchforth would spend the next day "Fixing my Gun," according to "the only known contemporary LDS record that mentions the Fancher party before the massacre."

Half starved, exhausted, a hundred miles south of Salt Lake City and hundreds of miles farther from a Gentile settlement, and now fully informed by their new members of the Mormon hysteria, the Fancher

Train proceeded with wariness. Every night the wagons were drawn into a circle, the wheels were chained together, and sentries were posted. "The Fancher company was not an aggregation of fools or lunatics," wrote one of the first observers of the event. "They knew that they were within the power of an enemy that was then preparing for war with the United States. Their failure to obtain food supplies, and the sullen behavior of the Saints would have convinced men of ordinary sense and caution that theirs was a dangerous situation."

At this point they had procured nothing. "Now and then, some Mormon, weak in the faith or braver or more fond of money than his fellows, would steal into the camp, in the darkness of night, bearing with him just what he was able to carry," according to Fanny Stenhouse. But such acts of humanity or greed were met with swift and cruel punishment. "It is true that occasionally some Mormon more daring than his fellows would sack up a few pounds of provisions, and under cover of night smuggle the same into the emigrant camp, taking his chances of a severed windpipe," wrote another.

The severe treatment of a band of God-fearing emigrants by God-fearing Mormons has bewildered historians and other writers for more than a century. Laden with young children, the train could not have credibly been feared as an advance guard of the U.S. Army. Nor had its members been accused of a crime or caused a disturbance, though some contemporary reports refer to the massive cattle herd as destructive of private property. Some of the earliest observations drew unwanted attention to the obvious—the train was resplendent in its supply of arms, ammunition, clothing, household goods, longhorn cattle, fine well-groomed horses, and what one fellow emigrant called "considerable funds."

At Nephi they tried to purchase flour from Red Bill Black, who owned the local mill, but were refused. Averaging only seven miles a day on the rough wagon road, with scorching daytime temperatures and unrelenting sun further enervating them and their animals, they followed the Juab Valley on the western slope of the San Pitch Mountains. Their wagons were now empty of food, and they survived on their own slaughtered beef cattle. They passed the tiny settlement of Buttermilk Fort on the north end of the Pahvant Range and moved on another ten miles to the onetime Utah capital of Fillmore City. "They had but three or four settlements yet to pass through," wrote "Argus," an anonymous source, "and then their way would pass over the most to be dreaded of all the American deserts, where there would be no possibility of obtaining a pound of food."

Finally, they passed through rough volcanic terrain, arriving at Corn Creek on August 25, where "they saw the first kindly look and heard the first friendly word" since they had left Salt Lake City twenty-one days earlier. "And, strange to say, those friends were Indians." Federal agent Garland Hurt had been teaching Chief Kanosh's Pahvant tribe European agricultural methods. The band sold the Fancher-Baker party thirty bushels of corn and "sent them away in peace."

That night, George A. Smith camped forty yards away from them on the creek. He was returning to the capital from his trip south, where he had carried Young's order to John D. Lee and other militia leaders. Accompanying Smith on the journey to Salt Lake City were Jacob Hamblin and several Indian chiefs from the south. Smith would claim twelve years later that three men from the Fancher-Baker party came to their camp, including "the Captain of the company," much aroused by the presence of Indians not native to the immediate vicinity. "I replied that if their party had not committed any outrage upon the Indians there would be no danger," Smith professed to have told them, though many historians view the entire exchange with skepticism. Whatever the truth of the discussion between the parties, the Fancher-Baker party "hurried to get away," according to David L. Bigler, stepping "up their rate of travel to more than twelve miles a day, about as fast as an ox train with a large herd could go."

Leaving Corn Creek, they now faced the most difficult terrain of the Southern Trail, climbing two six-thousand-foot mountain passes before dropping down through piñon-dotted ridges into the isolated town of Beaver. Here they were unable to buy food and hay, and continued their forlorn journey. They moved steadily for forty-eight hours, through Red Creek and rolling toward Parowan, passing imposing granite rocks— thrown up by "some convulsion of nature," one explorer later wrote— etched with ancient hieroglyphs. Named for a Book of Mormon warrior, Parowan sat at the base of the rugged Hurricane Cliffs. Built around a mountain-fed stream, the town of a hundred residents was surrounded by a six-foot-thick earthen wall rising to twelve feet, which sheltered the Mormon homes and gardens. But William Dame had ordered the walls closed so that the party could not enter the town and see the militia assembled there—"which militia," wrote one observer, "afterwards assisted in their destruction, for which preparations were even now made." The evidence of "so much drilling and marching, and the abundance of firearms in public hands might well alert them to the fact that they faced far more danger from the Mormons than they did from the Indians," wrote Wise.

Perhaps even more strategic was the necessity for Mormon militia leaders to shelter the brethren from the true domestic nature of the wagon train. If the party entered the town, "the ordinary Saints of Parowan would soon realize that here were no boisterous, dissolute, irreligious 'mobocrats,' " wrote one historian, "but sober, 'homespun,' God-fearing family people, much like themselves—with the result that the emigrants would be all too likely to win the sympathy of the very militiamen who soon might have to be used in an attack on the train."

Circling the town on the western edge of the fort, they camped on a stream in the shadow of the town's impenetrable adobe wall. The local gristmill refused to grind the corn the travelers had acquired in Corn Creek, but they were somehow able to purchase a small amount of wheat. The "Good Samaritans," as the few who took pity on them were called in later reports, met harsh retribution by fellow Saints. When a "little Englishman" tried to sell them some provisions, a local Mormon leader "advanced before him, and, pressing the edge of a bowie-knife against his throat compelled him to retreat."

William A. Leaney, a Parowan resident, recognized the artist William Aden as the son of a doctor who had once saved his life from an anti-Mormon mob while he was on a previous mission to Paris, Tennessee. Leaney took pity on the Gentiles and invited the young Aden to his home. He instructed his wives to harvest some onions for the young man and presented them to Aden in gratitude for his father's previous generosity. Dame dispatched two enforcers, who beat Leaney senseless with a picket from his own fence.

From Parowan the party made their way southwest to Cedar City, where it seemed their fortune might have changed. Reaching the most populous of all the towns in the southern territory on one of the first days of September, they were able to purchase fifty bushels of wheat. There, a man named Joseph Walker agreed to grind all their corn, wheat, and grain on hand. When Bishop Philip Klingensmith sent a Mormon elder to order Walker to stop, Walker responded with defiance uncharacteristic of the settlers. "Tell the bishop that I have six grown sons, and that we will sell our lives at the price of death to others before I will obey his order." Walker was excommunicated for his actions, though he remained a faithful Mormon for the rest of his life.

The emigrants left late the next day and set up camp three miles outside Cedar City in a cooperative field. Resting only one night, they began their exit from Mormon country the next morning, eager to reach the long-sought oasis of Mountain Meadows, where, they were told by local Mormons, they would be able to obtain food. The trail wound from Cedar City to Iron Creek and on to Little Pinto Creek through pine trees and tall sagebrush. From the rise at Jacob Hamblin's ranch on Meadow Creek they could see the luxuriant alpine grasses of the meadow they thought would be their deliverance.

On Friday, September 4, they crossed the rim of the Great Basin. On Saturday they moved slowly down into the five-mile-long valley. Opening from a narrow entrance to the east and expanding into a network of creeks and cottonwoods, the meadow closed with a bottleneck exit into the rugged Beaver Mountains to the west. "This little mountain paradise . . . was altogether the most beautiful place in all the rout [sic]," Parley Pratt had written in his journal in 1851. "Some 1000 or 1500 acres of bottom or meadow lands were spread out before us like a green carpet, richly clothed with a variety of grasses, and possessing a soil both black, rich, and quick. The surrounding hills were not abrupt, but rounded off, in a variety of beauteous landscapes and everywhere richly clothed with the choices of bunch grass and bordered in the higher eminances [sic] with cedar and nut pine sufficient for fewel [sic]."

The travelers set up camp near a large spring at the southern end "shut in by smooth rounded hills," and for the first time in their long and burdensome trek from Arkansas to the Spanish Trail they relaxed their guard. Fancher's uncharacteristic and disastrous failure to post armed sentries and outriders through the night would puzzle later historians, the laxity inexplicable in light of the hostility they had endured thus far. Among the captain's fatal mistakes was not to encircle the fresh spring within their campsite, a decision based on the swampiness of the ground; another error was the haphazard arrangement of wagons, apparently to allow more privacy for individual families. The party retired to their tents under a virtually full moon.

On Sunday, the morning began with the Sabbath service held in the expansive tent that had faithfully been transported across the country. After church William Aden sketched a scene of domestic tranquillity—

the women laundered, sewed, mended clothing, aired out bed linens, and prepared their spartan meals; the children ran and played in the warm high-altitude sun; the men gathered firewood, carried buckets of water from the stream, and repaired the wagons. One young woman in advanced pregnancy finally rested comfortably, expecting to deliver her child momentarily in this sylvan Eden of cottonwood glades.

Here the emigrants believed they would be able to recuperate and regroup, putting the trepidation of the past weeks behind them. A month of leisurely grazing would fatten the livestock for the ultimate crossing of the desert. They planned on being at their new homes in the land of golden opportunity by late fall.

CHAPTER TEN

Mountain Meadows,
September 7–11, 1857

T HEY ROSE at dawn. Soon there was the clamor of cookware and
crackling fires, and the smell of brewing coffee and roasting game
drifted through the brisk air. Carefree and relaxed, a number of men
warmed themselves at the edge of the community campfire. "While
eating breakfast of rabbit and quail a shot rang out and one of the
children toppled over," Sarah Baker would recall. Hideous shrieks
emanated from a ravine to their south as a barrage of gunfire rained on
the unprotected camp from all directions. Within moments, seven men
had fallen dead. Fancher's throat had been struck by a musket ball, rendering him helpless, and minutes later his twenty-five-year-old nephew,
Matt, took command, shouting orders to circle the wagons. Baker was
also seriously wounded, as were twenty others.

Taken completely by surprise, the emigrants marshaled their forces
with stunning alacrity and composure. The experienced frontiersmen
in the group brought order to the bedlam with breakneck speed,
shouting orders to the women and children to take cover and scram-
bling to gather their weapons, all the while returning fire to the unseen
enemies. Adept with the rifle, and accustomed to Indian skirmishes,
the Arkansans successfully warded off their assailants, and no further
injuries were sustained after the first shocking volley. "Unguarded as
they were at the moment of the attack," wrote a witness, "they had
traveled too far over roads infested with Indians to become confused."

The men corralled the forty wagons into a circular barricade, shoveling trenches in order to sink the wheels down to the axletrees and

pulling the tongues inward. As the men threw up earthen mounds in front of the wagons, the women dragged the wounded and dying into the center of the fortification, where a pit was dug to shelter them. The adults maintained their calm, but panic infected the more than fifty children. As the injured moaned and the young cried helplessly, the others constructed a rough but formidable siege works. The riflemen in the company mobilized and responded with a fierce and effective counterattack, shooting at their enemies hiding in the nearby hills—"fighting like lions," one of the emigrants later recalled.

Soon after daybreak the firing came to a standstill and the travelers began assessing their situation. A spring was outside their corral at a perilous hundred-yard distance. They could not see their cattle and oxen grazing in the valley beyond. Some of the horses and mules that had been tied to the wagons now lay dead on the ground, the survivors rearing and struggling to free themselves. For a train of such fastidiousness in planning, tenacity in the face of unexpected privations in Utah Territory, and seasoning and expertise on the part of its leaders to have so egregiously let down its guard would mystify future analysts. Having left the last hostile Mormon settlement behind them, having believed assurances from Jacob Hamblin and other Mormons of the safety of Mountain Meadows, and having assumed the docility of the Paiutes, the Fancher-Baker party had been lulled into the falsest sense of security. Moreover, while the war whoops that had been heard indicated an Indian attack, that conclusion was at odds with the assessment Fancher, Baker, and the other veteran pioneers had made from previous expeditions west—they knew the southern Paiutes to be a notoriously complacent, peaceful, and generally unarmed tribe.

The meadow was a mirage of serenity. Far from being a sanctuary, it was instead a perfect death trap. Surrounded by rocky outcroppings that provided cover for attackers, hills that afforded the enemy a bird's-eye view of the camp, and only two tapered exits at either end, it was strategically flawless for the site of an ambush. In fact, Mountain Meadows was known among Mormons as "a preferred location for the quiet execution of unpleasant tasks," according to one historian, and the site was the inspiration behind the infamous Mormon euphemism for blood-atonement killings—sending the victim "over the rim of the basin."

The siege that began on Monday continued through Tuesday with a halfhearted round of sniper fire. The emigrants listened to the cattle herd bellowing in the distance as the enemy began their roundup. The defenders continued to strengthen their redoubt, but every foray to the spring for fresh water was met with gunfire. The sporadic salvos indicated a strange perseverance amidst a partial retreat, as if the enemy were biding time while it mustered its forces. By Wednesday the suffering had become acute. More of the wounded had died, and the smell of decaying corpses and carcasses became unbearable. The lack of water and food was reaching a crisis point, as the emigrants huddled together under the blistering sun by day and a biting chill by night. A bullet that penetrated the corral tore the lobe from the left ear of three-year-old Sarah Baker, sitting on her father's knee. The emigrants knew they would all die if the siege didn't end soon. The wounded "tossed from side to side with anguish," a journalist wrote two years later.

The attack began again with a fury, and it was clear their enemies had received a significant bolstering of troops. "Still the beleaguered Arkansans fought well and bravely," according to a nineteenth-century newspaper account, "but at this time, on the third day of the battle, the pangs of unassuaged thirst drove them almost to the verge of despair." In a forlorn move, hoping to appeal to the humanity of their enemies, the emigrants dressed two little girls in "spotless white" and sent them with a bucket toward the spring. Both were shot dead in an instant.

The party decided they could no longer remain in their defensive position but had to seek help from the outside world. William Aden daringly volunteered to make his way north to recruit assistance from a party of emigrants known as the Dukes Train, which had been following a few days behind them. Aden and a companion called the Dutchman stole quietly into the night, leading their horses for several miles until they could safely mount. Galloping toward Cedar City, they saw a campfire at Richards' Springs, where, they surmised, the other pioneers might have arrived. Aden dismounted and approached three men who had risen to greet him. One, a Mormon elder named William C. Stewart, asked Aden what he wanted. He and the two others, Benjamin Arthur and Joel White, listened as Aden described the assault in the meadow. The Dutchman stayed on his horse. When Aden finished his plea, "Stewart shoved a pistol to Aden's breast and killed him," a participant in the events later testified. As the Dutchman wheeled on his horse he was shot by White but managed to flee and return to the Fancher camp.

Whatever knowledge the party had prior to that night about the makeup of their enemies, the Dutchman's awful tale would have further confirmed for them that Mormons were involved in their plight. Given the numerous apostates who were traveling with the wagon train—longtime residents of the territory who were hoping to escape the excesses of the reformation and whose views would have been considered in any group discussions about the predicament—the party would have long suspected Mormon participation by now. However, the evidence does not suggest that the emigrants knew the full magnitude of the force arrayed against them, a force composed of a highly organized and well-trained military unit acting on order of church officials. Still, their understanding of the situation would have taken on a new perspective by Wednesday night.

Thursday morning, a renewed attack began, and in the hail of fire two men ran to the stream with buckets, miraculously returning with fresh water for the party. "The bullets flew around them thick and fast, but they got into their corral in safety," an eyewitness recalled. Within the encampment the men began digging a pit in the hope of reaching water. After toiling for several hours they had dug a trench six feet wide and five feet deep, but they still had not reached an underground spring and decided to abandon the project to conserve energy for the continuing battle.

In the early afternoon they saw a white man crossing the valley onto a bluff just west of the corral. They hurriedly made a white flag and hoisted it in the middle of their corral, where it could be seen for miles. Then they dispatched two little boys to find the elusive figure in the nearby hills. But the boys' search was futile; the man, John D. Lee, knew he had been spotted and hid from the children. "They came to the place where they had last seen me and hunted all around," Lee later wrote, "but being unable to find me, they turned and went back to the camp in safety."

From his vantage point behind a large rock, Lee had a full view of the corral. He watched as two men left the camp to cut wood. The courage of the Arkansas emigrants, chopping firewood in a rain of gunfire, caused Lee to "weep like a child," he would recall. "The men all acted so bravely that it was impossible to keep from respecting them." For two hours Lee watched the emigrants, "feeling all the torture of mind that is possible for a man to suffer who feels merciful, and yet knows, as I knew then, what was in store for that unfortunate company." At the nearby Hamblin ranch, some of the Mormon militiamen pitched horseshoes to pass the time while they waited for still more reinforcements.

In intensifying desperation, the emigrants convened Thursday evening and decided on a dangerous but grave course of action. Alexander Fancher, barely able to speak from the throat injury he had sustained on the first day of the siege, now implored three of the group's healthiest, most skilled, and most experienced scouts to make a furtive trek across the Mojave Desert. The three heroic scouts are generally identified as Captain Baker's son John H. Baker and the two renowned horsemen of the group, Tilghman Cameron and Hampton Fancher. Legend has it that Captain Fancher's fabled bay stallion, Ebony King, as well as Cameron's racing mare and the other fine bloodstock, had been run off and stolen during the initial onslaught.

Sneaking out at night, they would head for California, where they would notify the world of the barbaric situation. The likelihood of those left behind surviving the week or more it would take for a rescue party from the west to arrive was remote at best—assuming the messengers safely escaped the meadow—so they turned their attention to a sort of last rites and final accounting for a civilized nation.

The entire company gathered for the momentous reckoning. They drew up a petition addressed to "the Masons, Odd Fellows, Baptists, and Methodists of the States, and to all good people every-where," describing the uninterrupted four-day siege by men "well supplied with powder and weapons." Beseeching immediate salvation from their fate, the emigrants recognized the improbability of a rescue, begging, in the event, for justice to be brought to their attackers. There followed a list of all emigrants' names, ages, birthplaces, locations of previous homes, occupations, religions, and positions in the wagon train. The number of clergymen, physicians, farmers, drovers, wranglers, and children was stated. The document also itemized all the personal property, including jewelry, currency, gold, weapons, wagons, and livestock. All the survivors signed the petition, the adults representing an impressive array of churches and Masonic lodges in Arkansas.

Kneeling in a circle, they all prayed together for the last time, "a white haired old Methodist pastor" presiding over the downcast group. After emotional farewells, the scouts slipped into the nearby ravine. No shots were fired as the men made their getaway, but Ira Hatch, one of the Mormon militiamen positioned nearby, spotted them. Mormons would later report that all three men were tracked and murdered in their sleep, and rumors would circulate that either John D. Lee or Jacob Hamblin destroyed the historic petition; though, like much of the rest of the story, the truth would be mired in a lack of solid evidence.

A strange calm settled across the valley as dawn broke on Friday, and for the first time in five days the gunfire seemed to have come to a total standstill. The Fancher-Baker party had no food or water, their ammunition stores were nearly depleted, their two captains were wounded, three of their ablest men were off on a vain quest across a wasteland, the bodies of several others were decomposing in their midst, and many were suffering the agony of untreated wounds. The group would now need a miracle to survive. Suddenly, such a miracle seemed to appear.

As the sun moved to midmorning, the emigrants spotted a large body of white men coming up the road carrying the white flag of truce along with an American flag. "All is joy in the corral . . . a general shout is raised," according to a later investigation. Ecstatic, the emigrants dressed eight-year-old Mary Dunlap in a white dress and sent her out waving a little white handkerchief in a further token of armistice. "Delighted with the approach of armed men bearing the American flag," a federal agent would later say, "they hailed the spectacle with joy. For this approach means rescue and deliverance." Three wagons could be seen, Mary's younger sister Rebecca would later recall, and then one man rode out alone waving a white flag as his horse trotted toward the besieged camp—"held by all civilized nations and peoples, from time immemorial, as an emblem at once of peace, of truth, of honour." Matt Fancher walked out to meet the rider, an English convert to Mormonism named William Bateman. Just weeks earlier Bateman had been threatened with excommunication for apostasy, but had been granted one last chance to prove his penitence by carrying out church orders at Mountain Meadows. Placed "in the front ranks," as Prophet Heber Kimball put it, Bateman and fellow backsliders would be put "to the test."

Bateman told Fancher that a Mormon named John D. Lee wanted to enter the emigrants' camp to negotiate a treaty. When Fancher agreed, Bateman circled the white flag above his head like a lasso, signaling to Lee that the emigrants had agreed to the cease-fire and to discussing a resolution. Astride a fine horse, Lee rode toward the motley and emotional assembly, using secret Masonic signals to further convey comradery. It was now noon. Dismounting, he introduced himself as a federal Indian agent, hoping to gain their trust as a fellow patriotic American, as well as a constituted military officer of the American territory of Utah. He was also a major in the Mormon militia, he told them; thus he had the unique ability to mediate between the emigrants and the Paiutes, who Lee claimed were angry with the party and were the aggressors in the conflict. Lee "said the Indians had gone hog wild but the Mormons would try to save us and take us all to Cedar City, the nearest big Mormon settlement if our men would give up their guns," a survivor would report more than eighty years later. "Nothing less than the surrender of their provisions, arms and cattle will pacify their wrath," the emigrants were told.

Drawing on his most persuasive and articulate powers, and relying on skills honed over decades of proselytizing, preaching, convincing, and cajoling, John D. Lee faced the most formidable task of his life—to win a total surrender. "My position was painful, trying and awful," Lee said of the encounter that would haunt him for two decades. "My brain seemed to be on fire; my nerves were for a moment unstrung; humanity was overpowered as I thought of the cruel, unmanly part that I was acting . . . I wished that the earth would open and swallow me where I stood. God knows my suffering was great. I cannot describe my feelings. I knew that I was acting a cruel part and doing a damnable deed." Lee knew there was no honor or chivalry by any code of civilized conduct, military or civilian, in decoying and ambushing unarmed men, women, and children. Yet he would carry out his role masterfully.

"As I entered the fortifications," Lee wrote, "men, women and children gathered around me in wild consternation. Some felt that the time of their happy deliverance had come, while others, though in deep distress, and all in tears, looked upon me with doubt, distrust and terror." The emigrants were busy burying men Lee described as "two men of note," who had apparently just died of earlier wounds. Wrapping the bodies in buffalo robes, the emotional party placed them in a single grave. Lee sat on the ground outside the corral waiting, where "a large fleshy lady" came to him twice and described the five-day siege. Seven of their men had died, she told him, and forty-six others had been wounded. Suddenly impatient, Lee urged them to finish the burial ceremony and make a hasty decision. Whatever initial misgivings he endured had given way to a renewed zealotry. "My faith in the godliness of my leaders was such that it forced me to think that I was not sufficiently spiritual to act the important part I was commanded to perform. My hesitation was only momentary. Then feeling that duty compelled *obedience to orders,* I laid aside my weakness and my humanity, and became an instrument in the hands of my superiors and my leaders."

For between three and four hours Lee coaxed the party to surrender their weapons—"mostly Kentucky rifles of the muzzle-loading style," he noted—and even in the end dissension was rife and passionate. "If you give up your arms you are a fool," said one. "If you do you are dead men," implored another. The recommendation of the many apostates in the camp would never be known, or whether they considered their fellow Mormons capable of such cold-blooded treachery. Sixty members of the Mormon militia were waiting beyond the closest hill, Lee promised, who would escort them to Cedar City, where their weapons and belongings would be returned to them. Though Matt Fancher, who was now the group's leader, and a gravely injured Jack Baker saw no alternative, the dying Alexander Fancher uttered a dramatic final order. "Good God no, Matt!" he pleaded with his nephew. But the captain's entreaty was dismissed as delirium.

"Well our men did not have much choice," a survivor said in explaining the denouement. "It was either stick it out and fight till the last of us were killed or starved or take Lee up on his proposition, even tho it did seem fishy." Even if the emigrants distrusted Lee, even if they believed Mormons had been culpable in the siege, they had been reduced to such absolute hopelessness that placing their fate in the hands of their foes seemed the only solution. "Their ammunition was about all gone," Lee noted. "I do not think there were twenty loads left in their whole camp. If the emigrants had had a good supply of ammunition they never would have surrendered, and I do not think we could have captured them without great loss, for they were brave men and very resolute and determined."

Even at the end, most of the emigrants probably thought that at the worst they were surrendering to a force bent on no more than plunder. No amount of preparation, intelligence, bravery, perseverance, or heroism could have equipped them for what they were facing. No other event in American history paralleled it, and that their captors—fellow Christians—would be capable of the act that followed would have been unthinkable to the condemned party. Mormon agent John D. Lee "looked into the faces of the intended victims, then betrayed their desperate trust in his humanity and the near-sacred promise of the white flag," as one writer put it.

Once the Arkansans agreed to place themselves under Lee's protection, the operation took on a sudden urgency. Militiaman Daniel McFarlane galloped in to say the Indians might change their minds if the surrender did not occur instantly. What happened next would give rise to contradictory testimony that continued for more than a century. But what is indisputable by all accounts is that the work of death was carried out with planned and organized swiftness and precision. One of the murderers later remembered that by his gold pocket watch the killings of some 140 men, women, and children had taken no more than three minutes.

Lee ordered the unarmed, unresisting men and the famished women and children to divide into three groups and then signaled to his troops that they were ready to march. Two wagons approached the compound driven by militiamen Samuel McMurdy and Samuel Knight. Separating the women and children from their husbands and fathers, and further dividing the healthy from the wounded, the Mormons directed them with an eerie exactitude. Into McMurdy's wagon were loaded all of the weapons, covered with featherbeds, and possibly some of the children under eight years old—in accordance with Mormon doctrine, this is the age of "innocence," and the year in which they are baptized. Knight's wagon was loaded with at least five wounded men and a teenage boy, as well as other younger children, according to some accounts. "The wounded and young children including me and my two sisters and brother were put in another wagon," Sallie Baker told a reporter many years later. "My mother and father were wounded and were in the wagon with us children."

It was late afternoon by the time the pitiful procession got under way. First the two wagons set out in the direction of the California Road, with Lee walking between them. McFarlane led the women and older children, following a quarter of a mile behind the second wagon on foot. "They made the men wait until the women and children were a good ways on ahead before starting the men out single file about ten feet apart," Sallie Baker remembered. The men were a half mile behind the women, moving in a column and commanded by Major John Higbee on horseback, each walking next to an armed Mormon guard.

The first wagon dipped over a knoll just as the women and children walked into a "low swale where the road led through heavy underbrush," one writer said, then the two groups disappeared from the sight of their men and hurried past members of the Nauvoo Legion who had been formed by Lee into a square. When the emigrant men reached those troops, they smiled and waved, letting out a cheer of gratitude to their supposed protectors. The men came to a smooth open patch surrounded by oak brush; suddenly, Higbee sat erect in his saddle, fired a shot into the air, and gave the fateful order to his brethren: "Halt! Do your duty!" Or, as some later reported, it was not Higbee but either Lee or Klingensmith who shouted, "Halt! Do your duty to Israel!" With that, each Mormon shot the emigrant man next to him. The Mormon apostate refugees, who were still wearing their endowment garments, were "blood atoned" by the ritual slitting of throats. "Higbee, I wouldn't do this to you," a wounded apostate pleaded with the man he recognized as a Cedar City elder. "You would have done the same to me or just as bad," Higbee reportedly said before cutting the man's throat.

Most of the men died instantly, and those who attempted to escape were "picked off by a second firing" or chased by armed horsemen who had been bringing up the rear. At the sound of the shots, the women and children began yelling and running. Higbee then gave the order to kill them all. "It was my duty, with the two drivers, to kill the sick and wounded who were in the wagons and to do so when we heard the guns of the troops fire," Lee claimed. "As we heard the guns, I ordered a halt and we proceeded to do our part." Implausibly, Lee contended that a premature firing of his weapon precluded him from taking part in the wholesale butchery that was going on around him. "I fully intended to do my part of the killing," Lee claimed, but it was all finished by the time he regained his composure.

"From the survivors went up such a piercing, heart-rending scream—such a shriek of blank despair—then the flight of all except one young woman, who sprang to Lee, and clung to him for protection," read one account of the mayhem. The children in the first wagon huddled together. One-year-old Sarah Dunlap was shot in the elbow, sending all of the children into a frenzy. "One of the Mormons ran up to the wagon, raised his gun and said 'Lord my God, Receive their spirits. It is for Thy Kingdom that I do this,' " reported Sallie Baker. She then watched as McMurdy fired at two men who were comforting each other, killing them both with one bullet. She saw the wagon driver bludgeon a fourteen-year-old boy to death with the butt of a gun. "In the midst of all the confusion the two Dunlap girls Ruth, 14, and Rachel, 16, made a wild dash across the valley to some scrub oak thinking they were safe but evidence showed they suffered far worse than the other women." Afterward it was reported that the two sisters were raped, stripped of their clothing, and then brutally murdered by Lee after they promised to love him and obey him all their lives—a charge Lee would deny for the rest of his own life. Rebecca and Louisa Dunlap saw their twin sisters, Lucinda and Susannah, killed, and would later identify their murderers.

"The knife and sword and bayonet completed the work commenced by the bullet," as one writer put it. Mothers clung to their infants, trying to shield them from the fatal blows. Two women who held each other were slain with one sword thrust. "One young girl sprung from the wounded and dead beside her and fell upon her knees before one of the murderers, a young man," according to later testimony, "who, touched by a momentary compassion, or other feeling, raised her to her feet and declared he would save her, when his father, one of the leaders in the massacre, and believed by many to have been Lee, stabbed her to the heart in his son's arms."

Captain Jack Baker held four-year-old Nancy Huff in his arms as he was killed; the little girl then watched her mother "shot in the forehead and fall dead." She looked on helplessly as teenage girls begged their murderers to spare them, to no avail. Vina, "the prettiest of the three Baker girls," was last seen by one of her sisters being led away, her beautiful long black hair hanging straight. One eyewitness reported "children clinging around the knees of the murderers, begging for mercy and offering themselves as slaves for life could they be spared. But their throats were cut from ear to ear as an answer to their appeal." Another witness reported that two attractive young girls were told that if they danced nude their lives would be spared, yet after doing the macabre performance they too were put to death. "You don't forget the horror," one of the survivors said. "And you wouldn't forget it either, if you saw your own mother topple over in the wagon beside you, with a big red splotch getting bigger and bigger on the front of her calico dress."

For his part, Lee would always claim that he never personally killed anyone that day, and he portrayed himself instead as the Good Samaritan saving children from the clenches of certain death. His later confessions were full of heartrending tales of how he heroically, and single-handedly, spared lives of innocents. But others insisted that he acted reprehensibly.

After most of the killing had been completed, it was decided who was "old enough to tell tales," as the Mormons put it, which led to several more execution-style slayings of children. "The Mormons may have had a horror of killing anyone under the age of eight, which by definition constituted shedding innocent blood," as one historian wrote, "but they apparently were more concerned about disposing of any child old enough to be a credible witness." "In these essentials, all accounts agree," Juanita Brooks concluded. "The points of difference come in placing the responsibilities for giving and executing the orders."

When the slaughter had stopped, an unknown number of children—Lee insisted there were sixteen, others said seventeen, and some reports indicated more than twenty—were the sole survivors as the sun was slipping quickly behind the mountains. Philip Klingensmith, the bishop from Cedar City, came on horseback to help manage them. Lee would later testify that he ordered Knight and McMurdy to dump all the dead bodies into a pile and then transport the surviving children four miles north to Jacob Hamblin's ranch, where Hamblin's wife Rachel and their Paiute servant, Albert, awaited them. Jacob was said to be in Salt Lake City being blessed by Brigham Young with a new polygamous wife at the time of the massacre on his ranch. Rachel had been hearing what she called "a great number of guns firing" since Monday, but on this Friday, at sundown, she had "heard a fire greater than before and more distinct . . . when the last of them were killed." Then the wagon loaded with the hysterical children arrived at her home.

An interrogator would later marvel at Rachel's lack of affect and strange absence of emotion about the massacre. "Of the shooting of the emigrants, which she had herself heard, and knew at the time what was going on, she seemed to speak without a shudder, or any very great feeling." But when she turned to the plight of the orphans "who were brought by such a crowd to her own house . . . two of the children cruelly mangled and the most of them with their parents' blood still wet upon their clothes, and all of them shrieking with terror and grief and anguish, her own mother heart was touched."

John Calvin Miller, six, was among the children, and with him were his sister Mary, four, and one-year-old brother, James. John was the only one of them who would talk, but he could not remember their last name, only that he was there when their mother and father and two other brothers were murdered, and that he saw the men who shot them. Georgia Ann Dunlap was eighteen months old. Her parents and seven sisters and brothers had just been executed in front of her eyes, and she was now alone with her five-year-old sister, Prudence Angelina, who could not stop sobbing. Emberson Tackitt, four, had watched his mother hacked to death, while his father, two older brothers, an aunt, and three cousins were being shot and their throats cut a few yards away. Like John Miller, Emberson had also seen many of the murderers clearly enough to identify them, but he knew to keep silent just then. His younger brother, nineteen-month-old William Henry, who was in his mother's arms when the attack began, lay dazed and whimpering in one of the wagons.

Gushing blood from the gunshot wound that had mangled her ear, Sarah Frances Baker, three, her five-year-old sister, Mary Elizabeth, and the youngest of the surviving infants, nine-month-old William, had just watched the slaughter of their parents and a seven-year-old sister. Felix Marion Jones was eighteen months old. Within a few minutes his family had been wiped out, and he would not be able to remember anything about his murdered mother, father, and sister. Christopher "Kit Carson" Fancher, five, along with his twenty-two-month-old sister, Triphenia, had seen their wounded father shot in his litter and their mother murdered with an ax, while six brothers and sisters under the age of nineteen were being killed nearby. Nancy Sophrona Huff, at four, was the sole survivor of a family of six annihilated in the same ways.

One child died as they arrived at Hamblin's ranch. Another, one-year-old Sarah Dunlap, had had her left arm nearly severed by a musket ball. Clinging frantically to her, their dresses soaked in blood, were her sisters Rebecca, six, and Louisa, four. They had all seen the slaughter of their seven brothers and sisters, as well as both parents, and Rebecca had pried her baby sister from the arms of their dead mother.

Rebecca and Louisa had also watched as the Mormon killers, disguised as Indians, washed off their war paint in one of the meadow streams. They would eventually be among the first witnesses to report this occurrence, thereby attributing the murders to white men rather than Paiutes. But for now, the sisters knew better than to utter a word about that. "My father was killed by Indians," little Kit Carson Fancher would tell a journalist two years later. "When they washed their faces they were white men."

As night fell, the field of carnage was a ghastly sight, the bodies still oozing blood into the meadow. The wolves and coyotes gathered in packs under a new moon, yipping in anticipation. Lee walked past a group of women's bodies, then past a pile of dead children he thought were between the ages of ten and sixteen. "The bodies of the women and children were scattered along the ground for quite a distance before I came to where the men were killed," he later remarked. He began a mental tabulation of the casualties, which he ultimately estimated to be 121 souls, including those killed earlier in the corral and the three who had tried in vain to escape. Neither that tally nor any later count would include the Mormon "backouts" murdered that day.

When Lee reached his fellow Danites, John Higbee and Bishop Klingensmith were standing near where the largest group of men had fallen. "The boys have acted admirably," Higbee told Lee. "They took good aim, and all of the Gentiles but three fell at the first fire." Higbee then announced it was time to examine the bodies for valuables. With the encroaching darkness, a more thorough search would have to wait until the following day, but Higbee seemed eager to begin the process. Lee claimed that he stood by in silent dread as Higbee, Klingensmith, and William C. Stewart searched the bodies for jewelry, money, and watches. It isn't clear if Lee told the truth.

When the preliminary scavenging was completed, Lee, Higbee, and Klingensmith addressed the soldiers at their nearby camp. Fifty "grim, silent men," as one account described the Mormons who had participated in the deed, waited for their commanding officers to impart some words of wisdom and direction. Much now had to be decided, "the most important of which were the story they would tell to their shocked neighbors and the stand they would take before an outraged nation." We "made speeches, and *ordered* the people to keep the matter a secret from the *entire* world," Lee said. "Not to tell their wives, or their most intimate friends, and we pledged ourselves to keep everything relating to the affair a secret during life. We also took the most binding oaths to stand by each other, and to always insist that the massacre was committed by Indians alone. This was the advice of Brigham Young too."

The scheme to blame the atrocity on the Indians—even to use the term "massacre," one so often associated with Indian barbarity—was indeed conceived, crafted, and disseminated with the characteristic meticulousness for which Brigham Young was famous.

Several families of the Shivwits Paiute band had witnessed the siege from the surrounding hills, where they had gone for their traditional fall harvest of piñon nuts. This fact was either not known or not given much consideration by the killers, who were busily taking their collective vow of silence. But for the tribe, the massacre would have far-reaching and devastating consequences. Peaceful farmers and root diggers, the Paiute of the Great Basin had survived for a thousand years crafting bones into tools and eating seeds, insects, squirrels, rabbits, and birds. Lean and agile, but armed with the crudest of weapons, they could bring down one of the ubiquitous mule deer of the Beaver Mountains only if they hunted as a group. Usually naked, they sometimes dressed in buckskin hides or wore rabbit skins as a cape. September was the most important season of the year to the Paiute, having religious as well as celebratory significance, and they clung unwaveringly to the associated rituals. The nut gatherers carried their possessions on their backs from the lower elevations of the desert into the cool high mountain country. After seeing the events on September 11, they instinctively sensed they were in danger. A Paiute descendant of an eyewitness, recalling what his grandfather had told him when he was as a child, said, "We knew we would be blamed. We had seen too much. We knew we'd either be killed by the Mormons or by the Americans, and either way we could no longer stay there." Some members of the tribe left that night with the belongings they had with them, many migrating into what is now eastern Nevada and northern Arizona; some went as far north as Wyoming and Montana. Their dispersal irrevocably strained their native culture—one more victim of the terrors let loose in the valley that day. Like the Mormon killers, the Paiute Indians protected the secret from generation to generation, their few oral histories over the next century laced with the fear and reticence of telling all they knew about the massacre.

The officers commanded their troops to camp on the field among the dead, the men consigned to a night of sleeplessness that would haunt most of them forever, according to their later diaries and other accounts. Legion guards were posted throughout the night to keep at bay the predatory animals, or even men from their ranks who might be lured to plunder. Lee, Higbee, and Klingensmith then rode back to the Hamblin ranch, where they ate supper among the din of the wailing orphans. "I was nearly dead," Lee said later, recalling that he slept soundly through the night.

PART THREE

THE LEGACY

CHAPTER ELEVEN

Deseret, September 12, 1857

B EFORE DAWN on Saturday, Lee awakened to hear William Dame and Isaac Haight arguing loudly. The two senior Nauvoo Legion officers, respective presidents of the Parowan and Cedar City churches, had arrived at the ranch sometime in the night and had fallen into a dispute about the details of the episode and how it would be reported to Brigham Young. Dame, the thirty-eight-year-old high-strung militia commander, was cowed by Haight, who held a lower military rank but was ecclesiastically superior; the religious hierarchy superseded the civil or military divisions of the church. Haight was arguing against reporting the full details of the massacre—especially the large number of women and children—to Young, and he seemed surprised that Dame intended to do so. Haight told Dame that if his intentions were to report the massacre, he "should never have ordered it done." When they noticed Lee and the others staring at them, their discussion came to an abrupt stop, the two men apparently not wanting their private dispute to be heard by the other participants. Lee, Dame, Haight, Klingensmith, Higbee, and Judge James Lewis, who had arrived in the night from Parowan, set out for the meadows on horseback; William Stewart drove the McMurdy wagon. Samuel Knight stayed at the ranch with the children and his inconsolable wife, Caroline, who had recently given birth to their own child at the Hamblin ranch. Alternating between coherence and delirium, Caroline repeatedly called for her young husband and then rejected him at the smell of blood on his clothing.

The first bodies they came to in the early-morning haze were the disfigured women and children. All color drained from Dame's face. "Horrible! Horrible!" Dame said sotto voce, stricken by the reality that confronted him. Lee sidled closer to him, eager, as he said, to hear Dame's reaction as well as any further discussion between the two commanders, because he had been so surprised by the conflict between the men. "Horrible enough," Haight said loudly, "but you should have thought of that before you issued the orders."

"I didn't think there were so many of them [women and children]," Dame is reported to have said, "or I would not have had anything to do with it." He then collapsed in distress, which infuriated Haight, who thought Dame's posturing and denial of responsibility theatrical and perilous to protecting the secrecy of the massacre and the shielding of the participants.

Lee later wrote of this second altercation:

> "I must report this matter to the authorities," Dame told Haight.
>
> "How will you report it?" said Haight.
>
> Dame said, "I will report it just as it is."
>
> "Yes, I suppose so, and implicate yourself with the rest?" said Haight.
>
> "No," said Dame. "I will not implicate myself, for I had nothing to do with it."
>
> Haight then said, "That will not do, for you know a d——d sight better. You ordered it done. Nothing has been done except by your orders, and it is too late in the day for you to order things done and then go back on it, and go back on the men who have carried out your orders. You are as much to blame as any one, and you know that we have done nothing except what you ordered done. I know that I have obeyed orders, and by G——d I will not be lied on."

The verbal exchanges on the killing field that morning would become the subject matter of conflicting affidavits, trial testimony, diaries, military tribunals, and criminal investigations over the next decades. What was consistent in all contemporaneous accounts was Dame's apparent surprise, remorse, and attempted disavowal; Haight's determination to lay the blame squarely on Dame; and Lee's resolve to portray himself as a scapegoat who merely followed orders. Mormon historians and church leaders have long pointed to Dame's use of the word "authorities" as evidence that Young had not ordered the attack. Other scholars have contended that Dame's incredulous stance was a calculated effort to shield himself and his higher authorities—under orders from those authorities, General Daniel Wells and ultimately commander-in-chief Brigham Young—from culpability. "You throw the blame of this thing on me," Haight yelled at Dame, "and I will be revenged on you if I have to meet you in hell to get it!"

Worried about the fifty or sixty other soldiers, many of whom had donned war paint the day before and who now, though with feigned disinterest, were in fact anxiously eavesdropping on their bickering commanders, Lee decided it was time to "stop the fuss," as he put it, and get on with rounding up the rest of the booty. The meadow was a sea of mutilated bodies and bloody debris. Wagons were now dismantled and featherbeds ripped open in search of gold; utensils, tools, and home furnishings that had been strewn about were collected. The plunder proceeded with a strange quiet. Women from Cedar City and nearby settlements arrived to remove the calico dresses and lace pinafores of the women and children, pulling off their expensive shoes, and ripping earrings, brooches, and rings off the corpses, most to be turned over to the church.

"Their fine stock, their pleasure vehicles, their musical instruments, and abundant and elegant outfit, excited the cupidity of the sacerdotal robbers," the *Salt Lake Daily Tribune* later reported, "and hence to the gratification of their gloomy ferocity, was added the inducement of capturing rich spoils."

The bodies were piled in heaps with little or no attempt to bury them. "They worked in pairs," Lee recalled, "two to a body, carrying the men to the rifle-pits of their encampment, now somewhat enlarged and cleaned out to hold more." Nephi Johnson, a twenty-four-year-old Indian interpreter who implausibly claimed he was unable to participate in the slaughter because his horse got away, mustered enough courage to recommend a controversial course of action. "You have made a sacrifice of the people," he told his leaders, "and I think we should burn the wagons and turn the cattle loose for the Indians, and go home like men."

Paiute witnesses would contend that they watched as the Mormons dumped a large number of bodies into a nearby ravine, burning them in a massive and putrid-smelling funeral pyre, but a mass grave of the victims would never be found, and a traveler who passed over the terrain some weeks later saw no evidence of burials or burnings. John L. Ginn reported well-preserved bodies that "lay just as they had fallen, each wound that had caused death being immediately over the corresponding pool of coagulated blood on the ground," and with eyes "picked out by crows." Jacob Hamblin, who claimed to have returned from Salt Lake City a week later, reported seeing "nineteen wolves pulling out the bodies and eating the flesh." Witnesses who visited the scene eight days later testified that the bodies had been heaped into three distinct piles—those who had been stabbed, shot, and had their throats cut. "There was no clothing left on man, woman or child, except that a torn stocking leg clung to the ankle of one."

Haight, Higbee, and Dame would argue as well over the distribution of goods. The bloody clothing and bedding that had been gathered by the women and others were taken to the cellar of the church tithing office in Cedar City, where they would be referred to, according to one version of events, as the "property taken at the siege of Sevastopol." The leaders warned their men against personal looting, and one private reported that when he retrieved a gold-filled pouch Higbee grabbed it from him, pocketed it himself, and threatened to slit the man's throat if he uttered a word about it. As for the reported $100,000 worth of gold said to be on the train, most of what was retrieved—the actual amount would never be revealed—was turned over to the church treasury in Salt Lake City. The forty wagons were given to local Mormons for use in hauling lead ore from Nevada. The carriages emblazoned with stags' heads were transported to Salt Lake City, where at least one of them was used by Brigham Young. Approximately nine hundred head of cattle were corralled near Cedar City, branded with the church's "cross," and driven north to the capital. An unknown number were branded with "JDL" and kept by John D. Lee. The clothing and shoes were doled out to the church faithful, and the wives of the militia leaders wore the women's finery for many years to come. The huge cache of seized weapons, and the finest horses, were divvied up among militia leaders.

By late afternoon on Saturday, the work on the field neared completion. The men were called together at the nearby spring, where they were "provided towels and soap, and each man washed himself thor-

Joseph Smith, founder of the Mormon religion, had his first vision in 1820, at the age of fourteen. Three years later he would report being surrounded by "a pillar of light" during a visitation from the angel Moroni, who directed him to do God's work on earth.

Left: In a bitter succession contest following Smith's death in 1844, Brigham Young ascended as heir. Young would build a theocratic dictatorship, personally directing all affairs of church and state, and even arranging the plural marriages of his "worthy male" followers.

Retreating "from Christians," as Brigham Young called his enemies, Young led two thousand of his Mormon followers out of Nauvoo, Illinois, in 1846. The refugees had been unable to live in peace with their neighbors, and would eventually settle in the Salt Lake Valley.

Young's personal residences in Salt Lake City exuded the prosperity and domestic tranquility the prophet hoped his followers would emulate. Most saints of the era lived in distinctly less regal homes, however, constructing primitive earthen "dugouts" for their wives and many children.

Left: Captain John W. Gunnison led the first U.S. Army survey into the Salt Lake Valley in 1849. He then wrote a best-selling book about the Mormons, which he considered sympathetic and they considered malicious. Mormon leaders refused to assist him when he returned in 1853 to map part of the route of the transcontinental railroad. His murder that year would be blamed by Brigham Young on Ute Indians, but Gunnison's family and federal officials in Utah believed Young and other church leaders were responsible for the death.

Right: Thomas Leiper Kane, circa 1865. He was a frail neurotic capable of feats of endurance. A public champion of Brigham Young's endangered theocracy, Kane was a furtive agent and defender of the sect from its early days.

This anonymous engraving of the Mountain Meadows Massacre is the most famous depiction of the slaughter.

John Cradlebaugh successfully pursued the perpetrators of the Mountain Meadows Massacre with indefatigable tenacity and courage, thereby earning the lasting enmity of Mormon leaders.

John D. Lee was the only person held accountable for the Mountain Meadows Massacre. Though Lee used treachery to convince the emigrants to surrender, and participated in the slaughter, he was a scapegoat. For his part, he maintained until his death that he had merely followed the orders of his military and ecclesiastical superiors, and that Brigham Young had sacrificed him in a "cowardly, dastardly manner."

Young dined regularly with his numerous wives, who constantly vied for the coveted role of "favorite." This illustration was drawn for *Harper's Weekly* in October 1857—a month after the Mountain Meadows Massacre—and accompanied an article entitled "Scenes in an American Harem."

A contingent of the U.S. Army under the command of General Albert Sidney Johnston camped at Fort Bridger during the winter of 1857–58, starving on half-rations, weakened by Mormon guerrilla attacks, and bivouacked in blizzard conditions. The troops planned to advance into Salt Lake City as soon as the weather permitted to confront Mormon defiance of the government.

General Johnston's army entered the Salt Lake Valley in late June 1858, marching through the streets of Zion and past the home of Brigham Young. From dawn until dusk, the troops poured into the city, where they were greeted by silence and a few unfurled American flags.

In the fall of 1859, Young granted an unprecedented interview to *New York Tribune* editor Horace Greeley. Greeley portrayed the Mormons as victims of persecution, and neglected to ask the prophet any questions about the Mountain Meadows Massacre.

In May 1859, Major James H. Carleton's soldiers erected a primitive rock-cairn memorial at the scene of the massacre. On a transverse beam they carved the words: "Vengeance is mine: I will repay, saith the Lord." Exactly two years later, Brigham Young visited the site and declared, "Vengeance is mine and I have taken a little." With that, some of his followers dismantled the cairn. In 1864, U.S. soldiers rebuilt it.

"Center on my heart, boys. Don't mangle my body," John D. Lee told his executioners in 1877. Lee had chosen a firing squad as his method of death, instead of the decapitation that for Mormons symbolized atonement, for he felt he had committed no sins for which he needed to atone.

"The curse of God seems to have fallen upon it, and scorched and withered the luxuriant grass and herbage," John D. Lee's lawyer wrote of Mountain Meadows in 1877. Today, the meadow is dotted with scrub pine and sagebrush, and the lush cottonwoods have disappeared. Descendants of those killed there believe it is hallowed ground befitting of a national monument.

All photographs and illustrations are from the author's personal collection, with the exception of the portraits of Thomas Leiper Kane and John Cradlebaugh, which are courtesy, respectively, of the American Philosophical Society and the Nevada Historical Society.

oughly in what was a more than symbolic rite," Lee recalled, "soaping and lathering his hands and arms to the elbows and his face and neck." Then they moved into a large circle where Lee, Haight, Dame, and Higbee made speeches. Haight told the men that they had been "privileged to keep a part of the covenant to avenge the blood of the prophets." The leaders thanked God for delivering the enemy into their hands and thanked the men for their zeal in performing the difficult task. At this point the leaders revealed to the men that the official version of events to be disseminated to the outside world, if indeed any dissemination became necessary, was that the uncontrollable warlike Paiutes were responsible for the massacre. The commanders impressed upon their soldiers the "necessity of always saying the Indians did it alone, and that the Mormons had nothing to do with it," Lee recalled. They vowed to keep Mormon participation secret from everyone, including their families. The only people who were to know would be the participants, and the three men in the Salt Lake City hierarchy—Brigham Young, Daniel Wells, and George A. Smith. The group "voted unanimously that any man who should divulge the secret . . . should suffer death." Enclosing the four leaders in the middle of the circle, each of the brethren placed his left hand on the shoulder of the man next to him and raised his right hand to form a right angle. The leaders faced the four points of the compass, and Haight, the highest-ranking ecclesiastic present, led them in the most solemn pledge to kill anyone who violated the oath of secrecy. When Dame blessed the men and concluded with "Amen," they relaxed and listened to further orders. All were to proceed to the Hamblin ranch in formation, two to a wagon, where the orphans would be distributed. Any of the leaders who desired to take a child would then be free to do so, and, if there were enough remaining children, other soldiers could request them.

Lee and Klingensmith oversaw the distribution of the human plunder. The leaders took first choice of their own favorites. Lee took Kit Carson Fancher (whom he renamed Charlie), a young girl, and possibly an infant as well. Klingensmith chose two for himself. Conscious of the threat the children might still pose as eyewitnesses if they stayed together and were able to discuss the event, the leaders went to great lengths to separate brothers and sisters. When Rachel Hamblin pleaded for the Dunlap sisters to stay together, Lee relented, and the three little girls remained under her care at the Hamblin ranch.

. . .

A pall fell over the Mormon settlements of southern Utah as word spread of what was called "the blood feast of the Danites." The bickering and shifting of blame did not end with the collective vows of secrecy, but rather intensified as each participant claimed he had not murdered anyone and then proceeded to incriminate his fellow perpetrators. The seeping details of the massacre could not be fully contained.

"Every witness that claims that he went to the Meadows without knowing what he was going to do has lied, for they all knew, as well as Haight or anyone else did," Lee later claimed in a confession, while continuing to maintain his own innocence. "And they all voted, every man of them, in the Council, on Friday morning, a little before daylight, to kill all the emigrants."

The details about who gave the orders for the massacre and what the role was of every major figure have been argued for a century and a half. As Will Bagley has written, "reliable history requires accurate data. In the case of Mountain Meadows, we have a record irrevocably colored by dubious folklore and corrupted by perjury, false memory, and the destruction of key documents." Still, within the context of the era and the history of Brigham Young's complete authoritarian control over his domain and his followers, it is inconceivable that a crime of this magnitude could have occurred without direct orders from him. Virtually every federal officer who became involved in future investigations of the massacre would conclude that Young personally ordered the atrocity, used his position to shield the killers who had followed his instructions, and personally directed the elimination of all evidence incriminating himself and his closest advisors. The evidence of Young as an "accessory after the fact" is abundant, though documentation of his earlier role as orchestrator of the massacre is elusive. Many historians believe that Young wrote a letter to his military commanders in the south ordering that the Fancher Train be "used up"—but that letter, like much else, never surfaced. Juanita Brooks fervently contended that Lee "would have carried out no orders which he thought would be contrary to the wishes of Brigham Young." There can be no question that Lee took very seriously and literally the instructions from Young's personal emissary George A. Smith only weeks earlier, which may too have been in the form of a letter that has long since disappeared.

The contention that the Mormons believed the train to be an advance guard of the U.S. Army is ludicrous, given the numbers of women and children. It is certain that the Fancher-Baker party was lured under false pretenses and treachery to the remote ambush site of Mountain Meadows for the purpose of annihilation and plunder; that the genocide was carried out as part of a military operation of a highly disciplined, rigidly hierarchical theocracy of a would-be nation-state; and that it was never the independent initiative or act of renegade terrorists or Indians, as some Mormon advocates have said.

There were numerous reports after the massacre that the slaughter of those in the Fancher Train, in addition to similar planned offensives against emigrant parties on the Southern Trail, was plotted in detail at William Dame's "woodpile" in Parowan at the beginning of September. It is widely believed that this group, called the Tan Bark Council and composed of Dame, Haight, and an unknown third man, selected Mountain Meadows as the site of the massacre and that the entire company was to be murdered. A few days later, however, after a lively debate, the conspirators decided to spare the "innocent blood" of those under the age of eight, over the objection of Haight, who contended "there will not be one drop of *innocent* blood shed, if every one of the damned pack are killed."

Several participants claimed consistently in later trial testimony, affidavits, or diaries that they were ordered by their military commanders to report to Cedar City on Sunday evening, September 6. It is known that at Sunday service that day Haight, trying to whip up public support for the planned carnage, incited his congregation with specific reference to the Fancher Train: "I am prepared to feed to the Gentiles the same bread they fed to us. God being my helper I will give the last ounce of strength and if need be my last drop of blood in defense of Zion." Some of the murderers reported that a divine revelation from Brigham Young was read aloud at this gathering "commanding them to raise all the forces they could muster and trust, follow those cursed gentiles . . . attack them, disguised as Indians, and with the arrows of the Almighty make a clean sweep of them, and leave none to tell the tale."

After the church service, Haight called a special meeting of the High Council in which he promised "a celestial reward" to those who followed his orders. An emotional discussion about "doing away with" the emigrants ensued, in which one Laban Morrill reputedly faltered, fearing for his own life then and afterward. Several others also opposed what seemed to them an outlandish act of evil, prompting a disgusted Haight to break up the meeting and gather with only those men he felt he could trust. "It was not safe for a man to be too outspoken or vigorous in his stand against them," recalled a Mormon who defied Haight's order. "I was afraid of both the church and the military authorities," Bishop Klingensmith would later testify. "I feared personal violence; I feared I would be killed. I had to obey Haight and his counsel." Klingensmith claimed to have had "power only on small temporal cases" in his role as bishop, even though he had been a member of the church since 1844 in Nauvoo, and had migrated with the earliest groups from Council Bluffs to Salt Lake City.

Lee claimed to have been "lampooned" by Haight when at the massacre he at first refused to lure the emigrants with a flag of truce. "Joseph Smith said that God hated a traitor, and so do I," Lee said he told Haight. "Before I would be a traitor I would rather take ten men and go to that camp and tell them that they must die, and now to defend themselves, and give them a show for their lives; that would be more honorable than to betray them like Judas." Other leaders ridiculed Lee's sensitivity. "They said I was a good, liberal, free-hearted man, but too much of this sympathy would be always in the way; that every man now had to show his colors; that it was not safe to have a Judas in camp." When he found "every eye" upon him, Lee finally acquiesced, he said.

At the gathering of core loyalists in Cedar City sometime during the week of the siege, Haight ordered the men to arm themselves, paint their faces like Indians, and report to a site near the Hamblin ranch at a designated time on Friday, September 11. Whatever qualms Lee might have had apparently disappeared, for several witnesses remembered him before and after the massacre strutting around Cedar City displaying the red sash symbolic of his status with the Danites and as a major in the Nauvoo Legion in the old Missouri days. The night of the meeting, he and Haight camped together and planned the upcoming attack.

There were numerous and moving stories of those who refused to participate. As letters, diaries, and other surviving documents make clear, the southern settlements were full of God-fearing men of conscience who could not abide wholesale murder of civilians.

Helen Brockett, a ninety-two-year-old descendant of a Salt Lake City Mormon, was told by her grandmother that her great-grandfather J. J. Davidson had been ordered by Brigham Young to go south to participate in the slaughter. "Young called in the Avenging Angels and told them to use bows and arrows to shoot the people in the back after they were already dead to make it look like Indians did it." Instead, Davidson "backtracked through a river bed" and fled to California. For years afterward he lived in fear of Young's retribution.

Many failed to appear at the meadow that morning, while others came but declined to carry out their orders. John Higbee later testified that Lee called these resisters "cowards" and ordered them to sit on the ground. Others were summoned to Mountain Meadows to help bury the victims of an "Indian massacre," but became suspicious when told they were to bring weapons rather than shovels. Arriving at the scene they found to their dismay that they were expected to participate in the death march and gun down innocent men. William Bradshaw escaped that fate. When he appeared with a spade, he said, "Haight asked [me] where was my gun?" Bradshaw responded that he didn't need a gun to bury the dead, prompting Haight to call him a fool and order him to stay behind.

Weeks before, facing dissension and defections within the ranks, as well as an alarming resistance among the faithful—many of whom had only recently arrived from Scandinavia and England and had neither firsthand experience with the earlier persecutions nor a burning passion to avenge the blood of the prophets—Haight had used his pulpit to begin a defamation campaign against the Fancher Train. The slander was carefully crafted, well placed, and oft-repeated, the claims exaggerated with each retelling. It was said the group was from Missouri, the state that had threatened to exterminate the Mormons. Then it was said these Missouri "wildcats" had been personally responsible for the assassination of Joseph Smith, and were brandishing the gun that had been used to kill him. The emigrants were also alleged to have named two of their longhorn steers "Heber" and "Brigham."

Word spread from settlement to settlement. Some on the train, it was said, had participated in the Hauns Mill Massacre of Mormons in Missouri nearly twenty years earlier. Word also spread that among those traveling with the group were the killers of Parley Pratt, who had been stabbed to death on the Arkansas-Oklahoma border a few months earlier. A story that took hold claimed that Pratt's widow, Elenore McLean, was in Salt Lake City when the train camped nearby, and identified Pratt's murderer among the emigrants. And if all those accusations failed to excite Mormon hostility against the Fancher

Train, rumors circulated that the men used profane language and the women were prostitutes.

The allegations are at odds with all the contemporaneous evidence from those who had any contact with the train along the trail. "It is abundantly proven that the emigrants were orderly, peaceable, Sabbath-loving and generally Christian people, holding religious services frequently," an 1877 account of the incident concluded, based upon the statements of those who had met them at Fort Bridger. Even Jacob Hamblin would later testify that "they seemed to be ordinary frontier 'homespun' people." Historian David White concluded that "every one of the many charges of bad conduct by the Fancher Train . . . comes directly or indirectly from Mormon sources whose motives must be questioned."

After the fact, there was great uncertainty among Mormon leaders about how the crime would be viewed, both by the Gentile world and by the Mormons themselves, despite the earlier efforts to demonize the Fancher-Baker party. Now, the church hierarchy had to redouble its efforts to castigate the Paiute Indians, establishing a clear motive for why they could be said to have perpetrated the crime. To serve that end, the myth of the "poisoned springs" was invented.

The rumor was spread that members of the wagon train had laced a stream near Corn Creek with poison, leading to the death of some Pahvant Indians and inciting them to rally support among their fellow natives in the Paiute tribe to seek revenge on the party. An ox was said to have been poisoned as well. Though the poison tale was never told the same way twice, the fabrication gathered the most momentum of all the charges laid to the emigrants. The story was ultimately denied by Indian witnesses including Chief Kanosh, discredited by military and other government investigators, and dismissed by various journalists and historians, but the Mormons tenaciously kept the fiction alive. For without the poison tale, the credibility of Indian hostility toward the emigrants completely dissolved, and with it a motive for the atrocity.

Indian leaders themselves denied involvement just as vehemently, claiming any who participated were hired assassins and renegade mercenaries who had been promised payment in clothing, guns, and cattle by the Mormons. "The Mormons killed everyone, even women and children," according to one Paiute oral history. The Mormons asked two Indians who observed the atrocities to help them pack up all the booty. The Mormons kept the horses and milk cows, and they told the two Indians that if they saw any round gold pieces (coins) lying on the ground the Indians were not to pick them up because they were poison and would kill them. However, the Mormons picked up the coins and put them in a sack and kept them. "They hid everything else in a tunnel in a round red place down there someplace."

"No Indians were ever poisoned," Chief Beaverite, the brother of Kanosh, would say. In an interview with the Associated Press, Beaverite denounced the Mormons as cowards. "No Indians in Utah had any animosity against the whites . . . I know all these Indians. I know all the Indian traditions. I know what I tell is true."

Even the Mormon Nephi Johnson much later confessed to the truth: "White men did most of the killing."

Long before the bodies were shoved into mass graves, efforts were under way to conceal any role Brigham Young or the church hierarchy might have had in the episode. With so many innocents dead, and the likelihood of details of the slaughter reaching the rest of the nation, Young's deniability would be crucial if the church was to go on.

The prophet's alibi revolved around the infamous Haslam Ride, a 496-mile trip by horseback said to have been completed in a miraculous one hundred hours. Church officials have long contended that an angry Isaac Haight dispatched James Holt Haslam on a "Spanish horse" on the morning of September 7, after church elders such as Laban Morrill resisted the order for the slaughter. Haslam was said to be carrying a letter to Young stating that John D. Lee had the emigrants corralled and requested direction from the leader as to how the Mormon militia should proceed. Much controversy has surrounded the plausibility of this story, not only concerning the breakneck pace of eighty-six miles per day, but the actual date and time that Haslam departed, as well as the details of the document he purportedly carried. No such letter has ever surfaced, and Young himself claimed to have lost it. Haslam said that Mormon leaders provided him with fresh horses along the way—hence his pace—that he delivered the letter at dawn on September 10, and that he left at one p.m. with Young's response after sleeping briefly. Haslam later testified: "Brigham's message was 'Go, don't spare horse flesh, those men must be spared, let them go in peace.' Got back to Cedar on the Sunday following and learned the deed was done."

Though the original letter Haslam carried to Young disappeared, the contents of Young's response were widely disseminated. "In regard to the emigration trains passing through our settlements, we must not interfere with them until they are first notified to keep away," Young wrote in a letter to Haight from the "President's Office, Great Salt Lake City, Sept. 10, 1857." Continuing, he ordered the southern militia to allow the emigrants to pass unmolested. "You must not meddle with them. The Indians we expect will do as they please but you should try and preserve good feelings with them."

Citing this as evidence that Young did not order the massacre—contradicting what virtually every later federal investigator would establish—was a brilliant plan. What remained unaddressed in this letter is why militia members from southern Utah would need specific orders from their church president *not* to massacre travelers passing through their territory.

As further evidence that the Indians were vengeful toward the emigrants, the church documented in the *Journal History of the Church* on September 1 the details of a one-hour meeting that day between Young and twelve Indian chiefs in Salt Lake City. "Bro Jacob Hamblin arrived in G.S.L. City from the Santa Clara Mission with 12 Indian chiefs who had come to see Pres. Young," according to the entry. Among those present were two brothers of the deceased Chief Walker, Kanosh and Ammon, as well as Paiute chiefs Tutsegabit and Youngwuds, and representatives of the Piedes and several other bands from the Santa Clara and Virgin River areas of southern Utah. "A Spirit Seems to be takeing possesion of the Indians to assist Isreal [sic]," Young wrote in his diary for that date. Then he referred to the members of the Fancher Train as if they were from a foreign country. "I can hardly restrain them from exterminating the 'Americans.' " These were the same Indian chiefs who had given the wagon train its "first kindly look" and "first friendly word" only days earlier at Corn Creek.

No written account of this crucial meeting was known to exist until more than 140 years later, when in 1999 a scholar located in church archives the journal of Young's Indian interpreter and brother-in-law, Dimick Baker Huntington. Huntington, who had played such an instrumental role in tampering with the jury in the Gunnison massacre trial, now surfaced again. His diary repudiates the Mormon leader's lifelong denials and makes clear that on September 1, Young was met with disconcerting resistance from the Indians as he tried to enlist their support against the wagon train. Church officials have steadfastly maintained that the chiefs left that day in time to travel nearly three hundred miles to marshal their warriors, and begin the massive attack on the Arkansas pioneers just six days later.

Paiute chiefs Tonche and Jackson later told federal investigators that they carried with them a letter from Young ordering the emigrants to be killed, though no such document was ever found. Why they would willingly carry such a letter, after expressing their reluctance to participate in the slaughter, is unclear.

Within days of the massacre, Indian agent Garland Hurt's informants from various tribes had provided him with a complete account of the Mormon-led atrocity, and further warned him that the Nauvoo Legion was marching to capture him. "Some half dozen of the natives rushed into my office room, exclaiming, 'Friend! Friend! The Mormons will kill you!' and pointed to the window on the eastern side of the house. On looking out, to my surprise, I saw seventy-five or one hundred armed dragoons stationed in the road about a mile from the house." Protected by a handful of Ute warriors, Hurt—the last non-Mormon federal official remaining in Utah—escaped into the mountains and arrived at Fort Bridger two months later starving and exhausted. "I am glad we did not get him," one of the Mormon militiamen reflected, "for more than likely he would have been killed if we had."

Upon learning of Hurt's escape, Young set out to vilify him as he had defamed the earlier "runaway officials" who had been driven out six years earlier. Hurt's official report of the massacre was the first and most accurate on the record. "The Indians insisted that Mormons, and not Indians, had killed the Americans," Hurt wrote.

The Sunday following the massacre, John D. Lee left on horseback for his home at Fort Harmony, feeling he had participated in God's work and determined to honor his vow of secrecy for the rest of his life. Jauntily riding through the gates of the fort, he proclaimed loudly: "Thanks be to the Lord God of Israel, who has this day delivered our enemies into our hands." Three or four days later he was visited by Isaac Haight. "We are in a muddle," Lee claimed Haight told him. "Haslem [sic] has returned from Salt Lake City, with orders from Brigham Young to let the emigrants pass in safety." Haight's version went on, "I sent an order to Higbee to save the emigrants, after I had sent the orders for

killing them all, but for some reason the message did not reach him."
Lee thought this a significant new development, for the stage was being
set for Haight and his superiors in Salt Lake City to place the sole
blame for the massacre on Higbee, Lee, and others in the field that day
while providing Young, Haight, and Dame with an alibi.

Lee, who always claimed not to have known about the Haslam Ride
until this time, personally doubted its veracity, for Lee fully believed
that Brigham Young already knew about, and had indeed ordered, the
killing of the emigrants. So seeking Young's guidance at such a late
hour served no purpose, in Lee's consideration, except to provide
Young with deniability. He recognized the significance of this new
development immediately, saying they were all in what he called "a bad
fix." Later that week he returned to Cedar City to meet with other
church leaders and to receive new orders. The High Council had met
and determined that he should be the one to ride to Salt Lake City and
officially report the full details of the massacre to Young. Lee did not
think it appropriate that he be the sole person to report such gruesome
details to Young, when his own role in the massacre was to follow the
orders of his superior officers. Balking, Lee responded that Dame, as
the militia commander, should submit a written report instead. "I told
him that it was a matter which really belonged to the military department, and should be so reported." Dame refused, according to Lee,
arguing that "the written word is too apt to fall into the wrong hands,
and it is too easily misunderstood."

Lee was the chosen emissary, Haight said, because of his intimacy
with the prophet. "You are closer to Brother Brigham than anyone
else," Lee said Haight told him. Lee became further confused about the
actual extent of Young's prior knowledge of the planning of the massacre when Haight, as his spiritual leader, assured him that he would
not be violating the sworn covenant by revealing the details to Young.
"It is of his right to know of everything that goes on in this church,"
Dame said of Young. His uneasiness grew when Haight further
instructed Lee not to "expose any more of the brethren than you find
absolutely necessary." Haight then promised Lee a "celestial reward"
for his service. "The time will come when all who acted with us will be
glad for the part they have taken," Haight told him, "for the time is
near at hand when the Saints are to enjoy the riches of the earth." Lee
finally agreed to undertake the task. He considered it an indisputable
fact "that the Mormons were to conquer the earth at once . . . that the

millennium had come, and that Christ's reign upon earth would soon begin."

Driving a wagon with a team of horses belonging to the dead emigrants, and with the bright-eyed Kit Carson Fancher on the seat beside him, Lee set off for his home, where he would make preparations for his journey north. Back in Harmony, he gave the child to his young wife Caroline, ordering the boy to obey her and help her with the family chores. "Show him what love and affection you can," Lee told Caroline. "He is an orphan child, remember, and deserves all the kindness we can give him."

Another of Lee's wives, Rachel, noted in her diary that Lee left for Salt Lake City on September 20. Along the way he met Jacob Hamblin, who was returning to Mountain Meadows with his new wife, Priscilla Leavitt. According to Hamblin's later testimony, Lee revealed to Hamblin the details of the Mormon extermination of the Fancher Train, despite the secret oath. James Gordon, an old friend and neighbor of Lee's, reported Lee stopped to visit him en route to the capital. Carrying a "high-topped black silk hat" stuffed with loot from the massacre, according to Gordon, Lee poured out fine jewelry and gold watches on the family table for all to admire.

Lee said he traveled for ten days before reaching Salt Lake City, but official church records show he arrived at Brigham Young's private residence on September 28. The primary accounts of the historic meeting the following day come from John D. Lee's confession written twenty years later and the journal entry of church historian Wilford Woodruff. The two are diametrically opposed.

Lee said he gave Young, who was frail and recovering from a recent illness, "a full, detailed statement of the whole affair, from first to last," including the identity of every Mormon participant in the massacre and how many emigrants each man had killed. "I described everything about it. I told him of the orders Haight first gave me. I told him everything. I told him that 'Brother McMurdy, Brother Knight and myself killed the wounded men in the wagons, with the assistance of the Indians.' " This statement, which Lee wrote later, was in contrast with his claims that he never killed anyone that day; nor did he later attribute significant participation by Indians.

Young asked Lee many questions and told him that Haight had previously informed him that there was no innocent blood in the entire party "for they were a set of murderers, robbers and thieves." This confirmed in Lee's mind that Young already knew the details of the slaughter. The prophet was pensive but scrutinizing every detail. Others entered the room during the conversation, each interruption causing Young to signal Lee to silence. When Lee had completed his report, Young responded: "This is the most unfortunate affair that ever befell the Church. I am afraid of treachery among the brethren that were there," now suggesting to Lee that Young had in fact not ordered the attack. He then ordered Lee to take yet another vow of silence. "You are *never* to tell this again, not even to Heber Kimball. It *must* be kept a secret among ourselves. When you get home, I want you to sit down and write a long letter, and give me an account of the affair, charging it to the Indians. You sign the letter as Farmer to the Indians, and direct it to me as Indian Agent. I can then make use of such a letter to keep off all damaging and troublesome inquiries." Lee followed those orders explicitly, hoping to earn, he said, "that Celestial reward that had been promised to me."

Young declared he was troubled by the murders of women and children. "This whole thing stands before me like a horrid vision," Lee said Young told him. Asking Lee to leave him in prayerful reflection, Young said he would comment further the following day. Before withdrawing, Lee made an impassioned plea on behalf of himself and all the Mormon militia at Mountain Meadows who believed they were acting under orders of Young and "in strict conformity with the oaths that we have all taken to avenge the blood of the Prophets."

Woodruff made an entry in his diary notable for its complete sanitation of Mormon responsibility. But there is no evidence that Woodruff witnessed the meeting except for his own claim nearly thirty years later, which many later historians found dubious. This would be the official church version into the twenty-first century:

John D. Lee . . . arrived from Harmony with an express and an awful tale of blood. A company of California emigrants, of about 150 men, women and children. Many of them belonged to the mobbers of Missouri and Illinois. They had many cattle and horses with them, and they traveled along south. They went damning Brigham Young, Heber C. Kimball and the heads of the Church; saying that Joseph Smith ought to have been shot a long time before he was. They wanted to do all the evil they could, so they poisoned beef and gave it to the Indians, and some of them died; they poisoned the springs of water, and several of the Saints died. The Indians became enraged at their conduct and they surrounded them on the prairie, and the emigrants formed a bulwark of their wagons, and dug an entrenchment up to the hubs of their wagons, but the Indians fought them five days until they had killed all the men, about sixty in number. Then they rushed into the corral and cut the throats of the women and children, except some eight or ten children which they brought and sold to the whites. They stripped the men and women naked and left them stinking in the sun. When Brother Lee found it out he took some men and went and buried their bodies. It was a horrid, awful job. The whole air was filled with an awful stench. The Indians obtained all the cattle and horses and property, guns, etc.

The Woodruff document goes on to assert that Lee assured Brigham Young that there was no "innocent blood in the camp" and further denigrated the emigrants. "Brother Lee said . . . he had two of the children in his house, and he could not get but one to kneel down in prayer-time, and the other would laugh at her for doing it, and they would swear like pirates." Inadvertently, the reference to "innocent blood" implicated the Mormons, for, as David Bigler later wrote, the Indians would have had no "concern over the shedding of innocent blood."

Lee returned the following day, as Young had ordered, and found the prophet to be "quite cheerful," he said later. According to Lee, Young now told him that he had taken the matter directly to God: "God answered me . . . I have evidence from God that He has overruled it all for good, and the action was a righteous one and well intended." Assured, as Lee wrote later, that "Brigham Young was then satisfied with the purity of my motives in acting as I had done at the Mountain Meadows," he left for Harmony.

CHAPTER TWELVE

Camp Scott, November 16, 1857

O N THE DAY James Haslam claimed to have arrived in Salt Lake
City bearing details of the siege at Mountain Meadows, Brigham
Young gave U.S. Army Quartermaster Captain Stewart Van Vliet a
strangely polite guided tour of his personal residences and church
property. The U.S. Tenth Infantry had been marching toward Utah Territory from Fort Leavenworth for two months to install the slate of new
federal officials appointed by President Buchanan. It was too late in the
season for the unit, now under the command of Colonel Albert Sidney
Johnston, to proceed to Salt Lake City before winter, and yet they were
dangerously low on the necessary supplies for setting up winter quarters. So the War Department dispatched the diplomatic Van Vliet to
meet with Young and enlist his aid.

Van Vliet's primary goal was to arrange a locale near the capital for
the expedition to camp throughout the coming winter and to procure
provisions for his troops and livestock, as well as lumber to build structures. His orders were to obtain a site "sufficiently near to be effective
in supporting the civil authority" but distant enough "to prevent an
improper association of the troops with the citizens." He was also
there to gauge the mood of the Mormons.

Van Vliet was a perfect choice as emissary. As an officer with General
Kearny during the Mexican War, he had personally recruited many
Mormons from Council Bluffs for the Mormon Battalion, and was
highly regarded by them. Still, the Mormons considered his mission pre-
sumptuous at best and treacherous at worst. The precarious condition

of the army unit was known to Young; members of the Nauvoo Legion had told him that the troops could not survive without the Mormons' help. The expedition was strung out across the Great Plains, with Johnston himself joining the rear guard at Fort Leavenworth just as Van Vliet entered Salt Lake City. Van Vliet left his military escort behind and rode into the capital alone as a gesture of peace. The decade-old city he found that autumn of 1857 consisted of some twenty thousand inhabitants, mostly women, spread out over six square miles of cottonwood and poplar groves.

During a series of affable and courteous exchanges, Young had seen to it that Van Vliet heard nothing of Mountain Meadows. Mormon leaders worried that if Van Vliet relayed news of the situation to Johnston, an invasion of Utah Territory would be expedited, with reinforcements and supplies dispatched at once. Young kept the government emissary preoccupied and entertained.

Just days after Van Vliet's arrival, though, Young changed abruptly from pleasant host to defiant adversary. He harangued the captain with the familiar account of persecutions against his people and likened the U.S. troops to yet another persecuting force. Now that the United States was "about to pursue the same course," as Young told Van Vliet, he and the Mormon people were determined to resist the troops by military force. Van Vliet, whose orders included assuring Young that the government wanted no conflict and had no quarrel with their religion, was stunned.

On Sunday, September 13, Young invited Van Vliet to attend church services, where an imposing congregation greeted the officer. The sermon was delivered not by Young, who exclaimed he was too furious to conduct the service, but by another church elder, who forbade the troops from entering the territory. The army would meet an "overpowering source," Van Vliet recalled the elder proclaiming. The preacher then called on all present to raise their hands if they were willing to "apply the torch to their own buildings, cut down their trees, and lay waste their fields." Van Vliet estimated more than four thousand people enthusiastically responded.

In an oblique but unrecognized reference to the massacre at Mountain Meadows just two days earlier, Young told Van Vliet privately, "if the government dare to force the issue, I shall not hold the Indians by the wrist any longer . . . you may tell the government to stop all emigration across the continent, for the Indians will kill all who attempt it." Young then denied the request for supplies, vowing that nothing would be sold to the troops, who could now look forward to a long winter of starvation and deprivation at their winter quarters.

Shaken, Van Vliet warned Young that the Mormons might indeed be successful against the troops soon to be bivouacked at Fort Bridger, but such resistance would only serve to further galvanize the U.S. government, which would commit its full force and strength against the Mormon opposition. Van Vliet reported to his superiors, according to T. B. H. Stenhouse, that he told Young that if the Mormons would accept the installation of the new federal agents for the territory—including Young's replacement as governor, the obese Mormon sympathizer Alfred Cumming—Van Vliet would use his best efforts to stave off the expedition and avoid the bloodshed. He even promised to personally withdraw from the army if the government proceeded against the Mormon people. Van Vliet left the following day to report to his superiors the failure of his mission and the rebellious atmosphere. He concluded in his report to Captain A. Pleasanton that the Mormons would no doubt be successful in preventing the army from entering the territory before the following spring.

The army seemed formidable because of its sheer numbers, but it was in fact quite vulnerable. Its divided units, straggling at intervals along the trail, were tempting targets, short on provisions and composed of a haphazard collection of infantry and dragoons, and operating under unsure commanders from Johnston all the way up to the president.

In Young's Zion, meanwhile, the scorched earth policy had gone into immediate effect, as the prophet sermonized that he would make "a Moscow of Utah, and a Potter's Field of every canyon." On September 15, the day after Van Vliet left to join the troops more than a hundred miles away, at Fort Bridger, Young essentially declared war against the United States, issuing his famous proclamation: "Citizens of Utah—We are invaded by a hostile force who are evidently assailing us to accomplish our overthrow and destruction." As governor and federal superintendent of Indian affairs, Young issued three distinct orders: "1st. Forbid all armed forces of every description from coming into this Territory, under any pretence whatever; 2nd. That all the forces in said Territory hold themselves in readiness to march at a moment's notice to repel any and all such invasion. 3rd. Martial law is hereby declared to exist in this Territory from and after the publication of this proclamation, and no person shall be allowed to pass or repass into or through, or from the Territory without a permit from the proper officers." By the church leader's order, any Mormon man who defied the proclamation would be put to death. Young then dispatched one of his generals to deliver the proclamation to Johnston.

The same proclamation had been issued and distributed August 5, 1857, along with the orders into the outlying settlements prohibiting the sale of provisions to the Fancher-Baker wagon train. While the earlier proclamation implicated Young and church leaders in the hostility that led to the massacre at Mountain Meadows, reissuing the document with a later date was important for the alibi, providing some distance between the killing of the emigrants and direct orders from the church leadership. Historians have disagreed about the conflicting dates for many years, ascribing various motivations, rationalizations, and significance to them. "The date of the proclamation was changed from August to September for the purpose of destroying the plain evidence that the massacre of the emigrants was authorized by the proclamation, inasmuch as the emigrants had no 'permit' to pass through the territory," according to writer Josiah Gibbs. Copies of signed and dated proclamations for both August 5 and September 15 existed in church archives throughout the next century.

On September 15, Young and his commander Daniel Wells issued specific orders to the military leaders in Zion. "We intend to desolate the Territory," they told the officers, "and conceal our families, stock and all our effects in the fastnesses of the mountains, where they will be safe, while the men waylay our enemies, attack them from ambush, stampede their animals, take the supply trains, cut off detachments, and parties sent to canyons for wood, or on other service."

The Mormon forces were immediately sent to fortify Echo Canyon, an eighteen-mile-long narrow and steep gorge they believed the U.S. Army would soon enter. The men were drilled and inspired with the ardor of being God's warriors—Swedes, Danes, Englishmen, and pioneer Americans—but when they trudged into the knee-deep snows of the canyon, some did so without shoes or heavy coats, as clothing was scarce at the time. While the women began sewing uniforms for the crude militia, most men reported wearing carpets, blankets, and old clothes. But their decade in the rugged Wasatch Mountains had hardened them, and they knew almost every canyon, ridge, and precipice in a formidable terrain the likes of which the American troops had never seen.

They built stone fortresses and dug trenches to protect the riflemen. They dammed rushing streams as obstacles and placed huge boulders on cliffs to be hurled down upon the enemy. The immediate strategy was to keep the army from entering the canyon until the heavy snows in upcoming weeks would make it impassable. In Salt Lake City and the outlying settlements the Saints began preparations to abandon their homes, as Young sought locations in what is now Idaho and southeastern Nevada for a mass migration. He ordered all non-Mormon merchants to leave the territory, while continuing to recall all the Saints from California and Nevada.

Meanwhile, small guerrilla forces on swift horses and under the direction of Danite chiefs William Hickman and Porter Rockwell began harassing the army. Setting fire to the government's wagons and stampeding its cattle herds, the Avenging Angels created havoc for the already demoralized American troops.

On October 3 the Danites burned Fort Bridger, then set fire to the grass surrounding the army post, threatening the survival of the government's grazing livestock. On October 5, forty-four Danites raided an army supply train, burning the seventy-five wagons loaded with three thousand pounds of desperately needed bacon, coffee, flour, ham, and other foodstuffs, and running off fourteen hundred head of the army's cattle. The army troops moved two miles away and from the smoldering Fort Bridger established a new camp, which they named for the army's commanding general, Winfield Scott. A squadron of dragoons protected the remaining supply trains, and by late fall, when Johnston and the rest of the army made its way from South Pass to Camp Scott, a struggle for survival in the early blizzards began.

When Van Vliet returned to Washington in November, he reported the precarious situation to the secretary of war. "At present Governor Young exercises absolute power, both temporal and spiritual, over the people of Utah, both of which powers he and the people profess to believe emanate directly from the Almighty."

Meanwhile Young, despite his bellicose behavior, was still hoping for a peaceful solution to what he feared could result in the destruction of his people. Preachings of the Second Coming aside, the prophet was also an indefatigable pragmatist. If he could stave off the army until spring, he would have time to calculate how to save face with his flock while maneuvering for what he hoped would be a peaceful political détente with Washington. Then, months later, he could agree to install his malleable successor while appearing a victor in his own right. But to effect such an arrangement, his handling of the Mountain Meadows Massacre would be paramount. To aid him in that task he relied once again, with the most fateful consequences, on his beloved and trusted Gentile friend Thomas Leiper Kane.

A wearied Samuel Richards reached Kane's home in the fall of 1857 carrying a message from Brigham Young. No one was home. It was an autumn evening, and the Kane family had relocated to their country estate in the mountains of Elk County, Pennsylvania. Richards found the diminutive philanthropist there, sickly as usual but characteristically responsive to the plight of the Mormons.

Kane, now thirty-two and a lawyer, sported a mustache and a goatee, and was grieving the recent death of his revered and famous explorer brother, Elisha. Elisha had died suddenly in Havana just months earlier and had been given a hero's treatment at home. His body lay in state at Independence Hall as the flag hung at half-mast at the U.S. Capitol. Thomas, now married and the father of two small children, was pressured firmly by his wife and father not to take up the cause of the Mormons again. Having been engrossed in family concerns after Elisha's death, Kane had been distracted from the gravity of the situation in Utah. "When I came down upon the world again, which was in October (1857)," he wrote, "and learned the true state of affairs at that time, I was inexpressibly shocked." The letter from Young had convinced him "beyond question that the Mormons were determined to resist our troops."

Coincident with the message from Young, Kane was approached by George Plitt, an intimate friend of President Buchanan's who wanted to discuss with him "the Utah difficulties," as Kane later recalled. Plitt urged Kane to proceed at once to Washington to meet with Buchanan and from there to travel as a "commissioner of peace" to Utah. It was not clear to Kane at the time if Plitt had made the overture at Buchanan's behest. Only recently, Kane had heard "some sort of threat about what would be done if I undertook again to lecture the President."

Now, he felt called by duty to both his country and the Mormon cause to offer his services as a mediator between Buchanan and Young. He faced a daunting task to convince Buchanan that the Mormons were a peace-loving people, when so much evidence to the contrary had reached officials in the War Department, and to persuade Young that he should step down as governor of Utah and accept Kane's original recommendation of Alfred Cumming as his replacement.

As it was, three prominent Mormon apostates were advising Buchanan. Rumors of a Mormon massacre were filtering into the capital as Buchanan addressed Congress during the first week in December about the Mormons' escalating rebellion. But Congress had little enthusiasm for a religious civil war and postponed Buchanan's request for four new regiments and an expanded military budget for what was being called the Utah War. As information mounted about the disaster building at Camp Scott, with the prospect of untold numbers of soldiers perishing in the upcoming winter, the president began seeking a peaceful and honorable solution with new fervor. Now Philadelphia district attorney James Van Dyke contacted his friend Buchanan on Kane's behalf. Recounting several discussions he had had with Kane, Van Dyke wrote to the president of Kane's belief that he could "accomplish an amicable peace. He is willing to make an expedition to Salt Lake this winter even at his own expense, if hostilities have not advanced to such a point as would render useless any efforts on his part."

Resigning his well-paid position as a federal court clerk—an act that embittered his wife, Elizabeth, who had little regard for Brigham Young and thought polygamy a scourge—a fragile Kane set off for Washington. He had written a letter to Buchanan to which he received no response but was determined to use the full force of his father's political sway to secure a meeting with the reluctant president. "Quixotically brave," as one historian described the wiry little man, Kane was further impelled by a need to prove himself on the heels of the glory surrounding his always more celebrated, and now martyred, brother.

Thanks to intelligence information about Brigham Young's army gathered by Mormon contacts, Kane's appeals to Buchanan were finally successful. On Christmas night, the president ushered him into the White House for a private meeting Kane would never forget. Having opposed the army's push forward beyond Fort Laramie, Buchanan now feared a political and public relations calamity. "He had heard of the intentions of the Mormons to assail our little army at a very early day," Kane recalled. "He knew they must succumb. He knew that disaster to the army would be before the country a disgrace to his administration." Kane impressed upon Buchanan that he intended to go to Utah with or without government sanction, and that if he were burdened with an official title the Mormons would reject him as a spy. He refused any compensation for the journey. Finally, Buchanan told Kane he could promise Brigham Young that Buchanan would grant a full pardon to the Mormons in exchange for allowing the army to set up camp near Salt Lake City and install the new federal officers.

On the last day of the year, Buchanan penned two shrewdly contradictory letters on Kane's behalf, one to convey Kane's quasi-official status to the commanders at Camp Scott, and another to convince Young that Kane was *not* an agent of the U.S. government. The president thought the mission "hopeless."

Within weeks of the tragedy at Mountain Meadows, stories began appearing in California newspapers. On October 10, 1857, the *Los Angeles Star* ran the sensational headline "Horrible Massacre of Emigrants." Saints arrived at the Mormon outpost at San Bernardino bearing news of the slaughter. The large apostate population in California spread the reports like wildfire, and by October 15 the *San Francisco Herald* had also published a story. Mail carriers, other emigrants, and defecting Mormons trickled into southern California with fresh accounts, some with eyewitness testimony about the killing field itself. A party of eleven men escaping Utah passed through the meadow on October 2 and reported the scene upon their arrival in California. "Saw two piles of bodies, one composed of women and children, the other of men." All were nude, and the children ranged in age from one month to twelve years old. "The throats of some were cut, others stabbed with knives, some had balls through them." A man named John Aiken had passed through Mountain Meadows soon afterward and signed a chilling affidavit upon his arrival in San Bernardino: "I saw about twenty wolves feasting upon the carcasses of the murdered."

Soon the news began making its way to the East Coast press. The Fanchers waiting in Visalia for their many family members sent word back to Arkansas that a disaster had befallen the party, and relatives in

Harrison beseeched the federal government to investigate the reports. "The whole United States rang with its horrors," Mark Twain later wrote of the excitement.

Though reporting in lurid detail the tips pouring into the newsrooms, the papers issued caveats about the stories: "we confess our unwillingness to credit such a wholesale massacre," one editor wrote. Editorials clamored for the U.S. government to take immediate action to protect emigrants crossing through Utah Territory. Calling it "the Mormon massacre," the *San Francisco Daily Evening Bulletin* appealed to the federal government for the punishment of Young and his theocracy. "The blood of American citizens cries out for vengeance from the barren sands of the Great Basin." Young dismissed the furor as the fantasy of lying, corrupt, and craven newspapermen—a "prolonged howl of base slander" designed to "excite to a frenzy a spirit for our extermination."

As droves of Saints were leaving California for Utah, called back by Young to help defend Zion, a matching number were leaving Utah over a crisis of conscience spurred by the events at Mountain Meadows. In a devastating irony, both those coming and going were doomed to pass over the site of the slaughter, many haunted for the rest of their lives by the skulls and long locks of women's hair strewn about.

The southern settlements could not contain the disaffection in the populace. "I knew instinctively, as did many others, that something was being hidden from the mass of the people," remembered a child who would grow up to become Brigham Young's nineteenth wife. No community was more impacted than Cedar City, which was in a state of shock, losing half its population within a year. "The extra wagons in the tithing office yard and the orphaned children in so many homes made them all acutely conscious of the tragedy at the Meadows," wrote Juanita Brooks. "There were now on the tithing office shelves many pairs of shoes tied together and arranged by size; there were quilts and blankets, cooking utensils and dishes, and some clothing. There were muted whisperings of bloody shirts and dresses that were soaked in many waters, washed in suds, and ironed ready for wear, and of women who became nauseated or turned faint over their task but remained tightlipped and stoic." When the goods were auctioned off on church property, the reality was stark. Following a mass exodus, the town dwindled to a mere twenty families, according to census records. Rumors persisted that many residents simply disappeared, and that those men who had refused to participate in the slaughter were themselves "hewn down." Nephi Johnson would later testify that he knew of people who had "come to harm" for resisting the order to kill the emigrants. Residents shunned the meadow itself, as if it were now haunted and would bring a curse upon all who trespassed.

Meanwhile, others passing through the territory remarked on the new prosperity among the settlers. A drover named Hugo Hickman had observed the "poverty and rags" worn by the residents of Cedar City in early 1857. But now he "was greatly surprised to see the people so well dressed, in States Jeans [jeans made in the United States instead of homespun in Zion], Silks and Satins . . . rich in clothing, cattle, wagons, julery [sic] and money." Hickman wrote in his diary that a local friend told him "all the property and clothing" he saw "knocking around came from the Mountain Meddows." In the desperate poverty of southern Utah, where shoes were scarce and women's finery even rarer, the spoils from the wealthy Fancher Train brought opprobrium to the massacre leaders and their wives, who flaunted their windfall.

In New Harmony, John D. Lee set out to write the official account of the massacre, laying the blame, as Young had directed him to do, upon the Indians. Though Lee had been led to believe that he was the first to inform Young of the event, remarks made by Young in their private meeting had suggested that Haight had earlier provided the prophet with details. In addition, two Paiute chieftains, Tutsegabit and Youngwuds, had told the prophet of the murders less than a week after it had happened. Then, on September 20, a full week before Lee had visited Young, Chief Walker's successor, Arapeen, had also reported the massacre to Young and been told by Young to help "himself to what he wanted" from the spoils of the slaughter. When the chief refused, contending the "Mericats" had not hurt him or his people, Young called him a "squaw."

Lee dutifully submitted his report to Young, addressing him as "Ex-Officio and Superintendent of Indian Affairs" and dating the document November 20:

Dear Sir: My report under date May 11th, 1857, relative to the Indians over whom I have charge as farmer [Indian agent], showed a friendly relation between them and the whites, which doubtless would have continued to increase had not the white *mans* been the first aggressor, as was the case with Capt. Fancher's company of emigrants, passing through to California about the middle of September last, on Corn Creek, fifteen miles south of Fillmore City, Millard County. The company there poisoned the meat of an ox, which they gave the Pah Vant Indians to eat, causing four of them to die immediately, besides poisoning a number more. The company also poisoned the water where they encamped, killing the cattle of the settlers. This unguided policy, planned in wickedness by this company, raised the ire of the Indians, which soon spread through the southern tribes, firing them up with revenge till blood was in their path, and as the breach, according to their tradition, was a national one, consequently any portion of the nation was liable to atone for that offense.

About the 22d of September, Capt. Fancher and company fell victims to their wrath, near Mountain Meadows; their cattle and horses were shot down in every direction, their wagons and property mostly committed to the flames. Had they been the only ones that suffered we would have less cause of complaint. But the following company of near the same size had many of their men shot down near Beaver City, and had it not been for the interposition of the citizens at that place, the whole company would have been massacred by the enraged Pah Vants. From this place they were protected by military force, by order of Col. W. H. Dame, through the territory, besides providing the company with interpreters, to help them through to the *Los Vaagus* [sic]. On the Muddy, some three to five hundred Indians attacked the company, while traveling, and drove off several hundred head of cattle, telling the company that if they fired a single gun that they would kill every soul. The interpreters tried to regain the stock, or a portion of them, by presents, but in vain. The Indians told them to mind their own business, or their lives would not be safe. Since that occurrence no company has been able to pass without some of our interpreters to talk and explain matters to the Indians.

Friendly feelings yet remain between the natives and settlers and I have no hesitancy in saying that it will increase so long as we treat them kindly, and deal honestly toward them. I have been blest in my labors the last year. Much grain has been raised for the Indians.

To add credence to the letter, Lee audaciously attached fraudulent claims totaling $2,200 to be submitted to the federal government for payments made to himself, William Dame, Jacob Hamblin, and Philip Klingensmith. The vouchers requested reimbursement for cattle, wagons, and other loot from the Fancher Train that Lee claimed was distributed by him to the Paiutes as part of the Mormons' contract with the government to suppress Indian hostility. Brigham Young signed the vouchers knowing full well, according to Juanita Brooks, they were charging the government with material which came from the murdered emigrants. When the Indians later claimed they never received any items, investigations by Congress held up payment to the Mormons for nearly a decade.

In Lee's report, which would become the official version promoted by the church, Dame and the Mormons were heroes who had tried to save the lives of the emigrants. The fact that Lee placed the date of the massacre on September 22 only added to the confusion and cast the church's proclamation in a different light.

Less than three weeks after the massacre, Lee had submitted another false claim with the Office of Indian Affairs in the amount of $3,527.43 for goods and services provided the Indians "near Mountain Meadows." The inventory in support of this claim again referred to the booty from the massacre and included the clothing belonging to the slaughtered women and children.

Lee traveled north again in December as a delegate, along with Isaac Haight, to the constitutional convention that would prepare the application of Utah for admission as a state. Throughout the term of the legislature, Lee was in the nearly constant company of Brigham Young, who "treated me all the time," Lee recalled, "with great kindness and consideration." In his message to the legislature, Young made his first public remarks about the murdered emigrants, denouncing them as thieves who had fallen at the hands of the Indians.

It would not be until January 6, 1858, that Young would finally report the incident to the federal commissioner of Indian affairs, laying the blame again on the wagon train's provocations and the Indians. The next day he rewarded his adopted son and loyal servant, John D. Lee, with a seventeenth wife, a twenty-two-year-old English beauty named Emma Batchelor. After a round of festivities in the capital, where Haight also received a new wife, the two couples returned together by carriage to the southern colonies. There, under the orders of Young, they were to prepare the Saints for the U.S. Army's advance, which was expected as soon as the snow thawed, into the Salt Lake Valley.

Accompanied only by a servant, whose last name he assumed, Thomas Kane booked passage as "Dr. Osborne" from New York City on the *Moses Taylor* on January 5, 1858. His intended route would take him across the isthmus of Panama, up to San Francisco, and over the Sierra Nevada to Salt Lake City. Though Kane abhorred traveling by sea, his commitment to saving the Mormons overrode all fear and discomfort. On January 14 he arrived at his designated port of entry in oppressive heat, and was delighted to abandon ship for a modern railroad that took him across Panama. The next day he was back at sea "in helpless headache and sickness." On January 29 he arrived in San Francisco.

The following day he embarked by sea for San Pedro near the small Spanish settlement of Los Angeles in southern California, suddenly altering his route, which brought him under the suspicion of U.S. military officers in San Francisco. "He was to proceed from that place to Salt Lake City and Bridger by the way of Fort Hall," wrote a government informant. "Instead of taking this route, against the remonstrances of our officers whom he found there and with whom he was directed to put himself in communication, he went down to San Pedro or San Diego and procured an outfit there to go to Utah by the southern route." Despite the secret if ambiguous private charge he carried from President Buchanan, Kane remained suspect at least in army eyes, and local officers had him under surveillance from the time his vessel docked in San Francisco.

On his two-day boat trip to San Pedro he encountered soldiers who, like many in California, had heard about the Mountain Meadows Massacre and were in high dudgeon, boasting of their eagerness to march against the Mormons. Kane proceeded to San Bernardino, where he intended to find Mormon guides who would take him to Salt Lake City. But his secret was betrayed, and his arrival caused an uproar in a town populated mostly by apostate Mormons, the faithful having already returned to Zion. A Los Angeles correspondent for the *Alta California* exposed Kane's true purpose: "Mr. O announced himself as a botanist and in pursuit of science generally. When it became known that he wished to be expressed through to Salt Lake City and that he had made very liberal offers of payment, the suspicions of the best citizens were aroused. The people of this outpost are very easily excited whenever the Mormons are in question. Many of them have been Mormons and they are more watchful than other communities. They wish to revenge themselves upon the whole sect for the delusion which once seized themselves."

The militant anti-Mormons called a meeting and appointed a committee to interrogate Kane and to prevent his mission as peacemaker. He was apprehended at his hotel and would have come to harm had the hotelier not interceded on his behalf. He left that night by horseback, accompanied by his black servant and three Mormon men. Kane feared he was being followed, so his entourage avoided the customary route, which would have taken him directly to Mountain Meadows. Though Kane made no reference to the massacre in his detailed journals, he was clearly aware of the volatility of the issue, both from the soldiers' remarks on the boat and the antagonism of the people in southern California against him as a Mormon emissary. But his Mormon guides skirted the scene of the crime, and when Jacob Hamblin accompanied him to Corn Creek, Hamblin arranged for Kane to interview Kanosh. Kanosh dutifully repeated the poison story to an apparently gullible Kane, even identifying the Indian ringleaders. The alibi would be critical in assuring Kane's continued and crucial allegiance to the Mormons, and Kanosh embellished the tale with full comprehension of its significance.

To prepare Brigham Young for Kane's arrival, Hamblin sent Indian runners ahead with a letter from Kane to Young:

My Dear Sir:

I trust you will recognize my handwriting. The date of my letter will apprise of my journey hither. That I have made it in six weeks from New York will persuade you that I am on no fool's errand, and have no want of confidence in my ability to convince you what is the true feeling of our people and the President toward yourself and the good citizens of Utah. I send this to you by express to urge you to postpone any military movement of importance until we meet and have a serious interview. If you are unprepared to see the expediency of doing so, I entreat it as a favor—in requital of the services which I rendered your people in their less prosperous days—in the name of the sincerity with which I yet remain, Their friend to serve them faithfully.

A. Osborne.

When he arrived on the outskirts of Salt Lake City, Kane sent another message to Young:

My dear Governor Young:

Your friend of old times is now within an hour's march of your dwelling, where he asks you to name an early hour for the interview which he has travelled so far to seek:—And, so near you, having no more occasion for the name of his colored servant, Osborne, signs himself,

Yours faithfully,
Thomas L. Kane

By the winter of 1857–58, every major newspaper in America was covering the Utah War. Vivid accounts from the New York correspondents who camped with the army near Fort Bridger depicted the devastating condition of the troops starving on half-rations. Unprepared for the blizzards and weakened by the guerrilla attacks, the army lost between fifty and two hundred of their animals each day at their camp of death.

Arriving in Utah on February 25, Kane was escorted to a meeting of church leaders at the Beehive House. He explained to them that he had come at his own expense and at great personal risk bearing an important message from President Buchanan. Kane then shocked his audience by begging for sympathy toward the army "now suffering in the cold and snows of the mountains."

Still, it was Brigham Young whom Kane had traveled all this way to see, so although the ever fragile envoy could barely speak from fatigue, he implored Young to continue their meeting in private. They met at eight p.m. and were closeted alone together for thirty minutes; the meeting was so secret that even Young's closest advisors, who often accompanied the prophet, were not allowed to attend. "I was requested by Col. Kane to consider [the conversation] as strictly confidential,"

Young noted. Though the details of the discussion have never been published, the diaries of both Kane and Young suggested Kane vouchsafed an apology from President Buchanan for failing to notify Young in advance of his replacement as territorial governor. "Colonel Kane admitted that this was a grave omission," Young wrote, "and one that but for the habitual negligence of the officers of the Departments at Washington might justly be regarded as an act of injustice to the Mormon people and of personal contumely to myself." For his part, Kane wrote in a letter to his younger brother that he "did a lot of little things such as apologizing to Brigham Young for a personal insult which I thought myself he had received, but the main performance of my embassy was that I gave Brigham Young and some of his best friends, my word of honor . . . that the President of the U.S. was not a liar." Young accepted the copy of a letter provided him by Kane "as the personal apology," as Young put it, "of Mr. Buchanan."

Kane then presented Young with the president's three conditions for a peaceful settlement: that Cumming and the other federal officers would be installed immediately and the Mormons would submit to them; that all federal property in Utah would be turned over to the federal agents; and that a military post would be established in the immediate vicinity of Salt Lake City. In exchange, Buchanan would pardon all Mormons for all federal offenses—a sweeping and enticing amnesty that would include the slaughter at Mountain Meadows, the treasonous rebellion of Young, the guerrilla attacks on the army troops, and all other blood-atonement murders and criminal infractions across the territory. If the Mormons refused the olive branch, Kane impressed upon Young the likelihood that at the first sign of spring the troops would force their way through the canyons and occupy Salt Lake City.

Kane reminded Young that Cumming had been Kane's handpicked choice, and that the new governor's diffidence and pliability would assure Young's continued de facto rule over the Mormons. Cumming would pose no threat to the status quo, Kane assured Young; Cumming, with his affability and doltishness, would be far more palatable than someone else the government might decide to install in their midst.

In his private correspondence, Kane confided the heated dissension in the inner circles of the Mormon hierarchy. And though Kane bragged of his immediate success in convincing Young to send provisions to the army and accept the peaceful installation of Cumming, the private truce met stiff opposition by more radical factions in the church. Kane wrote that Young and others reportedly favored a peaceful solution, while reactionary apostles and militia leaders such as George Smith and William Dame were determined to resist the army. Smith wrote Dame, "Mr. Buchanan would like us to feed [the army] and not destroy them until he can get sufficient reinforcements to them to destroy us. . . . Bah!"

For two weeks, from February into early March, Young sought a consensus among his apostles to accept Buchanan's proposal. By then Kane had regained his strength sufficiently to carry the message of peace from Salt Lake City over the snow-laden mountains to Johnston at Camp Scott. Though Young offered Kane "some of his Norwegians" with sledges and showshoes, Kane left instead with the Danite assassin Porter Rockwell as his lead scout. "I did see then," wrote Kane, "if I had doubted it before how completely these mountaineers had our foolish herds of 'soldiers' at their mercy."

At the end of the second day, as he and his companions were setting up camp, two messengers from Brigham Young rode in with a letter to Kane. Young had just learned, he wrote, that "the troops are very destitute of provisions." Softening his earlier stance, Young now offered to send two hundred head of cattle and twenty thousand pounds of flour, "to which they will be perfectly welcome, or pay for, just as they choose."

When Kane arrived alone at Camp Scott on March 12, he faced stiffer opposition from his own countrymen than he had in Deseret. Johnston was even less receptive to Kane than Young's hardliners had been. If many of the Mormons considered Kane a spy, Johnston thought him an interloper and traitor. As Kane rode into camp, he reined his mule so close to Johnston's tent that when Johnston emerged he was wedged between the animal and his tent, a scene that insulted and embarrassed him.

Kane's arrogance and comparatively effeminate manner was offputting to Johnston. He had a burning passion against the Mormons—his men were "inflamed against the alleged atrocities" such as the Mountain Meadows Massacre, and he had no inclination to discuss peace with Kane. Even Kane's hard-won concessions from Young to provide the army with provisions were rebuffed by Johnston. "Whatever might be the need of the Army under my command for food, we would neither ask nor receive from President Young and his confederates any supplies while they continue to be enemies of the Government," Johnston wrote in a note he had delivered to Kane's tent.

The animosity between the two men reached absurd proportions, as they scribbled formal letters back and forth between their tents, separated by one hundred yards, Johnston refusing to meet personally with Kane, whom he considered a Mormon. Kane's meddling was resented by the troops; one major called him an "ass" and ordered a sergeant to keep him under surveillance. Tempers flared between the two men, prompting Kane to cryptically invite Johnston to a duel—an invitation that was, fortunately, intercepted before delivery. Averting violence in that instance, Kane continued to court disaster. Kane in turn was infuriated by his virtual "house arrest," calling the army men "monomaniacs." One night, after consorting with a Mormon courier some miles from camp, Kane fired shots to alert the sentinels of his return. "A patrol of the guard was sent out immediately," Captain Jesse Gove reported, "and one of my men shot at Mr. Kane and just missed him." Both Kane and Gove thought the soldier had intended to kill Kane, which prompted Kane to abandon his efforts with the military and focus instead upon the civil authorities in camp, particularly Alfred Cumming.

By April 3, Kane had convinced Cumming to travel to Salt Lake City without a military escort to be peacefully installed as governor. Johnston and his soldiers were disgusted. The *"entente cordiale,"* as one author called it, between Cumming and Johnston was now irrevocably broken. "If Gov. C. has been so far fooled by this nincompoop of a Mr. Col. Kane, he is a bigger fool than I thought him to be," Gove wrote. Johnston was intractable in his disdain for the Mormon cause. He saw the Mormons as "confederates in rebellion against the federal government," and thought Cumming had been co-opted by them. Johnston was increasingly determined to bring the Mormons to total submission.

Cumming was escorted by Porter Rockwell and Kane into Salt Lake City on April 12, and was greeted by parades and serenaded by such patriotic songs as "The Star-Spangled Banner" and "Yankee Doodle." The "best lodgings and best brandy were provided for his Excellency," was how one writer described the display. Cumming would take his orders from Kane, who was directing the new governor's every utterance, not letting him out of his sight for a moment, not even to sleep. On Kane's advice, Young personally introduced Cumming to an audience of four thousand Saints. "I have come out here to see that justice is done to you," thundered the new governor to the crowd. Kane bragged to Young that he "had caught the fish, now you can cook it as you have a mind to."

As Young continued his plans to relocate the Saints of northern Utah, still threatening to set fire to Salt Lake City before the army invaded, Cumming turned his attention to what he called "that damned atrocity." On April 24, an alarmed General Wells wrote to Young that Cumming intended to investigate the Mountain Meadows affair and planned an immediate trip to the southern settlements to conduct interviews. But assurances by Young that he intended to get to the bottom of it, and a firm intercession by Kane, convinced Cumming to abandon the probe as quickly as he had begun it. It would not be the only time an investigation into the tragedy was started and stopped, compromised and forsaken. The pattern would continue for the next century and a half.

By May, the sun warmed Camp Scott, now teeming with new reinforcements and the legendary captains Marcus Reno and Randolph Marcy. Brigham Young's choices were unmistakable: the Mormons had to conquer or retreat. Convinced that armed resistance would meet disaster, Young decided instead to try to win the public sympathy of the nation—a populace that was ambivalent toward the Mormons' plight. He ordered his followers to take three years' supply of food and disappear into the wilderness rather than succumb to a federal military force camped near their city. "I am your leader, Latter Day Saints," he told them, "and you must follow me; and if you do not follow me you may expect that I shall go my way and you may take yours if you please."

Thousands of Mormons left Salt Lake City, some one hundred men staying behind to torch the abandoned fields and homes as soon as the army entered the valley. Cumming couldn't keep tears from streaming down his face at the sight of the refugees. "He would tell the story of poverty and rags, of 'the poor women and innocent children' travelling barefooted and covered with dust, till they looked more like Indians than Caucasians," a friend remembered. The image of thousands of American men, women, and children, dressed in shreds and fleeing their homes under pursuit of an overpowering American military force, was almost more than President Buchanan could bear. To make matters worse, the *New York Times* now branded the whole affair "Buchanan's Blunder." Moreover, the Utah War was wracked with corruption so egregious some were calling it the "Contractor's War."

"Whatever our opinion may be of Mormon morals or Mormon manners," the *Times* editorialized, "there can be no question that this voluntary abandonment by 40,000 people of homes created by wonderful industry, in the midst of trackless wastes, after years of hardships and persecution, is something from which no one who had a particle of sympathy with plucky fortitude and constancy can withhold his admiration."

Meanwhile, by the summer of 1858 the American public had lost all interest in the West, now turning its attention to the impending crisis in the southern states. Bowing to public opinion, Buchanan dispatched two "commissioners of peace" to Utah bearing a face-saving pardon for all offenses committed during the rebellion if the Mormons would profess their allegiance to the United States. The Kane family was deeply insulted, afraid the appointments would "take all the wind out of Tom's sails." Orchestrating well-placed leaks in national newspapers, the family sought to elevate Kane's role to what his wife called "the Napoleon of Peace." But Kane's ego seemed to have survived the slight. "Next to myself—this is modest—our country owes more to Brigham Young than to any other human being in our generation," he grandiosely wrote in a letter home.

Learning of his father's death, Kane left Salt Lake City for Washington before the climax of the crisis that had brought him there. "It is the cream of creams," he said in praise of Young's choice of flight over fight. "You have taken the right course, and I want you to keep it." Bearing messages from Cumming to President Buchanan, Kane was escorted as far as Council Bluffs by six mounted riflemen selected by Young.

The daring "Dr. Osborne" had saved the Mormons once again, this time from possible annihilation. Whether he was genuinely deluded or simply chose what he thought was a justifiable peace effort to save thousands of lives on both sides, Kane's intervention would ensure that the Mountain Meadows Massacre—the largest single atrocity in the history of the United States to that point—would never be fully investigated. "Kane alone had the duplicity, the diplomacy, the social standing, and the absolute devotion to the Mormon cause which were required to bring the kingdom through this crisis without disaster," wrote Young biographers Frank Cannon and George Knapp.

In a highly personal and candid letter written to a younger brother that spring, Kane made what seemed to be a guarded reference to the Mountain Meadows Massacre. "All we, like sheep, have gone astray," he wrote. "B. Young, painter and glazier also went astray at one time— but if not since a certain day last fall, at least since the 1st of March 1858 he has been laboring for his salvation upon his knees, without the honors of a noble Christian."

In the end, the Utah War would be one of the strangest military and political episodes in the nation's history. Buchanan's commissioners of peace arrived carrying the president's proclamation and terms of pardon—which Brigham Young and the Mormons quickly accepted— and by June 26, 1858, the army staged its "occupation" of Salt Lake City. The "rebellion" now at an end, twenty-five hundred soldiers in perfect and peaceful order marched through the deserted streets of Salt Lake City, the inhabitants having fled en masse. "All day long, from dawn till after sunset, the troops and trains poured through the city," recalled an army correspondent, "the utter silence of the streets being broken only by the music of the military bands." The troops continued for thirty-five miles to the southwest, where Johnston selected a perma- nent post in the Cedar Valley. Christening it Camp Floyd, for the cur- rent secretary of war, Johnston ordered the construction of one of the largest military posts anywhere in the United States.

With the despised U.S. Army now fully ensconced in Zion, the Mormons awaited new direction from their prophet. On July 4, Young faced the depressing task of liberating his followers from their refugee camp fifty miles south. "All who wish to return to their homes in Great Salt Lake City are at liberty to do so," he proclaimed. Many had exhausted their resources in the "Move South," as it was called in church histories, and had no choice but to remain in the temporary set- tlements and eke out a new living. But the majority loaded their wagons and slowly made their way back to the fields and homes they had deserted.

A demoralized Young withdrew into isolation. Flanked by body- guards, he surrounded his properties with Danites. The once flamboy- ant and ubiquitous prophet now became for a time an apprehensive recluse. War averted, he still could not escape the specter of Mountain Meadows. Despite Cumming's best efforts to let the matter die, others sought to keep it alive; for the next two decades Young would be inextricably enmeshed in the management of secrets and alibis. In some ways, the matter would never die.

On the last day of 1857, as President Buchanan provided Thomas Kane with two letters for the purpose of resolving the government's dispute with Young, William C. Mitchell of Dubuque, Arkansas, wrote to Arkansas senator W. K. Sebastian. His was one of many letters written by relatives of the Fancher Train victims urging the U.S. Senate to open an investigation into reports of a Mormon massacre in Utah Territory. The more vivid the accounts making their way to national newspapers, the more outraged the citizenry became. Vigilante militias with the sole purpose of confronting the Mormons sprang into action throughout California and Nevada, and in Arkansas the rage of the relatives was palpable, with volunteer companies organizing in a dozen counties. The "Nevada Rifles" and "Sierra Rangers" were thirsting for vengeance against the Mormons at the same time Kane was conniving a deal for amnesty.

By January 1858, confirmation of the murders of the prominent and well-liked Arkansas families had reached their native state. In February, an emotional public meeting was held in Carroll County to appeal to the federal government to investigate the crime and punish the Mormons. In a call to arms, the citizens vowed to raise four military companies to go immediately to Utah and rescue the surviving orphans rumored to be held captive. The gathering was widely publicized and aroused the interest of Congress. "I have just received the published proceedings of a public meeting . . . in relation to the massacre of their friends and relations," Commissioner of Indian Affairs A. B. Greenwood wrote to Secretary of War John B. Floyd on March 6. "[I]t is alleged that these barbarous wretches have now in their custody some fifteen children . . . and they [the relatives] earnestly invoke the aid of the government to enable them to recover the children." Greenwood hoped Floyd would "be able to communicate something that will to some extent relieve the friends of those who have been so brutally murdered."

"This department has, at present, no information respecting the massacre alluded to," Floyd responded, somewhat unbelievably considering the publicity the murders had spawned. Floyd nonetheless vowed to transmit immediately to Johnston the *Arkansas State Gazette* story about the alleged murders. Johnston, Floyd informed the congressman, would be ordered to "adopt such measures for the recovery of the children said to be still in captivity."

Congressional oversight of the massacre intensified. Despite the uneasy truce between the Mormons and the troops, Johnston still remained under orders from the secretary of war to investigate the mass murder and retrieve the surviving children. With this exploratory zeal in the air, Brigham Young emerged from his solitude to preempt a federal probe. He and Kane had given Cumming their word that Young would see that the crime was investigated. Since then, Young had come under increasing criticism by national publications for failing to investigate the massacre, just as the *Deseret News* was excoriated for neglecting to report the occurrence long after the event was well known throughout the country.

To conduct the "investigation," Young chose George A. Smith, the very church agent who the previous summer had carried orders to Cedar City leaders to incite their people to avenge the blood of the prophets. Smith's efforts were an exercise in public relations and limiting the political repercussions. John D. Lee had detailed the facts of the crime to Young ten months earlier, and Jacob Hamblin had fully informed Smith of the events in June 1858. "[Apostle] Smith was sent south not to learn the truth," wrote one historian, "but to devise an explanation church leaders could provide to external enemies, non-Mormon allies, and the increasing number of loyal members who had questions about the affair." Smith began his inquiry with a visit to the scene of the massacre on July 29. Despite having viewed the gruesome remains, Smith went to lengths to characterize the victims as cowards.

A group of inquisitors, including several church leaders under Smith's direction, interrogated various participants from Cedar City and the surrounding settlements. Smith dined and sojourned with the very men responsible for the mass murder. Staying at the Harmony home of John D. Lee the night of August 3, Smith accepted a gift of gold from his host. On August 6, Smith wrote his report, entitled "The Emigrant and Indian War at Mountain Meadows, Sept. 21, 22, 23, 24, and 25, 1857," again mysteriously moving the dates forward by more than a week. Pro forma, the blame was laid to the Indians and the emigrants, and Dame and Haight were seen as benevolent interveners who heroically saved some of the children from death. Smith said there were "some 200 Indians engaged in this fight, a large number of the dead killed with arrows; the residue with bullets, the Indians being armed with guns and bows." He included a curious reference: "It is reported that John D. Lee and a few other white men were on the ground during a portion of the combat, but for what purpose or how they conducted or whether indeed they were there at all, I have not learned." Smith submitted his investigative conclusions to Brigham Young in a letter dated August 17.

His public obligation to investigate the massacre fulfilled, Young reentered public life. Cumming was satisfied with the church's official investigation, but, of course, the matter had hardly been put to rest.

CHAPTER THIRTEEN

Cedar City, April 7, 1859

JOHN C. KREIDELBACH was born in Germany in 1750 and emigrated as a young man to the United States. He was a well-educated man and spoke five languages. He served as a private in the Revolutionary War and was taken prisoner by the British and held near Baltimore, where he escaped into the Maryland countryside. He Americanized his name and made his way to Pennsylvania, where he married, fathered eight children, and became the first German Reformed minister in the area. His fourth child, Andrew, moved to Circleville, Ohio, as a young man, and married the daughter of a prominent farmer. There, on February 22, 1819, she gave birth to John Cradlebaugh.

John was a serious and curious child, an avid reader who set his sights on scholarship at an early age. At some point he lost an eye, but the handicap was never disabling. From a family of means—his father built and operated the Canal Hotel on the Ohio Canal—Cradlebaugh was able to enroll at both Kenyon College and the new Miami University at Oxford, Ohio. He returned to Circleville in 1839 at the age of twenty, where he read law with a prominent local attorney and was admitted to the Ohio bar the following year.

Sometime in the mid-1840s he married the beautiful Angeline Ring from nearby Lancaster, who was thirteen years his junior. In 1847 his young wife gave birth to their first child, a daughter, and the next year she bore a son. John, active in local politics and involved with issues of public education, was elected to the Ohio State Senate in 1850 as a Democrat from a newly created district. He moved his thriving family to the state capital of Columbus when he began to serve his term, and there Angeline became pregnant again. The delivery was difficult, and Angeline remained weak and bedridden until two months later, when she and the baby died on the same day. John was devastated.

The widowed father of a four-year-old daughter and a three-year-old son, Cradlebaugh chose not to run for reelection to the legislature, returning instead to the family home in Circleville. Practicing law for the next few years, he devoted himself to his business and his children. But tragedy struck again in 1855 with the death of his daughter.

He attempted to cope by immersing himself in politics. A gifted orator, he gave a speech in the spring of 1858 in support of President Buchanan's controversial position limiting the extension of slavery in new western states and territories; this brought Cradlebaugh a degree of national renown and the attention of Buchanan himself. It was an exceptional speech at a moment when few politicians were speaking out in defense of the new president's efforts to balance the increasingly irreconcilable conflict between North and South. When the president rewarded Cradlebaugh with a federal judgeship in Utah Territory, Cradlebaugh saw it as an opportunity to put his painful past behind him and begin life anew at thirty-nine with his ten-year-old son.

Arriving in November 1858 at a way station owned by Ephraim Hanks, Cradlebaugh would be the last of the new federal officers to reach Utah—the others had arrived at Camp Floyd with Johnston's force five months earlier. What struck those who first encountered Cradlebaugh in Utah Territory was his unpretentious manner and his sympathy toward the Mormons as persecuted Christians. At Hanks's tavern he gave up his comfortable carriage to a Mormon woman heading to Zion, and he and his son traveled the final miles by foot. Hanks recalled Cradlebaugh's saying he wanted no favoritism extended him.

He was welcomed by the Mormons as a bright and refreshing addition, unencumbered by the anti-Mormon prejudices that burdened so many of the other new federal officials. "The judge possessed but one eye," Hanks wrote, "and that is a very good one."

In January 1859 the judicial districts in Utah Territory were redrawn at the suggestion of Cumming, and Cradlebaugh was reassigned from Salt Lake City to the remote territory of what is now western Nevada, where the legal system was in chaos. Vigilante justice arising from mining disputes from the Comstock Lode and Indian violence from the Washoe and Pyramid Lake tribes had made the area around Genoa a wild and lawless landscape. While awaiting the official reappointment, Cradlebaugh was given a three-month period in Utah to investigate some of the more notorious recent crimes in the territory, including the Mountain Meadows Massacre. Almost immediately, Cradlebaugh heard accounts that Mormons had been involved in the mass slaughter, and he, along with U.S. Attorney Alexander Wilson, turned his attention to the crime.

Richard "Cat Fish" Cook and Henry Higgins, apostates from the south, were the first to voluntarily provide firsthand testimony to Cradlebaugh about the massacre. Higgins told Cradlebaugh he had seen twenty-five Mormons under the direction of John Higbee and Philip Klingensmith heading on horseback toward Mountain Meadows, where the Arkansas emigrants were encamped. He then saw the same men returning with the plunder from the massacre. Cradlebaugh provided Higgins with asylum at Camp Floyd when the informant expressed his fear of retribution at the hands of the Mormons.

The judge's first attempt to hold court was on March 8, 1859, when he convened a federal grand jury in Provo to hear testimony about the Parrish and Potter murders during the reformation—"the best documented case of killing for the sin of apostasy," according to historian Polly Aird. The case indicated that "the direction of the plot involved the entire church reporting line from Brigham Young down." Other cases involved the execution-style killing of six California emigrants, the castration and murder of another apostate, and other blood-atonement killings by Danite Porter Rockwell. At Cradlebaugh's request, Johnston's Tenth Infantry acted as a *posse comitatus* in furnishing security for the federal officials, witnesses, and grand jurors. But when the proceedings got under way, Mormons protested the soldiers' presence, and Cumming ultimately demanded that Johnston order his forces removed from the immediate vicinity. Johnston refused, fueling the hostility that already existed between the civil and military authorities since the earlier days at Camp Scott. Johnston and his men had viewed the civilian appointees to the territory as Mormon puppets. Cradlebaugh, who felt his witnesses had been threatened and intimidated, said no true justice could occur without their physical protection.

For two weeks he battled the grand jurors, many of whom were the very men he believed to be participants in the crimes he was investigating, and when they refused to return indictments, the increasingly fiery judge dismissed them in disgust. "I always supposed that I lived in a land of civil and religious liberty," he said to the jurors, "in which we were secured by the Constitution of our country the right to remove at pleasure from one portion of our domain to another, and also that we enjoyed the privilege of 'worshipping God according to the dictates of our own conscience.' But I regret to say, that the evidence . . . clearly proves that, so far as Utah is concerned, I have been mistaken in such supposition. Men are murdered here. Coolly, deliberately, premeditatedly murdered—their murder is deliberated and determined upon by church council-meetings, and that, too, for no other reason than that they had apostatized from your Church, and were striving to leave the Territory." Calling grand jurors the "tools, the dupes, the instruments of a tyrannical Church despotism," he dismissed them and released the prisoners. The disappointed judge returned to Camp Floyd with a handful of protected witnesses under the escort of the Tenth Infantry.

If Cradlebaugh had begun his service to Utah Territory with an open mind and ready acceptance of the Mormons, he was now an inflamed adversary. A deeply religious man, he found that his ideas of Christianity were far different from those of this sect, that his own deeply held view of angels bore no similarity to those of the Avenging Angels of Mormondom. Unlike Thomas Kane, of like background and political sophistication, Cradlebaugh could not justify the alleged atrocities at the hands of religious leaders as the inevitable result of previous persecutions. Nor could he abide the betrayal of justice by such blatant corruption. He turned his attention to the Mountain Meadows Massacre convinced, as he would later report to Congress, that "the Mormon church is guilty, of the crimes of murder and robbery as taught in their books of faith." He launched his probe in secrecy and with a new sense of urgency, as the diffident Cumming sought Washington's help to limit Johnston's authority. Cradlebaugh knew that without military protection the likelihood of bringing to justice the perpetrators of the massacre would be severely compromised. Still, he fully expected the Buchanan administration to stand firm in terms of what Cradlebaugh saw as right and wrong.

Concurrent with the ongoing criminal investigations, the military bureaucracy was continuing its efforts to retrieve the surviving children, an activity spawned by the requests from Arkansas relatives. Dr.

Jacob Forney, the superintendent of Indian affairs, had received via Johnston the secretary of war's orders to locate and rescue the survivors. Forney had written earlier to his newly appointed agent in the south, Jacob Hamblin, asking him to "endeavor with all diligence to discover the remainder of the children supposed to be living. All such must be recovered whether among white or Indians at any sacrifice." Forney chose Hamblin for the task because he had been told by the Mormons that the children resided with the Indian families who had killed their parents, and he felt Hamblin, as a longtime resident and Indian agent, would best be able to find them. Upon receipt of these orders, Hamblin began rounding up the children. It is not known how Brigham Young reacted to this new development. Knowing exactly which Mormon families had possession of the children—in fact, the three Dunlap sisters had remained with Hamblin's family since the day of the massacre—Hamblin claimed to federal agents that the orphans were in the hands of the Indians. Further, with a brazenness that had already come to mark the Mormon "investigation" of the massacre, Hamblin filed fraudulent claims for reimbursement from the U.S. government for payments he claimed he had to make to Indians to buy back the children.

"Jacob Hamblin by order of Forney," John D. Lee wrote in his diary on March 2, 1859, "took from my house Chas Fancher, one of the children of the unfortunate company that was massacred by the Indians." Lee too would file a fake voucher with the federal government for ninety-six dollars—two dollars a week for the forty-eight weeks he said the Indians had extorted money from him for Kit Carson Fancher's room and board.

Setting out in early March, while Cradlebaugh was still attempting to hold court in Provo and Hamblin was rounding up survivors, Forney made his way toward Mountain Meadows accompanied by massacre participant Ira Hatch. Stopping in the various communities along the way to take affidavits regarding the conduct of the Fancher Train and gathering information about the whereabouts of the survivors, Forney met hostility in Nephi and Corn Creek.

Owing his position to the political patronage of Thomas Kane, Forney had begun his task with sympathy toward the Mormon cause, even downplaying fears expressed by his predecessor, Garland Hurt. "These fears are imaginary," Forney had written of Hurt's charges that his life was in danger from the Avenging Angels. "I have never been treated kinder than by these people." But his initial determination to shield church leaders from culpability would eventually give way to the overwhelming evidence of Mormon responsibility. On March 18 he reported back to Washington that he had "received highly important and reliable information of the Mountain Meadow butchering affair." In addition to locating seventeen children, Forney estimated "that there was distributed a few days after the massacre, among the leading church dignitaries, $30,000 worth of property." Despite his obvious disdain for the Indians of the territory and favoritism to the Mormons, he nonetheless acknowledged it "has been exceedingly convenient to implicate the Indians."

Forney's own inquiry had convinced him that Mormons, and not Indians, had been responsible for the slaughter. He reported in August 1859 to his superior in Washington, A. B. Greenwood, that allegations the emigrants had poisoned any streams or oxen were blatantly false. "In my opinion," Forney wrote Greenwood, "bad men, for a bad purpose, have magnified the natural circumstance for the perpetration of a crime that has no parallel in American history for atrocity." Forney also reported that the children had never been in the possession of the Indians, but "were sold out to different persons in Cedar City, Harmony, and Painter Creek." Regarding the bogus vouchers and other claims for reimbursements, Forney said, "I cannot condescend to become the medium of even transmitting such claims to the department."

Captain James Lynch, a veteran of the Mexican War and an experienced frontiersman, had left Camp Floyd in March 1859 with thirty-nine emigrant men en route to what is now Arizona. Under Johnston's orders, Lynch and several other commanders were escorting a burgeoning traffic of apostates now fleeing Zion—"refugees from the Mormon Kingdom who had sought the army's protection because they feared their former coreligionists," as one historian described them. The flow of Mormon refugees would become the largest emigration up to that time, overshadowing even the California gold rush of 1852. Advertisements directed at apostates appeared in the Salt Lake City newspapers and were posted throughout the city. "Having through His Excellency Governor Cumming," read one, "asked of Gen. Johnston a military escort to conduct us beyond the lines of danger, on our road to California, and the same being readily granted, we respectfully solicit all who wish to avail themselves of this security, and can be ready for an early start, to convene at the California House."

When Lynch and his contingent reached Beaver City on March 27, they came upon Forney, who had been abandoned by his Mormon guides. He informed Lynch that he was on his way to Mountain Meadows to gather the children but was afraid to proceed, having been warned by Hatch and the others that inhabitants near Mountain Meadows "would make a eunuch of him." Lynch "cheerfully placed the whole party at his [Forney's] command," Lynch later reported. But Lynch was astonished and a bit distrustful that Forney had hired Hatch to begin with. "It was strange that he should have employed Mormons, the very confederates of these monsters, who had so wantonly murdered unoffending emigrants, to ferret out the guilty parties."

Accompanying Forney to Mountain Meadows, Lynch was shocked at the scene of carnage still evident. He reported,

> For more than two square miles the ground is strewn with the skull bones and other remains of the victims. In places the water has washed many of these remains together, forming little mounds, raising monuments as it were to the cruelty of man to his fellow man. Here and there may be found the remains of an innocent infant beside those of some fond, devoted mother, ruthlessly slain by men worse than demons; their bones lie bleaching in the noonday sun, a mute but an eloquent appeal to a just but offended God for vengeance. I have witnessed many harrowing sights on the fields of battle, but never did my heart thrill with such horrible emotions, as when standing on that silent plain contemplating the remains of the innocent victims of Mormon avarice, fanaticism, and cruelty.

Lynch, through his association with Cradlebaugh at Camp Floyd, where Mountain Meadows witnesses had been interviewed and protected, had no doubts about Mormon responsibility for the massacre.

Lynch and Forney proceeded to Hamblin's nearby ranch house, where the surviving children had been assembled. Lynch's emotions overcame him at the sight of the small survivors. "In a most wretched and deplorable condition," he described them, "with little or no clothing, covered with filth and dirt, they presented a sight heart-rending and miserable in the extreme." He was particularly affected by three-year-old Sarah Dunlap, who had gone blind and had lost the use of her left arm from the musket ball that had nearly detached it at the elbow. It was a sight that would stay with him the rest of his life.

Lynch took the ten orphans to Cedar City, where they waited for three days while clothing was made for them, "half-starved, half-naked, filthy, infested with vermin." At Cedar City they retrieved two more children, and another at nearby Painter Creek. Lynch conversed with the children, whom he described as traumatized but ecstatic to be back in the safety of "Americans." He learned from them that they had never been among Indians, but rather had been living with the very men they had seen kill their mothers and fathers, brothers and sisters. "The children pointed out to us the dresses and jewelry of their mothers and sisters that now grace the *angelic* forms of these murderers' women and children," Lynch later testified.

Lynch found that three of the children "retain a very vivid impression of much connected with the massacre." Eight-year-old Rebecca Dunlap, the oldest girl to survive the massacre, identified her father's murderer to Lynch when she saw the man during a brief stopover at the settlement of Santa Clara, and told Lynch as well that a young Indian man who resided with Jacob Hamblin had killed two of her sisters. Rebecca also contradicted Hamblin's long-standing alibi that he had been in Salt Lake City at the time of the massacre. She said Hamblin was the man she had pleaded with to spare her life, and she "even remembered the color of Jacob's suit," by one account. Rebecca later recalled that when the children were brought to the Hamblin ranch, one of the little boys had been shot in the leg and was crying. "The men stopped the wagon. One got out . . . took the little boy by his feet and knocked his brains out against the wagon wheel." She also told of Mormons robbing the corpses. "If a ring wouldn't come off easily, they cut off the finger."

Now with thirteen survivors, the party made its way to the Harmony home of John D. Lee, where Lynch thought Forney fawned over the massacre ringleader. When one of the young boys in tow, six-year-old Emberson Milum Tackitt, identified oxen belonging to his father now in the possession of Lee, and Rebecca and Emberson pointed out jewelry and clothing of their murdered mothers being worn by Lee's wives, Lynch refused to accept any hospitality from the man he would

call a "notorious murderer—THIS SCOURGE OF THE DESERT."
Forney, however, dined with Lee, earning the lifelong condemnation of
Lynch.

Rumors persisted that more children were with the polygamous
wives of Mormon leaders, but Lynch and Forney were unable to locate
them, and Hamblin swore that no more had survived. In fact, Philip
Klingensmith had taken a pretty blond infant—believed to be the
youngest Fancher child—whom he renamed "Priscilla" and gave to his
wife Betsy to raise. But when Hamblin collected the children, Priscilla,
along with other missing "mystery children," was not among them.

Though reluctant to return to Salt Lake City without knowing for
certain that all the survivors had been rescued, Lynch finally concluded
that all who could be found had been found. In late April, the
entourage made its way back north through the unfriendly Mormon
colonies.

While the cargo of children ambled toward the capital, Johnston
ordered Captain Reuben P. Campbell, "in command of one company
of dragoons and two of infantry," to proceed to Santa Clara near
Mountain Meadows. "The motive for dispatching this force," Johnston
wrote to Winfield Scott, "is to give protection to the numerous travelers
who will pass over the southern route during the spring . . . and also to
make inquiries respecting murders which were said to have been perpetrated by Indians last fall."

Johnston assigned a medical officer to the combined companies and
rations for the troops for fifty days. When Cradlebaugh learned of the
expedition, he asked Johnston if he could accompany Campbell to
Cedar City to obtain sworn testimony regarding the Mountain Meadows Massacre, and asked that the small detachment provide security
for the witnesses. "I determined to visit that part of my district, and, if
possible, expose the persons engaged in the massacre," Cradlebaugh
later wrote. Johnston readily agreed, and U.S. Marshal William Rogers
was assigned to accompany the group in order to arrest the murder sus-
pects. Traveling with them, hidden in a covered wagon, were numerous
officers and witnesses of the court.

On April 21, the soldiers rolled out of Camp Floyd toward the Southern Trail. They were to meet up with Brevet Major James H. Carleton,
who was under orders from his commanding officer at Fort Tejon in

California to proceed with the First Dragoons to Mountain Meadows to "bury the bones of the victims of that terrible massacre."

Earlier in the month, Cradlebaugh had issued bench warrants that sent Lee, Higbee, Haight, Dame, Nephi Johnson, and others scattering to hiding places from the mountains around Harmony to what is now Zion National Park and to the tiny settlement of Pioche in southeastern Nevada. But Cradlebaugh's investigation had been compromised by Mormon sympathizers who had knowledge of the probe—including Cumming—and confidential information from the Cradlebaugh investigation systematically found its way to the Mormon leaders in the south; Lee received express messages almost daily informing him of the most sensitive details of the inquiry. Before the Santa Clara Expedition, as it came to be known, had left Salt Lake City, Lee knew about the troops marching south.

On April 30, after negotiating a spring snowstorm in the mountains, the contingent met up with Captain Lynch, Dr. Forney, and the "babies," near Beaver, and Cradlebaugh had an emotional interchange with the surviving children. "Oh, I wish I was a man, I know what I would do," an eight-year-old boy exclaimed to Cradlebaugh. "I would shoot John D. Lee. I saw him shoot my mother." Campbell reported what he had gleaned in his conversations with the group. "These children say that they have never been with the Indians," he wrote to Johnston. "A good deal of information can be derived from them in relation to the massacre, as some of them are old enough to remember the affair very well."

The next day Forney sent a dispatch to Johnston as well, now referring to sixteen children in his possession, having found three more survivors near Beaver. Describing a "very laborious and difficult trip," Forney said the children ranged in age from three and a half to nine years old. Most significantly, Forney said, "at least four of the oldest of the children *know,* WITHOUT DOUBT KNOW, enough of the material facts of the Mountain Meadow affair, to relieve this world of the *white* hell-hounds, who have disgraced humanity by being mainly instrumental in the murdering of at least one hundred and fifteen men, women, and children." His days with the victims seemed to have altered his sympathetic attitude toward the Mormons.

While Forney was on his mission to the southern settlements, Congress had been debating compensation and remuneration for the return of the children to their relatives. Ten thousand dollars were allocated for transporting the children from Utah to Arkansas. Russell, Majors and Waddell—the mammoth western freight company at the center of corruption charges against the Buchanan administration—made a humanitarian gesture to transport them by ox caravan free of charge. But Johnston and Forney both thought such an ordeal would be traumatic for the already abused children; instead, Johnston ordered spring wagons and ambulances to convey them in relative comfort, and a military escort of three companies to assure their safety. Along the way, Forney had grown attached to his small charges, and wanted to take responsibility for completing his mission of returning them with ample protection. "These unfortunate fatherless, motherless, and penniless children certainly demand more than an ordinary degree of sympathy," Forney wrote Johnston. "I have secured the services of four females to accompany them to Leavenworth. I will also provide suitable clothing, blankets, and such appliances as will be deemed necessary."

As the children were brought into Camp Floyd, where they would live with the soldiers for several weeks while preparations were finalized for their journey to relatives, the Carleton and Campbell contingents moved toward their rendezvous point at the Santa Clara River near Mountain Meadows. Campbell and his men, including Cradlebaugh and Rogers, were the first to reach their destination. On May 6 their wagons entered the meadow, and they set up camp near the site of the initial siege of the emigrants. "Nothing of interest occurred," Campbell wrote to Assistant Adjutant General F. J. Porter at Fort Bridger, "until my arrival at the Mountain Meadows." Disturbed by the scene, and shocked that there had apparently been no attempt by local Mormons to bury the dead, Campbell managed to convey the horrible scene in unembellished terms. "Here I found human skulls, bones, and hair, scattered about, and scraps of clothing of men, women, and children. I saw one girl's dress, apparently that of a child ten or twelve years of age."

For two days the men gathered the skeletal remains for burial and made such investigation as was possible with the decomposed body parts. Rogers filled "a two bushel basket of women's hair that was strewn around among the sage brush," he later reported, and determined how some of the victims had been shot—"the ball entering the back part of the head and coming out the front." In the party was Dr. Charles Brewer, assistant surgeon with the U.S. Army, who sought to determine the cause of death of the dozens of corpses. Twenty-five hundred yards from the corral where the emigrants had circled their wagons, Brewer found the largest number of "skeletons," which he determined to be men. Following a border of scrub oak 350 yards farther he came upon the bodies of numerous women and children "left to decay upon the surface," the young ranging from age six to twelve. "Here, too, were found masses of women's hair, children's bonnets, such as are generally used upon the plains, and pieces of lace, muslin, calicoes, and other material, part of women's and children's apparel." At that location Brewer buried thirteen skulls "and many more scattered fragments," marking the graves with "mounds of stone."

Most of the victims were strewn "about upon the plain," Brewer noted, and he set about gathering them to conduct a physical examination. "Many of the skulls bore marks of violence, being pierced with bullet holes, or shattered by heavy blows, or cleft with some sharp-edged instrument. . . . Some of the skulls showed that fire-arms had been discharged close to the head."

Brewer's pathological inquiry would be the first evidence submitted to the U.S. government that the victims had been killed in orchestrated executions, many by point-blank shots to the head, which contradicted the Mormon claims that Paiute Indians armed with arrows had been the murderers. Brewer would pronounce it "the most brutal butchery ever perpetrated on this Continent."

Visiting the site of the slaughter further galvanized Cradlebaugh's resolve. "Who can imagine the feelings of these men, women, and children, surrounded, as they supposed themselves to be, by savages," he ruminated. "Fathers and mothers only can judge what they must have been. Far off in the Rocky mountains, without transportation—for their cattle, horses, and mules had been run off—not knowing what their fate was to be, we can but poorly realize the gloom that pervaded the camp." The troops became nauseated at the bleak task, the young men overcome by their emotions. "Many brave men shed tears as they stopped to pick up all that remained of their fellow creatures," a nineteenth-century historian recalled. "Garments of babes and little ones, faded and torn, fluttering from each ragged bush, from which the warble of the songster of the desert sounds as mockery," was how one of the soldiers depicted the scene. "Human hair, once falling in glossy ringlets around childhood's brow or virtue's form, now strewing the plain in masses, matted, and mingling with the musty mould."

After sleeping two nights in the ghastly field, the contingent moved twenty miles southwest, where they camped for a week on the Santa Clara River. Once there, Campbell "sent for Jackson, the chief of the tribe said to be most hostile to the Americans." Cradlebaugh's tent became an interrogating room, as he hosted Jackson and other Indian chiefs, "who gave me their version." His interviews with local Paiutes and Mormon witnesses would confirm his investigative conclusions that church leaders under both ecclesiastical and military orders had conducted the entire operation.

Admitting that some members of their tribe were "engaged in the massacre," the chiefs contended that they were not there at the beginning and had later responded to the scene under written orders from Brigham Young. Only after the Mormons were entrenched in an unsuccessful battle with the wagon train did they solicit Paiute assistance. "A white man came to their camp with a piece of paper," Cradlebaugh reported he was told, "which, he said, Brigham Young had sent, that directed them to go and help whip the emigrants." The Indian witnesses said they were reluctant to participate because the emigrants "had long guns, and were good shots," and the Indians had no arms. They identified Lee, Haight, and Higbee as the "big captains" and said the Mormon militia had donned Indian war paint.

Cradlebaugh attached great credibility to the Paiute testimony. "The Indians in the southern part of the Territory of Utah are not numerous, and are a very low, cowardly, beastly set, very few of them being armed with guns. They are not formidable. I believe all in the southern part of the Territory would, under no circumstances, carry on a fight against ten white men."

Having recorded the available testimony from the Native Americans, the detachment moved north toward Cedar City, where they would wait for Carleton to arrive from Los Angeles. They stopped to camp again at Mountain Meadows. Brewer and others searched the field for additional evidence and anything that might identify the victims. "No names were found upon any article of apparel, or any peculiarity in the remains, with the exception of one bone, the upper jaw, in which the teeth were very closely crowded, and which contained one front tooth more than is generally found," Brewer reported.

In Cedar City, Cradlebaugh set up a makeshift judge's chambers in a vacant house—inhabitants had fled the city in droves—and announced to the community his intention to take testimony from anyone who had knowledge relating to the massacre, arrest those responsible, and adjudicate the cases. "As soon as it became known that Judge [Cradlebaugh] intended to hold a court, and that he would have troops to insure protection, and to serve writs if necessary, several persons visited him at his room, at late hours of the night, and informed him of different facts connected with the massacre," Rogers said in recalling the atmosphere.

"I was visited by a number of apostate Mormons who gave me every assurance that they would furnish an abundance of evidence in regard to the matter, so soon as they were assured military protection," Cradlebaugh reported. The informants feared for their lives and begged for anonymity and confidentiality in exchange for their cooperation. They asked to meet only at night, and for Cradlebaugh "not to recognize them" if he encountered them during daylight. One man in particular confessed his involvement in the slaughter, said his "mind and conscience" had been "tormented," and he was now willing to stand trial. Some of the witnesses "claimed that they had been forced into the matter by the Bishops," according to Cradlebaugh.

"Previous to the massacre, there was a council held at Cedar City," one man told Cradlebaugh, "which President Haight and Bishop Higby [sic] and Lee attended. At this council they designated or appointed a large number of men residing in Cedar City, and in other settlements around, to perform the work of dispatching these emigrants. The men appointed for this purpose were instructed to report, well armed at a given time, to a spring or small stream, lying a short distance to the left of the road leading onto the meadows, and not very far from Hamblin's ranch, but concealed from it by intervening hills. This was the place of rendezvous; and here the men, when they arrived, painted and otherwise disguised themselves so as to resemble Indians." This witness proceeded to recount for the judge in chilling detail the hour-by-hour siege and slaying of the emigrants. He then provided Cradlebaugh with the names of twenty-five Mormon participants.

The judge also received evidence that at least two more surviving children were in the vicinity, and dispatched agents to try to locate them. Chief Kanosh insisted in interviews with the investigators that a teenager between fourteen and seventeen years old and a three-year-old child were hidden in Cedar City. Rogers, along with eight quartermaster's men under Campbell's command, began a search for the children, going door to door in the nearby settlements. "I told them that if the children were in the country at all, every house would be searched if they were not given up," the marshal said. Finally, after being hired by Rogers, Jacob Hamblin delivered one more child to the troops in Cedar City, a boy of about two.

Cradlebaugh also inventoried the emigrants' property stored at the Cedar City church. "The bed clothes upon which the wounded had been laying, and those taken from the dead, were piled in the back room of the tithing office and allowed to remain for so great a length of time that when I was there, eighteen months after, the room was still offensive."

Now convinced beyond a reasonable doubt that he had solved the mystery of the "catalogue of blood, the cowardly, cold-blooded butchery and robbery at the Mountain Meadows," Cradlebaugh issued warrants for the arrest and immediate trial of thirty-eight men, including Lee, Haight, Dame, and Higbee. But Johnston received orders from Washington that would neutralize Cradlebaugh's investigation. President Buchanan had reacted suddenly and swiftly to political pressure from Thomas Kane and Cumming and moved to abolish the authority of Johnston's soldiers as a *posse comitatus* for Cradlebaugh's civilian proceedings. Kane, who Buchanan believed had "saved the nation from the expense and horror of a domestic war," as one historian put it, carried great cachet with the administration. So Buchanan took seriously Kane's declaration that Cradlebaugh was abusing his power by using Johnston's troops as protection for his courtroom and witnesses. In any case, the president's attention had turned to the brewing civil war between the North and South, and he had little tolerance for a crusading judge who was not satisfied to "hear patiently the causes brought before" him, as Attorney General Jeremiah S. Black portrayed the expedient decision.

In the event, a dismayed Johnston received his orders from Secretary of War Floyd: "Peace now being restored to the Territory, the judicial administration of the laws will require no help from the army under your command." Even before Carleton's expedition had arrived at Mountain Meadows, Campbell had been ordered to return to Camp Floyd. Infuriated, Cradlebaugh was forced to acknowledge that he could not carry out his public duties under such circumstances. Reluctantly he joined the disheartened troops for the long march back to Salt Lake City. But first, they would rendezvous with Carleton at Mountain Meadows and leave a small but final tribute to the innocent men, women, and children who lost their lives there.

. . .

Born in 1814 in Maine, James Henry Carleton was among the most distinguished of American military officers. Breveted during the Mexican War, the dark-haired, light-eyed commander was known for his meticulous attention to detail, his articulate speech, and his gifted prose. He had fought the notoriously vicious Jicarilla Apache with Kit Carson in what is now northern New Mexico, and studied cavalry tactics in the Crimean War between Russia and the British allies. But nothing in his forty-three years of life had prepared him for the violence and savageness he found at Mountain Meadows.

Arriving with his troops on May 16, 1859, Carleton converged with Campbell and his forces, Cradlebaugh and his marshals, and a sundry group of witnesses seeking protection from the army. They all set up camp at the spring near the emigrants' corral. "The scene of the massacre, even at this late day, was horrible to look upon," a stunned Carleton would write. "Women's hair, in detached locks and in masses, hung to the sage bushes and was strewn over the ground in many places. Parts of little children's dresses and of female costume dangled from the shrubbery or lay scattered about; and among these, here and there, on every hand, for at least a mile in the direction of the road, by 2 miles east and west, there gleamed, bleached white by the weather, the skulls and other bones of those who had suffered."

The next day he put his men to work. They measured the scene of the carnage "from the ditch near the spring to the point upon the road where the men were attacked and destroyed" at approximately one mile. "Major Henry Prince drew a map of the ground about the spring where the entrenchment was dug, and embracing the neighboring hills behind which the Mormons had cover."

Learning of the newly issued orders for the troops to return to Camp Floyd, and the emasculation of Cradlebaugh's criminal case, Carleton conversed at length with Cradlebaugh about the overwhelming obstacles in the judge's attempted prosecutions. "Judge Cradlebaugh says that with Mormon juries the attempt to administer justice in this Territory is simply a ridiculous farce," Carleton recalled. "He believes that the Territory ought at once to be put under martial law." Carleton commiserated with Cradlebaugh, and determined to conduct his own investigation into the matter pursuant to the orders he had received in California. "The judge can not receive too much praise for the resolute and thorough manner with which he pursues his investigation," he would remark.

Campbell informed Carleton that his men had collected and buried the bones of twenty-six of the victims. In addition, Brewer told Carleton that he had personally overseen three more burial sites—one with eighteen bodies, another with twelve, and another with six. Over the next few days, Carleton took a wagon and a party of men and scoured the sagebrush and ravines in a square-mile section. That hunt resulted in locating the "disjointed bones" of thirty-four more bodies. "The number could easily be told by the number of pairs of shoulder blades and by lower jaws, skulls, and parts of skulls, etc.," he reported. Nearly every skull he retrieved "had been shot through with rifle or revolver bullets."

When as many bodies as could be found were loaded into a wagon, Carleton directed the driver to a burial site. "A glance into the wagon, when all had been collected, revealed a sight which can never be forgotten," he recalled. He ordered the bones deposited in a grave "on the northern side of the ditch." His troops then set out to gather large granite stones in the neighboring foothills to construct a proper cairn. "I caused to be built . . . a rude monument, conical in form and 50 feet in circumference at the base and 12 feet in height." At the base Carleton's men placed a "slab of granite set in the earth" and inscribed the following words: "Here 120 men, women, and children were massacred in cold blood early in September, 1857. They were from Arkansas."

The troops now cut down two cedar trees from the surrounding escarpment, which they assembled into a rough-hewn but elegant cross twenty-four feet in height. On the transverse beam, which they would place facing north, a soldier carved the words "Vengeance is mine: I will repay, saith the Lord."

In a solemn ceremony, the troops raised the Christian symbol before departing the sacred ground in silence.

CHAPTER FOURTEEN

Mountain Meadows, May 25, 1861

J OHN CRADLEBAUGH fought back with the fury of a humiliated
man. On the stormy night of June 4, 1859, accompanied by an
escort of ten men, he left Camp Floyd for Genoa, Nevada, to assume
his seat on the federal bench in the Western Judicial District of the territory. There he received a hero's welcome, with discharged cannons
and a band. He convened his first court in a hayloft over a livery stable,
and from that unlikely venue warned of the dangerous yoke of Mormondom. As tensions mounted between the inhabitants of eastern and
western Utah Territory over the authority of the Mormon Church to
govern the West, Cradlebaugh agitated for Nevada's independence.
"He spoke and acted with the fearlessness and resolution of a Jackson," the *Territorial Enterprise* of Virginia City described him, and the
free-spirited Nevadans rewarded him with the position of the territory's first delegate to the U.S. Congress. "We have the utmost repugnance, the most hearty aversion to anything which places us within the
pale of Mormon Law," the *Enterprise* editorialized. Cradlebaugh's
efforts would be interrupted when he was seriously wounded as a
Union soldier at the Battle of Vicksburg.

Three weeks after Cradlebaugh left Camp Floyd, fifteen of the
orphaned children were piled into covered carriages for the long trek
back to Arkansas. Leaving on June 27, 1859, they were escorted by
Companies A and C of the Second Dragoons, commanded by Captain
Richard H. Anderson. Anderson transported them as far as Fort Leavenworth, where William C. Mitchell, an Arkansas state senator, met

them. The two oldest boys, John Calvin Miller and Emberson Milum Tackitt, remained behind with Jacob Forney in order to testify in the event of a criminal case against the Mountain Meadows perpetrators.

Forney gave specific instructions to the army to take special care of the group, making sure they were well fed and comfortable. "They should have little or no bacon or beans, but little fresh meat, plenty of rice, sugar, milk, butter, and eggs," he wrote. "I have furnished for the party dried and can peaches, 70 pounds of butter, and about 100 pounds of butter crackers." Forney designated one of the women as "chief nurse," and ordered three of the men he had hired to "render all needful assistance of their comfort getting wood and water, and putting up the tent or tents."

Mitchell had been hired by the government to retrieve the children at Fort Leavenworth. He embraced the task wholeheartedly, eager to see his grandchildren Prudence Angeline and Georgia Ann Dunlap. Hiring a female nurse, Mitchell left Carroll County, Arkansas, in early August with two two-horse wagons to bring them the rest of the way. Expecting to rendezvous with the caravan on September 1, Mitchell was thrilled that it arrived at the army camp a week early. "The little children were in fine health," Mitchell reported of the five boys and ten girls.

On September 15 a wildly emotional crowd of friends and relatives greeted them at Carrolton, Arkansas. "You would have thought we were heroes," Sallie Baker would recall years later. "They had a buggy parade for us through Harrison." Mitchell lined the children up on a courthouse bench and identified them as best he could. Not all could remember their last names or the names of their parents, but the close-knit community sought to determine who their parents might have been, recognizing certain family traits and expressions. Though the children's memories were uneven, the one recollection they all had in common was that it had been a white man who rode into their camp bearing a white flag of truce.

Mitchell took his granddaughters home, and the three Dunlap girls were claimed by their uncle James Douglas Dunlap. Hampton Bynun Fancher took charge of his cousin Kit Carson and Kit's sister, Triphenia Fancher. Friends and distant relatives adopted the remainder.

"When we got around to our house," Baker reminisced,

Grandma Baker, the one who refused to go to California, was standing on the porch. She was a stout woman and mighty dignified, too. When we came along the road leading up to the house she was pacing back and forth but when she caught sight of us she ran down the path and grabbed hold of us, one after the other and gave us a powerful hug. Leah, our old Negro mammy, caught me up in her arms and wouldn't let me go. She carried me around all the rest of the day, even cooking supper with me in her arms. I remember she baked each of us children a special little apple turn-over pie . . . I remember I called all of the women I saw "mother." I guess I was still hoping to find my own mother, and every time I called a woman "mother," she would break out crying.

Meanwhile, Forney was getting frustrated. "In my opinion there is but a slender prospect of even a court being held soon," Forney wrote to the commissioner of Indian affairs in Washington on November 2, 1859. "Your advice of the disposition of these children [the two who had stayed behind as witnesses] is respectfully solicited."

Forney expressed his interest in adopting Emberson Milum Tackitt, whom he called "Ambrose Miram"—which was probably how the little boy pronounced his name. The child "informs me that he has no near relations," Forney wrote. "I am, consequently, anxious to take this boy into my family and do for him as for a child." Forney received a succinct one-line response: "Bring the boys to Washington," Commissioner A. B. Greenwood wrote on November 30, 1859.

Forney and the two boys arrived in Washington on December 12, where they were interviewed by government officials, but stayed only one day. No record of the children's testimony was maintained, and they were immediately turned over to an army major, who took them to Fayetteville, Arkansas. Forney's request to adopt Emberson was apparently denied.

The orphans were back in Arkansas, Cradlebaugh was exiled to the no-man's-land of northern Nevada, and the Mountain Meadows Massacre was marginalized. Brigham Young took no further action. In the fall of 1859, President Buchanan and Attorney General Black repeatedly beseeched Thomas Kane to obtain information relating to it. Kane, still an outspoken and indefatigable defender of the Mormons, pleaded with Young to provide him with affidavits and evidence that he could give to the administration to prove the Mormons innocent.

Working into the night on December 8, George A. Smith and other church historians culled together the exonerating evidence from Smith's "investigation" of the massacre.

"Neither yourself, nor any one acquainted with me, will require my assurance that, had I been appraised of the intended onslaught at the Meadows, I should have used such efforts for its prevention as the time, distance, and my influence and facilities, should have permitted," Young wrote to Kane. "The horrifying event transpired without my knowledge, except from after report, and the recurring thought of it ever caused a shudder in my feelings . . . the facts of the massacre of men, women, and children are so shocking and crucifying to my feelings, that I have not suffered myself to hear any more about them than the circumstances of conversation compelled." Apparently satisfied with Young's response, Kane and Buchanan halted their inquiries.

In a rare and nationally disseminated interview in the fall of 1859, Young explained the church's history of persecution to a sympathetic *New York Tribune* editor, Horace Greeley. Young "compares the Mormons to the apostles and Buchanan to Pontius Pilate," Greeley reported. It was the first time Young had granted such an interview, and Greeley basked in a cordial welcome. The famous correspondent asked the prophet nothing about the Mountain Meadows Massacre, reporting instead on the theology and Young's claims that although he had become a millionaire, "no dollar of it was ever paid me by the church."

With the election of Abraham Lincoln in 1860—and the lead-up to war—the massacre receded in national importance. When the Civil War broke out in 1861, Cumming left Utah Territory, ultimately claiming that Young had "lied to and deceived him" about the massacre. Speaking of his powerlessness in Zion, he drew his final assessment: "Cumming is Governor of the Territory, but Brigham Young is Governor *of the people*. By ———, I am not fool enough to think otherwise." Years later Cumming would tell the *Salt Lake Daily Tribune* he believed Young "to have been the prime mover in the conspiracy that consummated that massacre, and that he ought to have been indicted as an accessory before the fact." Cumming went on to describe Young as "one of the damndest rascals that ever went unhung."

The conflict revived Young's millennialist fervor. Citing Joseph Smith's 1832 prophecies that "the wars . . . will shortly come to pass" and the "slaves shall rise up against their masters," Young told his followers the Second Coming was nigh.

As the federal troops left Utah for forts and battlegrounds through-out the North, Young was once more in command of his empire. Glo-rying in his return to absolute power over the territory, he made his first journey in five years to the southern settlements, ostensibly to explore the possibility of establishing a new cotton industry in the fertile valleys there. "A key purpose of the May 1861 excursion," however, according to a Mormon historian, "was to insure that southern Utahns under-stood the need for silence on the subject of Mountain Meadows." Now Young would visit John D. Lee at his new home in Washington, Utah.

Lee had prospered mightily in the years since the massacre, acquir-ing land, livestock, wives, and money, and he was eager to display the wealth to his "father." He had built a mansion in Washington, using lumber from Parowan, native mica for the windows, and millstones hauled from the local mountains by a full-time crew of ten men. His molasses mill earned him forty dollars a day during harvest, he owned a productive twenty-acre cotton farm in nearby Toquerville, and the 1860 census indicated he was worth $49,500. His wives and children were the best dressed in the county, and though he had often reveled in the fate of the evil Arkansans—"like the Ancient Mariner, he went up and down compelling every person whom he met to listen to his story of an emigrant train that had been murdered by the Indians," a con-temporary reported—he could not escape the stigma.

There were many in the community who shunned Lee and his family, and few confronted him to his face. Stories of his brutality were ram-pant, including one particularly gruesome tale later recounted by one of his wives that she had seen him slit the throat of a child survivor of the massacre who had spoken out of turn. The young victim had com-mented on Lee's wife Emma wearing the silk dress and gold jewelry of the girl's mother. In Lee's orchard, "figs ripened black over the grave" of the murdered child, according to local legend. Hostile neighbors turned their cattle into his grain fields and diverted his irrigation ditches.

The "Ballad of John D. Lee" was chanted secretly to the strumming of a banjo, though never in his presence.

> *They melted down with one accord*
> *Like wax before the flame*
> *Both men and women, old and young*
> *O Utah, where's thy shame?*
> *By order of Old Brigham Young*

This deed was done, you see
And the captain of that wicked band
Was Captain John D. Lee
By order of their President
This bloody deed was done
He was the leader of the Mormon Church
His name is Brigham Young.

Whatever opprobrium attended Lee in certain social or church circles, Brigham Young did not waver in the support and admiration of his
adopted son. When Young's twenty-three carriages approached Lee's
estate on the last day of May 1861, Lee saddled his finest horse and
rode out to meet the prophet. Lee was greeted warmly and accepted
Young's invitation to ride privately with him in his personal wagon. As
his wives prepared the feast of butchered beef and sheep, and arranged
sleeping quarters for fifty of the president's entourage, Young absolved
Lee of any guilt in the massacre, according to Lee's account of their
meeting. The murdered emigrants, Lee later claimed Young told him
that day, were the relatives of those who had killed the martyred
prophets, and therefore had "merited their fate."

Six days earlier, Young told Lee, as the suite passed through Mountain Meadows on the way from Cedar City to Washington, Young had
ordered the caravan to come to a stop at Major Carleton's cairn. "It
was a very cold morning much ice on the creek," church historian Wilford Woodruff entered in his diary for May 25, 1861. Wearing a heavy
overcoat against the chill, Young walked up to the cross. Silently study-
ing the inscription, "Vengeance is mine: I will repay, saith the Lord,"
Young responded aloud in an imposing voice: "Vengeance is mine and I
have taken a little." He then gave the Danite signal, raising his right
arm, the fist pointing to the sky, and as he turned toward his wagon one
of his followers threw a lasso over the cross. The man spurred his horse
into flight, and the rope pulled the cross onto the ground, dragging it
until it splintered into a dozen pieces. "In five minutes there wasn't one
stone left upon another," an elder who was present remembered. "He
didn't have to tell us what he wanted done. We understood."

Mark Twain pronounced the territorial government of Utah a "hopeless failure" after he visited Salt Lake City in 1861. Calling Young "an

absolute monarch" who "laughed at our armies," Twain wrote irreverent accounts of the massacre and its aftermath for the *Territorial Enterprise*. Convinced that the Mormons were responsible for the slaughter, Twain "collated," as he called it, a set of eight damning circumstances: the Mormon participants who had confessed to Judge Cradlebaugh; the failure of Brigham Young, as superintendent of Indian affairs, to report the incident to government authorities in a timely fashion; the flight of the participants to avoid prosecution during Cradlebaugh's investigation; the failure of the *Deseret News,* "the church organ, and the only paper then published in the Territory, to notice the massacre until several months afterward, and then only to deny that Mormons were engaged in it"; the testimony of the surviving children; the children and property of the emigrants in the possession of Mormon leaders; the "freely and frequently made" statements of the Indians in the vicinity, as well as the evidence gathered by the Indian agent Forney and other federal officers; and the testimony of Captain R. P. Campbell.

If the U.S. government was willing to let the subject of the massacre die, a fresh band of journalists was clamoring for justice. A new Gentile-owned paper in Salt Lake City, the *Utah Reporter,* became the voice for the Fancher-Baker party.

With the completion of the transcontinental railroad in 1869, Gentiles had been pouring into the territory in record numbers. "The Saints found their Zion infiltrated and assailed by 'outsiders,' " a historian of the era said of the changing atmosphere. With the growing non-Mormon population in Salt Lake City and the free-press competition to the *Deseret News,* Young came under increasing scrutiny not only for his role in the massacre but for his financial dealings as well.

All the while, Young continued to have close and cordial relations with Lee, who boasted pretentiously of this. On an outing to Salt Lake City, Lee had been seen traveling with Young in his personal carriage—a public display considered grotesque by those who knew the carriage had belonged to one of the murdered emigrants. Sometime during 1867 or 1868, as Lee recalled it, Young dined with Lee at Lee's Washington home, typically requesting in advance that Lee prepare a banquet for him. "Cut me a chunk off the breast of the turkey," Lee said Young told him, "and a piece of the loin of one of the fat kids, and put some rich gravy over it, and I will eat it at 2 p.m." In the spring of 1869, during another tour of the southern settlements, the prophet warmly embraced Lee, much to the displeasure of local residents, and even publicly acknowledged him at a church meeting. Young and his retinue then spent the night at Lee's home.

It would be part of the larger historical tragedy of Mountain Meadows that the outside world would level collective blame and guilt at Mormons in general. For there were untold numbers of faithful and believing Mormons profoundly disturbed by the church's role in the slaughter and the subsequent dissembling, which they termed "lying for the Lord." Hierarchical church leaders were no less appalled than common Saints by what they increasingly saw as the dark blot on their religion. Amasa Lyman, a devout and kindhearted man who had been a high priest, apostle, and Danite since the early days at Kirtland, encouraged the participants in the massacre to "make a full confession and take the consequences." Lyman would be excommunicated.

The men who participated "in that almost unparalleled crime," as author Josiah Gibbs portrayed them, "were not murderers in the generally accepted definition of the word. They were irresponsible victims of gross superstition, and, almost without protest, they stained their souls with blood in the effort to perform the will of God, as they understood the order to commit murder."

In an explosive series in the summer of 1870 and continuing through 1871, the *Utah Reporter* began publishing anonymous "open" letters to Brigham Young from an author identified only as "Argus." Argus, a longtime Mormon familiar with the intricacies of the church doctrines, seemed to have personal knowledge of the Fancher-Baker party and inside information about the siege and slaughter. "Your militia took up their line of march in pursuit of them," Argus wrote to Young, "*your militia!* You, Brigham Young, were at that very time Governor of Utah, and Commander-in-Chief of the military forces of the Territory, and were drawing your salary as such from the treasury of the United States."

In a devastating depiction of the forces behind the attack, Argus revealed for the first time to a Utah audience the depth and breadth of the killings, as well as church command of the atrocity. "These soldiers did not come together by chance," he continued. Citing a sworn affidavit from a participant, Argus maintained the call to arms "was a regular military call from the superior officers to the subordinate officers and privates of the regiment . . . said regiment was duly ordered to muster, armed, and equipped as the law directs, and prepared for field operations." Then, in excruciating detail, Argus gave a day-by-day, moment-by-moment account of the starvation and dehydration of the emigrants, their betrayal with the flag of truce, and their precise execution at the command of "Halt. Do your duty!"

What followed, according to Argus, was the well-organized annihilation of everyone but seventeen children. When it was over, "all was still! Save the last death-strugglings of the unhappy victims, the cries of the remnant of little ones who had been left behind in the flight, and the heavy breathings of the soldiers, pale, trembling, and aghast at the horrid scene before and around them." Demons were set loose in some of the men, excited by the blood lust of the affair, the author claimed. "Well, sir," he wrote the prophet, "your soldiers, with many a coarse, ribald, vulgar jest, with many an obscene, beastly remark, stripped them entirely of their clothing, and the whole company were left nude and stark, and without burial!"

The Argus exposé fueled the growing dissension among a group of intellectual and wealthy Mormons who had broken off from Young. The group of businessmen and spiritualists challenged Young's economic policies, church corruption, and absolute theocracy, and had been demanding disclosure about the Mountain Meadows Massacre for more than a decade. Now loosely formed under their de facto leader, a brilliant entrepreneur named William Godbe, the Godbeites, as they came to be known, presented the most threatening challenge to Young's power. One of Utah's richest men, Godbe had in 1868 cofounded the *Utah Magazine,* the first literary journal in the territory to publish probing and insightful criticism of Young's political and spiritual reign. When Godbe and his followers were excommunicated and their publication boycotted by the faithful, they officially formed their movement into the Church of Zion.

On New Year's Day 1870, Godbe published the first issue of what was initially named the *Mormon Tribune* and would become the *Salt Lake Tribune.* With a powerful secular voice, the *Tribune* would launch a relentless attack on Young's regressive administration and a drumbeat of demands for a full investigation of the massacre.

Washington had long since abandoned interest in the mass murder—refusing even to adjudicate claims from the surviving children for compensation—but, ironically, Young was meeting the stiffest demands for church accountability from within his own ranks. The church had continued to blame the Indians and deny Mormon involvement into

1869, but after the Argus revelations, followed by the pressure from the independent *Tribune,* a noticeable shift in church policy went into effect. As more damning evidence surfaced, the church suddenly turned its focus away from the Indians and onto what they now portrayed as the overzealous and renegade fanatics of southern Utah spurred by war hysteria.

By early 1870, Young had begun to detach himself from Lee. Lee initially thought this distancing was an expedient Young had been forced into, rather than a true "cutting off." On February 24, Young and his caravan ventured south as far as Beaver, where Lee rode up to meet him. Joining the prophet at church services, Lee was surprised but not unduly alarmed at Young's uncharacteristic coolness toward him. In a private meeting after the service, Young said to Lee he should sell his Utah holdings and move out of the territory. But Lee's farms were prospering, and at fifty-eight years old he had neither the ambition, energy, nor desire to uproot and relocate. It would not be until eight months later that Young impressed upon Lee that his earlier instruction had been not an idle recommendation but a command.

In early September, Young came south with a group of explorers seeking an approach to the Colorado River east of Kanab. Lee joined the expedition, which included Young, Dame, Dimick Huntington, and the explorer John Wesley Powell. On the banks of the Kanab River, Young and Lee had a private conversation, in which Young reiterated the demand for Lee to move out of Utah and across the Colorado River into Arizona, where a Utah arrest warrant would have no validity. "I should like to see you enjoy peace for your remaining years," Young told Lee. "Gather your wives and children around you, select some fertile valley, and settle out here." When Lee balked, Young sharpened his tone. "It is my wish and counsel."

On October 8, Lee was formally excommunicated, though he did not learn of the sanction for several more weeks. In a unanimous decision, the twelve apostles severed all ties with Lee, who had been a devoted Saint for thirty-two years. When Lee received official notice of the action, he fell into a deep depression. "My love for the Truth is above all other things & is first with me," Lee recorded in his journal, "& believe that Prest. Young has Suffered this to take place for a wise purpose & not for any Malicious intent." In December, Lee approached Young at the southern community of St. George, which had been colonized in 1858, and demanded a rehearing. Young rebuffed his onetime "son," admonishing Lee to act like a man instead of a baby. "I . . . asked him why they had dealt so rashly with me," Lee later recalled, "without allowing me a chance to speak for myself; why they had waited seventeen years and then cut me off; why I was not cut off at once if what I had done was evil." Lee claimed to have been astonished when Young replied, "I never knew the facts until lately." Soon after this encounter Lee received an anonymous note, though he recognized the handwriting to be that of a church apostle: "Our advice is, Trust no one. Make yourself scarce & keep out of the way."

Not yet aware that "the entire blame of the massacre was shifted to [his] shoulders," as one historian put it, Lee faithfully followed church orders with the same disciplined servitude that had marked his decades-long dedication to the religion. Refusing to believe that Young had designated him the scapegoat for the entire affair, Lee was convinced that the prophet instead was protecting him by sending him away. Others too had gone into hiding, Lee knew, and he felt they were all shielding the church by their disappearances. Klingensmith lived at Dutch Flat, two miles southeast of Caliente, in what was now the state of Nevada, where he changed his name to P. K. Smith; Dame had gone on a mission to England; and Haight and his son-in-law Higbee had fled to Arizona.

Lee returned to Harmony at the beginning of 1871 and put all of his property up for sale. All but seven of his nineteen wives had died or abandoned him by then—several in response to his excommunication. It would take him a full year to liquidate his possessions and move. On December 23, 1871, accompanied by his wives Rachel and Emma and thirteen of his children, Lee settled amidst some of the world's most barren cliffs, at the confluence of the Colorado and Paria Rivers, where he reconciled himself to a life of exile.

"Oh, what a lonely dell!" Emma proclaimed at the desolation, christening their hideaway among the imposing sandstone walls, the rushing water, and immense landscape.

The night he arrived, he gathered the remnants of his family around him. "Do you know what night this is?" Lee asked them. When no one responded, Lee answered his own question. "This is the birthday night of our Prophet, Joseph Smith." Regaling them with the divinity of Smith and their one true religion, Lee then led the group in prayer. At the end, he implored his children to remain faithful Mormons for the rest of their lives—regardless of the fate of their father.

. . .

Though Lee did not know it, a case against him had been fortified months before he moved to Lonely Dell. On April 10, 1871, Philip Klingensmith appeared before the district court clerk of Lincoln County, Nevada, and provided a startling firsthand account of the massacre. He did so in the state of Nevada, he claimed, "for the reason that I believe that I would be assassinated should I attempt to make the same before any court in the Territory of Utah." Klingensmith's sworn affidavit, kept sealed by the federal court in Nevada for more than a year, was the first statement in court by a Mountain Meadows participant.

The confession by the former church bishop was a stark depiction of a coldly calculated slaughter at the hands of the Mormon militia. The affidavit made no mention of Indian involvement in the murders. When the *Cedar City Record* first reported its existence, in early September 1872, the news spread through Utah with a fury. By September 14, the affidavit had made its way into the hands of the *New York Herald*, which published it in its entirety under the headlines:

A MORMON MONSTROSITY

Letting in Light on the Mountain Meadows Massacre

A Participant in the Slaughter Confesses

*Men and Women Were Murdered in Cold Blood—
Only the Children Spared*

A DEMON'S FLAG OF TRUCE

Horrible Record of Bloodthirstiness

Klingensmith revealed that the militia had been "called out for the purpose of committing acts of hostility against" the emigrants. He claimed that Haight initially expressed a desire to let the wagon train pass in peace, but that he "had orders from headquarters to kill all of said company of emigrants except the little children." When the emigrants repulsed the initial attack, Lee called for more reinforcements, according to Klingensmith. A council held at Parowan with Dame resulted in additional troops joining the growing contingent at Mountain Meadows, as well as more men from Cedar City under Higbee's command. "Major Lee massed all the troops at a spring, and made a speech to them, saying that his orders from headquarters were to kill the entire company except the small children." Klingensmith then recounted how the decision was made to send a flag of truce into the emigrant camp and proceeded to describe the killing of the men, women, and children. His own orders, he claimed, were to gather and protect the youngest children during the melee.

When the killing was over, Lee reported the full details of the massacre to Young, according to Klingensmith. "Brigham Young was at that time the commander-in-chief of the militia of the Territory of Utah."

It was now clear to the church, if it hadn't been already, that deflecting blame onto the Indians would no longer carry any credibility, and Mormon leadership turned in earnest to laying total responsibility on one man: John Doyle Lee.

CHAPTER FIFTEEN

Mountain Meadows,
March 23, 1877

I N THE FALL of 1872, John D. Lee received lumber from the Mormon
Church to construct the first ferryboat for crossing the raging Colorado River. Twenty-six feet long and eight and a half feet wide, the
vessel provided Lee with a lively enterprise shuttling pioneers from
Utah into Arizona. The aging fugitive now called himself Major Doyle,
and turned Lee's Ferry into a profitable venture. Thanks to a series of
communications to him from Brigham Young, he felt assured that his
hideout was secure. Receiving "one confidential Letter of More importance than all," he recorded in his diary from the summer of 1872, he
was guaranteed that if he "continued faithful & true to that Mission,
that I never should be captured by My Enemies." He also claimed that
he was told he would receive "timely warning of the approach of Danger." In January 1874, Young appointed Lee the official ferryman,
promising to "pay you liberally for your Servises [sic]." Lee coveted this
scrap of paper, signed by both Young and George A. Smith, as "Evidence of the high minded Philanthropy that Ever characterize the
Nobleness of his Character."

Lee maintained contact with Young through messages sent to him
from Jacob Hamblin and Smith. In April 1874 he visited his beloved
prophet for the last time. Traveling to his old home in Washington, Lee
bathed and shaved and dressed in his finest Sunday clothes. Then he
rode by horseback to St. George, where Young received him "with the
kindness of a Father," Lee wrote. Joining Young and his family for an

extravagant family dinner, Lee knelt and prayed with Young before retiring to a private conversation in which the two men discussed the ferry operation. The next day, before their parting, Young confided in Lee, according to Lee, that he had heard rumors that Lee had taken up gambling, swearing, and other Gentile behavior. Lee denied the charge, and the prophet gave him a special blessing before their parting. "John, you must be careful & stand by your integrity."

Lee's fortune would change drastically in the next few months. In June, Congress approved the Poland Act, which withdrew criminal jurisdiction from Utah's probate courts—where it had resided with little effect for the past decades—and placed authority firmly in the hands of the U.S. attorney and the U.S. marshal. Now, for the first time, federal agents had the full power to prosecute the crimes of Mountain Meadows. In September the first grand jury convened under the newly enacted law indicted Lee, Dame, Haight, Higbee, Klingensmith, and four others on murder charges.

Lee had regularly visited his various wives and children in Utah Territory during the intervening years with virtual immunity. But now, Deputy U.S. Marshal William Stokes was in active pursuit and had organized a posse to arrest him. In early November, Stokes learned that Lee was at the home of his wife Caroline in Panguitch. Watching the property, Stokes's men saw Caroline talking to someone in a hen coop on the premises. As dawn broke on November 8, Stokes and his deputies made their move. They approached Lee's hiding place in a straw-covered pile. The marshal aimed his revolver and reportedly said, "If one straw moves, I'll blow your head off." At the same time, several women in the house had rifles aimed at the posse. Then, surprising them all, Lee said, "Hold on boys, don't shoot, I'll come out." He placed his own pistol in his holster and emerged brushing the straw from his shirt.

The man now called "the butcher in chief" by the *Salt Lake Daily Tribune* peacefully turned himself over to the federal agents. "Well boys, what do you want of me?" he asked them. When they read the warrant charging him with murder, he insolently replied, "Why don't you say wholesale murder? That's what you meant." The women and children in the house were crying with fear and excitement and yelling epithets at the agents, his oldest wife, Rachel, leveling a double-barreled shotgun at the officers. After an apparently brief discussion between

Lee, his older sons, and his wives about the chances for escape, Lee decided that with six men armed with rifles surrounding them any move would result in a bloodbath of his loved ones. Rachel refused to leave his side, and after insisting on making a big breakfast for her husband and his captors, she gathered a pile of blankets for the snowy journey north.

The marshal's men placed Lee in a covered wagon drawn by four horses and transported him to Beaver, where a raucous crowd had gathered in front of the Empire Hotel. People were shocked that the longtime Mormon official had actually been arrested for the massacre at Mountain Meadows. Placed in a jail cell under a strong guard, the gray-haired Lee was communicative and cheerful, and became loquacious when given an alcoholic drink, according to his guards. There the sixty-two-year-old father of fifty-six children and one hundred grandchildren settled in for an eight-month period of incarceration while awaiting his trial.

The *Tribune* trumpeted the capture and followed up with daily dispatches. "[W]e learn that the infamous John D. Lee, a priest of the Church of Jesus Christ, of Latter-Day Saints, and Brigham Young's special manager in the Mountain Meadows Massacre, was arrested at Panguitch," the *Tribune* reported on November 11. "It is already mooted in Church circles that Brigham Young, if accepted, will turn state's evidence against John D. Lee, in order to show a pretended love of justice in bringing the murderers to the gallows, but on the other hand speculations are rife among the Priesthood regarding the danger of exposure by the prisoner, who is reputed to be in possession of the fatal orders from Salt Lake City, which sent a hundred and twenty innocent beings into untimely and uncoffined graves." The newspaper, gaining brisk sales with the new sensation, editorialized that Lee's life was in danger from assassins. "It behooves the legal officers to take good care of their captive." Placing Lee in confinement but allowing Rachel to remain with him, the jailers feared for the safety of their famous prisoner. Stokes doubled his guard. "Lee knows too much for the safety of the Church," one news account said. " 'Dead men tell no tales.' "

Shortly after Lee's arrest, two Mormon men traveled to Lonely Dell and confiscated all of Lee's journals. An avid diarist throughout his life, Lee would later bemoan his loss of personal writings, claiming he had bestowed many of them on Young for safekeeping. "I could give many things that would throw light on the doings of the Church," Lee later wrote in jail. "But . . . nearly all of my journals have been made way with by Brigham Young; at least I delivered them to him and never could get them again."

In the fall of 1874, Fanny Stenhouse, a Godbeite, began a nationwide lecture series promoting her new book-length exposé on the Mormon Church, *Tell It All.* An American audience that had now turned its attention to Utah enthusiastically embraced her book, with its insightful preface by Harriet Beecher Stowe. In articles on the upcoming Lee trial published in various newspapers, she would be the first to question the federal government's failure over fifteen years to investigate the mass murder. "The treacherous assassination of this party of American citizens traveling along a national high-road," she wrote in an article published in the *Sacramento Record* and the *Chicago Tribune,* "and the indecent spoliation of their remains, have never been made the subject of inquiry by Congress and no President has ever recommended that judicial quest be made into the appalling crime."

Meanwhile, Lee's coconspirator William Dame had been apprehended as well. Captured at his Panguitch home, Dame was arrested and placed in the territorial penitentiary near Salt Lake City, where he was immediately provided a church-employed attorney. Initially fearing Lee intended to implicate Dame and the others, church officials closely monitored the cases.

Lee's repeated and publicized claims that Young had not ordered the massacre endeared him to church leaders and made him a folk hero among the faithful. Convinced that Lee intended to protect Young, or perhaps to ensure that he would not betray the prophet, the church provided Lee with two lawyers, Jabez G. Sutherland and George Caesar Bates. Three more attorneys joined the defense team, including W. W. Bishop from Pioche, Nevada. As the trial date neared, Lee became increasingly emotional and seemed to fear the worst. "Lee is feeling very badly and is in tears to-day," a correspondent reported on July 11, 1875.

Lee's day in court was dubbed the "Trial of the Century" and "the most important criminal case ever tried in the United States" by the national press. Excited by the rampant rumors that Lee intended to implicate Brigham Young and other high priests of the church, newspapers from around the country sent correspondents to cover the event.

Judge Jacob S. Boreman presided over the jury selection that began in the case on July 12, and out of more than a hundred potential jurors a body of eight Mormons, three Gentiles, and one "Jack Mormon"—a Mormon who is not devout but not apostate—was finally chosen. Though Sutherland and Bates were single-minded in their purpose to keep church leaders from becoming embroiled in the case, Bishop's priority was to see his client acquitted. The only way to do that, Bishop reasoned, was to show that Lee had followed direct orders from his military and spiritual commanders.

The stage was set for friction within the defense team, and when Lee announced just days before the trial was scheduled to begin that he intended to "make a full confession," the atmosphere became charged. Sutherland, Bates, and Bishop argued with one another over Lee's "confession," their interests at cross-purposes. In a consultation with prosecuting U.S. attorney William C. Carey, the two sides entered into what a later generation of lawyers would call plea bargaining. Carey agreed to drop charges against Lee if his confession was deemed honest and satisfactory. But when Lee claimed he was "merely an instrument in the massacre and acted under Dame's orders," as the *Salt Lake Daily Tribune* reported, Carey rejected the deal, since Lee would not be implicating the entire chain of command up to Brigham Young himself.

The case—now described as "assuming the shape of political negotiation"—was set for trial, and observers watched closely to see if Lee was prepared to expand his earlier confession. Rumors persisted that Lee, finally realizing he was being made a scapegoat, was no longer as complacent as he had been during his long incarceration. "Dame is the pet," a newspaper reported, "he has been soothed in the penitentiary by pleasant attentions, but Lee has been let severely alone in his solitary cell." As Lee agonized over his predicament, inside sources suggested he was on the verge of apostasy. "Alarm at the Camp of the Priestly Clan," one headline proclaimed. "The Church In Danger!" said another. The marshal ordered that Lee be protected from all interruptions as he worked for several days on a new, broadened statement of the facts. Lee's new confession provided additional evidence against Haight and Higbee, but exonerated Young and Smith, Young's crucial emissary to the southern settlements. This still did not satisfy the prosecutors, so Lee would have to stand trial.

On the morning of July 23, 1875, people poured into Beaver from the surrounding settlements. The overflowing crowd in the upstairs provisional courtroom at a local store forced the judge to move the trial to a nearby saloon. Journalists filled all the seats at two long tables, and the defense and prosecution each occupied additional tables. Along one wall sat the jurors, and some of Lee's numerous wives and children occupied another wall. Chairs were brought from nearby homes to seat the anxious spectators.

"Gentlemen of the jury: Eighteen years ago today a train of emigrants was wending its way from Arkansas to find a more genial home in California," prosecutor Carey began. "About 150 persons composed the company. It was the richest and best equipped train that ever crossed the Rocky Mountains." In an impassioned opening argument, taken in by an alert and often aghast audience, Carey provided a straightforward, chronological account of the shocking crime. Carey cited a few historic parallels—the 1857 massacre of British soldiers at Cawnpore, India; St. Bartholomew, where thousands of French Protestants were slaughtered by fanatic Catholics; the biblical extermination by Joshua of the entire city of Ai. "All these assassinations," he said, "are palliated by some adequate motive, but a motive for the slaughter of these emigrants at Mountain Meadows seems utterly wanting."

There followed a string of witnesses who testified they had been ordered by church leaders not to sell provisions to the Fancher Train. Some told of punishments they suffered for trading with the emigrants, ranging from beatings to being "cut off" from the church. Others testified about Smith's rousing sermons during and after the reformation, and his call to arms in the summer of 1857. One man described the gruesome scene he found when he passed through Mountain Meadows a few weeks after the slaughter. Another recalled Lee serving as auctioneer at the sale of the emigrants' goods in Cedar City. It amounted to a sordid tale of blood and violence, treachery and betrayal, that engaged a rapt audience.

But the star witness everyone craved to see and hear was Philip Klingensmith, the pale-eyed, lank, and muscular apostate who had cracked the case for the prosecution. Descended from a long line of Lutherans who spoke German in the home, Klingensmith had been born in Pennsylvania in 1814. He was baptized in the Mormon Church in 1841 and joined his fellow Saints in Nauvoo in 1844, where he worked as a blacksmith and helped build the temple. He received his patriarchal blessing there from the uncle of the martyred Joseph Smith, and was guaranteed that if he lived a humble and prayerful life, "not a hair of thy head shall fall by an enemy; bars, nor gates, nor prison walls, nor chains shall be able to hold thee." He relocated with the Saints to Salt Lake City in 1849, and in 1852 was ordered by Brigham Young to colonize Iron County. There, with his polygamous wives and children, he remained until the time of the Mountain Meadows Massacre.

Spirited into Beaver under cover of darkness, and with armed guards, Klingensmith feared for his life. It was assumed by the defense that he had been provided immunity from prosecution in exchange for his explosive testimony. He was the only Mountain Meadows participant who had voluntarily left the church and was willing to publicly break the covenant of silence taken on the ground after the killings. Prosecutors portrayed him as a truth teller motivated by a tortured conscience. Lee's attorneys suggested instead that he was acting out of pure self-interest.

In a slow and deliberate manner, all the more dramatic for its tone and escalating emotion and momentum, Klingensmith told a packed audience how the Mormon militia was called out to attack the Fancher-Baker party; how they stood in formation for three or four hours as Lee took the flag of truce to the emigrant corral—"an emblem held sacred by all civilized nations"; how Higbee, from horseback, gave the orders on the field and how the slaughter ensued. Expanding on his earlier affidavit, and in response to cross-examination, Klingensmith testified that Indians had been involved in the massacre—in his original confession he indicated Mormons had committed all the murders. He told how he traveled to Salt Lake City in October 1857 and in the presence of Lee and another witness discussed with Young the details of the murders and the distribution of the plunder. Klingensmith testified that Young ordered him to turn over all the loot from the massacre to Lee. The cattle had been branded with a cross—the church designation— Klingensmith said, and fifty of the steers were driven to Salt Lake City and traded to a man named Hooper, who was the congressional delegate from Utah Territory. In exchange for the cattle, Hooper provided boots and shoes for Saints in the south. Klingensmith said Young ordered him and the others never to discuss the massacre, even among themselves.

Cross-examined by Bishop, Klingensmith claimed he participated in the mass murder out of fear of "personal violence" if he had opposed his military and ecclesiastical commanders. That fear, he contended, was based on his personal knowledge of others who had been "put away"—the Mormon euphemism for blood-atoning murders. Klingensmith testified that he never personally witnessed Lee kill anyone on that fateful September day in 1857. The prosecution's primary witness, as it turned out, could not tie Lee to the actual death of any victim. And the allegation against Lee was that of "murder"—not a wider "conspiracy to commit murder" charge that would not enter the nomenclature of American criminal law until the next century.

That night, Lee was serenaded by the Beaver band, which sang to him from outside his jail cell. The streets of the town swelled with Lee sympathizers, prompting Stokes to call out special forces to keep peace in the inflamed community.

As the trial continued, the evidence of who actually issued the orders for the massacre became the center of attention. "The militia of southern Utah would never have been called out by Dame, Haight and Lee without orders from George A. Smith, who was Brigadier General of that district," one editorial avowed. "Mormons have never been known to make any important move without orders from 'headquarters', (meaning Brigham Young)."

But Smith and Young failed to appear. On July 28, Lee's attorneys stunned the court when they announced the receipt of an affidavit from a Salt Lake City surgeon claiming that both Young and Smith were too frail to testify. They would join the ranks of dozens of subpoenaed witnesses who never appeared and who could not be located by marshals. Of more than one hundred called, fewer than half would surface, and many of those came under duress. The testimony of Native Americans was never sought despite their potentially vital contribution, which can be attributed to the bigotry of the era.

On July 29, attorney Wells Spicer gave the three-hour opening statement for the defense, presenting what would be described as a "triangular argument." He charged the emigrants with "the suicidal folly" of stirring up the Indians in the first instance, cited the Utah War hysteria and the advance of Johnston's soldiers as the second mitigating factor, and, somewhat predictably, placed responsibility for all the killing on the Indians. Much to the chagrin of some of his fellow defense attorneys, Spicer also raised the uncomfortable specter that Lee had been following direct orders from the church hierarchy. Sutherland then closed the case for the defendant by maintaining the Mormons had no motive for killing the emigrants, and challenging Klingensmith's credibility.

Several reporters eager to hear an Indian reaction to the accusation interviewed a Pahvant observing the trial. The man, who identified himself as the son of a chief, accused the witnesses of lying, and denied involvement by his tribe or any others in the event.

Assistant prosecutor Robert N. Baskin summed up to a packed but silent courtroom. Calling the massacre "a crime against civilization and humanity," Baskin accused the Mormon Church of impeding every investigation into the incident and charged Young with being an accessory after the fact.

A somber Judge Boreman instructed the jury as to the degrees of murder and the essential ingredient of malice. He told them the burden of proof lay with the prosecution, and that the jurors had to believe beyond a reasonable doubt in reaching a conclusion of guilt or innocence.

The case went to the jury on August 5, and almost immediately gossip indicated they were hardened along religious lines—the eight Mormons and one Jack Mormon favoring acquittal, the three non-Mormons leaning toward conviction. On August 7, it became clear the jury was hopelessly deadlocked. The Mormon spectators erupted in cheers and applause when the announcement of a hung jury was made, and that night the community of one thousand inhabitants held a dance, to which all the jurors were invited.

If Lee and church leaders had believed an acquittal would settle the thirst for prosecution, they would be sorely disappointed. For what seemed to national journalists to be a blatant manipulation of justice only heightened the outrage of a public now widely informed about the atrocity. From New York to Sacramento, editorials cried foul. Charging that the jury was fixed, that the church had colluded to prevent key witnesses from testifying, and that dozens more either had perjured themselves or had had convenient lapses of memory, newspapers from coast to coast called for a new trial.

Judge Boreman ordered Lee transferred to the territorial penitentiary in Salt Lake City to await a second trial, charging the prosecution with failing to make its case and with lethargically pursuing crucial witnesses. For his part, Lee seemed to take the deadlock as evidence that Young had saved him, believing, as did most observers, that Young had had complete control over the outcome of the trial. On August 9, federal officers went for Lee at nine-thirty p.m., hoping to avoid a public demonstration. But even at that late hour, the streets of Beaver were lined with well-wishers. That evening Lee began making entries in a remarkable diary that would continue until April 18, 1876. Camping in the mountains along the way to Salt Lake City, Lee recorded seeing his first train near Nephi, which he described as "grand, romantic, and sublime." Lee wrote of his new jail cell, where he was shown to a straw bed with clean blankets in a compound surrounded by a four-foot-thick, eighteen-foot-high adobe wall. His fellow inmates included eleven convicts and three awaiting trial, most of them for murder. Lee spent September 6, his sixty-fourth birthday, in his forty-by-thirty-foot cell, writing feverishly in his diary. Serving time "for the Gospel's sake," as he depicted his ordeal, he found solace in his comparison to other martyred saints, apostles, and prophets.

Prosecutors and federal investigators, inspired with fresh zeal, visited him daily, promising him freedom if he would identify Young as the engineer of the massacre. Even as Lee's spirits plunged and his health declined, he became increasingly resigned to his fate as scapegoat for his beloved church. He would rather "rot & be Eat up with the bed bugs," Lee claimed he told Marshal Stokes, who offered to set him free if only Lee would confess to all he knew, "before I will dishonor myself by bearing false witness against any man, much less an innocent Man." Lee still believed Brigham Young would protect him from harm.

Between daily chores of milking, grooming horses, and shoveling snow, Lee set out to teach the illiterate inmates to read. Upon learning that Lonely Dell had fallen into disrepair in his absence, Lee sent a letter to Young via Daniel Wells asking for money for his wife Rachel to repair the road near the ferry. Neither Young nor Wells answered his plea. When the prison warden suggested to Lee that he could earn more than $2,000 by writing a short autobiography and promoting it on a national lecture tour, Lee gave the idea serious consideration as his feelings of abandonment swelled with each passing day. Ultimately he decided against it, being "loath to accept liberty & favours from those not of my religious faith." Still, he bemoaned the reality that in eighteen months of incarceration he had "tried with all the energy of my soul & body to call fourth [sic] aid from those who should stand by me, but as yet have failed to elicit their sympathy."

Suddenly some unidentified Mormons guaranteed a $15,000 surety bond for Lee's release from prison. On May 11, 1876, Lee was set free and was ordered to appear for his second trial in Beaver in September.

Returning to Lonely Dell, Lee rebuffed pleas from his sons to flee into Mexico. His wife Emma later claimed that Young himself advised her husband to leave the country.

Sumner Howard, a pious, wealthy, and accomplished Missouri criminal lawyer, had been appointed to replace William Carey as U.S. attorney. He assumed his new position with a fervent commitment to convicting Lee. Shrewd and politic, Howard realized that such a conviction would never be possible without the assistance of Young, and he had set out immediately to cultivate the prophet. Under pressure from his Washington superiors, who themselves were responding to national pressure, Howard would let nothing get in the way of his success.

Young fully realized that the Mountain Meadows Massacre would continue to plague him until someone was held accountable for the crime. In a calculated and mutually beneficial deal, Young and Howard came to terms. Young would make available all witnesses and evidence necessary for a conviction of Lee. In exchange, Howard would limit the testimony implicating Young, George Smith, and other church leaders in the affair, and drop charges against Dame. It was an extraordinary quid pro quo that neither side apparently committed to writing.

Lee, oblivious to this conspiracy to convict him, faced his future with unwavering loyalty to Young. Only when his church-retained lawyers withdrew from his defense did he slowly and disbelievingly acquire a new understanding of the forces at play. His Nevada lawyer, W. W. Bishop, continued to represent him, optimistically predicting another acquittal. But Lee was gloomy and depressed, feeling certain he was now the sacrificial lamb.

On September 11, 1876, the second trial of John D. Lee opened. The standing-room-only crowd watched as twelve Mormon men were sworn as jurors. True to his word, Howard immediately moved to have charges against Dame dropped. He then entered into evidence sworn statements from Young and Smith exonerating them and the church from any responsibility. Howard admitted Young's martial law proclamation to show the territory had been in a state of war at the time, as well as Young's 1858 report of the massacre to the Office of Indian Affairs laying blame on the Indians and Lee's report to Young attributing all guilt to the Indians.

In the upcoming days, even as the evidence mounted against him and Lee was devastated to hear that his favorite wife, Emma, had now abandoned him, he remained steadfast. "If my friends betray me," he said to a *Tribune* reporter, "I will not betray them, for I rely on an arm that cannot be broken."

The trial proceeded with extraordinary brevity, Howard calling only seven witnesses—all members of the church willing to testify against Lee but refusing to identify other participants in the crime. "While not a single faithful Mormon appeared for the prosecution at the first trial," wrote Will Bagley of the collusion to convict Lee, "enough loyal Saints testified at the second to make up a respectable congregation."

James Haslam testified he carried orders from Young for the emigrants to be saved. Jacob Hamblin, whom Lee would forever after call "Dirty Fingered Jake," claimed Lee confessed the entire crime to him and justified it because American troops were marching on Zion. But it was not until three more former friends—Nephi Johnson, Samuel McMurdy, and Samuel Knight—all swore they had personally witnessed Lee murder several men and women that Lee burst into tears.

The trial recessed, and a distraught Lee paced his jail cell, now cursing "the Mormons as traitors and villains," and claiming all of the murders mentioned had in fact been committed by the very men now laying the slaughter on him. The town was alive with gossip, the stacked case against Lee defying all earlier predictions. "Everybody stared at his neighbor," as one published report described the surprise, "and asked if the Church of Jesus Christ of Latter-day Saints and the District Attorney had ENTERED INTO A CONSPIRACY TO HANG LEE."

When the court reconvened, Hamblin took the stand again and claimed an Indian chief had told him he saw Lee slit the throat of one young girl and shoot another when he found them hiding in some bushes after the massacre—an apparent reference to the Dunlap sisters. No one challenged the hearsay testimony. Again, Lee wept.

Bishop called no witnesses for the defense, and in a brief but eloquent closing argument he maintained that Lee had been following military and ecclesiastical orders. Howard summed up with accolades for the Mormon Church in their unstinting cooperation with the prosecution.

It took the jury three and a half hours to reach a verdict: "Guilty of murder in the first degree."

Lee seemed to be the only one who was surprised. That night he wrote his newly estranged wife, Emma: "My worthy friend and able attorney, W. W. Bishop, felt that we were sold; he . . . had the promise that all was right from the leading men of the church."

An outpouring of sympathy for Lee erupted, and his guard was fortified amidst rumors that a mob intended to rescue him and spirit him out of the country. The day after the verdict, petitions circulated in the southern settlements begging Governor G. W. Emery for clemency. Citing Lee's age, ill health, and especially that he was "but one of many who are equally guilty with himself of the crime," his supporters received hundreds of signatures on their petitions.

On October 10, Lee appeared before Judge Boreman for sentencing.

"John D. Lee, have you anything to say why sentence of death should not be pronounced against you?"

"I have not," Lee responded in a firm steady voice.

Boreman entered an empathetic portrait of Lee as a victim of a "vast conspiracy" but a "willing participant" nonetheless. "The world has no sympathy for the perpetrators of so dastardly and cruel a butchery, and the Christian civilization of our age stands aghast at the long and persistent efforts to prevent the guilty from being brought to justice," Boreman said. Despite the sympathy "growing out of the belief that you have been deserted by the parties and the plotters of the crime, and left to be sacrificed," Boreman went on to say that "outraged justice requires" Lee's death sentence.

The judge then gave Lee a choice between three methods of execution: hanging, shooting, or beheading.

"I would rather be shot," Lee responded.

Since beheading was the preferred method for blood atonement according to Mormon doctrine, Lee's choice of execution by firing squad sent a clear signal to the faithful that he rejected a spiritual need to atone for any sins.

Lee was remanded to the territorial penitentiary while his attorney filed appeals, which postponed the scheduled October execution. Bishop, his staunch defender, encouraged Lee to write a history of the massacre and a true confession. The conviction had come as a shock to Lee, Young having assured him no harm would come to him. He transferred the false sense of security he felt during the trial to an equally baseless belief that Young would intervene at the eleventh hour to save him from execution.

He felt violated on so many different levels that he vacillated about where to focus his rage. He was a "son" betrayed by his "father"; a soldier betrayed by his commander; a husband betrayed by his wives; a parishioner betrayed by his priest. He had exhibited the loyalty and devotion unique to each of those roles, and been forsaken again and again. Like many men in his position throughout history, caught in the vise of what the next century would call "plausible deniability," Lee only gradually realized that he would pay with his life for the higher purpose of protecting his church. But once the reality took hold, he turned with a vengeance on those who had trespassed against him.

He asked his wife Rachel to bring him as many of his diaries as still existed at Lonely Dell, as well as all correspondence between him and Young, and especially to find a journal he had buried that contained the written orders from Dame and Haight to kill the emigrants. The few that could be found he turned over to his attorney; he thought that Young and his cohorts had destroyed the rest. By the end of the year he had turned his wrath on the prophet: "if he [Young] considered [himself] no accessory to the deed why would he bring men whose hands have been died [sic] in human Blood to swear away my life & make an offering of me to save his guilty Petts [sic]," Lee wrote to Emma on December 9, 1876. "[H]e thinks it a friendly act, to sacrifice me, to make me attone [sic] for the sins of his Pets as well as my own by shedding my blood . . . you know that is one of his peculiar ways of showing his Kindness to some men by killing them to save them but that Kind of Friendship is getting too thin, it is too much like the love that a Hungry wolf has for an innocent lamb."

During his final months in jail, Lee would write four conflicting and contradictory confessions. The accounts varied on the role of the Indians. What was consistent in them all was Lee's purpose at the meadow of following the orders of his military and spiritual leaders to avenge the blood of the prophets—the oath Lee considered sacred above all else since he had first become "the Life Guard of the Prophet Joseph Smith" in Nauvoo.

In September 1876 he sent more than one thousand pages in manuscript to Bishop with a directive to see that his life story be published after his death. "I wish you . . . to publish to the world the history of my life and of my connection with the affair for which I have been tried," he wrote to Bishop. He then asked that any profits that might derive from the book be divided among Bishop and Lee's family members.

Meanwhile, Howard's Washington superiors reprimanded him for the improper dealings with Brigham Young. The machinations had cost him "the confidence of every honest man in Utah in his integrity," according to the *Salt Lake Daily Tribune*.

On February 13, 1877, the supreme court of Utah Territory denied Lee's final appeal. "It has not yet been brought out clearly in the evidence that Brigham Young ordered this massacre of the Arkansas emigrants," the court concluded, "but the implication comes so near that he is convicted in the mind of every person who is acquainted with the facts."

The execution was set for March 23—"between 10 a.m. and 3 p.m."—at Mountain Meadows. The day before the execution, Governor Emery denied Lee's request for clemency. Claiming he could not justify issuing a pardon for such a heinous crime, Emery made his sentiments clear in his decision. "It is but a lame excuse for such a massacre that it was necessary to sacrifice those emigrants for the reason that an army was about to invade the Territory. The facts are the emigrants were a peaceable company of travelers, passing through the country, seeking homes still further west, and should have received the protection of every white person along their tedious journey, but instead of receiving such friendly assistance they were all, men, women and innocent children, foully murdered."

On the cold, windy morning of March 23, the condemned man wore a red wool shirt, hat, coat, and muffler to the place of his death. He had snored loudly during the wagon journey south, and had eaten a hearty breakfast. Though the rich grass had been ravaged over the past twenty years, the slope and bend of the valley was much the same as when he and his men rode in to attack the Fancher-Baker party. Now, not far from the ground where the unarmed victims had surrendered, Lee sat patiently and silently on his coffin as a photographer set up his equipment for the official pictures of the scene. The crumbling Carleton cairn was one hundred yards away.

A crowd of seventy-five spectators surrounded the site, mostly federal officers, newspaper reporters, troops under the command of Lieutenant George Patterson, and three church representatives. None of Lee's family members attended. When the camera was ready and the five-man firing squad was positioned anonymously inside a covered wagon, their rifles pointing through holes in the canvas, Lee rose slowly, wearily. He asked James Fennemore, the photographer, to provide a copy of the photograph to his three remaining faithful wives. He then spoke to the crowd: "I feel resigned to my fate. I feel as calm as a summer morning. I have done nothing designedly wrong. My conscience is clear before God and man, and I am ready to meet my Redeemer. This it is that places me on this field." He hesitated momentarily, gasping as he spoke of the "unprotected" family he would leave behind. He claimed for the final time that he had tried to save the emigrants, but said he understood he was being "sacrificed." "Death has no terror. I do not fear death. I shall never go to a worse place than the one I am in now."

Then, finally, he turned on his prophet. "I am a true believer in the gospel of Jesus Christ. I do not believe everything that is now practiced and taught by Brigham Young. I do not agree with him. I believe he is leading the people astray; but I believe in the gospel as it was taught in its purity by Joseph Smith in former days. I have my reasons for saying this. I used to make this man's will my pleasure, and did so for thirty years. See how and what I have come to this day. I have been sacrificed in a cowardly, dastardly manner."

He shook hands with a few men standing nearby, methodically removed his hat, coat, and muffler. The Reverend George Stokes knelt with him and prayed, and then the two men made their way over to the coffin, Lee leaning solidly onto the preacher's arm. A marshal blindfolded him, but at Lee's request left the prisoner's arms free. Facing the wagons he sat on his casket, raising his arms above his head.

"Center on my heart, boys. Don't mangle my body."

At the words *"Ready! Aim! Fire!"* five volleys broke the silent spring air. Lee fell back heavily into the rough-hewn coffin, his blood spilling through his endowment garments in the symbolism all Mormons understood. Lee's body was taken by wagon to Panguitch, where it was covered by his temple robes and buried in the local cemetery near the home of his wife Caroline.

EPILOGUE

Mountain Meadows Aftermath

"T HE CURSE of God seems to have fallen upon it, and scorched and withered the luxuriant grass and herbage that covered the ground twenty years ago," W. W. Bishop wrote of Mountain Meadows as it appeared on the day of the execution. "The Meadows have been transformed from a fertile valley into an arid and barren plain, and the superstitious Mormons assert that the ghosts of the murdered emigrants meet nightly at the scene of their slaughter and re-enact in pantomime the horrors of their massacre."

The *New York Herald* published an excerpt from *Mormonism Unveiled or Life & Confession of John D. Lee* within days of the execution. The book was basically the document Lee had given to Bishop for publication after his death, and it represented the first time Lee's story of the massacre would be told.

"As a duty to myself and mankind, I now confess all that I did at the Mountain Meadows Massacre without animosity to any one, shielding none and giving the facts as they existed," Lee wrote. "Those with me at that time were ACTING UNDER ORDERS from the Church of Jesus Christ of Latter-day Saints. The horrid deeds then committed were done as a duty which we believed we owed to God and our Church. We were all sworn to secrecy before and after the massacre. The penalty for giving information concerning it was death. As I am to suffer death for what I then did, and have been betrayed both by those who gave orders to act and those who were the most active of my assistants, I now give the world the true facts as they exist, and tell why the massacre was committed, and who were THE ACTIVE PARTICI-PANTS." The narrative proceeded to describe the mass murder in clear, matter-of-fact, chronological detail.

Brigham Young, upon learning of the report, immediately fired off a letter to the *Herald*. "If Lee has made a statement implicating me . . . it is utterly false. My course of life is too well known by thousands of honorable men for them to believe for one moment such accusations."

By May 1877, *Mormonism Unveiled or Life & Confession of John D. Lee,* with an introduction by Bishop, was a national best-seller. Lee had provided Bishop with the conclusion of the manuscript, according to Bishop, a week before his execution. Not surprisingly, the book was roundly dismissed as a fraud by church leaders, but has generally been determined valid and credible by later scholars of the event, though some have believed Bishop embellished it.

Before his death, Lee predicted Young would follow him to the other side within six months. "If I am guilty of the crime for which I am convicted, I will go down and out and never be heard of again," Lee told his family. "If I am not guilty, Brigham Young will die within one year! Yes, within six months."

On August 23—six months to the day after Lee's killing—Young gorged himself on green corn and peaches and fell deathly ill. Over the next six days he languished from what was believed to be cholera morbus, though later medical experts determined it to be an appendicitis attack. On August 29 at four p.m. he took his last breath and uttered his final words: "Joseph, Joseph, Joseph, Joseph," according to the *Deseret News*. But even his death, as his life, swirled in controversy. Rumors circulated in Salt Lake City that two of Lee's sons had poisoned him, but the stories gained no lasting purchase. More than twelve thousand Saints attended the tabernacle funeral and buried their prophet in a plain redwood box.

Young's longtime friend Thomas Kane maintained close personal contact with him and continued to defend Young and Mormonism until Young's death. Kane had volunteered for the Union Army and been severely wounded on Culp's Hill during the Battle of Gettysburg. A near invalid, Kane traveled in 1872 with his wife, two sons, and a cook to Salt Lake City to visit Young. Though Kane remained enamored of the prophet, his wife, Elizabeth, was less smitten. "Vulgarly speaking, I couldn't abide him!" she would write to a nephew in 1904, long after her husband was dead. "I used to be reminded by him of a great sandy cat with his yellow gray eyes. He was just as kind and hospitable to me as he could be, but I loathed him." Describing the unusual relationship between Kane and Young, she said both "had great magnetic power/hypnotic . . . and each influenced the other strongly."

John Cradlebaugh's Civil War wound would leave him disfigured and barely able to speak, which critically hampered his political career in Nevada. He died a penniless, broken man in 1872, driving a two-mule freight wagon between the high desert towns of Eureka and Elko. For seven years his family in Circleville sought to have his body returned to his native Ohio. He was finally laid to rest with his wife and children in the Circleville cemetery in 1879 after one of the longest funeral processions ever held in that community. His young son who had accompanied him to Utah Territory in 1859 had become a renowned journalist and colleague of American icons Mark Twain and Bret Harte.

Mountain Meadows and polygamy had threatened Utah's statehood for decades. With Lee held accountable for the crime, and the church finally denouncing polygamy with the Woodruff Manifesto of 1890, the U.S. government took a renewed look at the once rebellious theocracy. On January 4, 1896, President Grover Cleveland signed the proclamation adding a forty-fifth star to the U.S. flag.

Of all the stories to emerge from those horrible days in September 1857, few were as touching as that of the bloodied one-year-old Sarah Dunlap clinging to her two surviving sisters, blinded by an untreated infection, and maimed in the arm by a musket ball. James Lynch, the tall, courtly army officer who had ushered the surviving children from the colonies near Mountain Meadows to Camp Floyd in 1859, carried the memories of that little girl with him over the next decades. In 1893, having retired in Texas, he traveled to Arkansas to see if he could locate some of the survivors he remembered so clearly. One of the first stops he made, in Calhoun County, was at the home of Rebecca Dunlap, where he found the thirty-eight-year-old Sarah. Despite her blindness and handicap, she was known as one of the most beautiful, fun-loving, and gentle-spirited belles in Arkansas.

Their wedding, in December 1893, was one of the social events of the season in the Arkansas county. Sarah would live only eight more years, but it would be the happiest time of her life. Lynch told everyone they met how he had rescued her from the Mormons. He buried her under an ornate headstone in the Hampton, Arkansas, cemetery. When

he died, nine years later, he would be placed in an unmarked grave at
her side.

The August 3, 1999, backhoe excavation of skeletal remains of the
Mountain Meadows victims was only the latest episode in the stormy
aftermath of this singular American massacre. Behind it all remained
the unfinished search for meaning and responsibility that U.S. Army
Brevet Major James H. Carleton commenced a century and a half
before. Once the bones unearthed at Mountain Meadows were rein-
terred by official fiat in 1999, no other physical evidence, including bullets or wagon parts, was ever found.

"Typically with history, the winning side writes the story," said
Shannon Novak, a University of Utah forensic anthropologist, after she
had been ordered by the state of Utah to prematurely end her examination of the bones. Her efforts were "giving the dead a chance to speak."
She had recently returned from Croatia, where her analysis of a mass
grave led to the prosecution of Serbian war criminals. Earlier, her
examination of the bones of soldiers on the bloodiest battlefield of
Britain's fifteenth-century War of the Roses had shattered, according to
one account, "the romantic views of chivalry in medieval battle."

Neither Novak nor her colleagues had been prepared for the signs
of brutality revealed by the bones excavated at Mountain Meadows, or
for the political tug-of-war between scientific inquiry and a Mormon
Church eager to put the controversy as well as the remains to rest.
Reconstructing approximately eighteen skulls from the 2,605 pieces of
bone from twenty-eight victims—mostly women and children—the
scientists found startling new testimony in the first physical evidence
located in the twentieth century. It was evident that the murders had
been committed by white men rather than by the Paiute Indians commonly blamed for all of the attacks on the women and children, and
that Lee could not possibly have acted alone in a mass murder of this
order. Paiute leaders claimed the new forensic evidence supported their
own oral histories that the tribe had been "wrongfully blamed for
assisting in something that was not of their making," wrote Weber
State University cultural anthropologist Ron Holt and Paiute Tribe
education director Gary Tom in a recently published anthology of
Paiute chronicles.

When the examined bones were reburied on September 9, 1999, yet another plaque was installed by the church: IN THE EARLY MORNING HOURS OF SEPTEMBER 7, [1857,] A PARTY OF LOCAL MORMON SETTLERS AND INDIANS ATTACKED AND LAID SIEGE TO THE ENCAMPMENT. FOR REASONS NOT FULLY UNDERSTOOD, A CONTINGENT OF TERRITORIAL MILITIA JOINED THE ATTACKERS. THIS IRON COUNTY MILITIA CONSISTED OF LOCAL LATTER-DAY SAINTS ACTING ON ORDERS FROM THEIR LOCAL RELIGIOUS LEADERS AND MILITARY COMMANDERS HEADQUARTERED THIRTY-FIVE MILES TO THE NORTHEAST IN CEDAR CITY.

Through every successive version of the monument, the church has steadfastly denied any responsibility in the massacre on the part of its headquarters authorities in Salt Lake City, most notably Brigham Young. "That which we have done here must never be construed as an acknowledgement on the part of the church of any complicity in the occurrences of that fateful day," declared church president Gordon B. Hinckley at the 1999 dedication.

In 2000, the U.S. Forest Service rejected a proposal by the Church of Jesus Christ of Latter-day Saints to exchange land that the church owned in southwestern Utah for a parcel that would encompass much of Mountain Meadows. The land sought by the church was believed to include a mass grave of the emigrant women and children murdered at the site. The battle for control over the site and the protection of unmarked graves remains volatile, with many descendants of the Fancher Train pushing the U.S. Park Service for a memorial similar to that built for the victims of the bombing of the Oklahoma City federal building. Until the Oklahoma City bombing in 1995, Mountain Meadows had been the largest civilian atrocity to occur on American soil.

Lonely Dell, January 22, 2002

ALLEN MALMQUIST, a sixty-year-old U.S. Park Service volunteer, was swathed in protective gear for the unpleasant task of removing years' worth of animal droppings from the historic site. It was the morning of January 22, 2002. At first, he thought the lightweight forged sheet of lead he uncovered was but one more piece of refuse. But when he unrolled it he recognized a legendary signature.

"The first thing I saw was that it was signed J. D. Lee," Malmquist reported. As he stood there at the fort John D. Lee had built in 1872, taking part in the restoration project at Lonely Dell, Malmquist immediately grasped the significance of the finding.

He straightened the twelve-by-eighteen-inch "scroll" and read the stunning inscription:

> AT THE PAHREAH
> I HAV NOW LIVE LONGER THAN
> ECCPECTED THO I AM NOW ILL.—I DO
> NOT FEAR ATHORTY FOR THE TIME IS
> CLOSING AND AM WILLING TO TAK
> THE BLAME FOR THE FANCHER.—
> COL. DANE—MAJ. HIGBY, AND ME—ON ORDERS
> FROM PRES YOUNG THRO GEO SMITH
> TOOK PART—I TRUST IN *GOD*—I HAVE NO
> FEAR—DEATH HOLD NO TEROR—LORD HAV
> MERCI ON THIS RESLESS SOUL—
> > BY MY OWN HAND—
> > J. D. LEE—JAN 11–1872

The Park Service announced the finding on March 6, and initiated an archaeological examination of the artifact. They locked the lead sheet—what the *Salt Lake Tribune* christened the "Lead Scroll"—in a government vault and established a "chain of custody," as one of the rangers called it, to protect it while the scientific investigation continued. But even before the research had been completed, representatives of the Church of Jesus Christ of Latter-day Saints denounced it as a fake.

The Park Service nonetheless pursued expert forensic inquiry in an effort to authenticate the scroll by dating the age of the lead. Scientists ultimately determined the lead was mined in Missouri prior to 1865, which lessened the likelihood that it was a fake. Still, skeptics dismissed it as a hoax. Scholars of John D. Lee's diaries pointed to the evidence that Lee had indeed been suffering from a life-threatening illness in the days and weeks around January 11, 1872. Researchers considered the crudely inscribed statement, carrying the possible weight of a "deathbed confession," within the larger context of its history.

Notes

The historian must always make judgments in the use of documentary and anecdotal material, including critical analyses of the motives and credibility of various witnesses. Never is this truer in the story of the Mountain Meadows Massacre than with the testimony of John D. Lee. Lee's autobiography has long provided one of the original and most compelling firsthand accounts of the massacre and its aftermath. He began as a loyal zealot and ended as an embittered and disillusioned scapegoat, clinging steadfastly to his faith in Mormonism until the end. Analyzing Lee's varying and often contradictory testimony is not so daunting a task when one compares what Lee wrote against the backdrop of the historical setting and moment. I have relied on Lee's claims only when they could be substantiated by additional sources—as is often the case—or when I judged them to be true and accurate compared to other historical evidence. In this fashion, it became clear when Lee was self-justifying and obfuscating to protect his leaders, his church, or himself, and when he was speaking the truth as he believed it to be. All unspecified attributions to "Lee" in the notes are to his *Mormonism Unveiled or Life and Confessions of John D. Lee,* 2001 edition.

After the first mention, attributions in the notes to single names are abbreviated to the last name of the source. The full citations to all sources identified in this way are found in the bibliography. For early Mormonism, I have drawn on the incomparable research of Fawn Brodie, as well as T. B. H. Stenhouse and Fanny Stenhouse, M. R. Werner, D. Michael Quinn, and the analysis by Robert D. Anderson. Also helpful were John E. Hallwas and Roger D. Launius, Stanley P. Hirshson, and Larry Coates. The Gunnison massacre was brilliantly examined by historian R. Kent Fielding in his *Unsolicited Chronicler.*

For details about the makeup of the Fancher Train, I have reviewed oral histories, diaries, and depositions of the descendants from historical societies in Arkansas. The depositions are referred to herein as the "Arkansas depositions."

The *Higbee History and Stories* is a collection of letters and documents relating to the Higbee family, and is located at the Sherratt Library in Cedar City, Utah.

The investigation of the massacre is richly documented in U.S. government files at the National Archives, in records of the Bureau of Indian Affairs and the U.S. Army, and in congressional reports and presidential messages. New material from Mormon records, including Dimick Huntington's journal, contributed to a new understanding of the events of 1857.

The details of the life of John Cradlebaugh were compiled from government documents, historical societies in his native Ohio, and records located in Nevada, where he served as territorial judge.

I reconstructed the John D. Lee trial by using the complete contemporaneous newspaper accounts, reviewing original trial testimony, and drawing from Juanita Brooks's pioneering biography of Lee, as well as her classic *The Mountain Meadows Massacre*.

The contemporary accounts of the excavation of bones at Mountain Meadows in 1999 was the subject of a thorough and courageous report by journalist Christopher Smith in the *Salt Lake Tribune* in March 2000. Those efforts led to renewed interest in bringing light to this dark subject.

PROLOGUE
JACOB HAMBLIN'S RANCH, SEPTEMBER 11, 1857

xvii. "The best grazing tract in Utah Territory": Brevet Major Carleton's *Special Report to Congress* in 1859.

xix. "The children cried nearly all night": Interview with Albert Hamblin in the Carleton, *Special Report*.

THE CAIRN, AUGUST 3, 1999

xx. Their first inclination: *Salt Lake Tribune*, March 12, 2000.

xx. "We were told": Author's confidential interview; see also Brooks, *John Doyle Lee*, 11.

xxi. "an unusual mix": *Salt Lake Tribune*, March 13, 2000.

PART ONE: THE GATHERING
CHAPTER ONE: PALMYRA, 1823

3. "a countenance truly like lightning": Fawn Brodie, *No Man Knows My History*, 39.

3. "That God had a work for me to do": Ibid.; see also Carl Carmer, *The Farm Boy and the Angel*, 19, and Robert Mullen, *The Latter-Day Saints*, 14.

3. "the everlasting Gospel": Brodie, 39.

3. "For behold the day cometh": T. B. H. Stenhouse, *The Rocky Mountain Saints*, 17.

3. "to be authentic": Brodie, 39.
4. "to the twelve tribes": James 1:5.
4. "a pillar of light": Carmer, 13.
4. "I felt much like Paul": Smith quoted in Carmer, 13.
4. spending his "leisure leading a band of idlers": Brodie, 16.
4. "a peripatetic magician, conjurer and fortuneteller": Carmer, 53.
4. "Jews throughout the world": D. Michael Quinn, *Early Mormonism,* 167.
5. "both the autumnal equinox": Ibid.
5. "the moon was also in Libra": Ibid.
5. he had been "commanded": Ibid.
5. he would be "cut off": Carmer, 23.
5. "the two smooth three-cornered diamonds": Brodie, 40.
5. "Joseph's former troubles were as nothing": T. B. H. Stenhouse, 22.
5. "No comet appeared in the sky": Brodie, 7.
6. "too absurd for belief": Thomas Paine, *The Age of Reason,* 47.
6. "As a result of Paine's work": Robert D. Anderson, *Inside the Mind of Joseph Smith,* 220.
6. "frankly gloried in his freedom": Brodie, 5.
6. "Crook-Necked Smith": M. R. Werner, *Brigham Young,* 17.
6. the "barber-surgeon": Brodie, 8.
6. compensatory fantasies: Robert D. Anderson, *Inside the Mind of Joseph Smith,* 20 ff.
7. "leaving behind a people scattered": Brodie, 14.
7. "convulsive revivals": Quinn, *Early Mormonism,* 136.
7. "runaway Negroes": George W. Bean, *Autobiography of George W. Bean,* 16.
7. "he detested the plow": Brodie, 18.
7. "digging for money for subsistence": Ibid., 136.
7. "lake-country prototype of Huckleberry Finn": Carmer, 51.
7. "would have made a fine stump speaker": Daniel Hendrix quoted in Brodie, 26.
7. "as if he had spent his whole life": Lucy Smith, *Biographical Sketches,* 85.
8. the "stream of prose": Brodie, 44.
8. "lacked subtlety, wit, and style": Ibid., 62.
8. "He began the book": Ibid., 49. The Book of Mormon relied on what biographer R. Anderson described as revivalist fantasy. The themes in the Book of Mormon have been described as "a responsiveness to the provincial opinions of the time," Brodie, 69.
9. "BLASPHEMY": Brodie, 82.
9. "catapult that flung Joseph Smith": Ibid., 83. Brodie depicted a country "seized by swiftly spreading fear that the Republic was in danger" from inside rather than outside its borders, ibid., 63. Mormon historian D. Michael Quinn described in *Early Mormonism* how religious revivals redefined established American religions.
10. "ripe for a religious leader": Brodie, 91. "Of all the American religious

books of the nineteenth century," progressive candidate Henry Wallace would say a century later, "it seems probable that the *Book of Mormon* was the most powerful." Wallace quote, ibid., 67.

10. written "a supernatural history": Anderson, Robert D., 242.

10. "had received the keys of the holy priesthood": Samuel Nyal Henrie, ed., *Writings of John D. Lee,* 58.

10. "poor man's awe of gold": Brodie, 187.

10. "except for his nose": Ibid., 32.

10. "mysterious illumination": Ibid., 101.

11. "fortune-teller turned baptizer": Ibid., 88.

11. "Joseph was offering the red man": Ibid., 93.

11. "a land flowing with milk and honey": *The Doctrine and Covenants of the Church of Jesus Christ of Latter-day Saints,* section 31.

CHAPTER TWO: KIRTLAND/FAR WEST, 1831

12. "pattern of colony building": Larry Coates, *In Mormon Circles,* 24 ff.

12. For details of Kirtland's economic moment and Smith "infected with the virus": see Brodie, 188–89.

13. the "redemption of Zion," "like as Moses": *The Doctrine and Covenants of the Church of Jesus Christ of Latter-day Saints,* section 103.

13. "Those, who like me": John D. Lee in Henrie, 43. The apostles are described as "virile men, with the tough and arrogant strength of youth": Brodie, 162.

14. "The breath of scandal": Ibid., 147.

14. "Emma was furious": *Mormon Portraits,* 57, quoted in Brodie, 459.

14. "Wives, submit yourselves": *Latter-Day Saints Messenger and Advocate,* November 1835.

15. "the wars that will shortly come to pass": Joseph Smith's December 25, 1832, prophecy, quoted in Quinn, *The Mormon Hierarchy,* 619.

15. "his horse turned toward Zion": Brodie, 199 ff.

15. "the antidemocratic tendencies": Hallwas and Launius, *Cultures in Conflict,* 8.

16. "the myth of persecuted innocence": Ibid., 139.

16. "developed an infamous reputation": Ibid., 93.

16. "on the point of land": Lee in Henrie, 15.

17. "a pale and listless mother": Juanita Brooks, *John Doyle Lee,* 21.

17. "It affected her," "a slave to drink," "thrown upon the wide world," "I was robbed of all," "treated worse than an African slave": Lee in Henrie, 21 ff.

17. "developed the love and pride": Brooks, *John Doyle Lee,* 23.

17. "Men who will lead you": Ibid.

18. "a strong sense of his own destiny": Henrie, 4.

18. "The night she lay a corpse": Lee, ibid., 33.

18. "the glory of the Latter Day Work": Ibid.

18. "Everything but my soul's salvation": Ibid.

18. "As he came up, his hair washed back": Brooks, *John Doyle Lee,* 31.
18. "war of extermination": Sidney Rigdon speech quoted in Brodie, 223.
19. "thirsting for action": Ibid., 222.
19. "knew that the two political parties": Lee in Henrie, 36.
19. "The sign of distress," "I had seen the *sign*": Ibid., 40–41.
19. "placing the right hand": Ibid., 39.
19. "set the match to the powder keg": Brooks, *John Doyle Lee,* 32.
19. "Alarm seized the stoutest hearts": Lee in Henrie, 45.
20. "I thought that one Danite would chase": John D. Lee, *Mormonism Unveiled,* 73.
20. "to divulge the name," "placed under the most sacred": Lee in Henrie, 38.
20. Smith's "Mohammed speech": Reprinted in Coates, 37.
20. "The Mormons must be treated as enemies": Brodie, 235; also quoted in Brooks, *John Doyle Lee,* 37.
20. "Don't shoot": Brodie, 237.
21. "next to a boon": Lee in Henrie, 79.
21. "Thou shalt have power": Lee's patriarchal blessing quoted in Henrie, 79.
21. "pray for strength": Lee, ibid., 80.
21. "You are brave and good men": Brooks, *John Doyle Lee,* 37.
21. "a fine chestnut stallion": Brodie, 255.

CHAPTER THREE: NAUVOO, 1840

22. "The name is of Hebrew origin": Letter to "Beloved Brethren" signed by Smith and other "Presidents of the Church," January 15, 1841, Hallwas and Launius, 29.
22. "the melancholy music": Brodie, 256. For depictions of life in Nauvoo, see Hallwas and Launius.
23. "gathering like bees": Brooks, *John Doyle Lee,* 48.
23. "resolving to make Missouri a byword": Brodie, 259.
23. "Your cause is just": Van Buren quoted, ibid., 260.
23. "It was the policy of Joseph Smith": Lee in Henrie, 94.
23. Smith "classed the poor in three divisions": Henrie, 170.
23. "each man required": Ibid., 94.
23. "a new religious civilization": *New York Herald,* January 19, 1842, editorial.
24. "Smith for being an insatiable libertine," "the exterminator shall be exterminated": William Wise, *Massacre at Mountain Meadows,* 57–58.
24. "jested about his outranking": Brodie, 271.
24. "gilt stars tossed there": Carmer, 91.
24. "So secret was its very existence": David L. Bigler, *Forgotten Kingdom,* 24.
25. "Theodemocracy, where God and the people": *Nauvoo Neighbor,* April 17, 1844, quoted in Brodie, 364.
25. "Using the same techniques": Coates, 47.
25. "It was hard enough to preach the gospel": Lee in Henrie, 135.

25. "whose business it was": Brodie, 315.

25. "Those who took Joseph's campaign seriously": Ibid., 367.

25. "theme of deceiving," "moved from one self-made crisis": Robert D. Anderson, *Inside the Mind of Joseph Smith*, 225.

25. "You don't know me," "No man knows my history": Joseph Smith Jr., *History of the Church*, 6: 243.

26. "Monogamy seemed to him": Ibid., 297.

26. "bring down the wrath of the Gentiles": Ibid., 298.

26. "after much hesitation": Brooks, *John Doyle Lee*, 56.

26. "initial period of shock": Brodie, 303.

26. "To men who loved their wives": Ibid., 300.

26. "allowed the most ordinary backwoodsman": Will Bagley, *The Blood of the Prophets*, 7.

26. "plunged into new sealings": Ibid., 27.

27. "My life is more in danger": Smith, *History*, 6: 152.

27. "men who knew too much": Bagley, 16.

27. "The paper had put him on trial": Brodie, 375.

27. "tried to be a law-abiding citizen": Lee in Henrie, 161.

27. "Here is wishing that all the mobocrats": Ibid., 162.

27. "attracted like flies": Brodie, 378.

27. "his blue and buff uniform," "Will you stand by me," a thunderous "Aye!": Ibid., 378–79.

28. "I call God and angels": Smith, *History*, 6: 498–500.

28. "Christlike sacrificial figure," "I am ready to be offered": Hallwas and Launius, 191.

28. "word for the brethren to hang on to" and accounts of Joseph Smith's final days in Nauvoo: Ronald K. Esplin, ed., *Life in Nauvoo*, 231–40.

28. "If my life is of no value," "I am going like a lamb": Smith, *History*, 6: 545 ff.

28. "behind every bayonet": Brodie, 393.

28. "Oh Lord my God": Details of the assassination of Joseph Smith vary, some accounts indicating he was executed after he struck the ground. See Brodie; Quinn, *The Mormon Hierarchy*; Smith; Hallwas and Launius; among the many.

29. "For never, since the Son of God was slain": Poem by Eliza Roxey Snow (1804–87), the most celebrated of Mormon poets. First published in *Times and Seasons* 5 (July 1, 1844). Quoted here from Hallwas and Launius, 237. For details of her polygamous marriage to Joseph Smith see Todd Compton, *In Sacred Loneliness*.

29. "The death of the modern Mahomet": *New York Herald* quoted in Brodie, 397.

29. "I hope I live to avenge": Allen J. Stout journal, June 28, 1844, Utah State Historical Society.

29. "If Smith anticipated the possibility of his death": D. Michael Quinn, *The Mormon Hierarchy*, 143.

29. "Who should rule the church": T. B. H. Stenhouse, 205.
30. "Pretenders began to assemble": Wise, 67.
30. "strange and solemn awe": Pratt quoted in Werner, 187.
30. "In the evening, while sitting in the depot": Young quoted in Werner, 187.
31. "supernatural radiance": Brooks, *John Doyle Lee*, 63.
31. "Brigham Young arose and roared": Lee in Henrie, 142.
31. begged Young "with tears, not to rob": Ibid., 148.
31. "Brigham Young was at the head": T. B. H. Stenhouse, 205.
31. "Instead of vaulting": Ibid., 209.
32. "There is a tinge of Cromwell": Ibid., 265.
32. "placed under the most sacred obligations": Lee in Henrie, 147.
32. "I swear by the eternal Heavens," "now," he said, "betray me": Ibid., 147.
32. "Joseph cut off my right hand": Larry C. Porter in Black and Porter, *Lion of the Lord*, 2.
33. "a word and a blow": Werner, 5.
33. "I learned to make bread": Ibid.
33. "go and provide for yourself": *Journal of Discourses* quoted in Black and Porter, 21.
33. "I have been a poor boy and a poor man," "honest, reliable work": *Journal of Discourses,* 4: 312.
33–34. "I am naturally opposed to being crowded": Young quoted from *Journal of Discourses* in Black and Porter, 24.
34. "unremitting warfare of theologies": Gordon Wood quoted in Black and Porter, 46.
34. "these eternal things": Esplin in Black and Porter, 25.
34. "as fine a specimen": Ibid., 45.
34. "to prevent my being pestered": *Journal of Discourses,* 8: 37.
34. "The light was perfectly clear": Young quoted in Black and Porter, 30.
34. "I distinctly heard": Kimball quoted in Black and Porter, 30.
35. "carried his wife to the rocking chair," "most unjust": Black and Porter, 42.
35. "sick, tired, and disgusted": *Journal of Discourses,* 6: 39.
35. "the more he wrestled with": Werner, 12.
35. "The Holy Ghost proceeding," "fire in my bones": *Journal of Discourses,* 1: 90; see also Black and Porter, 39.
35. "own little mill stream": Werner, 13.
35. "I had to go out and preach": *Journal of Discourses,* 1: 313–14.
35. "I was but a child," "I opened my mouth": Ibid., 13: 211.
35. "Simple language, short sentences": Esplin in Black and Porter, 41.
35. "Pump yourselves brim full": Daniel J. Boorstin, *The Americans,* 320.
36. "set out Quixote-like": Esplin in Black and Porter, 43.
36. "I wanted to thunder and roar out the Gospel": *Journal of Discourses,* 1: 313.
36. "In my prayer I spoke in tongues": Young quoted in Werner, 14.
36. "true Adamic language," "thus acquired status": Brodie, 126.

36. "That man will yet preside": Smith, *History of the Church*, 1: footnotes.
36. "If Brigham Young ever becomes president": Werner, 14.
36. "Engulfed by dissension": Stanley P. Hirshson, *The Lion of the Lord*, 61.
36. "maintained a half-worshipful": Brooks, *John Doyle Lee*, 63.
36. "organize all the young men": Lee in Henrie, 143.
37. "In the meantime, his 'destroying angels' ": Ibid., 145.
37. "Mormon road to Heaven": Nelson Winch Green, *Fifteen Years Among the Mormons*, 41.
37. "men were as thick as blackbirds": Hallwas and Launius, 318.
37. "more wealth, more art": Werner, 201.
37. "fearful burden of taxes": Brodie, 264.
37. "Though they missed their Prophet": Brooks, *John Doyle Lee*, 69.
38. "have no right to meddle": Quinn, *Mormon Hierarchy*, 650.
38. the "Kingdom of God has come": Parley Pratt's, "Proclamation of the Twelve Apostles."
38. "a remnant of the tribes of Israel": Ibid.
38. "gratis" to all "presidents, governors, legislators": Ibid.
38. "top stone laid with Praises": Brooks, *John Doyle Lee*, 69.
39. "the Saints were no less ruthless": Wise, 75.
39. "the grass grows and water runs": Brooks, *John Doyle Lee*, 72.
39. "an episode in the cosmic struggle": Hallwas and Launius, 321.

CHAPTER FOUR: WINTER QUARTERS—COUNCIL BLUFFS, 1846

40. "No one unacquainted with the history": T. B. H. Stenhouse, 218.
40. "able assistants": Brooks, *John Doyle Lee*, 73.
40. "I should have been his first": Lee in Henrie, 155.
40. "I was to seek": Ibid., 184.
40. "frigged all the women": Bagley, 21.
41. "Flee Babylon by land or by sea": Black and Porter, ix.
41. "from Christians": Werner, 206.
41. "The crossing of the river": Young's diary quoted in Hallwas and Launius, 325.
41. "American refugees fleeing a city": Bernard DeVoto, *The Year of Decision*, 75.
41. "their squalling a muted note": Ibid., 76.
42. "though his name was not to be used," "Mormons would agree in writing": Werner, 207.
42. "so cold that grass could not grow": Ibid., 208.
42. "A great deal of grumbling": Bean, 26.
42. the "leader of this band of misery," "lapped over twelve inches": Werner, 209.
42. "building the roads and the bridges": Dale L. Morgan, *The Great Salt Lake*, 178.
43. "If our Government shall offer": Young quoted in T. B. H. Stenhouse, 237.

43. "Whenever you find a good man": Young quoted in Albert L. Zobell Jr., *Sentinel in the East*, 3.
43. "His object in seeing me": Ibid.
43. "one of the most beautiful women": Ibid., 7.
44. "Leaving all responsibility upon servants": Thomas L. Kane, the Kane Collection at the American Philosophical Society, Philadelphia, Pennsylvania.
44. "My handsome brother": Thomas L. Kane to Brigham Young, September 24, 1850, in the Kane Collection.
45. "web of family connection": Mark W. Summers, *The Plundering Generation*, 3.
45. "to recover his health": Zobell, 10.
46. "Erratic appearance in such varying company": Ibid.
46. Kane "threatened the officers": Ibid.
46. "Practiced in the arts of diplomacy": Kane Collection.
46. "I do not know how I shall do it": Ibid.
46. "our urgent work": Ibid.
46. "This man never knowingly passed by anyone": Zobell, 11.
46. "A sentimental humanitarian": Wise, *Massacre at Mountain Meadows*, 82.
47. "I wished him Godspeed, as I always must": Kane Collection.
47. "the subject of emigration": Zobell, 4.
47. "tact and patience and a little maneouvring": David L. Bigler and Will Bagley, eds., *Army of Israel*, 55.
47. "valuable hints": Wendell J. Ashton, *Theirs Is the Kingdom*, 210.
47. "affairs at Washington": Zobell, 4.
48. "aloof attitude": Morgan, 181.
48. "Devoid of all personal magnetism," "taught him to deal expeditiously": Nevins, xiv.
48. "he carried out his program": Ibid.
48. "If, in a hostile mood": Ibid., 181.
48. "We are true-hearted Americans": T. B. H. Stenhouse, 239.
49. "actively courting British support": Bigler and Bagley, 22.
49. "Little's respectfully worded, but not so subtle": Ibid., 21.
49. "It was with the view to prevent": James K. Polk, *Diary of James K. Polk During His Presidency*, 1: 445.
49. *"carte blanche* as to what I could ask for": Ashton, 212.
49. "The call could hardly have been more inconveniently timed": T. B. H. Stenhouse, 245.
49. "This thing is from above, for our good": Black and Porter, 155.
49. "None wanted to enlist": Brooks, *John Doyle Lee*, 90.
50. "Go and serve your country": Werner, 216.
50. "ragged and hungry refugees": Bigler and Bagley, 23.
50. "President Young had pulled all the strings": Brooks, *John Doyle Lee*, 90.
50. "A considerable portion of the camp": Morgan, 182.

50. "Reminded of the Seine": Ashton, 214.
50. "exhibit much of queer life": Kane correspondence quoted in Bigler and Bagley, 54.
50. "animated conversation": Zobell, 15.
50. "In three days the force was reported": Kane's "Historical Discourse," quoted in T. B. H. Stenhouse, 245.
51. "we should go into the Great Basin": Young quoted in Morgan, 183.
51. "a more merry dancing": Kane's "Historical Discourse," T. B. H. Stenhouse, 245.
51. "decorous maidens," "neatly darned white stockings": Ibid., 245–46.
51. "for his benevolent design": Ibid., 247.
51. "prolatary Little," "It is necessary to impress him": Thomas L. Kane letter to John Kintzing Kane, July 22, 1846, quoted in Bigler and Bagley, 63.
52. "the graveyards on the bluffs": DeVoto, 451.
52. "with all the beauty of that of David and Jonathan": Ashton, 206.
52. "not an hair of thine head": Ibid., 217.
52. "small, nervous hypochondriac": Hirshson, 80.
53. "a heavy toll for all that the mill ground": Lee in Henrie, 187.
53. "Bonaparte crossed the Alps": Werner, 218.
53. "dangerous but responsible mission": Brooks, *John Doyle Lee,* 95.
53. "President Young, how does this compare": Lee in Henrie, 183.
53. "Come, cheer up": Ibid., 184.
54. "considered Brigham Young infallible": Charles Kelly, ed., *Journals of John D. Lee,* 9.
54. "Buffalo, elk, deer, antelope": Ibid., 117.
54. "The angels of God": John R. Young, *Memoirs of John R. Young* (Salt Lake City: 1920), 16.
54. "entitled to the Keys of the Priesthood": Quinn, *Mormon Hierarchy,* 658.
54. "Distressed in the stomach and bowels": Lee journals in Kelly, 90.
55. "It is hard coming to life again": DeVoto, 454.
55. "I turned away": Ibid.
55. "Stirred up to do this": Quinn, *Mormon Hierarchy,* 248.
55. "an immense bookkeeping": DeVoto, 99.
55. "The only comfort we had": Bean, 27–28.
56. "In the cove of mountains": Frémont's report, quoted in Wise, 78.
56. "farmers, artisans, and craftsmen": Ray Allen Billington, *The Far Western Frontier,* 198. The exact date of Brigham Young's departure from Winter Quarters is alternately placed anywhere from April 1 to May 26 by various participants, writers, and historians.
56. "including the mules and harness": Lee in Henrie, 187.
56. "He accepted them": Werner, 219.
57. "preserved their illusion": DeVoto, 457.
57. "an inescapable, depressing quality": Werner, 220.
58. "a choice and rich land": T. B. H. Stenhouse, 256.

58. "God has made the choice": Paul D. Bailey, *Sam Brannan and the California Mormons,* quoted in Billington, 199.

58. "This last group had spent precious time": Brooks, *John Doyle Lee,* 138.

58. "chain of defiles": Stanley B. Kimball and Violet T. Kimball, *Mormon Trail,* 49.

58. "broad and barren plain": Billington, 199.

58. "Zion shall be established": Lee quoted in Brooks, *John Doyle Lee,* 139.

59. "A hard, resistant folk": DeVoto, 466.

59. "laying the foundation": Marc Reisner, *Cadillac Desert,* 2.

60. "The communal food gatherers": Bigler, 39.

60. "It would be a history": DeVoto, 469.

CHAPTER FIVE: SALT LAKE CITY, AUGUST 24, 1849

61. "trigonometrical and nautical survey": Morgan, 224.

62. "deliberately snubbed": Mark Twain, *Roughing It,* 425.

62. Bounded on the "west": T. B. H. Stenhouse, 274.

62. "they would never permit any survey": Fielding, *The Unsolicited Chronicler,* 44 ff.

63. "The idol of his school": Nolie Mumey, *John Williams Gunnison,* 9.

63. "Cicero's Select Orations": Ibid., 11.

63. "nearly one thousand pages a week": Ibid., 13.

63. "One of the U.S. Army's brightest ornaments": Bigler, 82.

63. "Under much apparent indifference": Morgan, 225.

64. "No means would be left untried": Ibid.

64. "the true object of the expedition": Ibid.

64. "kindness was shown": Lieutenant J. W. Gunnison, *The Mormons, or Latter-Day Saints, in the Valley of the Great Salt Lake,* 64.

64. "having inhospitable tracts": Ibid.

65. "unsaintly Saints": Morgan, 230.

65. "We are very quiet": Gunnison letters quoted in Fielding, *The Unsolicited Chronicler,* 47.

65. "the snows of a cold February": Ibid.

65. "Wood can scarcely be had": Ibid.

65. "It was conceived": Gunnison, 157.

65. "I shall have some curious notes": Gunnison letters, March 1, 1850, as quoted in Kent Fielding, *Unsolicited Chronicler,* 46.

66. "let them severely alone": Gunnison, 157.

66. "charges against Brigham Young's": T. B. H. Stenhouse, 275; as written in a letter to Stenhouse from Fillmore.

66. Fillmore's decision to appoint Brigham Young: See *Utah Historical Quarterly* 48 (spring 1980).

66. "scowls and insults": T. B. H. Stenhouse, 275; as written in a letter to Stenhouse from Fillmore.

66. "Taylor is dead and in hell": Hirshson, 111.
67. "profoundly ignorant": House Exec. Doc. 25, 15, as quoted in Bigler, 59.
67. Their "conduct shows": Ibid.
67. "Prophet of hell": U.S. Congress, *Congressional Globe,* May 20, 1852.
67. "moonshine, fright and homesickness": Letter from Gunnison to Carrington, as quoted in Fielding, 66.
67. "reason to regain its sway": Ibid., 65.
68. a "tempest" of persecution: Gunnison, 29.
68. "Smarting under a bitter recollection of violence": Ibid., 156–57.
68. "Separated now from those who can persecute them": Ibid., 159.
68. "If they were allowed to govern themselves": Fielding in preface to *The Unsolicited Chronicler.*
68. "Mormonism is an eclectic religious philosophy": Gunnison in Fielding, *Unsolicited Chronicler,* 8.
68. "they see the great city of New York": Gunnison, 165.
68. "a criminal code": Ibid., 83.
69. "common mountain law": Ibid., 72.
69. "They make it both a religious and social custom": Ibid., 71.
69. "long enough among the Mormons": T. B. H. Stenhouse, 275.
69. "disruption and jealousies," "contemplation of plurality": Gunnison, 157–59.
69. "the pinnacle of post-mortal existence": Coates, 81.
70. "Some women": Gunnison, 69.
70. "Out of this matter grows an immense power": Ibid., 71.
70. "lead to the downfall": Ibid., 61.
70. "no matter how severe": Fielding, *Unsolicited Chronicler,* 6.
70. "I . . . am astonished": Ibid., 10.
70. "to test that hospitality a second time": Wise, 137.
71. "As their interest lies": Gunnison quoted in Fielding, *The Unsolicited Chronicler,* 49.
71. "a quality of madness": David Haward Bain, *Empire Express,* 35.
71. "crossing the North Platte into the South Pass": Gunnison, 152.
72. "gambling, stock-jobbing": Bain, 47.
72. "having his first leisure and rest": Robert Shlaer, *Sights Once Seen,* 30.
72. "The crowning work of the century": Gunnison, 153.
73. "prominently before the public": Fielding, *Unsolicited Chronicler,* 135.
73. "hurrying everyone from the President on down": Ibid., 5.
73. "Not since Napoleon": William H. Goetzmann, *Army Exploration in the American West,* 305.
73. "Mohametans of the Nineteenth Century": Fielding, *Unsolicited Chronicler,* 5.
73. "the anxious eye of the statesman": Ibid.
73. Young "never had taken the trouble": Ibid., 138.
73. "The Government knew all too well": Wise, 137.

74. "You know full well my desire to do justice": Gunnison quoted in Fielding, *Unsolicited Chronicler,* 6.
74. "was inflammatory": Ibid., quoting *St. Louis Intelligencer,* June 5, 1853.
75. "These people, I understand, do not spare me": Fielding, *Unsolicited Chronicler,* 10.
75. "volumes on parchment": Ibid., 49.

CHAPTER SIX: SEVIER RIVER, OCTOBER 26, 1853

76. "From their earliest memory": Bigler, 63.
76. "These Utah Indians went by different names": Bill Hickman, *Brigham's Destroying Angel,* 57.
77. "The Mormons got permission": Ibid.
77. "beneath the dignity of a warrior": Report of Indian Agent E. A. Graves, June 8, 1854; as quoted in Fielding, *Unsolicited Chronicler,* 76.
77. "not a braver tribe": Garland Hurt quoted in Bigler, 66.
77. "This [Wa-kara] is the man who, regarded in the mountains": Gunnison, 149.
78. "As he rode at the head of his braves": Hubert Howe Bancroft, *History of Utah,* 473–74.
79. "used the fear of Indian aggressions": Fielding, *Unsolicited Chronicler,* 84.
79. "protection against the mobs and armies": Ibid., 88.
79. "white and delightsome people": *The Book of Mormon,* 2 Nephi 30:6.
79. "I send you some tobacco," "When you get good natured again": Brigham Young to "Capt. Walker," July 25, 1853, quoted in Andrew Love Neff, *History of Utah to 1869,* 374.
80. "It was a strange sight": Gwynn H. Heap, *Central Route to the Pacific,* 79–80.
80. "blocked up with wagons": Ibid., 95.
80. "I was determined to carry out the instructions": John D. Lee to Young, September 24, 1853, *Governor Young's Letter Book,* LDS archives.
81. "to control and aid the emigrant travel": Gunnison, 150.
81. "With a buffalo-skin and piece of charcoal": Ibid., 151.
81. "furnishing the Indians with powder and lead": Hickman, 91.
81. "Bridger had eluded too many Blackfeet": Bigler, 79.
81. "but the whisky and rum": Hickman, 92.
81. "They came into our camp looking for protection": Journal of Martha Spence Heywood, as quoted in Bigler, 81.
82. "began suddenly to burn": Translation of Dr. J. Schiel as quoted in Mumey, 56.
82. "The chief gave a long speech": Ibid.
82. "these poor objects of humanity": U.S. House of Representatives, *Explorations and Surveys,* 76.

82. "leaving no place on the horse unoccupied": Fielding, *Unsolicited Chronicler,* 122.
83. "a bleary eyed, hard faced old savage": Mumey, 147 ff.
84. "across five mountain ranges": Ibid., 51.
84. "On reaching this plain a stage is attained": Gunnison in Fielding, *Unsolicited Chronicler,* 136.
84. "We have arrived in the vicinity of the Mormons": Gunnison quoted in Mumey, 52.
85. "only a single Indian who scampered away": Ibid., 157 ff.
85. "Heavy snowstorms raced from time to time": Ibid., 55 ff.
86. "too confiding and unsuspecting," "an unusual sense of security": Astronomer Sheppard Homans in letter to the *New York Times,* December 12, 1853.
86. "through wetlands lined with willows": Bigler, 83.
87. For details of the Gunnison Massacre, see Fielding, *The Unsolicited Chronicler* and Mumey.
87. "I have always held myself": Martha Delony Gunnison to W. W. Drummond, April 14, 1857, in Fielding, *Unsolicited Chronicler,* 366 ff.
87. "My dear strange friend": W. W. Drummond to Martha Delony Gunnison, April 27, 1857: Ibid.
90. "under the orders, advice, and direction of the Mormons": Drummond's letter of resignation to the attorney general, March 30, 1857: Ibid.
90. "Into this cauldron of suspicion": James W. Loewen, *Lies Across America,* 96.

PART TWO: THE PASSAGE
CHAPTER SEVEN: HARRISON, MARCH 29, 1857

93. "Are you as tired": Burr Fancher, *Westward with the Sun,* 243.
93. "Good grass coupled with a mild climate": Ibid., 244.
94. "keep one's nose out of religion and politics": Ibid., 228.
94. "If they owed you money, they would pay you": Ibid., 223.
94. "an abundance of good mast": Author interview with Burr Fancher, June 27, 2000.
95. "A restless wind": Fancher, 243.
96. "There was plenty of wood and water and grass": B. G. Parker, *Recollections,* 44.
96. "purchased a team of horses": Fancher, 245.
96. "the brothers would have their California ranch": Ibid., 247.
97. "farmer, cattleman, and slave owner": Arkansas depositions.
97. "a bevy of families": T. B. H. Stenhouse, 427.
97. "whining people would soon erode": Fancher, 248.
97. "Sober, hard-working": Fanny Stenhouse, *Tell It All,* 324.
97. a "wage in cattle": John H. Baker in Arkansas depositions.

98. "Arkansas is plenty good": Mary Ashby Baker in Arkansas depositions.

98. "seen signs," "it's death to go": Anna Jean Backus, *Mountain Meadows Witness*, 105.

98. "head of fine stock cattle": Arkansas depositions.

98. "An industrious man and a shrewd, good trader": Ibid.

98. "a considerable amount of cash and personal property": Ibid.

98. "A good outfit and his family was well provided for": Ibid.

98. a "very large amount of gold coin": Mountain Meadows Monument Foundation newsletter.

99. "guns, pistols, Bowie knives": Ibid.

99. "heavily loaded wagon": in Arkansas depositions.

100. "where the huge spring gushed from the hillside": Fancher, 249.

100. "Joyous people, longing for the better, richer life": Jim Lair, *The Mountain Meadows Massacre*, 196.

100. "Several riding carriages": T. B. H. Stenhouse, 424.

100. "exceedingly fine company": Ibid., 427.

101. "A prize to tempt unscrupulous men": Lair, 182.

101. "it was less traveled": Bigler, 160.

101. "crossing the White River": Fancher, 249.

101. "fifty or sixty souls": Parker, *Recollections of the Mountain Meadow Massacre*, 6.

101. "cutting down trees," Indian attacks: Author interview with B. Haines, October 22, 2000.

102. "Because of its size and [the] vigilance of its leader": Wise, 168.

102. "traveled leisurely, with the view of nursing": T. B. H. Stenhouse, 427.

102. "observed as a day of sacred rest": Ibid.

102. "There, on the low, boundless prairies": Ibid.

102. "from becoming bored with their routines": Fancher, 249.

102. "to keep a supply of vitamins available": Ibid., 250.

102. "long-standing Mormon solicitations": Ibid.

103. "From that day": Bigler, 162.

CHAPTER EIGHT: DESERET, AUGUST 3, 1857

104. "a rising tide of fanaticism": Frank J. Cannon and George L. Knapp, *Brigham Young*, 261.

104. "We cannot afford to purchase wagons and teams": Brigham Young quoted in Hirshson, 152, from the *Millennial Star,* December 22, 1855.

105. "an LDS version": Coates, 62.

105. "A tall, thin, repulsive-looking man": *New York Times*, September 21, 1857.

105. "an orgy of recrimination and rebaptism" and "hewn down": For details on the Reformation, see Josiah F. Gibbs, *The Mountain Meadows Massacre*, 8 ff.

105. "Have you shed innocent blood?": The questions for the Saints can be

found in Gustive O. Larson, "The Mormon Reformation," *Utah Historical Society Quarterly* 26 (January 1958). See also Hirshson, 155, and Bigler, 127.

106. "the era's prodigious reign of terror": Coates, 65.

106. "Almost all things are purified": Hebrews 9:22

106. "A season of community madness": Cannon and Knapp, 266.

106. "I want their cursed heads cut off": Juanita Brooks and Robert Glass Cleland, eds., *A Mormon Chronicle,* 1: 98–99.

106. "The killing of Gentiles": Lee, 278.

106. "grown cold in the faith": Cannon and Knapp, 268.

106. "Ever since that event": *New York Times,* May 20, 1857, quoted in Wise, 290.

106. castrated him "in a brutal manner": Bigler, 132.

107. "although what they had done was common knowledge": Ibid., 133.

107. "Vague rumors": Werner, 376.

107. "If Brigham Young did not intentionally provoke war": Bagley, 77.

107. "loathsome ulcer": Douglas quoted in T. B. H. Stenhouse, 347.

107. "The knife must be applied": Zobell, 82.

107. "Cautious and unimaginative": Gienapp profile of James Buchanan in Brinkley and Davis, The *Reader's Companion to the American Presidency,* 179.

108. "sacred balance": "James Buchanan," *The Columbia Encyclopedia,* 6th ed., 2001.

108. "public sentiment favoring both a firm assertion": Kenneth M. Stampp, *America in 1857,* 200.

108. "These people repudiate the authority": House Exec. Doc. 71, 118–20.

109. "The people of Utah": For James Buchanan's speech to Congress, December 9, 1857, see John Bassett Moore, ed., *Works of James Buchanan,* vol. 10.

109. "under the orders, advice, and direction": Resignation letter from Judge Drummond to Attorney General Jeremiah Black, April 2, 1857, published by the *New York Times* on April 2, 1857.

109. "tampering with the Indian tribes": Moore, vol. 10.

110. For details of the role of Adam in the endowment ceremonies, see Fred E. Bennett, *The Mormon Detective,* 62ff.; Green, 46ff.; Hirshson, 134ff.; Brodie, 279ff.; and Deborah Laake, *Secret Ceremonies,* abstract.

110. "seduce girls and females": Quinn, *Mormon Hierarchy,* 573.

110. "He was not woman-crazy": Stanley, 163.

111. "Closely guarded": Steven Pratt, "Eleanor McLean," 227ff.

111. "staunch his wounds": Fielding, *Unsolicited Chronicler,* 382.

112. "overheated emotions in Utah": Bigler, 146.

113. "Whisperings ran through the crowd": Juanita Brooks, *The Mountain Meadows Massacre,* 18.

113. "With such glory before their wondering eyes": T. B. H. Stenhouse, 352.

113. "God Almighty helping me": Kimball's speech reported in the *Deseret*

News, August 12, 1857. See also Brooks, *Mountain Meadows Massacre,* 19.

113. "This American continent will be Zion": Young quoted in Fielding, *Unsolicited Chronicler,* 383.

114. "some suitable position": July 28, 1857, letter from General Harney to Brigham Young, quoted in Stampp, 203.

114. "Buy all the powder, Lead, and Caps": Brigham Young correspondence dated August 15, 1857, reproduced in Brooks, *Mountain Meadows Massacre,* 27.

114. "Seek by words of righteousness": Brigham Young to Jacob Hamblin, August 4, 1857, reproduced in Brooks, *Mountain Meadows Massacre,* 34.

114. For a study of Indian depredations during 1856–57, see John D. Unruh Jr., *The Plains Across: The Overland Emigrants and the Trans-Mississippi West, 1840–1860* (Urbana: University of Illinois Press, 1979).

115. "we are invaded by a hostile force": August 5, 1857, proclamation reproduced in Fielding, *The Unsolicited Chronicler* 395; C. V. Waite, *The Mormon Prophet,* 44; and in numerous other sources. T. B. H. Stenhouse wrongly places the date of the proclamation at September 15, 1857.

115. "report without delay any person": August 6, 1857, order from Brigadier General Franklin D. Richards quoted in Brooks, *Mountain Meadows Massacre,* 20.

115. "violent and treasonable proclamation": Waite, 46.

115. "looking forward to the time": Fanny Stenhouse, 323.

116. "Muskets, 99," "the command feel calm": Dame to Wells, August 23, 1857, reproduced in Brooks, *Mountain Meadows Massacre,* xvii–xviii.

116. "Both men were tried and trusted": Bigler, 164.

116. "full of hostility and virulence": August 17, 1857, journal entry of Rachel Andora Woolsey Lee, Henry E. Huntington Library, San Marino, California.

116. "I have been sent down here by the old Boss": Lee, 228.

116. "Suppose an emigrant train should come along": Ibid.

116. "red-hot for the gospel": Ibid., 230.

116. "he laughed heartily," "will do just as you say": Ibid.

116. "to prepare the people for the bloody work": Ibid.

117. "General George A. Smith held a high rank": Ibid.

117. "the direct command of Brigham Young": Ibid.

CHAPTER NINE: THE SOUTHERN TRAIL,
AUGUST 8–SEPTEMBER 4, 1857

118. "expected to refit and replenish": Fanny Stenhouse, from an interview with Eli B. Kelsey, 325.

118. "advice of the Mormons," "The two were to rejoin": Malinda Cameron Scott Thurston deposition, Brooks, *Mountain Meadows Massacre,* xxii.

118. "rode about Salt Lake City": Fancher, 251.

119. "On the morning of the 5th of August": Malinda Cameron Scott Thurston deposition.
119. Malinda later testified: Ibid.
119. "a historian sympathetic to the Mormons": Bagley, 98.
119. "Few men have played a more decisive part": Wise, 298, referring to Hubert Howe Bancroft, *The History of the Pacific States*, vol. 21, *Utah, 1540–1886* (San Francisco: History Company, 1889), 543–71.
120. "This, considering their need of provisions": T. B. H. Stenhouse, 326.
120. "The Mormons claimed": Parker, 7.
120. "turn [the Indians] loose": Ibid.
120. "keep my temper and appear cool": Ibid., 9.
120. "I can now see that I was in a very close place": Ibid., 8.
121. "all information about the emigrants' conduct": Bagley, 99.
121. "Once the Fancher party left Salt Lake": Ibid.
121. "It was no secret": Wise, 189. See also "Argus" in T. B. H. Stenhouse, 432.
121. "essayed to trade off some of their worn-out-stock": "Argus," T. B. H. Stenhouse, 432.
122. "scenic paintings for the Provo Dramatic association": Gibbs, *Mountain Meadows Massacre*, 12.
122. "well calculated to inflame": Discursive Remarks, quoted in Bagley, 116.
122. "who had joined the California emigrant train": "The Emigrant Massacre," *San Francisco Herald*, October 15, 1857.
122. "the reception was still the same": Fanny Stenhouse, 326–27.
122. "The company of Gentiles": Diary of Samuel Pitchforth located by David L. Bigler and quoted in Bigler, 166.
122. "the only known contemporary LDS record": Depiction of the Pitchforth diary, Bagley, 404.
123. "The Fancher company was not an aggregation": Gibbs, *Mountain Meadows Massacre*, 17.
123. "Now and then, some Mormon, weak in the faith," "It is true": Fanny Stenhouse, 327.
123. "considerable funds": "The Late Horrible Massacre," *Los Angeles Star,* October 17, 1857.
123. Red Bill Black: Gibbs, *Mountain Meadows Massacre*, 16.
123. "They had but three or four settlements": "Argus," T. B. H. Stenhouse, 432–33.
124. "they saw the first kindly look": Ibid., 433.
124. "sent them away in peace": Ibid.
124. "the Captain of the company," "I replied": Smith to St. Clair, November 24, 1869, quoted in Bigler, 167, though Bigler writes "the letter must be treated skeptically."
124. "hurried to get away": Ibid., 167.
124. "some convulsion of nature": S. N. Carvalho, *Incidents of Travel and Adventure,* 273.
124. "which militia": Fanny Stenhouse, 327.

125. "so much drilling and marching": Wise, 202.

125. "the ordinary Saints of Parowan": Ibid.

125. a "little Englishman": "Argus," T. B. H. Stenhouse, 434.

125. "Tell the bishop that I have six grown sons": Gibbs, *Mountain Meadows Massacre,* 18.

126. "This little mountain paradise": Parley Pratt's "Journal of the Pacific Mission, April 25, 1851," published in *California Historical Quarterly* (March 1935). Quoted in Reva Stanley, *The Archer of Paradise,* 247, with all misspellings.

126. "shut in by smooth rounded hills": Major Henry Prince, who mapped the area in 1859, quoted in Bigler, 168.

CHAPTER TEN: MOUNTAIN MEADOWS, SEPTEMBER 7–11, 1857

128. "While eating breakfast": Sarah Baker memoir, *Higbee History and Stories,* Gerald R. Sherratt Library, Southern Utah University, Cedar City, Utah.

128. "Unguarded as they were": "Argus," T. B. H. Stenhouse, 435.

129. "fighting like lions": Rebecca Dunlap memoir.

129. "a preferred location for the quiet execution": Bagley, 121.

130. "tossed from side to side with anguish": *Harper's Weekly,* August 13, 1859.

130. "Still the beleaguered Arkansans," *San Francisco Chronicle,* November 22, 1874.

130. "Stewart shoved a pistol": Remarks attributed to John M. Higbee in the *Salt Lake Daily Tribune,* March 28, 1877. For details of the Aden murder, see also Bagley, 147; Fancher, 255; Wise, 226; Brooks, *Mountain Meadows Massacre,* 71.

131. "The bullets flew around them": Lee, 237.

131. "They came to the place": Ibid.

131. "weep like a child": Lee, "The Howard Document," in Kent Fielding, *The Tribune Reports,* 281.

131. "The men all acted so bravely": Lee, 238.

132. "well supplied with powder and weapons": C. P. Lyford, *The Mormon Problem,* 296–99.

132. "white haired old Methodist pastor": Pacific Art Company, *History of the Mountain Meadows Massacre,* 6.

133. "All is joy in the corral": U.S. House of Representatives, *Utah and the Mormons,* February 7, 1863.

133. "Delighted with the approach of armed men": Judge Carey's opening address in the John D. Lee trial, reprinted in Fielding, *Tribune Reports,* 105.

133. "held by all civilized nations and peoples, from time immemorial": "Argus," T. B. H. Stenhouse, 437.

133. Placed "in the front ranks": Heber C. Kimball, *Journal of Discourses* 4, August 16, 1857, 375.

134. Lee "said the Indians had gone hog wild": Sallie Baker quoted in 1940, found in *Higbee History and Stories.*
134. "Nothing less than the surrender of their provisions": Judge Carey's opening address in the John D. Lee trial, reprinted in Fielding, *Tribune Reports,* 105.
134. "My position was painful": Lee, 245.
134. "As I entered the fortifications": Ibid.
134. "two men of note": Ibid.
134. "a large fleshy lady": Lee in the "Howard Document," quoted in Fielding, *Tribune Reports,* 284.
135. "mostly Kentucky rifles": Lee, 246.
135. "If you give up your arms you are a fool": Bagley, 145.
135. "Well our men did not have much choice": Sallie Baker, *Higbee History and Stories.*
135. "Their ammunition was about all gone": Lee, 246.
135. "looked into the faces of the intended victims": Henrie, 416.
136. "The wounded and young children including me and my two sisters": Sallie Baker, *Higbee History and Stories.*
136. "They made the men wait": Ibid.
137. "low swale": Brooks, *John Doyle Lee,* 215.
137. "Higbee, I wouldn't do this to you": Backus, *Mountain Meadows Witness,* 136.
137. "picked off by a second firing": Brooks, *John Doyle Lee,* 215.
137. "It was my duty": Lee, 248.
137. "I fully intended to do my part of the killing": Ibid., 249.
137. "From the survivors": "Argus," T. B. H. Stenhouse, 438.
137. "One of the Mormons": Sallie Baker, *Higbee History and Stories.*
138. "In the midst of all the confusion": Ibid.
138. "The knife and sword and bayonet": *San Francisco Chronicle,* November 22, 1874.
138. "One young girl sprung from the wounded": Ibid.
138. "the prettiest of the three Baker girls," "shot in the forehead": Nancy Huff memoir, quoted in Bagley, 147.
138. "children clinging around the knees": Carleton, *Special Report,* 11.
138. "You don't forget the horror": Sarah Baker memoir, quoted in Bagley, 150.
139. "Mormons may have had a horror": Bagley, 154.
139. "In these essentials, all accounts agree": Brooks, *Mountain Meadows Massacre,* 75.
139. "Of the shooting of the emigrants": Ibid., 5.
140. "My father was killed by Indians": Bagley, 154.
141. "The bodies of the women and children": Lee, 250.
141. "The boys have acted admirably": Lee, *The Mormon Menace,* 328.
141. "grim, silent men," "the most important of which": Brooks, *Mountain Meadows Massacre,* 96.
141. "made speeches, and *ordered* the people": Lee, 251.

142. "We knew we would be blamed": Confidential interview with author.
143. "I was nearly dead": Lee, 252.

PART THREE: THE LEGACY

CHAPTER 11: DESERET, SEPTEMBER 12, 1857

147. "should never have ordered it done": Brooks, *John Doyle Lee*, 219.
148. "Horrible," "Horrible enough": Ibid.
148. "I didn't think there were so many": Lee, 253.
148. The exchange between Haight and Dame: Lee, 252–53. Also see Lee, *Mormon Menace*, 330; Brooks, *John Doyle Lee*, 219; Brooks, *Mountain Meadows Massacre*, 110 ff.
149. "You throw the blame of this thing on me": Lee, *Mormonism Unveiled*, 245–46.
149. "Their fine stock, their pleasure vehicles": Fanny Stenhouse, quoted in *Salt Lake Daily Tribune*, January 19, 1875.
149. "They worked in pairs": Brooks, *John Doyle Lee*, 219.
149. "You have made a sacrifice of the people": Ibid., 220.
150. "lay just as they had fallen": Brooks, *Mountain Meadows Massacre*, 128.
150. "nineteen wolves pulling out the bodies": Ibid.
150. "property taken at the siege of Sevastopol": J. P. Dunn, *Massacres of the Mountains*, 264. For details about the distribution of property see also Brooks, *Mountain Meadows Massacre* and *John Doyle Lee*, and Fancher.
150. "provided towels and soap": Brooks, *John Doyle Lee*, 220–21.
151. "privileged to keep a part of their covenant": Ibid., 221.
151. "necessity of always saying the Indians did it alone": Lee, 254.
152. "Every witness that claims": Ibid., 250.
152. "reliable history requires": Bagley, xvi.
152. Lee "would have carried out no orders": Brooks, *Mountain Meadows Massacre*, 80.
153. "there will not be one drop of *innocent* blood": Lee, 218.
153. "I am prepared to feed to the Gentiles": Brooks, *John Doyle Lee*, 207.
153. Regarding a divine revelation from Brigham Young, author C. V. Waite wrote in 1866 that his revelation "commanding them to raise all the forces" came from Young as "Great Grand Archee, or God": Waite, 66.
154. "It was not safe for a man to be too outspoken": Perry Liston quoted in Brooks, *Mountain Meadows Massacre*, 55.
154. "I was afraid of both the church and the military authorities": Klingensmith testimony at the first John D. Lee trial, *History of the Mountain Meadows Massacre*, 15.
154. "Joseph Smith said that God hated a traitor": John D. Lee statement reprinted in *History of the Mountain Meadows Massacre*, 26.
155. "Young called in the Avenging Angels": Author's telephone interview with Helen Brockett, October 18, 2002.

155. Testimony of William Bradshaw in the John D. Lee criminal trial reported in the *Salt Lake Daily Tribune,* July 28, 1875.
156. "It is abundantly proven,": *History of the Mountain Meadows Massacre,* 3.
156. "they seemed to be ordinary": Carleton, *Special Report,* 3.
156. "every one of the many charges": David A. White, ed., *News of the Plains,* 218.
156. the poison tale was never told the same way twice: Bagley, 119. Forney claimed the poison tale was "entitled to no consideration": Forney to Greenwood, August 1859, "The Massacre at Mountain Meadows," *Harper's.*
156. "The Mormons killed everyone . . . They hid everything else.": La Van Martineau, *The Southern Paiutes,* 62.
157. "White men did most of the killing": Nephi Johnson's confession comes from the diaries of Francis M. Lyman, which are in the possession of the First Presidency of the Mormon Church. Bagley quotes Johnson in *Blood of the Prophets,* 166, and calls the admission "the most significant new evidence to appear since Juanita Brooks completed her work on Mountain Meadows."
157. the infamous Haslam Ride: "I have made diligent search for it," Young would say of the Haslam letter; Brigham Young's testimony in John D. Lee's trial, quoted in White, 221.
157. "'Go, don't spare horse flesh'": Haslam testimony at John D. Lee trial, *Salt Lake Daily Tribune,* September 16, 1876.
158. "In regard to the emigration trains": Brigham Young letter to Isaac Haight from church records, reproduced in Brooks, *Mountain Meadows Massacre,* 63. Historian White would call Young's answer a "shrewd reply. If it arrives in time it will correct a policy gone wrong. If it is too late, it will cover his tracks. It also leaves the Indians unrestrained and culpable" (White, 222).
158. "Bro Jacob Hamblin arrived": *Journal History of the Church,* quoted in Brooks, *Mountain Meadows Massacre,* 41.
158. "A Spirit Seems to be takeing possesion": Brigham Young's diary, September 1, 1857, quoted in White, 219. Huntington wrote of the Indians' meeting with Brigham Young: "It made them open their eyes. They sayed that you have told us not to steal. So I have, but now they have come to fight us & you, for when they kill us then they will kill you." *Dimick B. Huntington Journal,* September 1, 1857.

Garland Hurt would write in a report to Washington that Young frequently and systematically attempted to enlist the aid of the Indians against Americans. "I have frequently been told by the chiefs of the Utahs that Brigham Young was trying to bribe them to join in rebellion against the United States by offering them guns, ammunition, and blankets." Garland Hurt's report reprinted in U.S. House of Representatives, 1858, *Message from the President of the United States, The Utah Expedition,* 204.

159. "Some half dozen of the natives": *The Utah Expedition,* 206.

159. "I am glad we did not get him": David L. Bigler, "Garland Hurt, the American Friend of the Utahs," *Utah Historical Quarterly* 62 (spring 1994), 149 ff.

159. "The Indians insisted that Mormons": Garland Hurt's report, reprinted in *The Utah Expedition,* 203.

159. "Thanks be to the Lord": Brooks, *Mountain Meadows Massacre,* 139.

159. "We are in a muddle": Lee, *Mormonism Unveiled,* 256.

160. "a bad fix": Ibid., 257.

160. "I told him that it was a matter": Ibid.

160. "the written word is too apt to fall into the wrong hands," "You are closer to Brother Brigham than anyone else": Brooks, *John Doyle Lee,* 222.

160. "It is of his right to know of everything": Ibid.

160. "expose any more of the brethren": Lee, *Mormonism Unveiled,* 257.

160. "that the Mormons were to conquer the earth": Ibid.

161. "Show him what love and affection you can": Brooks, *John Doyle Lee,* 222.

161. "high-topped black silk hat": Ibid., 223.

161. "a full, detailed statement," "I described everything about it": Lee, *Mormonism Unveiled,* 257.

161. "for they were a set of murderers": Ibid.

162. "This is the most unfortunate affair," "You are *never* to tell this again": Ibid.

162. "that Celestial reward": Ibid., 258–59.

162. "This whole thing stands before me": Ibid., 259.

162. "in strict conformity with the oaths": Ibid.

162. "John D. Lee . . . arrived from Harmony": Wilford Woodruff's journal, reprinted in Scott J. Kenney, *Wilford Woodruff's Journal,* vol. 5, 102; and Brooks, *Mountain Meadows Massacre,* 141. The original journal is in the archives of the church historian. Lee claimed his meeting with Young was not attended by any other person. Woodruff only claimed to have been present when, on October 24, 1884, he swore: "I was in the office of Governor BY, in SLC, when John D. Lee, who had just arrived from the south . . . was invited by the Governor to the back office; I was requested to accompany him": Charles W. Penrose, *The Mountain Meadows Massacre,* 51. That ex post facto claim by Woodruff is considered skeptically by many historians.

163. "concern over the shedding of innocent blood": Bigler, 175.

163. "quite cheerful," "God answered me," "Brigham Young was then satisfied": Lee, *Mormonism Unveiled,* 259.

CHAPTER TWELVE: CAMP SCOTT, NOVEMBER 16, 1857

164. "sufficiently near to be effective": Orders from Captain Pleasanton, Assistant adjutant to General Harney, to Quartermaster Captain Stewart Van Vliet, quoted in Fielding, *Unsolicited Chronicler,* 398.

165. A description of Salt Lake City and its population and gender breakdowns can be found in *Harper's Weekly,* July 11, 1857.

165. "about to pursue the same course": Van Vliet quoted in T. B. H. Stenhouse, 357.

165. "overpowering source," "apply the torch": Ibid.

165. "if the government dare": Bancroft, 505 ff.

166. "a Moscow of Utah": Brigham Young quoted in Werner, 391.

166. "Citizens of Utah": Brigham Young proclamation, alternately dated August 5 and September 15, 1857, original copies located in Special Collections, Marriott University Library, University of Utah. Reprinted in Fielding, *Unsolicited Chronicler,* 395; T. B. H. Stenhouse, 358–59; and numerous other locations. That any man who defied Young's orders would be put to death was made evident in his statement "When the time comes to burn and lay waste our improvements, if any man undertakes to shield his, he will be sheared down" (Young quoted in Waite, 50).

167. "The date of the proclamation was changed": Gibbs, *Mountain Meadows Massacre,* 11.

167. "We intend to desolate the Territory": Young and Wells to David Evans, September 16, 1857, reprinted in Bigler, 148.

168. Details of the burning of Fort Bridger were recounted by notorious Danite chief Bill Hickman in his 1904 confessions, *Brigham's Destroying Angel.*

168. "At present Governor Young": Van Vliet to Secretary of War, quoted in T. B. H. Stenhouse, 364.

169. "When I came down upon the world again": Ibid.

169. "the Utah difficulties": Ibid.

169. "some sort of threat": Ibid.

170. "accomplish an amicable peace": Van Dyke to Buchanan, December 29, 1857. Buchanan Papers, Library of Congress, Manuscript Division.

170. "Quixotically brave": Bigler, 185.

170–171. "He had heard of the intentions of the Mormons": Thomas Leiper Kane, from the Kane Collection.

171. President Buchanan letter, December 31, 1857: Kate B. Carter, "Colonel Thomas L. Kane and the Mormons," *Treasures of Pioneer History* (October 1956). The two December 31, 1857, letters from President James Buchanan to Thomas Leiper Kane would serve to ingratiate Kane to both sides. "I would not at the present moment, in view of the hostile attitude they have assumed against the United States, send any agent to visit them on behalf of the government," he wrote in one. In the other, he wrote: "it affords me pleasure to commend you to the favorable regard of all officers of the United States whom you may meet in the course of your travels." Both letters are reprinted in Zobell, 104–5 and exist in the James Buchanan Papers.

171. "Saw two piles of bodies": Dunn, 266.

171. "I saw about twenty wolves": Affidavit of John Aiken, signed and notarized in San Bernardino on November 24, 1857, quoted in Brooks, *Mountain Meadows Massacre,* 126.

172. "The whole United States rang with its horrors": Twain, 428.

172. "we confess our unwillingness": *Los Angeles Star,* October 10, 1857.

172. "The blood of American citizens": *San Francisco Daily Evening Bulletin,* reprinted in Brooks, *Mountain Meadows Massacre,* 146.

172. "prolonged howl": Young quoted in Bagley, 185.

172. "I knew instinctively, as did many others": Ann Eliza Young, *Wife No. 19,* 229.

172. "The extra wagons in the tithing office yard," "There were now on the tithing office shelves many pairs of shoes": Brooks, *John Doyle Lee,* 225.

173. "come to harm": Werner, 416.

173. "was greatly surprised": Anna Jean Backus, *Through Bonds of Love,* 39.

173. help "himself to what he wanted": *Dimick B. Huntington Journal,* September 20, 1857.

173. Letter from John D. Lee to Brigham Young, reprinted in Lee, 260. The voucher for $3,527.43 submitted to the Office of Indian Affairs is contained in the *Accounts of Brigham Young, Superintendent of Indian Affairs in Utah Territory,* House Exec. Doc. 29.

175. For details on the vouchers, see Brooks, *The Mountain Meadows Massacre,* 150 ff, and Bagley, 254 ff.

175. "treated me all the time": Lee, 263.

176. "He was to proceed from that place": Statement written by a government informant who was watching Kane's movements in San Francisco. From the Kane Collection.

177. "Mr. O announced himself": A reprint of *Alta California* story in the Kane Collection.

178. "now suffering in the cold and snows": Kate B. Carter, "Colonel Thomas L. Kane," 76.

178. "I was requested by Col. Kane": Ibid.

179. "did a lot of little things such as apologizing": Ibid.

180. "Mr. Buchanan would like us": George Smith to William Dame, March 3, 1858, quoted in Bagley, 199.

180. "I did see then": Kane correspondence with Young, the Kane Collection.

180. "the troops are very destitute": Brigham Young to Thomas Kane, March 9, 1858, quoted in Leroy R. Hafen and Ann W. Hafen, *The Utah Expedition,* 269.

180. "inflamed against the alleged atrocities": Charles P. Roland, *Albert Sidney Johnston,* 207.

180. "Whatever might be the need": Johnston to Kane, March 15, 1858; see Roland, 207.

181. The "*entente cordiale*": T. B. H. Stenhouse, 383.

181. "If Gov. C. has been so far fooled": Ibid., 145.

181. "confederates in rebellion": Sherman L. Fleek, "Thomas L. Kane," 42.
181. "best lodgings and best brandy": Waite, 55.
182. "I have come out here to see that Justice is done to you": *New York Herald,* July 2, 1858.
182. "had caught the fish": Ashton, 245.
182. "that damned atrocity": *Salt Lake Daily Tribune,* November 1, 1876.
182. "I am your leader": In Brigham Young's instructions and remarks in March 1858, reprinted in Hirshson, 179.
182. "He would tell the story": T. B. H. Stenhouse, 398.
183. "Whatever our opinion": *New York Times* editorial quoted in Zobell, 166.
183. "take all of the wind," "the Napoleon of Peace": Richard D. Poll, *Quixotic Mediator,* 20–21.
183. "Next to myself": Kane Collection.
183. "It is the cream of creams": Carter, 79.
183. "Kane alone had the duplicity": Cannon and Knapp, 299.
184. "All we, like sheep, have gone astray": Kane Collection.
184. "All day long, from dawn till after sunset": T. B. H. Stenhouse, 396.
184. "All who wish to return": Fielding, *Unsolicited Chronicler,* 446.
185. "I have just received the published proceedings": A. B. Greenwood to John B. Floyd, March 6, 1858, U.S. Senate, *Message of the President of the United States, Communicating in Compliance with a Resolution of the Senate, Information in Relation to the Massacre at Mountain Meadows, and other Massacres in Utah Territory,* 2.
185. "This department has, at present," "adopt such measures for the recovery": John B. Floyd to A. B. Greenwood, March 11, 1858, quoted in *Message of the President,* 4.
186. "[Apostle] Smith was sent south": Bagley, 212. The George Smith report, dated August 6, 1858, quoted in Brooks, *Mountain Meadows Massacre,* appendix, 242.
187. "It is reported that John D. Lee": Brooks, *Mountain Meadows Massacre,* appendix, 247.

CHAPTER THIRTEEN: CEDAR CITY, APRIL 7, 1859

189. "The judge possessed but one eye": Bigler, 189.
190. "the best documented case of killing," "the direction of the plot": Polly Aird, "Escape from Zion," 202.
191. "I always supposed": Cradlebaugh's final address to the Provo grand jury, quoted in T. B. H. Stenhouse, 408.
191. "the Mormon church is guilty": U.S. House of Representatives, *Utah and the Mormons,* 17.
192. "endeavor with all diligence": Forney to Hamblin, August 4, 1858, National Archives, Indian Affairs—Utah Superintendency.
192. "Jacob Hamblin by order of Forney": John D. Lee diary, March 2, 1859, quoted in Brooks, *Mountain Meadows Massacre,* 173. The original Lee

diaries are owned by the Henry E. Huntington Library, San Marino, California.

192. "These fears are imaginary": Forney to Greenwood, August 1859, Senate Exec. Doc. 42, "Forney's Report," in *Message of the President of the United States,* 45.

193. "has been exceedingly convenient" Ibid., 52–53.

193. "In my opinion": Ibid., 76.

193. "were sold out to different persons": Ibid., 79.

193. "refugees from the Mormon Kingdom": Aird, 197.

193. "Having through His Excellency": *Valley Tan,* May 17, 1859.

194. "would make a eunuch of him," "cheerfully placed the whole party," "It was strange": Captain James Lynch affidavit, July 27, 1859, in *Message of the President of the United States,* 84.

194. "For more than two square miles": Ibid., 81.

194. "In a most wretched and deplorable condition": Ibid.

195. "half-starved, half-naked": Statement of John Lynch furnished to the Secretary of War, July 21, 1877, National Archives.

195. "The children pointed out to us": In *Message of the President of the United States,* 82.

195. "retain a very vivid impression": Statement of John Lynch furnished to the Secretary of War, July 21, 1877, National Archives.

195. "even remembered the color of Jacob's suit," one of the little boys had been shot, "If a ring wouldn't come off easily": Backus, *Mountain Meadows Witness,* 162–65.

196. "notorious murderer—THIS SCOURGE OF THE DESERT": In *Message of the President of the United States,* 82.

196. "in command of one company of dragoons," "The motive for dispatching this force": Johnston to Scott, April 27, 1859, in *Message of the President of the United States,* 4.

196. "I determined to visit that part of my district": U.S. House of Representatives, *Utah and the Mormons,* 17.

197. "bury the bones of the victims": U.S. House of Representatives, *Mountain Meadow Massacre,* 1.

197. "Oh, I wish I was a man": Said by John Calvin Sorel to Cradlebaugh. U.S. House of Representatives, *Utah and the Mormons,* 20.

197. "These children say": Campbell to Johnston, April 30, 1859, in *Message of the President of the United States,* 8.

197. "very laborious," "at least four of the oldest": Forney to Johnston, May 1, 1859, in *Message of the President of the United States,* 8.

198. "These unfortunate fatherless, motherless, and penniless children": Forney to Johnston, June 15, 1859, ibid., 10.

198. "Nothing of interest occurred": Campbell to Porter, July 6, 1859, ibid., 15.

198. "a two bushel basket," "the ball entering the back": *Salt Lake Daily Tribune,* November 21, 1874.

199. "skeletons," "left to decay," "Here, too, were found masses," "many more scattered fragments," "mounds of stone," "upon the plain," "Many of the skulls bore marks," "the most brutal butchery": Brewer to Campbell, May 6, 1859, ibid., 16–17.

199. "Who can imagine": U.S. House of Representatives, *Utah and the Mormons*, 18.

199. "Many brave men shed tears": John Young Nelson, *Fifty Years on the Trail*, 129.

199. "Garments of babes": *Hutchings' California Magazine*, September 1859. Also in *Harper's Weekly*, August 13, 1859.

200. "sent for Jackson": Campbell to Porter, July 6, 1859, in *Message of the President of the United States*, 15.

200. "who gave me their version," "engaged in the massacre," "A white man came to their camp," "had long guns, and were good shots," "big captains," "The Indians in the southern part": U.S. House of Representatives, *Utah and the Mormons*, 17.

200. "No names were found": Brewer to Campbell, May 6, 1859, in *Message of the President of the United States*, 17.

201. "As soon as it became known": Statement of William H. Rogers, the *Valley Tan*, February 29, 1860. Reprinted in Brooks, *Mountain Meadows Massacre*, 274.

201. "I was visited," "claimed that they had been forced": U.S. House of Representatives, *Utah and the Mormons*, 20.

201. "Previous to the massacre": Statement of William H. Rogers, *Valley Tan*, February 29, 1860, reprinted in Brooks, *Mountain Meadows Massacre*, 275.

201. "I told them that if the children were in the country," Ibid., 272.

202. "The bed clothes," "catalogue of blood": U.S. House of Representatives, *Utah and the Mormons*, 20 ff.

202. "saved the nation": T. B. H. Stenhouse, 413.

202. "hear patiently the causes": Black to Cradlebaugh and Sinclair, May 17, 1859, "Correspondence between the judges of Utah and the Attorney General or President, with reference to the legal proceedings and conditions of affairs in that Territory," Senate Exec. Doc. 32.

202. "Peace now being restored": Floyd to Johnston, May 6, 1859, in *Message of the President of the United States*, 9.

203. "The scene of the massacre": Carleton, *Special Report*, 15.

203. "from the ditch near the spring": Ibid., 16.

203. "Judge Cradlebaugh says that with Mormon juries": Ibid.

204. "The judge can not receive too much praise," "disjointed bones," "The number could easily be told," "had been shot through": Ibid., 15.

204. "A glance into the wagon": Aurora Hunt, *Major General James Henry Carleton*, 174.

204. "on the northern side of the ditch," "I caused to be built": Carleton, *Special Report*, 15.

CHAPTER FOURTEEN: MOUNTAIN MEADOWS, MAY 25, 1861

205. "He spoke and acted with the fearlessness": *Territorial Enterprise,* April 28, 1859.
205. "We have the utmost repugnance": Ibid., October 8, 1859.
206. "They should have little or no bacon," "chief nurse," "render all needful assistance": Forney to Whiting, June 28, 1859, in *Message of the President of the United States,* 63.
206. two two-horse wagons: Mitchell to Greenwood, July 5, 1859, ibid., 67.
206. "The little children": Mitchell to Greenwood, October 4, 1859, ibid., 90.
206. "You would have thought we were heroes": Sallie Baker, *Higbee History and Stories.*
206. "When we got around to our house": Ibid.
207. "In my opinion," "Your advice of the disposition," "informs me that he has no near relations": Forney to Greenwood, November 2, 1859, in *Message of the President of the United States,* 91.
207. "Bring the boys to Washington": Greenwood to Forney, November 30, 1859, ibid., 92.
208. "Neither yourself, nor any one acquainted with me": Brigham Young to Thomas Kane, December 15, 1859, Brigham Young Collection, LDS Archives, 325–28.
208. "compares the Mormons," "no dollar of it was ever paid me": *Harper's Weekly,* September 3, 1859.
208. "lied to and deceived him," "Cumming is Governor": T. B. H. Stenhouse, 445.
208. "to have been the prime mover in the conspiracy": *Salt Lake Daily Tribune,* interview with Alfred Cumming, November 1, 1876.
208. "the wars . . . will shortly come to pass": Smith's December 25, 1832, prophecy, quoted in Quinn, *The Mormon Hierarchy,* 619.
209. "A key purpose": Bagley, 246.
209. "like the Ancient Mariner": Ann Eliza Young, *Wife No. 19,* 251.
209. "figs ripened black": Charles S. Peterson. "Life in a Village Society, 1877–1920," *Utah Historical Quarterly* (spring 1981), 86.
209. *"They melted down with one accord":* Numerous and varied versions of "The Ballad of John D. Lee" passed down through generations, though, as historian Juanita Brooks wrote: "Indeed, after a hundred years some who will furnish the words or sing it privately will not allow their name to be used; it went the way of most folk songs, being passed from one to another by memory" (Brooks, *John Doyle Lee,* 251–52).
210. "merited their fate": Ibid., 267.
210. "It was a very cold morning": Wilford Woodruff's journal, reprinted in Brooks, *Mountain Meadows Massacre,* 182. The original journal is in the archives of the church historian.
210. "Vengeance is mine": Several accounts of this incident exist, with only small variations of text. The clearest evidence of its occurrence comes from the Woodruff journal entry for May 25, 1861.

210. "In five minutes there wasn't one stone left": Elder Dudley Leavitt, who was present, told this version to his family. See Brooks, *Mountain Meadows Massacre,* 183.

210. a "hopeless failure": Twain, 427.

210–211. "an absolute monarch," "laughed at our armies," "the church organ," "freely and frequently made": Ibid., 431. These were the same conclusions reached by author C. V. Waite in her 1866 book, *The Mormon Prophet.*

211. "The Saints found their Zion": Fielding, *Tribune Reports,* xiv.

211. "Cut me a chunk off the breast": Lee, 266.

212. "make a full confession": Obituary of Amasa Lyman, *San Bernardino Times,* February 9, 1877, quoted by Bagley, 262.

212. "in that almost unparalleled crime": Gibbs, *The Mountain Meadows Massacre,* 16.

212. "Your militia took up their line of march," "These soldiers did not come together by chance": "Argus," T. B. H. Stenhouse, 435.

213. "all was still": Ibid., 438.

213. "Well, sir, your soldiers": Ibid., 439.

Historians have speculated that "Argus" was in fact Charles W. Wandell, a church member since 1837. Disfellowshipped in 1864 for "prospecting," he became a vocal opponent of the church and was believed to have been a participant at Mountain Meadows. T. B. H. Stenhouse, a well-known Godbeite, reprinted the "Argus" letters in his 1871 book *The Rocky Mountain Saints.* Protecting the identity but vouching for the accuracy of the report, Stenhouse included the following note in his book:

> As no statements of such importance as those made by this writer could possibly be cited in a work of this kind without knowing who he was, and whether he was likely to be in possession of the information that he claimed to know, for some months the Author sought anxiously, but ineffectually, to discover the writer's name; the publisher very property concealed it. At an unlooked-for moment the thread was accidentally found, and "Argus" frankly avowed that he wrote the "open letters," and assured the Author that before a Federal court of justice, where he could be protected, he was prepared to give the evidence of all that he had asserted. It need only be added that "Argus" has probably been for thirty years a Mormon, has resided many years in Utah, has been a high-priest in the Church, and has held responsible civil positions in the Territory.

In 1858, in a letter to his family, Captain Jesse A. Gove, with the Tenth Infantry at Fort Bridger and special correspondent with the *New York Herald,* confided in his wife: "I sent letter to N.Y. Herald, signed 'Argus.' You may see it. Send me the Daily Herald after you read it" (Gove, 141). In another letter home Gove wrote, "I am very tired, having written a long letter to the Herald signed 'Argus.' I wrote one last mail. Keep it quiet" (Gove, 145).

214. "I should like to see you enjoy peace," "It is my wish and counsel": Brooks, *John Doyle Lee,* 289.

214. "My love for the Truth": Ibid., 294.

215. "I . . . asked him why they had dealt so rashly": Lee, 270.

215. "Our advice is, Trust no one": Brooks, *John Doyle Lee,* 296.

215. "the entire blame of the massacre": Ibid., 187.

215. "Oh, what a lonely dell!": Brooks, *Emma Lee,* 57.

215. "Do you know what night this is?": Ibid., 307.

216. "A MORMON MONSTROSITY": *New York Herald,* September 14, 1872. Philip Klingensmith affidavit, April 10, 1871, reprinted in full in T. B. H. Stenhouse, 439–42; Brooks, *Mountain Meadows Massacre,* 238–42; Backus, *Mountain Meadows Witness,* 274–77; and *New York Herald,* September 14, 1872.

CHAPTER FIFTEEN: MOUNTAIN MEADOWS, MARCH 23, 1877

Note: Many of the *Salt Lake Daily Tribune* reports can be found in Robert Kent Fielding's superb compilation of contemporaneous press accounts, *The Tribune Reports of The Trials of John D. Lee for the Massacre at Mountain Meadows.*

218. Receiving "one confidential Letter": Robert G. Cleland and Juanita Brooks, eds., *Mormon Chronicle,* 200. If Brigham Young was indeed the author of this letter, its existence has not been made available to scholars pursuing the subject.

218. "pay you liberally for your Servises," "Evidence of the high minded Philanthrophy": Brooks, *John Doyle Lee,* 333.

218–219. "with the kindness of a Father," "John, you must be careful": Ibid., 334.

219. "If one straw moves": Details of John D. Lee's arrest were widely reported in the *Salt Lake Daily Tribune,* November 13, 1874, under the headline "Thrilling Particulars of the Arrest of John D. Lee." See also Brooks, *John Doyle Lee,* 335 ff., and William Bishop, ed., *Mormonism Unveiled,* 297 ff.

219. "the butcher in chief": *Salt Lake Daily Tribune,* November 14, 1874.

219. "Well boys, what do you want of me": Brooks, *John Doyle Lee,* 336.

220. People were "shocked" at Lee's arrest, according to Bishop, 297 ff.

220. "[w]e learn that the infamous John D. Lee": *Salt Lake Daily Tribune,* November 11, 1874.

220. "Lee knows too much": Ibid.

220. "I could give many things": Lee, 265.

221. "The treacherous assassination": Fanny Stenhouse, reprinted in Fielding, *Tribune Reports,* 40.

221. "Lee is feeling very badly": Ibid., and *Salt Lake Daily Tribune,* July 11, 1875.

221. "the most important criminal case": *Salt Lake Daily Tribune,* July 19, 1875.

222. "make a full confession": Ibid., July 14, 1875.

222. "merely an instrument": Ibid.

222. "assuming the shape of political negotiation": Ibid.

222. "Dame is the pet": Ibid., July 16, 1875.

222. "Alarm at the Camp": Ibid., July 13, 1875.

222. "The Church In Danger": Ibid., July 18, 1875.

223. "Gentlemen of the jury," "All these assassinations": Ibid., July 23, 1875.

223. "not a hair of thy head": Klingensmith's patriarchal blessing, Backus, *Mountain Meadows Witness*, 38.

224. "an emblem held sacred": Carey's opening statement, ibid., 106.

224. "personal violence," "put away": Klingensmith testimony in the first trial of John D. Lee has been reported in Brooks, *Mountain Meadows Witness*, 191 ff.; Lee, 339 ff.; Fielding, *Tribune Reports*, 109 ff. An original transcript of the full text of the testimony at the trial can be found at the Henry E. Huntington Library, San Marino, California.

225. "The militia of southern Utah": Fielding, *Tribune Reports*, 123.

225. "the suicidal folly": Ibid., 141.

226. "a crime against civilization": *Salt Lake Daily Tribune*, August 6, 1875.

227. "grand, romantic, and sublime": Brooks, *John Doyle Lee*, 343.

227. "for the Gospel's sake": Ibid., 345.

227. "rot & be Eat up": Ibid., 346.

227. "loath to accept liberty," "I tried with all the energy": Ibid., 352.

228. For claims that Young advised Lee to flee, see Brooks, *John Doyle Lee*, 358.

228. For details about the conspiracy to convict Lee, see Bagley, 300, and the *Salt Lake Tribune Reports* published in Fielding, 207 ff.

229. "If my friends betray me": *Salt Lake Daily Tribune*, September 14, 1876 (see Fielding, *Tribune Reports*, 208).

229. "While not a single faithful Mormon": Bagley, 304.

229. "the Mormons as traitors and villains": *Salt Lake Daily Tribune*, September 17, 1876.

229. "Everybody stared at his neighbor": *Salt Lake Daily Tribune*, September 13, 1876.

230. "my worthy friend": Brooks, *John Doyle Lee*, 365.

230. "but one of many": Ibid.

230. "vast conspiracy": Judge Boreman's sentencing of Lee was reprinted in the *Salt Lake Daily Tribune*, October 11, 1876.

231. "if [Young] considered [himself] no accessory": John D. Lee to Emma Lee, December 9, 1876, from John D. Lee Collection, Henry E. Huntington Library.

231. "I wish you . . . to publish": Lee to Bishop, September 30, 1876. Lee, 34.

232. "the confidence of every honest man": *Salt Lake Daily Tribune*, September 20, 1876. (See Fielding, *Tribune Reports*, 233.)

232. "It has not yet been brought out": *Salt Lake Daily Tribune*, February 14, 1877.

232. "It is but a lame excuse": Emery's denial of Lee's request for clemency, *Salt Lake Daily Tribune*, March 22, 1877. (See Fielding, *Tribune Reports*, 261.) Lee's execution was reported by correspondents at the scene for the *Salt Lake Daily Tribune*. The stories are reprinted in Fielding, *Tribune Reports*, 261 ff.

EPILOGUE

MOUNTAIN MEADOWS AFTERMATH

237. "The curse of God": Lee, 390.
237. "As a duty to myself and mankind": *New York Herald*, March 21, 1876. Reprinted in the *San Francisco Chronicle, Salt Lake Daily Tribune,* and *Pioche Record*, Pioche, Nevada.
238. "If Lee has made a statement": *New York Herald*, March 23, 1876.
238. "If I am guilty": Bagley, 319.
238. "Joseph, Joseph": Hirshson, 320.
238–239. "Vulgarly speaking," "had great magnetic power": Letter from Elizabeth Kane to nephew "Francis," February 15, 1904, from the Thomas Leiper Kane Papers.
240. "Typically with history," "giving the dead": Shannon Novak, *Salt Lake Tribune*, March 13, 2000.
240. "the romantic views of chivalry": *Salt Lake Tribune*, March 13, 2000.
240. "wrongfully blamed": Forrest S. Cuch, *A History*, 131 ff.
241. "That which we have done here": *Salt Lake Tribune*, March 2000 series.

The backhoe incident, as the *Tribune* described it in a probing three-part series in March 2000, was "another sad chapter in the massacre's legacy of bitterness, denial, and suspicion." That series of articles prompted what the *New York Times* described in January 2001 as a "formal dressing-down" of the paper's publisher by church president Gordon Hinckley, and has been cited as a primary reason the church intervened in a convoluted business transaction in which the rambunctious *Tribune* was sold to a company expected to be more congenial to church interests. Founded in 1871 by dissident Mormons who were then excommunicated by Brigham Young, the *Tribune* has been the independent voice of the non-Mormon minority of Utah for more than a century. But like the reburied remains, that voice seemed about to be stifled as well. The scientists ordered to stop their examination were furious, but powerless to challenge the political suppression. Some Utah officials reportedly argued with the governor, including Jones, who by his own account contended that hasty reinterment of the pioneers' remains would be "ethnocentric and racist" when Native American remains discovered in excavation were routinely subjected to analysis.

The brief episode of revelation and suppression sparked heated charges and countercharges throughout 1999 and 2000. Hundreds of victims' relatives throughout the country petitioned the state of Utah to retrieve the remains of their ancestors; some demanded DNA testing. More than twenty-eight thousand "hits" over a matter of months were recorded on a once obscure Internet Web site about the massacre. Arkansas governor Mike Huckabee, on behalf of the descendants residing in his state, requested federal stewardship of the site, which would remove it from church control. Still others sought to have the meadow declared a National Historic Landmark. "It's like having Lee Harvey Oswald in charge of JFK's tomb," said Scott Fancher, a descendant of one of the leaders of the wagon train.

The Massacre that Won't Die

For more than a century, the events surrounding the massacre remained the subject of wild rumors and whispered recollections in Utah. Reports circulated for decades that John D. Lee's executioners were shooting blanks, and that church leaders helped him escape to Mexico. Rumors in Arkansas at the end of the twentieth century claimed Lee wore a crudely fashioned bulletproof vest that saved his life.

Lee was keenly aware of the biblical edict that the sins of the father would be visited upon the sons. Folktales in Utah suggested that Brigham Young had placed a curse on Lee and his progeny "unto the third and fourth generation." Perhaps no one man felt the legacy of shame more than Stewart Udall, former U.S. secretary of the interior, who had the serendipity, as he told the author, to be a great-grandson of both Lee and Jacob Hamblin. It would be Udall's soul-searching mediation that would bring the emigrants' descendants together with the descendants of the participants in the massacre. At the dedication of the new monument at the site in 1999, with great emotion he read a poem he had written on the subject:

Now descendants of the slain

And sons and daughters of the slayers
come, arm in arm, to end the tragic story,
to share a burial rite, perform a
ceremony of atonement.

But how to cleanse the stained earth?

To erase old griefs and grievances?

To quench long-dying embers of anger?
To forgive unforgivable acts?

The balm they bring is love,
the only ointment God offers
to heal wounds too deep for healing.

LONELY DELL, JANUARY 22, 2002

242. "The first thing I saw": *Salt Lake Tribune,* March 9, 2002.
243. "chain of custody": Confidential interview with the author, February 10, 2002.

Bibliography

BOOKS

Ahmanson, John. *Secret History: A Translation of Vor Tids Muhamed*. Chicago: Moody Press, 1984.

Anderson, Nels. *Desert Saints: The Mormon Frontier in Utah*. Chicago: University of Chicago Press, 1942.

Anderson, Robert D. *Inside the Mind of Joseph Smith: Psychobiography and the Book of Mormon*. Salt Lake City: Signature Books, 1999.

Arrington, Leonard J. *Brigham Young: American Moses*. New York: Alfred A. Knopf, 1985.

Ashton, Wendell J. *Theirs Is the Kingdom*. Salt Lake City: Bookcraft Company, 1945.

Backus, Anna Jean. *Through Bonds of Love: In the Shadow of the Mountain Meadows Massacre*. Orem, Utah: AJB Distributing, 1998.

——. *Mountain Meadows Witness*. Spokane, Wash.: Arthur H. Clark, 1996.

Bagley, Will. *The Blood of the Prophets: Brigham Young and the Massacre at Mountain Meadows*. Norman: University of Oklahoma Press, 2002.

Bain, David Haward. *Empire Express: Building the First Transcontinental Railroad*. New York: Viking, 1999.

Bancroft, Hubert Howe. *History of Utah*. San Francisco: History Company, 1889.

Beadle, J. H. *Western Wilds and the Men Who Redeemed Them*. Philadelphia: Jones Brothers and Company, 1878.

——. *Life in Utah; or, The Mysteries and Crimes of Mormonism, Being an Exposé of the Secret Rites and Ceremonies of the Latter-Day Saints*. Philadelphia: National Publishing Company, 1870.

Bean, George W. *Autobiography of George W. Bean and His Family Records*. Salt Lake City: Utah Printing Company, 1945.

Beck, Warren A., and Ynez D. Haase. *Historical Atlas of the American West.* Norman: University of Oklahoma Press, 1989.

Bennett, Fred E. *The Mormon Detective.* Chicago: Laird and Lee, 1887.

Bigler, David L. *Forgotten Kingdom: The Mormon Theocracy in the American West, 1847–1896.* Logan: University of Utah Press, 1998.

Bigler, David L., and Will Bagley, eds. *Army of Israel: Mormon Battalion Narratives.* Logan: Utah State University Press, 2000.

Billington, Ray Allen. *The Far Western Frontier, 1830–1860.* New York: Harper & Row, 1956.

Birney, Hoffman. *Zealots of Zion.* Philadelphia: Penn Publishing Company, 1931.

Bishop, William, ed. *Mormonism Unveiled; or the Life and Confessions of the Late Mormon Bishop, John D. Lee.* St. Louis: Bryan, Brand & Company, 1877.

Bitten, Davis, and Gary L. Bunker. *The Mormon Graphic Image, 1834–1914: Cartoons, Caricatures, and Illustrations.* Salt Lake City: University of Utah Press, 1983.

Black, Susan Easton, and Larry C. Porter, eds. *Lion of the Lord: Essays on the Life and Service of Brigham Young.* Salt Lake City: Deseret Book Company, 1995.

Boorstin, Daniel J. *The Americans.* New York: Vintage Books, 1965.

Bowden, Charles. *Stone Canyons of the Colorado Plateau.* New York: Harry N. Abrams, 1996.

Bringhurst, Newell G., ed. *Reconsidering* No Man Knows My History: *Fawn M. Brodie and Joseph Smith in Retrospect.* Logan: Utah State University Press, 1996.

———. *Brigham Young and the Expanding American Frontier.* Boston: Little, Brown, 1986.

Brinkley, Alan, and Davis Dyer, eds. *The Reader's Companion to the American Presidency.* Boston: Houghton Mifflin, 2000.

Brodie, Fawn M. *No Man Knows My History: The Life of Joseph Smith, the Mormon Prophet.* New York: Alfred A. Knopf, 1990.

Brooks, Juanita. *John Doyle Lee: Zealot, Pioneer Builder, Scapegoat.* Logan: Utah State University Press, 1992.

———. *Emma Lee.* Logan: Utah State University Press, 1978.

———. *The Mountain Meadows Massacre.* Norman: University of Oklahoma Press, 1962.

Brooks, Juanita, and Robert Glass Cleland, eds. *A Mormon Chronicle: The Diaries of John D. Lee, 1848–1876.* Salt Lake City: University of Utah Press, 1988.

Burton, Richard F. *The City of the Saints.* New York: Harper and Brothers, 1862.

Bushman, Richard L. *Joseph Smith and the Beginnings of Mormonism.* Chicago: University of Illinois Press, 1984.

Cannon, Frank J., and George L. Knapp. *Brigham Young and His Mormon Empire*. New York: Fleming H. Revell, 1937.

Carleton, J. H. *The Mountain Meadows Massacre*. Spokane, Wash.: Arthur H. Clark, 1995.

Carmer, Carl. *The Farm Boy and the Angel*. Garden City, New York: Doubleday & Company, 1970.

Carvalho, S. N. *Incidents of Travel and Adventure in the Far West*. New York: Derby & Jackson, 1857.

Cleland, Robert G., and Juanita Brooks, eds. *Mormon Chronicle, the Diaries of John D. Lee, 1848–1876*. Salt Lake City: University of Utah Press, 1983.

Coates, Larry. *In Mormon Circles: Gentiles, Jack Mormons, and Latter-day Saints*. Reading, Mass.: Addison-Wesley Publishing Company, 1991.

Compton, Todd. *In Sacred Loneliness: The Plural Wives of Joseph Smith*. Salt Lake City: Signature Books, 1998.

Cooley, Everett L., ed. *Diary of Brigham Young, 1857*. Salt Lake City: Tanner Trust Fund, 1980.

Corbett, Pearson H. *Jacob Hamblin: The Peacemaker*. Salt Lake City: Deseret Book Company, 1952.

Cuch, Forrest S., ed. *A History of Utah's American Indians*. Salt Lake City: Utah State Division of Indian Affairs, 2000.

DeVoto, Bernard. *The Year of Decision, 1846*. New York: St. Martin's Press, 2000.

Dunn, J. P. *Massacres of the Mountains: A History of the Indian Wars of the Far West, 1815–1875*. New York: Archer House, 1886.

Durham, Michael S. *Desert Between the Mountains: Mormons, Miners, Padres, Mountain Men, and the Opening of the Great Basin, 1772–1869*. New York: Henry Holt, 1997.

Egan, Timothy. *Lasso the Wind*. New York: Alfred A. Knopf, 1998.

Elder, William. *Biography of Elisha Kent Kane*. Philadelphia: Childs & Peterson, 1858.

Ellison, Robert W. *Territorial Lawmen of Nevada*. Vol. 1, *The Utah Territorial Period, 1851–1861*. Minden, Nev.: Hot Springs Mountain Press, 1999.

Euler, Robert C. *The Paiute People*. Phoenix: Indian Tribal Series, 1972.

Fancher, Burr. *Westward with the Sun*. Albany, Oregon: Fancher & Associates, 1999.

Faulring, Scott H., ed. *An American Prophet's Record: The Diaries and Journals of Joseph Smith*. Salt Lake City: Signature Books, 1989.

Fielding, Kent. *The Unsolicited Chronicler: An Account of the Gunnison Massacre, Its Causes and Consequences, Utah Territory, 1847–1859*. Brookline, Mass.: Paradigm Publications, 1993.

Fielding, Kent, ed. *The Tribune Reports of the Trials of John D. Lee for the Massacre at Mountain Meadows*. Higganum, Conn.: Kent's Books, 2000.

Fletcher, Patricia K., Lee Whiteley, and Jack E. Fletcher. *Cherokee Trail Diaries:*

A New Route to the California Gold Fields and Another New Route to the California Gold Fields. Fletcher Family Foundation, 1999.

Freece, Hans. P. *The Letters of an Apostate Mormon to his Son.* New York: Hans P. Freece, 1908.

Furniss, Norman F. *The Mormon Conflict, 1850–1859.* New Haven, Conn.: Yale University Press, 1960.

Geer, Thelma. *Mormonism, Mama, and Me.* Chicago: Moody Press, 1979.

Gehm, Katherine. *Sarah Winnemucca: Most Extraordinary Woman of the Paiute Nation.* Phoenix: O'Sullivan Woodside, 1975.

Gibbons, Francis M. *Wilford Woodruff: Wondrous Worker, Prophet of God.* Salt Lake City: Deseret Books, 1988.

Gibbs, Josiah F. *The Mountain Meadows Massacre.* Salt Lake City: Salt Lake Tribune Publishing Co., 1910.

———. *Lights and Shadows of Mormonism.* Salt Lake City: Salt Lake Tribune Publishing Co., 1909.

Goetzmann, William H. *Army Exploration in the American West, 1803–1863.* New Haven, Conn.: Yale University Press, 1965.

Golder, Frank Alfred. *The March of the Mormon Battalion, From Council Bluffs to California.* New York and London: Century Co., 1928.

Gove, Captain Jesse A. *The Utah Expedition 1857–1858.* Concord: New Hampshire Historical Society, 1928.

Gowans, Fred. R. *Fort Bridger: Island in the Wilderness.* Provo, Utah: Brigham Young University Press, 1975.

Green, Nelson Winch. *Fifteen Years Among the Mormons.* New York: H. Dayton, 1859.

Gunnison, Lieutenant J. W. *The Mormons, or Latter-Day Saints, In the Valley of The Great Salt Lake: A History of Their Rise and Progress, Peculiar Doctrines, Present Condition, and Prospects, Derived from Personal Observation During a Residence Among Them.* Philadelphia: Lippincott, Grambo & Co., 1852.

Hafen, Leroy R., and Ann W. Hafen, eds. *The Utah Expedition 1857–1858: A Documentary Account of the United States Military Movement Under Colonel Albert Sidney Johnston and the Resistance by Brigham Young and the Mormon Nauvoo Legion.* Glendale, Calif.: Arthur H. Clark Company, 1958.

Hallwas, John E., and Roger D. Launius. *Cultures in Conflict: A Documentary History of the Mormon War in Illinois.* Logan: Utah State University Press, 1995.

Hammond, Otis G., ed. *The Utah Expedition, 1857–1858: Letters of Capt. Jesse A. Gove.* Concord: New Hampshire Historical Society, 1928.

Hansen, Klaus J. *Quest for Empire: The Political Kingdom of God and the Council of Fifty in Mormon History.* Lincoln: University of Nebraska Press, 1981.

Heap, Gwynn H. *Central Route to the Pacific.* Philadelphia: Lippincott & Grambo, 1854.

Henrie, Samuel Nyal, ed. *Writings of John D. Lee.* Tucson: Hats Off Books, 2001.

Hickman, Bill. *Brigham's Destroying Angel.* Salt Lake City: Shepard Publishing, 1904.

Hirshson, Stanley P. *The Lion of the Lord: A Biography of Brigham Young.* New York: Alfred A. Knopf, 1969.

Holmes, Kenneth L. *Covered Wagon Women: Diaries and Letters from the Western Trails, 1851.* Lincoln: University of Nebraska Press, 1984.

————. *Covered Wagon Women: Diaries and Letters from the Western Trails, 1840–49.* Lincoln: University of Nebraska Press, 1983.

Hunt, Aurora. *Major General James Henry Carleton, 1814–1873: Western Frontier Dragoon.* Glendale, Calif.: Arthur H. Clark Company, 1958.

Kane, Elizabeth. *A Gentile Account of Life in Utah's Dixie, 1872–73. Elizabeth Kane's St. George Journal.* Salt Lake City: Tanner Trust Fund, 1995.

Kane, Thomas L. *The Mormons.* Philadelphia: Historical Society of Pennsylvania, 1850.

————. *The Private Papers and Diary of Thomas Leiper Kane: A Friend of the Mormons.* Edited by Oscar Osburn Winther. San Francisco: Gelber-Lilienthal, 1937.

Kelly, Charles, ed. *Journals of John D. Lee, 1846–7 and 1859.* Salt Lake City: University of Utah Press, 1984.

Kenney, Scott G., ed. *Wilford Woodruff's Journal.* Midvale, Utah: Signature Books, 1983.

Kimball, Stanley B., and Violet T. Kimball. *Mormon Trail: Voyage of Discovery.* Las Vegas, Nev.: KC Publications, 1995.

King, David S. *Mountain Meadows Massacre: A Search for Perspective.* Washington, D.C.: Westerners, Potomac Corral Great Western Series, No. 8, 1970.

Klein, Philip Shriver. *President James Buchanan: A Biography.* University Park: Pennsylvania State University Press, 1962.

Knecht, William L., and Peter L. Crawley. *History of Brigham Young, 1847–1867.* Privately printed, 1966.

Laake, Deborah. *Secret Ceremonies: A Mormon Woman's Intimate Diary of Marriage and Beyond.* New York: William Morrow and Company, 1993.

Lair, Jim. *The Mountain Meadows Massacre: An Outlander's View.* Marceline, Mo.: Walsworth Publishing Company., 1986.

Lee, John D. *Mormonism Unveiled or Life and Confession of John D. Lee and Complete Life of Brigham Young.* Albuquerque, N.M.: Fierra Blanca Publications, 2001.

————. *The Mormon Menace.* Introduction by Alfred Henry Lewis. New York: Home Protection Publishing Company, 1905.

————. *The Life and Confessions of John D. Lee, The Mormon.* Philadelphia: Barclay and Company, 1877.

Limerick, Patricia Nelson. *Something in the Soil: Legacies and Reckonings in the New West.* New York: W. W. Norton, 2000.

———. *The Legacy of Conquest: The Unbroken Past of the American West.* New York: W. W. Norton, 1987.

Linn, William Alexander. *The Story of the Mormons.* New York: Russell & Russell, 1963.

Lockley, Frederic. *The Lee Trial.* Salt Lake City: Tribune Printing Company, 1875.

Loewen, James W. *Lies Across America: What Our Historic Sites Get Wrong.* New York: New Press, 1999.

Lyford, C. P. *The Mormon Problem.* New York: Phillips and Hunt, 1886.

Martineau, La Van. *The Southern Paiutes: Legends, Lore, Language, and Lineage.* Las Vegas, Nev.: KC Publications, 1972.

McConkie, Bruce R. *Mormon Doctrine.* Salt Lake City: Bookcraft, 1966.

McCormick, John S., and John R. Sillito, eds. *A World We Thought We Knew: Readings in Utah History.* Salt Lake City: University of Utah Press, 1995.

McEuen, Douglas. *The Legend of Francis Marion Poteet and the Mountain Meadows Massacre.* Pleasanton, Tex.: Longhorn Museum, 1996.

Moore, John Bassett, ed. *The Works of James Buchanan: Comprising His Speeches, State Papers, and Private Correspondence.* Vols. 10, 11, and 12. Philadelphia and London: J. B. Lippincott Company, 1911.

Moorman, Donald R., with Gene Sessions. *Camp Floyd and the Mormons: The Utah War.* Salt Lake City: University of Utah Press, 1992.

Morgan, Dale L. *The Great Salt Lake.* Lincoln: University of Nebraska Press, 1986.

Mullen, Robert. *The Latter-Day Saints: The Mormons Yesterday and Today.* Garden City, N.Y.: Doubleday & Company, 1966.

Mumey, Nolie. *John Williams Gunnison (1812–1853): The Last of the Western Explorers; A History of the Survey Through Colorado and Utah with a Biography and Details of His Massacre.* Denver: Artcraft Press, 1955.

Neff, Andrew Love. *History of Utah to 1869.* Salt Lake City: Deseret News Press, 1940.

Nelson, John Young. *Fifty Years on the Trail: A True Story of Western Life.* Norman: University of Oklahoma Press, 1963.

Nevins, Allan, ed. *Polk: The Diary of a President, 1845–1849.* London, New York, and Toronto: Longmans, Green and Co., 1952.

Nichols, Roy Franklin. *Franklin Pierce: Young Hickory of the Granite Hills.* Philadelphia: University of Pennsylvania Press, 1958.

Pacific Art Company. *History of the Mountain Meadows Massacre, or the Butchery in Cold Blood of 134 Men, Women and Children.* San Francisco: Spaulding & Barto, 1877.

Paine, Thomas. *The Age of Reason.* New York: Citadel Press, 1974.

Parker, B. G. *Recollections of the Mountain Meadow Massacre.* Plano, Calif.: Fred W. Reed, 1901.

Penrose, Charles W. *The Mountain Meadows Massacre.* Salt Lake City: Deseret News Press, 1906.

Polk, James K. *The Diary of James K. Polk During His Presidency, 1845 to 1849*. 4 vols. Chicago: A. C. McClurg & Co., 1910.

Poll, Richard D. *Quixotic Mediator: Thomas L. Kane and the Utah War*. Salt Lake City: Brigham Young University Press, 1986.

Quinn, D. Michael. *Early Mormonism and the Magic World View*. Salt Lake City: Signature Books, 1998.

———. *The Mormon Hierarchy: Origins of Power*. Salt Lake City: Signature Books, 1994.

Reisner, Marc. *Cadillac Desert: The American West and Its Disappearing Water*. New York: Viking, 1986.

Remini, Robert V. *Joseph Smith*. New York: Viking, 2002. Advance uncorrected proofs.

Rich, Russell R. *Ensign to the Nations: A History of the Church from 1846 to the Present*. Provo, Utah: Brigham Young University Publications, 1972.

Ricketts, Norma Baldwin. *The Mormon Battalion: U.S. Army of the West, 1846–1848*. Logan: Utah State University Press, 1996.

Roland, Charles P. *Albert Sidney Johnston: Soldier of Three Republics*. Austin: University of Texas Press, 1964.

Rusho, W. L. *Lee's Ferry: Desert River Crossing*. Salt Lake City: Tower Productions, 1998.

Schindler, Harold. *Orrin Porter Rockwell: Man of God, Son of Thunder*. Salt Lake City: University of Utah Press, 1983.

Seegmiller, Janet Burton. *A History of Iron County*. Salt Lake City: Utah State Historical Society, 1998.

Shlaer, Robert. *Sights Once Seen: Daguerreotyping Frémont's Last Expedition Through the Rockies*. Santa Fe: Museum of New Mexico Press, 2000.

Sloan, Irving J., ed. *James Buchanan 1791–1868: Chronology—Documents—Bibliographical Aids*. Dobbs Ferry, N.Y.: Oceana Publications, 1968.

Smith, Lucy Mack. *Biographical Sketches of Joseph Smith the Prophet and His Progenitors for Many Generations*. Liverpool: Published for Orson Pratt by S. W. Richards, London, 1853.

Stampp, Kenneth M. *America in 1857: A Nation on the Brink*. New York and Oxford: Oxford University Press, 1990.

Stanley, Reva. *The Archer of Paradise: A Biography of Parley Pratt*. Caldwell, Idaho: Caxton Printers, Ltd., 1937.

Stansbury, Howard. A. *An Expedition to the Valley of the Great Salt Lake*. Philadelphia: Lippincott, Granbo & Co., 1852.

Stegner, Wallace. *Mormon Country*. Lincoln: University of Nebraska Press, 1970.

———. *The Gathering of Zion*. New York: McGraw-Hill, 1964.

Stenhouse, Fanny. *Tell It All*. Hartford, Conn.: A. D. Worthington & Co., 1874.

Stenhouse, T. B. H. *The Rocky Mountain Saints: A Full and Complete History of the Mormons, From the First Vision of Joseph Smith to the Last Courtship of Brigham Young*. London: Ward, Lock, and Tyler, 1871.

Summers, Mark W. *The Plundering Generation: Corruption and the Crisis of the Union, 1849–1861.* New York: Oxford University Press, 1987.

Tullidge, Edward W. *History of Salt Lake City.* Salt Lake City: Star Printing Company, 1886.

Turner, Wallace. *The Mormon Establishment.* Boston: Houghton Mifflin, 1966.

Twain, Mark. *Roughing It.* New York: Penguin, 1987.

Tyler, Sergeant Daniel. *A Concise History of the Mormon Battalion in the Mexico War, 1846–1847.* Salt Lake City, Utah, 1881.

Varley, James F. *Brigham and the Brigadier.* Tucson: Westernlore Press, 1989.

Waite, C. V. *The Mormon Prophet and His Harem.* New York: Riverside Press, 1866.

Walker, Dale L. *Legends and Lies: Great Mysteries of the American West.* New York: Tom Doherty Associates, 1997.

Walker, Ronald W. *Wayward Saints: The Godbeites and Brigham Young.* Urbana and Chicago: University of Illinois Press, 1998.

Wallace, Irving. *The Twenty-seventh Wife.* New York: Simon & Schuster, 1961.

Werner, M. R. *Brigham Young.* New York: Harcourt Brace, 1929.

Wheat, Margaret M. *Survival Arts of the Primitive Paiutes.* Reno: University of Nevada Press, 1967.

White, David A., ed. *News of the Plains and the Rockies 1803–1865.* Vol. 4. Spokane, Wash.: Arthur H. Clark, 1998.

Williams, Terry Tempest. *Leap.* New York: Pantheon, 2000.

Wise, William. *Massacre at Mountain Meadows: An American Legend and a Monumental Crime.* Lincoln, Nebr.: iUniverse.com, Inc., 2000.

Wixom, Hartt. *Hamblin: A Modern Look at the Frontier Life and Legend of Jacob Hamblin.* Springville, Utah: Cedar Fort, 1996.

Wyl, Dr. W. *Mormon Portraits or the Truth About the Mormon Leaders From 1830 to 1886.* Salt Lake City: Tribune Printing and Publishing Company, 1886.

Young, Ann Eliza. *Wife No. 19.* New York: Arno Press, 1972.

Young, John R. *Memoirs of John R. Young, Utah Pioneer, 1847, Written by Himself.* Salt Lake City, Utah: Deseret News, 1920.

Zobell, Albert L., Jr. *Sentinel in the East: A Biography of Thomas L. Kane.* Salt Lake City: Nicholas G. Morgan Company, 1965.

GOVERNMENT DOCUMENTS

U.S. House of Representatives. *Accounts of Brigham Young, Superintendent of Indian Affairs in Utah Territory.* Exec. Doc. 29, 1862, Serial 1128, 100–02.

———. *Affairs in Utah and the Territories. Letter from the Secretary of War Transmitting in Compliance with House Resolution of the 5th instant the report of Brevet Brigadier General James F. Rusling, Inspector for the Year Ending June 30, 1867.* Misc. Doc. 153. 40th Cong., 2nd sess., June 17, 1868.

———. *Contracts—Utah Expedition. Letter from the Secretary of War.* Doc. 99. 35th Cong., 1st sess., April 7, 1858.

———. *Exec. Report of the Secretary of War.* Exec. Doc. 40. 35th Cong., 2nd sess., February 26 and 28, and March 2, 1859.

———. *Explorations and Surveys for a Railroad Route from the Mississippi to the Pacific Ocean.* Report by Edward G. Beckwith. Exec. Doc. 18. 33rd Cong., 1st sess., 1855.

———. *Message from the President of the United States in relation to the condition of affairs in the Territory of Utah.* Exec. Doc. 44. 42nd Cong., 3rd sess., February 14, 1873.

———. *Mountain Meadow Massacre. Special Report of the Mountain Meadow Massacre by J. H. Carleton, Brevet Major, United States Army, Captain, First Dragoons.* Doc. 605. 57th Cong., 1st sess., 1859.

———. *Remonstrance of William Smith et. al., of Covington, Kentucky, against the Admission of Deseret into the Union.* Misc. Doc. 43. 31st Cong., 1st sess., December 31, 1849.

———. *Territorial Papers of the United States, 1789–1873.* Roll 15, Utah, December 31, 1849–June 11, 1870.

———. *Utah and the Mormons. Speech of Hon. John Cradlebaugh of Nevada on the Admission of Utah as a State,* February 7, 1863.

———. *Message from the President of the United States on The Utah Expedition.* Exec. Doc. 71. 35th Cong., 1st sess., 1858.

U.S. Senate. *Message of the President of the United States, Communicating in Compliance with a Resolution of the Senate, Information in Relation to the Massacre at Mountain Meadows, and other Massacres in Utah Territory.* Exec. Doc. 42. 36th Cong., 1st sess., May 4, 1860.

———. *Message of the President of the United States (regarding the correspondence between the judges of Utah and the Attorney General or President).* Exec. Doc. 32. 36th Cong., 1st sess., April 3, 1860.

———. *A Petition of 22,626 Women of Utah asking for the repeal of certain laws, the enactment of others, and the admission of the Territory of Utah as a State.* Misc. Doc. 42. 44th Cong., 1st sess., December 17, 1875.

SELECT PERIODICALS AND NEWSPAPER ACCOUNTS

"About Mountain Meadows Massacre Victims from North Arkansas." *Utah Historical Quarterly* (summer 1992).

Aird, Polly. "Escape from Zion: The United States Army Escort of Mormon Apostates, 1859." *Nevada Historical Society Quarterly* (fall 2001).

"Bones Found at Utah Site of Massacre 142 Years Ago." *New York Times,* August 15, 1999.

Brooks, Juanita. "The Mountain Meadows: Historic Stopping Place on the Spanish Trail." *Utah Historical Quarterly* 35:2 (spring 1967).

"The Calaboose in Salt Lake City." *Harper's Weekly,* November 6, 1858.

Cardon, A. F. "Mountain Meadows Burial Detachment, 1859: Tommy Gordon's Diary." *Utah Historical Quarterly* 35:2 (spring 1967).

Carter, Kate B. "Colonel Thomas L. Kane and the Mormons." *Treasures of Pioneer History* (October 1956).

Denton, Sally. "What Happened at Mountain Meadow?" *American Heritage* (October 2001).

Elder, William. "Biography of Elisha Kent Kane." *The Atlantic Monthly* (March 1858).

Esplin, Ronald K., ed. "Life in Nauvoo, June 1844: Vilate Kimball's Martyrdom Letters." *Brigham Young University Studies* 19 (winter 1979).

Fife, Austin L. "A Ballad of the Mountain Meadows Massacre." *Western Folklore* 12:4 (October 1953).

Fleek, Sherman L. "Thomas L. Kane: Friend of the Saints." *Mormon Heritage* (July 1997).

"Forty Years in the American Wilderness." *American Catholic Quarterly Review* 15:57 (January 1890).

Gorney, Cynthia. "Epilogue to a Massacre." *Washington Post,* September 17, 1990.

Greeley, Horace. *Harper's Weekly,* September 3, 1859.

Groesbeck, Kathryn D. "The Mountain Meadows Massacre." *True West* 6:4 (March–April 1959).

Hyde, John. "Salt Lake and Its Rulers." *Harper's Weekly,* July 11, 1857.

"Interesting Facts About the Mormons." *Harper's Weekly,* December 4, 1858.

Mackinnon, William P. "125 Years of Conspiracy Theories: Origins of the Utah Expedition of 1857–58." *Utah Historical Quarterly* 52:3 (summer 1984).

"The Massacre at Mountain Meadows, Utah Territory." *Harper's Weekly,* August 13, 1859.

Miller, David E. "Mormon Minute Men." *Salt Lake City Tribune,* December 29, 1957.

"Monthly Record of Current Events." *Harper's New Monthly Magazine* 19 (June 1859).

"The Mormons." *American Catholic Quarterly Review* 4:16 (October 1879).

"The Mountain Meadow Massacre." *Hutchings' California Magazine* 4:3 (September 1859).

"The Murder of the Deaf and Dumb Boy in Utah." *Harper's Weekly,* February 26, 1859.

Pratt, Steven. "Eleanor McLean and the Murder of Parley P. Pratt." *Brigham Young University Studies* 15 (winter 1975).

"Salt Lake City." *Harper's Weekly,* September 4, 1858.

"Scenes in an American Harem." *Harper's Weekly,* October 10, 1857.

Schindler, Harold. "Utah War Broke Hold Mormons Had on Utah Centennial," *Salt Lake City Tribune,* July 23, 1995.

"Sketches in Utah." *Harper's Weekly,* September 26, 1874.

"Tragic Story of Mountain Meadows Massacre Now Told by Sole Survivor." *The American Weekly.* Date unknown. In the possession of Special Collections, Gerald R. Sherratt Library, Southern Utah University, Cedar City, Utah.

"Troublous Times in Utah." *Harper's Weekly,* November 25, 1871.

"Views in and About Salt Lake City." *Harper's Weekly,* September 18, 1858.

"The War in Utah." *Harper's Weekly,* April 24, 1858.

Yates, Trudy R. "Go West, Young Man." *Pickaway Quarterly* 19 (fall 1977).

CHURCH DOCUMENTS

Arrington, Leonard J. *Kate Field and J. H. Beadle: Manipulators of the Mormon Past.* Lecture. Salt Lake City, March 31, 1971.

Dimick B. Huntington Journal 1857. LDS Historians Library, Salt Lake City, Utah.

The Doctrine and Covenants of the Church of Jesus Christ of Latter-day Saints. Salt Lake City: The Church of Jesus Christ of Latter-day Saints, 1921.

Governor Young's Letter Book. LDS Archives, Salt Lake City, Utah.

Journal History. Family and Church History Department, Church of Jesus Christ of Latter-day Saints.

Journal of Discourses. 26 volumes. London: Latter-day Saints Book Depot, 1854–86.

Proclamation of the Twelve Apostles. April 6, 1845. New York: Pratt and Bunnon, 1845. Liverpool: Wilford Woodruff, 1845.

Smith, Joseph, Jr. *History of the Church of Jesus Christ of Latter-Day Saints. Period I. History of Joseph Smith, the Prophet, by Himself.* 6 vols. Salt Lake City: Deseret News, 1902–12.

CORRESPONDENCE, PAPERS, MANUSCRIPTS, AND DIARIES

"Biographical Summaries About Nevada's Territorial, District, Supreme Court, and Federal Judges." Unpublished manuscript. Nevada State Archives, Carson City, Nevada.

Higbee History and Stories. Special Collections, Gerald R. Sherratt Library, Southern Utah University, Cedar City, Utah. (Including synopsis of interview with eighty-five-year-old massacre survivor Sallie Baker Mitchell in September 1940, and transcription of seventeen-page memoir written by Major John Higbee in February 1894.)

Huff, Nancy. Memoir. "The Mountain Meadows Massacre." *Daily Arkansas Gazette,* September 1, 1875.

Kane, Thomas. Collection of Correspondence and Diaries. American Philosophical Society, Philadelphia, Pennsylvania.

Lee, John D. Collection. Henry E. Huntington Library, San Marino, California.

Bibliography

Letter from Elenore McLean to Orson Pratt, May 22, 1857, published in the *Millennial Star,* July 4, 1857.

Rebecca Dunlap. Memoir. "Mountain Meadow Massacre." *Fort Smith Elevator,* August 20, 1897.

Shirts, Dr. Morris. "Mountain Meadows Massacre—Another Look." An expansion of a paper prepared for the People's History Writing Conference, Dixie College, St. George, Utah, February 1991.

————. "Mountain Meadow Massacre." Lecture presented in 1972; in possession of Special Collections, Gerald R. Sherratt Library, Southern Utah University, Cedar City, Utah.

Shirts, Dr. Morris, and Otto Fife. "Iron County Historical Society Lecture." January 22, 1972. Gerald R. Sherratt Library, Southern Utah University, Cedar City, Utah.

Acknowledgments

I first saw Mountain Meadows when I was a child. In the early 1960s my family frequently escaped the summer heat of southern Nevada to visit my godparents, Lindsay and Martha Jacobson, in Pine Valley, Utah. We never made the journey without my father's pulling over to the side of the road to show us the meadow. No markers existed, no memorials or other designations. The crumbling Carleton cairn was a pile of haphazard rocks. Yet my father never passed the spot without stopping. He didn't say anything about it except to make vague references such as "This is where the Mormons dressed like Indians and attacked a wagon train."

But somehow, even then, I knew the place carried a significance belied by its tranquillity. I never asked any questions. Though we were not Mormons, my father was descended from a long line of Mormon pioneers, beginning with his great-grandmother Jean Rio Baker, who had converted in London in 1849 and brought her seven children with her to Zion. She had been a concert pianist in France and England, and she carted a piano to Utah cross-country by wagon train. The piano is now exhibited at the church museum in Salt Lake City. She left the church for reasons that remain mysterious.

My father's grandmother Nicolena Bertelsen had made a solo trek from Denmark to Utah in 1851 as a nine-year-old girl. She walked from St. Louis to Salt Lake City, pushing her few belongings in a handcart. His mother, Hazel Baker Denton, was the eighth child in the second family of a polygamous marriage.

My heritage is one of strong and courageous pioneer Mormon women, and when I decided to write this book I was determined to approach the subject with a respectfulness worthy of those women.

I owe a debt of gratitude to many people who shared their particular insights, knowledge, and scholarship. I am especially grateful to R. Kent Fielding, who was unstinting in his pursuit of the truth of Mountain Meadows, no matter how unpalatable or shocking that truth might be; to Stewart Udall, who like a stern but caring father imparted advice, support, and notes of caution in his singular passion for seeking the truth; to wagon train descendants and relatives—Burr, Scott, and J. K. Fancher—for their ruminations and sharing. I am continually thankful to Will Bagley, whose generous cooperation with a fellow author is the mark of integrity, and a measure of his own commitment to the truth above all else.

This book would not have been possible without Gloria Loomis. Literary agents of such brilliance and principle are a rare breed in the twenty-first-century publishing world. I am indebted once again to my editor Jonathan Segal, whose clarity of vision and straightforward approach to letting a story tell itself has guided me through murky waters to my own clear stream. Richard Snow and Fred Allen at *American Heritage* were courageous in their commitment to this story and a pure joy to work with.

I am blessed with a circle of friends without whom not one word of this book could have been written. This gang of intrepid women makes it possible for me to balance a life of the mind with that of the material world. From picking little boys up at school, to bringing over a good bottle of wine, to feeding dogs and horses, or just laughing, hiking, camping, dancing, and skiing with me, they are my touchstones. To Janeal Arison, Shaune Bazner, Kathy Bond, Maxine Champion, Nancy Cook, Brooke Dulaney, Mary Frei, Felice Gonzales, Judy Illes, and Ellen Reiben—thank you. And to the "group"—Marla Painter and Mark Rudd, Sandy Blakeslee and Carl Moore, Lucy Moore and Roberto Gallegos—thanks for keeping me focused on the big picture. Bob Samuel made it possible to make my deadline by doing the lion's share of springtime Little League duty.

Roger Morris contributed keen and essential analysis to the early research, and generously read the manuscript at its various stages.

Finally, I am forever grateful to my family. My parents, Ralph and Sara Denton, have supported and championed my work with unflagging, if sometimes uncomfortable, loyalty. In our differences we have found the things that matter most. My three sons—Ralph, Grant, and Carson—are my light and inspiration. They have been solid troopers every step of the way, from the first moment they ran their little fingers over the etched names on the monument at Mountain Meadows. While their classmates spent school vacations at beaches or exotic faraway places, they piled into an aging Suburban for repeated trips to a 145-year-old massacre site. This book, in a thousand ways, is for them.

May 2002

Index

Abrams, Levi, 88, 89
Aden, William A., 122, 125, 126–7, 130, 263*n*
Age of Reason (Paine), 6
Aiken, John, 171
Aird, Polly, 190
Albert (Hamblin servant), 139
Allen, James, 49
Alta California, 176–7
America in 1857 (Stampp), 108
Ammon (Ute chief), 77, 158
Anderson, Richard H., 205–6
Anderson, Robert D., 6, 10, 247*n*
Arapene (Ute chief), 77, 173
"Argus," 123–4
   identity of, 274*n*
   massacre exposé of, 212–13
Arizona, 62
Arkansas State Gazette, 186
Army of the West, 47
Army Topographical Corps, 72
Arthur, Benjamin, 130
Associated Press, 157
Avenging Angels, *see* Danites

Bagley, Will, 107, 121, 152, 229, 266*n*
Bain, David Haward, 71
Baker, Abel, 98
Baker, George W., 98

Baker, John H., 132
Baker, John Twitty "Captain Jack," xxi, 97, 98, 101, 103, 118–19, 121, 128, 129, 135, 138
Baker, Manerva Beller, 98
Baker, Mary Ashby, 98, 206–7
Baker, Mary Elizabeth, 140
Baker, Sallie, 136, 137–8, 206
Baker, Sarah Frances, 128, 130, 140
Baker, Vina, 138
Baker, William, 140
"Ballad of John D. Lee," 209–10, 273*n*
Bancroft, Hubert Howe, 78, 119–20
Barton, Lance Corporal, 86
Baskin, Robert N., 226
Bateman, William, 133
Bates, George Caesar, 221–2
Beale, Edward, 80
Bean, George Washington, 42
Beaverite (Paiute chief), 157
Beckwith, Edward G., 74–5, 82–3, 85
Beecher, Lyman, 35
Beller, David, 98
Beller, Melissa, 98
Bellows, John, 86–7
Bennett, Gordon, 23
Bennett, John C., 23–4
Benton, Thomas Hart, 71–2

295

A NOTE ABOUT THE AUTHOR

Sally Denton is a descendant of Mormon pioneers. Since 1977 she has been an award-winning investigative reporter in both print and television, having written for the *New York Times,* the *Washington Post,* and the *Chicago Tribune.* She is the author of *The Bluegrass Conspiracy: An Inside Story of Power, Greed, Drugs, and Murder,* and, with Roger Morris, *The Money and the Power: The Making of Las Vegas and Its Hold on America, 1947–2000.* She was awarded a Lannan Literary grant in 2000, and received the Western Heritage Award in 2002 for her work on *American Massacre.* She lives in the Southwest with her three sons.

A NOTE ON THE TYPE

The text of this book was set in Sabon, a typeface designed by Jan Tschichold (1902–1974), the well-known German typographer. Based loosely on the original designs by Claude Garamond (c. 1480–1561), Sabon is unique in that it was explicitly designed for hot-metal composition on both the Monotype and Linotype machines as well as for filmsetting. Designed in 1966 in Frankfurt, Sabon was named for the famous Lyons punch cutter Jacques Sabon, who is thought to have brought some of Garamond's matrices to Frankfurt.

Composed by North Market Street Graphics, Lancaster, Pennsylvania
Printed and bound by Berryville Graphics, Berryville, Virginia
Map by David Lindroth, Inc.
Designed by Robert C. Olsson